Totalitarianism, Globalization, Colonialism

Totalitarianism, Globalization, Colonialism

The Destruction of Civilization since 1914

Harry Redner

Transaction Publishers
New Brunswick (U.S.A.) and London (U.K.)

Library of Congress Catalog Number: 2013039627
ISBN: 978-1-4128-5397-2
Printed in the United States of America

Library of Congress Cataloging-in-Publication Data

Redner, Harry.
   Totalitarianism, globalization, colonialism : the destruction of civilization since 1914 / Harry Redner.
      pages cm
   Includes bibliographical references.
   ISBN 978-1-4128-5397-2 (cloth : alk. paper) 1. Civilization, Modern--20th century. 2. Totalitarianism--History--20th century. 3. World politics--20th century. 4. East and West. 5. Globalization. I. Title.
   CB425.R337 2014
   320.53--dc23

                                                      2013039627

Contents

Introduction

A century after the start of the First World War, we can reflect on the changes to civilization in the period from 1914 to 2014, which we will call the twentieth century for purposes of historical analysis. The Great War released a flood of events that engulfed Europe first, then the rest of the world, and gave rise to one of the most traumatic centuries in human history. At times in this period, humanity itself came close to the abyss, in ways never possible before the advent of weapons of mass destruction. In sheer numerical terms it was the most bloody century in history; and even if the loss of life is measured in proportion to the total human population, it still ranks close to the top, perhaps exceeded only by the Mongol depredations in the thirteenth century.[1] For sheer slaughter, the first half of the century, 1914 to 1964, has rarely, if ever, been surpassed. It is true that in the next half-century calm was to a considerable extent restored, with only the occasional mass murder, usually in an out-of-the-way place. Perhaps mankind realized how close it had come to perdition just as the half-century was closing and recoiled from further killing. For the present, the danger of nuclear holocaust has receded, though it has not been completely removed.

However, our main interest is not in recounting the horrors of our time; rather, it is in examining their effects on civilization, a subject that is seldom addressed. These might have been much worse than in fact they were. A different outcome to the Second World War, an even greater catastrophe than the First, might have spelled a grave setback for civilization. If Hitler had won the war in the East, as he came within an ace of doing, Europe would have been under Nazi totalitarian domination for far longer than it actually was. Since America was likely to have developed nuclear weapons first, it would probably have used them to devastate Germany, with horrendous consequences for

European civilization in general. A similar outcome can be envisaged if, due to some quirk in weather or other mischance, D-day had failed and the Allies had been unable to land in Europe in time to prevent Stalin from overrunning the whole of Germany and most of Western Europe as well.[2] This, too, would probably have led to nuclear war and the utter ruination of Europe and other parts of the world.

All in all, it was "a damn close run thing"—to paraphrase the Duke of Wellington—that civilization survived beyond the twentieth century. And the danger has not passed. Disasters can still ensue from many quarters, whether through wars or environmental catastrophes or incurable diseases, or other still unsuspected calamities. However, these are not the issue with which we are concerned in this book. Our interest is not with what might have happened or what could potentially happen, but merely with what actually happened. Our aim is not to pursue some "end-of-civilization" thesis, the kind usually proffered in vatic tones fit for parody, in which whatever the writer happens to fear or loathe is set down as boding "the end of civilization as we know it." No such end-of-civilization thesis is entertained here.

The destruction of civilization with which we are concerned is an extended and enduring historical process with no foreseeable end. It is a slow withering away that could go on, cease, or reverse itself—we have no way of predicting in the long run which it will be. Best described as a de-civilizing process, it developed with frightening rapidity in the twentieth century and seems set to continue well into the twenty-first, for no countermovement is as yet discernible. We might hope for such a reversal, and we are duty bound to work for it, but we have no grounds for assuming it will necessarily occur. Civilization is now in the balance for the very first time in human history. How this balance tips will depend on the aspirations and unpredictable actions of future generations. All we can do is seek to influence them by safeguarding what is left of the civilization we inherited from our predecessors. Communication between the generations, as we pass on old and recent traditions, is clearly our key responsibility.

Among the relatively more recent traditions that are crucial for the future survival of civilization are those of the Enlightenment, as the outstanding historian Eric Hobsbawm declared: "I believe that one of the few things that stands between us and an accelerated descent into darkness is the set of values inherited from the eighteenth-century Enlightenment."[3] In a brief lecture delivered late in his life, Hobsbawm spells out what he means by "darkness," which he also calls "barbarism," utilizing the traditional terminology deriving from the fall of the classical civilization that, as we will show, is not altogether appropriate:

> The argument of this lecture is that, after about 150 years of secular decline, barbarism has been on the increase for most of the twentieth century. In this respect I understand "barbarism" to mean two things. First, the disruption and breakdown of the system of rules and moral behavior by which *all* societies regulate the relations among their members and, to a lesser extent, between their members and those of other societies. Second, I mean, more specifically, the reverse of what we may call the project of the eighteenth-century Enlightenment, namely, the establishment of a universal system of such rules and standards of moral behavior, embodied in the institution of states dedicated to the rational progress of humanity.[4]

In defining "barbarism," Hobsbawm has in effect also offered a cursory definition of its opposite, namely, civilization. In this view, which we share, civilization in modern times is primarily a matter of "the system of rules and moral behavior" and of "the rational progress of humanity"; or, putting it in a nutshell, of ethics and rationality, which, as we will show, are closely bound up with standards of higher literacy. It is, therefore, mainly in respect of ethics, rationality, and higher literacy that we need to assess the extent of the destruction of civilization in the twentieth century.

The first decisive event in this process of withering away was undoubtedly the First World War. Hobsbawm, like many others, sees this as the opening of the gates of hell:

> We may need to explain why nineteenth-century civilization did not recover from the First World War, as many expected it to do. But we know it didn't. It entered upon an age of catastrophe: of wars followed by social revolutions, of the end of empires, of the collapse of the liberal world economy, the steady retreat of constitutional and democratic governments, the rise of Fascism and Nazism. That civilization receded is not very surprising, especially when we consider that the period ended in the greatest school of barbarism of all, the Second World War.[5]

It is also not surprising that Hobsbawm is circumspect rather than forthright about one of the main causes of why civilization did not recover: the Bolshevik seizure of power in Russia and the resultant spread of Leninist-Marxism, for Hobsbawm himself and countless other intellectuals like him were lifelong devoted Marxists. This was the beginning of the age of totalitarianism of which Fascism and Nazism were alternate expressions. The Second World War, the descent into the lowest circles of hell, developed into the conflict between these two antagonistic forms of totalitarianism, Bolshevism and Nazism. It is essential to ask why thinkers like Hobsbawm should have espoused an ideology such as Bolshevism—as others espoused Nazism—and remained loyal to it. The commitment of intellectuals to devastatingly destructive ideologies remains a mystery; nevertheless, we will seek to elucidate it later in this work. Hobsbawm provides few clues as to this matter. However, he does outline the sequence of stages during which the de-civilizing process took place:

> I will now suggest a brief chronology of this slide down the slope of barbarization. The main stages are four: the First World War, the period of world crisis from the breakdown of 1917–20 to that of 1944–7, the four decades of the Cold War era, and lastly, the general breakdown of civilization as we know it over large parts of the world in and since the 1980s. There is an obvious continuity between the first three stages. In each of the earlier, lessons of man's inhumanity to man were learned and became the basis of new advances in barbarism.[6]

In this work we will refer to these first three stages as the *Events of the Twentieth Century*, and we will relate them to totalitarianism. This is the first of the main topics in our title, and we will devote most attention to it in the first part of the work. The fourth stage, that following the 1980s, we will discuss under the general heading of globalization, which is the second of the topics in the title and it will feature most prominently in the second part of this book. The third topic, that of colonialism, does not occur in Hobsbawm's brief summation, except perhaps implicitly in the phrase "the end of empires," which must refer to the de-colonialization that followed on the prior epoch of colonialism. We will explore how colonialism figured in the destruction of civilization in the third part of this work when we consider the fate of the non-Western civilizations, which Hobsbawm completely overlooked. Taken together, totalitarianism, globalization, and colonialism constitute the basic terms of our historical explanation for the ongoing destruction of civilization in the twentieth century.

Hobsbawm's assertion that with the destruction of civilization we are entering into a renewed state of barbarism certainly sounds odd. Barbarism is generally considered to be the state prior to civilization, one that ensues when a civilization collapses materially and organizationally and lapses back into what used to be called "savagery"—namely, a simpler state of social existence like that of tribalism or even feudalism. But clearly this is not what is happening in the world at present, and certainly not in Europe or America. There has been no material decline; on the contrary, Europe as well as America and many other parts of the world have entered into a state of general material affluence never before experienced in history. And the same holds true of their level of organization and social well-being; law and order is perhaps more prevalent than ever, personal security as well as individual rights have never been as safeguarded; democracy is spreading all over the world; literacy is almost universal; and information of every type is freely available. What we have elsewhere termed the Forces of Modernity—namely, industrial capitalism, the bureaucratic state, modern science, and technology—are responsible for these major advances, which most people consider to be progress.[7] Does this not also amount to an advance of civilization?

There are many thinkers who believe that it does; indeed, they hold that we now live in an advanced civilization that they call global or technological civilization, for it is one that spans the whole world, and it is based on the new technologies that enable rapid transportation and almost instant communication throughout the globe. Everywhere the same or very similar conditions obtain in respect of all major factors of importance in current conditions of human life. Whatever still distinguishes people from each other now seems secondary and of far less importance. Mostly, of course, these are the cultural, social, and individual differences that still exist and have not yet been completely eliminated. Is this, then, the brave new world toward which civilization has been steadily progressing, or is it something quite other that follows from the steady retreat from civilization to which Hobsbawm refers? Whatever it is, it is not barbarism. In our prior work we have called it a state beyond civilization or a condition of postcivilization.[8]

What we mean by this paradoxical designation will become clearer once we provide a theoretically adequate definition of civilization. The word itself is etymologically of Latin origin and did not come into use until the eighteenth century, first in its French form; but the idea behind it is as old as Classical civilization itself. In its root meaning it refers to the city (*civis* in Latin, *polis* in Greek), the locus of civilization, but not so much to the urban infrastructure itself, as to the way of life carried on within it by its citizens. This style of living came to be designated as civil or civilized. This idea was then transferred from its classical sources to analogous forms in numerous localities, during various ages, which also came to be called civilizations. However, many of these were not based on cities but on courts, which is a key marker in separating Western from Eastern civilizations.

Historically speaking we can also distinguish early and usually long-lasting civilizations, such as Sumer and Egypt, from later more developed ones, such as Greece, China, India, and eventually the Christian and Islamic ones. The difference between them is not merely a matter of chronology, for civilizations that arose very late, such as the pre-Columbian ones in America, are very like the early ones in the Old World. Rather, the main differentiating factor is whether a civilization derives from the breakthroughs of the Axial Age, a term devised by the philosopher Karl Jaspers to describe the key turning point of human history. It generally refers to the period between 700 and 300 BC approximately, and more specifically to the time around about 500 BC, when many of the most revered thinkers, prophets, and sages were near contemporaries: Pythagoras, Deutero-Isaiah, the Buddha, Confucius, and possibly Zoroaster as well, though his dating is uncertain.[9] It is from these that the philosophies, ethical systems, and religions that are still extant and current throughout the world derive.

The advanced civilizations of the world were founded directly or indirectly during the Axial Age based on the canonic texts, then devised and passed on in written form down the ages. It is these books that define for us the meaning of civilization. Civilization is primarily the forms of acting, thinking, and feeling adumbrated by these different traditions, and the subsequent developments based on them. Whatever else is needed to maintain a civilized form of life is secondary; this includes the material infrastructure of economic production, political organization, techniques of every description, and even scientific knowledge of a purely pragmatic kind—though not the theories themselves, for these are part of humanity's rational enlightenment. Civilization is primarily a matter of culture in the normative sense of that word, as when we speak of someone being cultured. There are cognate terms in all European languages, such as "kulturny" in Russian.

As Hobsbawm indicated, the civilization of the West is founded on a culture of ethics and rationality based on high literacy. This had its origins in Greek philosophy, Roman law, and Judaic monotheism. It developed into what is now commonly called the Judeo-Christian European civilization or the West for short, though that term can also be used for the whole sequence of Occidental civilizations, the Classical Greek and Roman, the Byzantine, and the European. The West, in both these senses, gave rise to a complex syncretic ethical system, in which a number of diverse components interact.[10] This was conjoined with numerous forms of rationality, which incorporated abstract theory and were couched in philosophic, scientific, and mathematical modes of representation.[11] From these two sets of features, which were more developed in the West than in any of its coeval civilizations, the culture of Modernity arose during the period of Renaissance and Reformation approximately and became the necessary precursor to our contemporary condition of globalization. The Enlightenment, whose passing Hobsbawm mourns, was the intermediate stage between early Modernity and our postcivilizational age. It will be our task to explain how this epochal transition took place and what agencies brought it about.

We can begin to understand what distinguishes civilization from postcivilization when we study the contrasting nature of literacy in both. Civilization is based on the high literacy of classical or canonic texts that embody the knowledge and wisdom of its culture and its fundamental beliefs—that is, both its rational and ethical norms. In the case of the West, these were incarnate in the first place in the works of the philosophers and prophets, or to be more specific in Plato and Aristotle, the Bible, and St. Paul. Later, all kinds of other foundational texts were added to these, such as the work of great poets, dramatists, and novelists, and in modern times also the works of natural philosophers or scientists like Newton and Darwin. All such texts used to play a basic role in education, and nobody would have been considered educated—that is, civilized—who was not knowledgeable about them, at least to some degree. This was the mark of civility, facilitating intelligent conversation and letter-writing. Depending on their education and ability, people obviously attained different levels of excellence in this respect, but it represented an ideal for all.

The decline of high literacy in our time is a striking symptom of the onset of a postcivilizational condition. Best described by the German term *Bildung*, literacy on this level is disappearing, even if it has not yet completely vanished. There is, of course, an almost universal literacy, which has never before been present in any society; this achievement, however, masks the fact that basic literacy involves a generally low level of comprehension. Everybody can read, but what most people choose to read is of questionable value. Certainly, the classical and canonic texts are hardly read or, if read, only perfunctorily by students having to satisfy examination requirements. Even standards of literacy in popular reading matter have fallen drastically over the course of the twentieth century. If we compare any newspaper, public address, popular novel, or piece of literature from before the First World War with present-day texts, we see a huge disparity in the literacy demanded by works from these different periods. Apart from print media, the other types of media, such as film, radio, TV, video, and even the Internet, require only moderate literacy, as they are based on electronic sound and image. Reliance on them has led to the impoverishment of education and to mass stupefaction, as the sociological studies of Benjamin Barber demonstrate.[12]

How can one speak of "civilization" under such circumstances? And yet this is what many theorists, both sociologists and historians, choose to call a global or technological civilization. They base themselves on the technological apparatus that is everywhere prevalent, like the so-called car culture that dominates the lives of people as soon as they become sufficiently affluent to afford a vehicle, or the now equally prevalent computer "literacy." They point to the economic integration of the world through global production, distribution, and marketing arrangements that enable a cornucopia of consumer goods to be available worldwide. They note the near-universality of law and order and the provisions that have been made to protect human rights from which all individuals benefit. They laud the free circulation of information and the availability of knowledge on any subject whatever, due to the new technologies of communication. This, they say, is what amounts to a technological civilization.

Yet the term "technological civilization" is an oxymoron. Civilization, as we have argued, cannot be based on technology or on any other material and even organizational factors, for it is primarily a matter of culture, that is, of ethics and rationality, linked to high literacy. No amount of sheer material progress of any kind can possibly constitute a civilization. Hence, a situation such as that of the present, where enormous material and organizational progress has taken place, but which is accompanied by a huge decline in culture, can only be called a postcivilizational condition, something that is beyond civilization as we have known it.

In the following discussion we are intent on explaining what has brought about such an unprecedented contradiction between the material and cultural sides of social life. We will focus first on what can be called the primary agencies of de-civilization: totalitarianism, globalization, and colonialism. Before discussing them singly, we will consider them briefly together. Then we will consider their deeper causes, above all the Forces of Modernity: industrial capitalism, the bureaucratic state, modern science, and technology. The relation between these three forces on the one hand, and totalitarianism, globalization, and colonialism on the other hand, is in fact the crux of our whole account. It is this relation that we hope to make fully explicit by the end of the work. And in the process we hope to explicate the unusual condition in which civilization now finds itself and explain why calling it a "technological civilization" is so misleading.

The three agencies of de-civilization are distinct historical processes, which overlapped during the twentieth century. Colonialism is the oldest, for it took place largely in the nineteenth century and led to the establishment of European empires or spheres of influence in Asia and Africa. Colonialism is different from colonization or what is known as white European settlement of the New World, which took place during the sixteenth century in South America and the seventeenth century in North America, and also much later in Australasia. Colonialism came to an end around the middle of the twentieth century, due largely to the costs and tribulations that the two world wars and the battle against totalitarianism exacted from the main imperial powers, Britain and France, though the liberation movements that arose in the aftermath of their initial defeats, especially at the hands of the Japanese in East Asia, were also decisive. Once victorious, these movements established the states that sought to form a common nonaligned policy and constitute a block of Third World countries—a term that we will, nevertheless, continue to use because it is so well known, even though the global political situation that it reflected in the twentieth century is no longer current.

Totalitarianism began in the Old World, where it had its most devastating impact on civilization, though it also ravaged parts of the Third World as well; only the New World was completely free of it. In Europe it flourished in the period between the two great wars, after which it continued in a somewhat muted form, stripped of radical evil, which we will call sub-totalitarianism. Because of its destructive effect on Western civilization, we will concentrate most of our attention on totalitarianism when dealing with the Old World. The first part of our work will be largely devoted to it.

Totalitarianism, which helped to bring about the end of colonialism, also brought about the conclusion of the European drive for global integration that flourished until the First World War and only really ceased with the Great Depression and the Second World War. This was the earlier phase of globalization in which Britain played the leading role as the major capitalist and imperialist power during the nineteenth century. The second and much more decisive phase of globalization began after the Second World War under the aegis of the New World, after it had come to the rescue of the Old World and saved Western Europe from totalitarian domination.

America had risen to global prominence during the course of the twentieth century and reached world mastery in all respects in the period after the Second World War. It then set about establishing global organizations to manage the political, economic, social, and cultural affairs of the world: the UN and its agencies, for example, and the IMF, the World Bank, the OECD, and many others. These became the basis of a renewed globalization to which more and more nations adhered as they became modernized and as they abandoned the restrictive anticapitalist policies of Communist totalitarianism and so-called Third World Socialism, especially after the death of Mao in China and the collapse of the Soviet regime in Russia. At present America still stands at the head of this drive to globalization, so much so that for most intents and purposes globalization and Americanization are almost synonymous.

However, it must be stressed that by the term "Americanization" we do not mean the full extent and scope of American civilization, which we will discuss in part II, but only those aspects of it that are readily transmissible to other countries, especially though not exclusively those of the Third World, since all countries have become to some extent Americanized, even the European ones. Americanization largely concerns the Forces of Modernity in their American version: free-market capitalism, the liberal-democratic state, Big Science, and high-tech technology. These have become ubiquitous and all pervasive; the global integration of the world is based on them.

Totalitarianism, globalization, and colonialism might have overlapped historically, but they were not causally connected to each other; the one did not bring about any of the others. However, they did influence each other indirectly in all kinds of subtle ways. As we have already stated, the battle against totalitarianism promoted de-colonialization in many different respects; not the least of these was American foreign policy, which was designed to counter Communist totalitarian inroads into the old colonial empires, by pressing for the liberation of the native peoples in order to free the European powers from their colonial burdens and enable them to concentrate their forces on the Cold War challenge in Europe. American action during the Suez war, conducted by France and Britain against Nasser in Egypt, provides the prime example of the implementation of this policy. At the same time it is clear that colonialism was by no means the unmitigated evil its opponents and detractors now present it as, for without it globalization as we now know it could not have taken place. Undoubtedly it had a harmful effect on native peoples and their traditional cultures and civilizations, but at the same time it constituted the first phase of modernization, without which the development of modern states and economies—though not yet societies—in the Third World would have been impossible.

Colonialism did not cause totalitarianism, though Hannah Arendt implied a causal relation by presenting imperialism as a precursor to totalitarianism, as if the latter somehow grew out of the former.[13] But this was not the case. As we will show, totalitarianism had a quite different causal origin to do with the First World War. Nevertheless, in many respects colonialism influenced and prepared the way for totalitarianism. This is especially evident in the case of Italian Fascism and German Nazism. Mussolini's belated drive for empire in Africa led directly to his attempt to conquer independent nations and establish colonial possessions in the Adriatic region, namely in Europe itself. Hitler was forthright about his plans to colonize Eastern Europe up to the Urals; he set out these plans in *Mein Kampf* and implemented them in the Second World War. He drew his inspiration from the British Empire in India, declaring that "what India was to England, the territories of Russia will be for us."[14] It is also likely that the German policy of treating certain Slavs (by no means all, for the Nazis practiced no consistency in racial matters) as subhumans was also inspired by the way blacks were treated in some African colonies, most notoriously in the Belgian Congo and in German South-West Africa. After the revolt of the Hereros, the governor there issued a *Vernichtungsbefehl*, stating that "every Herero, whether found with or without a rifle, with or without cattle, will be shot."[15] This declaration was a foretaste of the extermination policies practiced later in the East. However, one must not exaggerate such influences; the Bolsheviks, who had no such colonial racist models, were equally adept at extermination, most frequently of their own people, rather than vanquished foreigners.

Finally, and perhaps improbably, there is some evidence that totalitarianism had an indirect bearing on subsequent globalization.

The traumatic effect of the totalitarian experience had the predictable consequence of breaking down nationalistic ideologies and encouraging countries to open themselves up to global influences. This is most evident in the two nations that suffered calamitous defeats in the Second World War, Germany and Japan. The willingness of so many states to surrender a considerable degree of sovereignty to world entities, as well as to integrate themselves into larger units of agglomeration, came as a reaction to their negative experiences under totalitarianism. Without this, it is doubtful whether the European Union would have been constituted as soon as it was; that in itself is a move beyond the nation-state. The willingness of China after Mao and of Russia after Gorbachev to join an American-dominated global system is certainly due to the immense failures they experienced with their respective Communist regimes.

Unfortunately, the harm that totalitarianism did to civilization was beyond repair. There is no doubt that totalitarianism was the most damaging agency of civilization ever encountered in history. It far exceeded that wrought by barbarians in past ages—and this is another reason why Hobsbawm's term "barbarization" for the history of the twentieth century is such a misnomer. Something much more insidious took place. Totalitarianism attacked civilization in a way that no outside barbarians could ever have done, for this was an assault on civilization from within civilization itself, against which civilization was almost helpless to defend itself.

In the first place, as Hobsbawm avers, the totalitarians were bent on destroying the late Western civilization of the Enlightenment that had flourish so prolifically before 1914 in Europe and America, and promised to spread gradually to all other parts of the world. This was the culture of liberal-democracy, of the rule of law, of human rights and individualism, of civility in personal bearing and relationships, of humanistic education, of religious freedom and the separation of church and state, of high literacy and a cultivation of the arts, and of intellectual and scientific pursuits, based on the university as an independent institution. It was precisely this civilization that both the far Left and the far Right types of totalitarianism set themselves to destroy, declaring it to be merely bourgeois. And the bourgeoisie was what they most detested and strove to eradicate. Hence, they negated and sought to overturn every one of the previously mentioned features. Of course, the way the Bolsheviks did this was different from the way the Nazis set about it, but the effect was similar. The Bolsheviks began with the burning of churches and the Nazis with the burning of books, but in no time both turned to the burning of people. Radical evil became their common predilection.

Once they embarked on radical evil, they did more than impugn the Enlightenment values of Western civilization; the very basis of that civilization itself was overturned. Judeo-Christian morality was assailed, first by the Bolsheviks because it was Christian and therefore the religious opium of the people, and then by the Nazis because it was Jewish and therefore racially tainted. Instead, what is right and good was to be judged exclusively by the interests of the Revolution and the proletariat or the Party or the *Volksgemeinschaft*. The rule of law—which the West had inherited from the Greeks and Romans, and developed further in a unique fashion—was dismissed as mere juristic formalism. Instead, the ukase of the Leader or the will of the *Führer* had the force of law. The Greek heritage of philosophical rationality and scientific truth was also suborned by being made subject to political requirements. All philosophies that went against the prevailing ideologies were banned, and all scientific theories that departed from them or were propounded by the wrong people were also rejected. Thus Mendelian genetics in the one case and Einsteinian physics in the other were declared anathema. After all these travesties, what could remain of rationality or civilization in general?

Colonialism was nowhere near as virulently destructive as totalitarianism, but it, too, was harmful to civilization—in this case not so much Western civilization as those of non-European peoples. Most of these civilizations were already in decline when the European colonialists arrived, but they were never given a chance to recover. The Europeans tended to view all other civilizations as inferior to their own and to treat them as relics of a bygone age and a more primitive stage of development. This conclusion followed from theories of development or social evolution, buttressed by Social Darwinism and usually accompanied by some degree of racism, both of which were invoked during the late nineteenth-century colonial period. It is true that there were also tendencies in the opposite direction in favor of the original and primeval, extolling the perennial wisdom of the East, for example, or the high spirituality of Eastern religions, or the more refined beauty of oriental art, or the primitive expressiveness of the arts of Africa; however, such attitudes were only to be found among a minority of sympathetically inclined orientalists or modernist artists, or other connoisseurs of the non-European exotic. Most Westerners believed that other civilizations had little to offer the West, and they numbered among them such great minds as Hegel, Marx, and Mill, the latter himself a colonial administrator.

Colonialism did not act against other civilizations by forcibly eliminating or repressing them; on the contrary, the colonial authorities were usually indulgent to native traditions and beliefs, except for those that really deserved to be abolished, such as widow-burning in India or foot-binding in China. Rather, they demeaned them in the eyes of their own exponents, the natives themselves, by demonstrating in so many seemingly irrefutable ways that Western civilization was superior. As a result, those who could afford it, usually members of the elite, sought a Western education for themselves and their children. It was precisely those educated in this way, frequently in the home countries of the colonialists, who became the leading advocates for national independence and, where necessary, fighters for liberation from the colonial yoke. It is owing to such people that Third World countries acquired Western ideologies—preeminently in the opposed forms of liberalism and Marxism—and Western modes of government, whether democratic or Socialist; and it is thanks to them that Third World countries became, at least to some degree, imbued with Western forms of culture. But in this respect they were continuing the *mission civilizatrice* that the Western powers at their most enlightened undertook.

It is this Europeanization of the Third World, usually called "modernization," that made globalization possible. Only countries that were sufficiently modernized are capable of joining the systems of world order that govern the economy, politics, knowledge, education, culture, and other aspects of global society. Countries that have not yet caught up with these developments remain on the periphery of such world systems. Globalization brings to the whole world the Forces of Modernity—namely, industrial capitalism, the bureaucratic state, science, and technology—that the West developed over the last five centuries. At present these institutions are being disseminated in their latest form, the one devised in America and conveyed to the rest of the world via American initiatives such as the Marshall Plan or the numerous other projects it undertook in other regions of the world when its dominance in all these respects became so pronounced. This was when Europe itself was, so to speak, Americanized.

It is not yet clear what the full effects of globalization will be for civilization, but already the signs are ominous. Globalization furthers the material and organizational aspect of civilization at the expense of all others—the cultural, moral, intellectual, and spiritual ones. It allows the latter to function only insofar as they are adjuncts to the former. Thus, for example, it promotes a culture of media and advertising that is consonant with the marketing needs of industrial capitalism, but this makes for global culture to the detriment of every type of local culture.[16] This is clearly a de-civilizing propensity, but one that is different from any that has ever occurred before. It has nothing in common with barbarism in the anthropological sense, though it results in cultural manifestations that are so crude and primitive they merit being called barbaric in a looser sense.

Thus we are confronted with an overwhelming civilizational paradox: in the midst of unprecedented material affluence and organizational efficiency, utilizing the most advanced technologies and the most up-to-date scientific knowledge—in the midst, that is, of progress in that narrow sense—we are at the same time sinking into a cultural, moral, intellectual, and spiritual decline that is also unprecedented.[17] How did civilization become both so advanced and so debased? This book sets out to explain the historical origins of this condition, more properly called "postcivilization," in the violently contradictory processes of the twentieth century.

Notes

1. See Steven Pinker, *The Better Angels of our Nature, The Decline of Violence in History and its Causes* (Allen Lane, London, 2011), p. 200.
2. See Steven E. Ambrose, "D-Day Fails", in Robert Cowley (ed.), *The Collected What If? Eminent Historians Imagine What Might Have Been* (Putnam, New York, 2001), p. 347.
3. Eric Hobsbawm, "Barbarism: A User's Guide", in *On History* (The New Press, New York, 1997), p. 254.
4. Ibid., p. 253.
5. Ibid., p. 259.
6. Ibid., p. 256.
7. See Harry Redner, *Beyond Civilization: Society, Culture, and the Individual in the Age of Globalization* (Transaction Publishers, Piscataway, NJ, 2013).
8. Ibid., p. 16.
9. See Karl Jaspers, *The Origin and Goal of History*, trans. Michael Bullock (Routledge and Kegan Paul, London, 1953).
10. See Harry Redner, *Ethical Life: The Past and Present of Ethical Cultures* (Rowman and Littlefield, Lanham, 2001).
11. See Harry Redner, *A New Science of Representation: Towards an Integrated Theory of Representation in Science, Politics, and Arts* (Westview, Boulder, 1994).
12. See Benjamin Barber, *Consumed: How Markets Corrupt Children, Infantilize Adults, and Swallow Citizens Whole* (Norton, New York, 2007).

13. See Hannah Arendt, *The Origins of Totalitarianism* (Allen and Unwin, London, 1967).
14. Quoted in Niall Ferguson, *Empire: How Britain Made the Modern World* (Penguin, London, 2003), p. 334.
15. Ibid., p. 296.
16. See Harry Redner, *Conserving Cultures: Technology, Globalization, and the Future of Local Cultures* (Roman and Littlefield, Lanham, 2004).
17. See Harry Redner, *Beyond Civilization*, op. cit.

I

The Old World

1

Totalitarianism and Civilization

Section I—Look Back in Horror

......these two intertwined lives [Stalin and Hitler]
contain the essential horror of the century.
François Furet

...Oh, horror, horror, horror
Heart nor tongue can conceive nor name thee.
Macbeth

The further we recede from the twentieth century, the more we look back on it in horror. It was the most horrendous time in Western Civilization, perhaps in the whole of human history. For not only were hundreds of millions of lives cut short in wars, exterminations, and famines, but the very fabric of civilized life was severely damaged, not just temporarily during the time of troubles but permanently so. The two world wars were the epicenters from which devastation spread like waves of violence in all directions until they encompassed the whole earth. As the historian Arno Mayer writes:

> With these two monstrous conflicts the twentieth century very likely became the most violent century in recorded history. Its wars were so uniquely bloody and savage because they were an amalgam of conventional war, civil war and *Glaubenskrieg*. Culminating in Auschwitz, Dresden and Hiroshima, they punctured what remained of the pretense that advanced civilization was measured by man's progressive mastery of violence.[1]

The latter view, advanced by Norbert Elias in 1939 on the very eve of the Second World War, in his magisterial work, *The Civilizing Process*, has recently been taken up by Steven Pinker; we shall criticize such

3

theories of a "civilizing process" elsewhere in another work, but clearly everything we have to say in this work goes against it.[2]

The main source of the violence of the century was undoubtedly totalitarianism. It was the cause of what Mayer calls "conventional war, civil war and *Glaubenskrieg*," a synonym for totalitarianism seen in religious terms, which, as we shall show in the next chapter, is not altogether correct. We shall refer to this conjunction of events as the Events of the Twentieth Century for short. It is important to stress right from the start that these were events brought about by people, acting singly and in groups, and not just impersonal occurrences caused by forces or systems beyond the control of individuals, though such were also in operation. The question will, of course, arise as to how these two ways of looking at human behavior relate to each other, which we shall tackle in chapter 3, section III. Among the countless individuals involved, the most influential, and therefore most important, were the dealers of death, foremost among whom were Stalin and Hitler, at least in Europe; in Asia, Mao must also be included. It is to these lives that the "essential horror of the century," as Furet puts it, must be primarily attributed.

What made such individuals so omnipotent and prone to so much evil was not anything inherent in themselves, of course; they were in most respects ordinary men and in some even deficient, though exceptional in their talents for influencing people and so acquiring and wielding so much power. Rather, it was the Events of the Twentieth Century, the historical context in which they operated, that gave them the opportunity to rise to the very top and acquire the undisputed leadership of nations. Their abilities came into play because in the troubled and anguished times of that epoch there were masses of people waiting and wanting to be led. The movements and parties they formed or controlled were not altogether unprecedented. Similar ones had arisen before, but only in this period could they make a bid for supreme and unchallenged domination over everyone. They assumed the monstrous form of totalitarianism, which became the fate of the times, as Irving Louis Horowitz declares:

> If the century can be politically summarized in a word, one would be hard-pressed to find a more appropriate term than collectivism. . . .
> But beyond politics as such is the need to define the century in systemic terms, or in terms that go beyond the political in any conventional sense. In doing so the most appropriate word to be developed is "totalitarianism."[3]

It is to totalitarianism that we shall devote our initial attention in coming to an understanding of the destruction of civilization in the twentieth century. This does not mean that totalitarianism was everywhere dominant; it certainly was not in the New World. Nor does it mean that totalitarianism was in the end victorious—far from it; it was ultimately defeated, though it still survives. What it does mean is that the struggle surrounding it, the battle for or against it, consumed most of the energies and resources of nearly all people on earth. Nearly all Europeans were directly involved, most Asians were either directly or indirectly implicated, and North Americans were drawn in by the conflicts of both Europe and Asia. Only South Americans and Africans south of the Sahara were left relatively untouched.

As we shall see, totalitarianism did not begin of its own accord. For its start it had the First World War to thank, for which it was in no way responsible, since that was caused by quite other forces. Had there been no such war, totalitarianism would not have arisen, as we shall seek to substantiate in what follows. If the Great War was an accident of history, though one waiting to happen, then so was totalitarianism. It was in no way preordained or inevitable. However, once the war started and developed into the wholesale carnage that it became, then totalitarianism or something approximating it became very likely. As Norman Davies puts it, "despite the victory of the Western democracies, the most dynamic political product of the Great War lay in the anti-Western, anti-liberal and anti-democratic monster of totalitarianism."[4] Totalitarianism in other parts of Europe was the cost that Western Europe and America incurred for victory.

The outcome of the war in the East led directly to the Russian Revolution and the establishment of the Bolshevik regime, the first totalitarian one in history. From that beginning others followed. Bolshevik revolutions in Germany and Austro-Hungary failed, but "red" insurrection in Italy provoked in reaction the first Fascist totalitarianism. A second might have ensued in Germany, if Hitler, acting in conjunction with Ludendorff, the former chief of staff and near-dictator of Germany in the last stages of the war, had not been so precipitate and reckless in initiating a putsch in Munich in 1923; he had to wait ten more years to come legally to power with the compliance of Hindenburg, another great wartime general, who was president. Totalitarianism in China came much later under Mao, when with Stalin's help he defeated Chiang Kai-shek in the civil war in 1948. From that victory other Asian and African totalitarianisms followed.

Once totalitarianism was launched, it became the main driving-force of world events, with the one possible exception, the Great Depression, which was America's contribution to global turmoil and the precipitating cause of Hitler's election victory in Germany. The Great Depression inaugurated a period of great instability in most countries both internally, giving rise to strikes and repressions, and, externally, giving rise to military adventures. Totalitarianism and other forms of dictatorship were everywhere promoted. All these outbreaks of violence precipitated the world into the Second World War.

This war and its outcome are too well known to need repeating here. In brief, the defeat of the far-right totalitarians, the Nazis in Germany and the Fascists in Italy, led to the triumph of the far-left totalitarians, the Bolsheviks in Russia. The further spread of Communist totalitarianism in Europe, beyond the East where Soviet military might prevailed, was stopped by American military and economic intervention. Out of the resulting stalemate, largely due to the fear of mutual nuclear annihilation, arose the Cold War, which lasted until the Soviet Union collapsed in 1989. That was the end of totalitarianism in Europe, but not in China and other parts of Asia. Now a new kind of competition is emerging between America and China, so the history of totalitarianism is far from over, though it is perhaps not as decisive in the twenty-first century as it was in the twentieth.

Some historians, particularly German ones, now refer to the main period of totalitarian conflict as a European civil war, but that is a tendentious exaggeration that makes it seem as if this was a war of brother against brother, so it does not matter who was on which side during it. However, Europe in that period was not anywhere near unity. It was divided into separate states at war, as had been the case throughout European history, and it mattered crucially whether one was fighting for democracy or for totalitarianism. But there is, nevertheless, a point to this way of putting it, for ideological conflict, for or against the totalitarian ideologies, became endemic within every European country and every totalitarian movement had its imitators and supporters, so-called fellow travelers, everywhere. So in that respect there was a kind of ideological civil war going on, although it did not always lead to outright violence, hardly ever so after the Second World War once the Iron Curtain was down, except for the insurrections in East Europe, most notably in Hungary, Czechoslovakia, and finally Poland.

It was this type of ideological warfare that was so inimical to culture and so destructive to civilization in general. It became all-pervasive, and everything was caught up in its toils and traps. Nothing touched by it could any longer be presented as pure and innocent, unbiased and of good intent, or perfectly harmless and promoting no particular political cause. Everything became suspect; everyone was doubted, disbelieved, and accused of partisanship, whether intended or not. And there were most frequently good grounds for suspicion and doubt, for lies and deceptions of all kinds came to proliferate. Propaganda outstripped information; disinformation took the place of knowledge; even science could no longer be trusted, for it was often falsified. "Truth" became that which people could be persuaded to believe by any means whatever. In short, there was no truth, for who could be trusted to tell it? People of the highest integrity and achievement were caught up in the networks of lies and came to repeat them either unknowingly and innocently, or knowingly and cynically, or themselves no longer able to tell the difference. Philosophers, scientists, writers, artists, intellectuals of every stripe and color were complicit in making themselves available for one ideological cause or another. This was perhaps the most egregious degradation of civilization that Europe had ever suffered. Its spirit was broken and could never be fully repaired.

The "civil war" surrounding the totalitarian ideologies was by no means confined to Europe alone; it spread across the Atlantic to America as well. The need to wage the Cold War called forth a fierce, often fanatical anticommunism at home as well as abroad. Many Americans in high places resorted to totalitarian methods in order to combat totalitarianism. Such methods, practices, and tactics infused themselves by a kind of unthinking osmosis into many cultural spheres, invading areas of professional competence from which they had been ethically excluded before, such as universities, the arts, and the higher reaches of the press and media in general. Witch hunts, boycotts, blackballing became quite common. Those who defended themselves against possible charges or accusations, whether justified or not, had most often no hesitation in resorting to equivocations, prevarications, and outright lies. Thus, many became embroiled in tangles of suspicion and self-protective deceit.

This was particularly the case in academia, where the freedoms of research, publication, and self-expression became casualties of conformity, and truth became a sop to ideology. Presses and journals were suborned, often with the justification that a good cause was served, as might well have been the case, but it was rarely the case that the ends justified such means. Associations and organizations were infiltrated by spies and *agents provocateurs*. So who could be trusted? The knowledge that such things were done with impunity and could be done again can never be retracted. Now new concerns have arisen, given that electronic surveillance has become all-pervasive. "Big Brother is watching you" is no longer an idle threat confined to fiction. The problem of means and ends is once again uppermost in the so-called war on terror. What still remains of our civilization, after the battle against totalitarianism had destroyed so much of it, might now fall victim to the very effort to save it from fundamentalist barbarism.

It is true that those countries that did not fall under totalitarian domination did not suffer as much as those that did. And of the latter, the longer they were subject to totalitarian rule, the worse the outcome for their people and their culture. Western Europe had only a small dose of the totalitarian poison and could get over it much better than Italy or Germany. In Italy, the totalitarian poison was a much weaker version than in Germany, which suffered the full brunt of prolonged Nazi rule, and in East Germany totalitarianism continued in another form under Communism for much longer. East Europe in general was subject to the same kind of totalitarian yoke following the Second World War. Russia came off worst of all, for it had suffered totalitarianism since the Revolution and for a period of twenty-five years in its worst Stalinist form. What this has meant for Russian culture and its civilization can easily be gauged by comparing where it stood under the autocratic Czar Nicholas II and the aristocrats before the First World War and what it is like now under President Putin and the oligarchs.

In the next section we shall go on to investigate the numerous ways in which totalitarianism destroys civilization. It is not a matter of a single blow, such as barbarian hordes invading a country, leveling cities, and ravaging the land. Now the destructive impulse does not come from the outside but is internally generated; it comes from some kind of wrong turn within civilization itself that we do not fully understand. Why a civilization, apparently at its apogee, like Europe before 1914, should go so terribly wrong will be the main question to answer.

Section II—How Civilization Perished

Prior to 1914, Europe was at the height of its power and cultural achievement. Not only was it politically and economically dominant throughout the world, but European civilization seemed the only one with any claim to being considered a civilization. All the others, or what was left of them, were not only deemed to be inferior versions but were destined to disappear before the inexorable march of Progress. Central and Eastern Europe in particular were culturally in a remarkably flourishing state though backward in many other respects. Ruled by the three dynasties—Hohenzollern, Hapsburg, and Romanov—the main cities of their empires were as advanced culturally and intellectually as any others in the world: Berlin, Munich, and Dresden; Vienna, Budapest, and Prague; Moscow and St. Petersburg—these were the places where new and exciting things were happening. In the West only Paris and London could hold a candle to them. And as bad luck or fate would have it, these were precisely the places where the worst depredations of totalitarianism occurred. It is as if European civilization in the East was nipped in the bud by a Siberian winter wind before it could come to fruition.

Of course, a large part of the explanation for this misfortune is that these were the cities on the losing side in the First World War. The Events of the Twentieth Century took a particularly grim toll in these parts of Europe, for it was there that totalitarianism emerged and persisted far longer than elsewhere. If one can metaphorically speak of a civilization committing suicide, then this is what happened in those key parts of Europe. Our task will be to elucidate how and why this happened.

The process began in Russia as soon as the Bolsheviks seized power and the Cheka was constituted and set to work to eliminate or exile all those opposed to the Revolution or who could not bring themselves to pay lip service to the new regime. Later, under Stalin, it became much worse: intellectuals, writers, artists, scientists, and academics in general were decimated in the various purges that unrolled before and after the Second World War; the war itself was almost welcomed by such people as a temporary respite from terror. Only those who were prepared to denounce others or who were too useful or well-known to be liquidated were spared. The cultural devastation did not just touch on the elites, it also affected ordinary people in countless ways. The peasants were deprived of their traditional Orthodox faith and folk beliefs and customs bound up with it, such as the celebration of Christmas and Easter. Oddly enough, it was the aristocratic-bourgeois high culture of the czarist era, such as the Bolshoi ballet, that was retained, for that catered to the pretensions of the Party bosses who saw themselves as the inheritors of the glories of the past.

In Germany the cultural devastation was nowhere near as severe, and much of traditional culture was maintained, though little new

9

was added. However, it was severely purged of all undesirable influences and anything contributed by Jews, though even that was not honestly implemented: the words of "Die Lorelei" were attributed to Anonymous, and the Jewish provenance of Lorenzo da Ponte, Mozart's librettist, was left in obscurity. Otherwise, all condemned books were burned, a process begun by university students themselves, and paintings mocked in exhibitions of so-called degenerate art. As Heine had once prophesied, the burning of books was followed by the burning of people, though in the Nazi case there was a long interval between the two holocausts, during which some people could escape. Tens of thousands of Germany's best minds fled abroad, mainly to America, and an indeterminate number who had been ostracized by the new regime's *Gleichschaltung* decrees retired into what later became known as an inner emigration. However, the great majority remained at their posts and fully collaborated with what the authorities required of them. The betrayal of truth and reason that this represented could not be expiated after the war, for the same people returned to their positions to serve the occupation authorities and the new German governments on both sides of the ideological dividing line. As Eliot put it, "After such knowledge, what forgiveness?"

As a result of totalitarianism, civilization was devastated in Europe, but it was even worse in China, where there was almost nothing left. Mao's Cultural Revolution was as thorough a destruction of culture as had ever been undertaken, even by the first emperor, Shih Huang-ti, after whom Mao modeled himself. The Red Guards, whom he unleashed, were not merely directed to attack foreign Western influences in China, such as the Boxers had set out to do, they were set to smash the old culture itself. The "anti-Confucius campaign" of the mid-1960s resulted in rampages and sheer vandalism that destroyed temples and trashed monuments and works of art. It is said that the Forbidden City was only spared because of Chou En-lai's personal intercession. But nothing could save the hundreds of thousands of teachers, professors, students, intellectuals, and others who were humiliated into committing suicide or survived among the peasants in the countryside where they had been sent for their "re-education." For a short time China was literally without learning of any kind for the first time in its recorded history. Can it ever recover? We shall return to this question in chapter 8.

Europe, too, experienced an attack on its civilization such as had never occurred in its history. The totalitarian regimes set themselves the task of eradicating the fundamental values on which Western civilization had been founded. They very nearly succeeded. In the name of founding a new civilization of the future, both the Bolsheviks and the Nazis set about destroying as much as they could of the existing one. But there was no such civilization of the future; it was all a utopian dream—yet the destruction in the present was real enough. Building Socialism in the one country as the first stage in achieving Communism was a delusion; the reality was the totalitarian state. Conquering colonial territories in order to establish the Thousand-Year Reich was the megalomaniac ambition; the reality was a war on two fronts that Germany could not win. Molding the new humans of the future meant expunging the humanity of those in the present. Instead of the old humanism, which both totalitarianisms despised, there arose a new brutalism: hardness of body and toughness of mind to the point of insensitivity was extolled; conscience was equated with weakness. Thus were the past and the present sacrificed for a future that never came.

From the outset, both totalitarian movements were intent on destroying the legacy of the Enlightenment. Liberal democracy, the main political achievement of the nineteenth century, was despised and denounced. Individualism and human rights were condemned in the name of dethroning the bourgeoisie, the supposed ruling class. Instead, both totalitarianisms advocated their ideals of collectivity, the submergence of the individual in the proletariat or the *Volksgemeinschaft*. Everybody was considered a worker, the new ideal social being; and everyone would find fulfillment in performing a function in the collectivity. In relation to the collectivity, there were no such things as individual rights; the demands it could make on its members were in no way limited. Self-sacrifice on behalf of the collectivity was the highest fulfillment. Hence both totalitarian "religions," so to speak, advocated different versions of a cult of death.

As regards private property, the free market and capitalist enterprise there seemed to be a fundamental difference of principle between the two totalitarian ideologies. But in practice the divergence between them was not all that great. Both practiced a centralized control of the economy and its planning and directions in terms of goals set by five-year-plans. The reason for this similarity was that both economies were geared to heavy industry intent on rapid rearmament and the mobilization of the workforce for this overriding purpose. It is true that the Bolsheviks expropriated all private property and nationalized all productive facilities in their drive against capitalism, whereas the

Nazis did not go anywhere near as far. But the Nazis did expropriate Jewish-owned enterprises and denounced as "Jewish capitalism" the free market where this went against their plans. Once the conquests began, they appropriated everything they wanted as plunder in the conquered territories.

Karl Polanyi declared in 1935: "Revolutionary Socialism is but a different formulation and stricter interpretation of truths generally accepted in Western Europe for almost two thousand years. Fascism is their denial."[5] He could not have been more wrong. But at the time it was a typical error made by Communist fellow travelers. Though it might have been true of Marxism prior to 1914, it was no longer so of Stalinism in 1935. By that stage Stalin had already outdistanced Hitler in trampling on all the basic truths of Western civilization. At this point Hitler had only set up concentration camps and murdered Röhm and his associates. Stalin had established the Gulag system and carried out the liquidation of the Kulaks; and looking ahead, following the assassination of Kirov, which he might or might not have engineered (the evidence is inconclusive), he was setting himself up to carry out the Great Purge and to justify it by means of the theater of the trials of the Old Bolsheviks. At the same time, he was promulgating a constitution that was the most liberal in the whole world. This was a level of deceit, hypocrisy, and mass murder that Hitler did not equal until the start of the war. Western civilization had never experienced this kind of moral debasement.

Hitler's onslaught on Western morality was carried out in the name of his attack on the Jews. He dared not openly assault Christianity and its Judeo-Christian moral foundations, but he did seek to undermine it by promoting German Christianity, which amounted to a kind of Gnostic heresy. This went as far as the denial that Jesus was a Jew. The denial of basic Christian teaching of the sacredness of life and of God's love for all of mankind, without exception, was inherent in the Nazi racial doctrines and eugenic practices. The gospel of love was either restricted to those of the superior racial community, the Aryans, or it was rejected altogether, in line with Nietzsche's critique of Christian morality as slave morality. Right and wrong were considered relative matters, depending on what was in the interest of the Volk or the Aryan race in general, just as the Communists held it to be whatever was in the interest of the proletariat and the Revolution. No Western ethics could accommodate such doctrines, which, in effect, aimed to eliminate ethics altogether.

As for religion, Hitler repeatedly appealed to Providence and to God to justify what he was doing, but he made it patently apparent that in doing God's work he was merely realizing the Social Darwinist goal of ensuring the triumph of the fit and strong, namely the Aryans, over the weak and ill who deserved to perish. God was identified with Nature, "red in tooth and claw." This was a verbal pretense of religion that amounted to a denial of religion. As we shall argue later, the idea that the Nazis expounded a "political religion" or "secular faith" is mistaken; their fanaticism must be explained in quite other terms.

Stalin, too, made a verbal pretense to a credo based on moral principles, such as the brotherhood of Man and the equality of all human beings. But in the actuality of the class struggle—which Stalin declared had intensified just when all opposition had been eliminated, for this enabled him to carry out his purges—such principles were mere residual sentimentalities. Only those of the right class origins were treated as real human beings; those of "bad" origin were declared parasites and pests worthy of extermination, just as Hitler regarded the Jews. To be declared an aristocrat, bourgeois, or kulak peasant was almost tantamount to a death sentence. And almost anyone could fall into one or other of these categories at any time. The intensification of the class struggle doctrine was Stalin's great contribution to the "stricter interpretation of truths generally accepted in Western Europe for almost two thousand years," as Karl Polanyi maintained, but this new rigor was the rigor mortis of all such truths.

Truth, as has been said, is the first casualty of war, and reason is the second. Both were simultaneously the victims of totalitarianism, sacrificed to their higher goals. A *sacrificio intellectualis* used to be demanded of believers in the revealed religions, especially of Christians who followed Tertullian's dictum "*credo quia absurdum*." But the totalitarian "theologians" went much further than that; they demanded the acceptance of the Leader's pronouncements as the revealed truth, no matter how much these contradicted themselves. Every argument could be settled simply by quoting what the Leader had said, preferably in his latest speech, for it did not do at all, and was highly dangerous, to delve back into past speeches, lest the inconsistencies resulting from tactical zigzagging be exposed.

Like the revealed religions, the totalitarian creeds had their "sacred scriptures" that could also be quoted in support of whatever might be proposed. But, once again, care had to be taken that their interpretation was in conformity with that recommended by the Leader or the

13

authorized Party "theoreticians." The Bolsheviks were much more scholarly and systematic in these respects than the Nazis, who took a more lax and easy attitude to their sources. Thus for example, Hitler did not always see eye to eye with other interpreters of Nazism, such as Rosenberg, and he sneered in irony at Himmler's wilder ideas about the Aryan race, though only to his inner circle in private. It would have been suicidal to go against Stalin in this way. Only Stalin's version of the Marx, Engels, and Lenin canon could be pronounced in public or private, and anything in these voluminous writings that went against it had to be consigned to silence. Thus censorship was imposed even on the Communist classics according to which the Bolsheviks legitimated their rule.

Such an attitude to truth and reason played havoc with, even if it did not explicitly deny, all the conceptions of knowledge science, law, society, and politics current in Western civilization. Anything that was subject to rational principles, ones still adhered to by the founders of these movements, could no longer be invoked once the totalitarians came into power. A wholesale debasement of truth and reason resulted. In the sciences, Engels's exposition of a "dialectics of Nature" led under Stalin to a rejection of the science of genetics, declared to be bourgeois, and the patronage of the charlatan Lysenko, whereas such renowned geneticists as Vavilov were sent to the Gulag. There were scientists in the West with Communist sympathies, such as J. D. Bernal in England, who defended this procedure. Einstein's theories did not fare well in the Soviet Union either, for the reason that they were not in accord with Marxian dialectics. In Germany, the work of Einstein and any other scientist of Jewish origin was banned outright and condemned as "Jewish science," a category never encountered before in the West. Thus was the rational approach to scientific truth sacrificed to ideology.

The rational approach to law, another of the hallmarks of Western civilization enshrined in the tradition of Roman Law, was also negated. In Germany, the leading legal theoretician and political philosopher, Carl Schmitt, declared the law to be simply the Leader's will, for whatever the Leader pronounced had the force of law. Thus the idea of Natural Law or natural rights or any other moral basis to the law could never arise. In Russia, there could be no such moral foundation of the legal system either, for, according to Marxist teaching, law was simply the expression of the interests of the ruling class. Since the proletariat was, supposedly, the ruling class of the Soviet Union, its law was whatever favored this class, which ultimately was identified as the universal class embracing all of humanity. In practice, however, it was not the real proletarians, the workers, who were protected by law (strikes and trade unions, for example, were forbidden), but the power prerogatives and privileges of the Party and its *nomenclatura*, presided over by the Leader himself.

None of this would have been very surprising or so damaging to civilization if it had been confined to the totalitarian states for the limited period of their existence. But this was far from the case, as we saw in the previous section. There was strong support or at least sympathy for what was taking place under totalitarianism in all the liberal democratic societies, including Britain and America, on the part of fellow travelers of all types. Justifications and excuses were given even where there was disagreement with what was taking place. These were particularly common among so-called "committed" intellectuals, such as the philosopher Jean-Paul Sartre and his acolytes of Existentialism. The so-called civil war that raged among the intellectuals, writers, artists, and scientists in Western Europe was particularly damaging to Western civilization. For even those who were, so to speak, on the right side and attacked totalitarianism as a false god, such as Arthur Koestler, sometimes resorted to the same methods as their antagonists. Whoever touched totalitarianism, even to push it aside, was soiled with its filth.

Section III—Radical Evil

Prior to 1914, nobody foresaw the coming of totalitarianism, just as nobody could envisage what a difference this would make to Western civilization. The worst that anybody could imagine was that liberal democracy might succumb to Caesarism or Jacobin dictatorship, neither of which was seen as any great danger to civilization itself. After all, civilization had survived the French Revolution, and according to most—apart from a few clerical reactionaries—it had gained a new lease of life from it. There were those who believed that civilization was suffering from a bout of decadence due to the long period of peace and stability during the nineteenth century and that a war or revolution was necessary to save it from stewing in its own corruptions. Thus George Sorel wrote on the eve of World War I that "proletarian violence, carried on as a simple manifestation of class war, appears as a very fine and heroic theory; it is at the service of the immemorial interests of civilization; it is not perhaps the most appropriate method of obtaining immediate material advantages, but it may serve to save the world from barbarism."[6] Little could he realize at the time what he was actually advocating or what the unleashing of "proletarian violence" would do to civilization, first in Russia, then elsewhere in Europe, and eventually all over the world.

Sorel was one of those pre-1914 thinkers honored by both the Bolsheviks and the Fascists; on his death in 1924, both Lenin's and Mussolini's governments sent official representatives to his funeral. Mussolini himself said, "I owe most to Georges Sorel."[7] In the pre-1914 period, the Bolsheviks and what later became the Fascists were still ideologically very close to each other; both were variants of Socialism. In fact, all the subsequent totalitarian ideologies derived from Socialism or incorporated it in some shape or form. National Socialism is another such variant, combining Socialism, nationalism, racism, and anti-Semitism. But that, too, had already occurred long prior to the war. The combination of Socialism and nationalism was quite commonplace; Marx had already encountered and countered it in Ferdinand Lassalle, and the addition of anti-Semitism to the compound brought forth Engels's blast in his *Anti-Dühring* against the author of that name. These were, so to speak, the right-wing deviations from Socialism; left-wing deviations occurred at the same time, as when Lenin departed from the orthodox Marxism of Plekhanov and the other Russian Social Democrats to establish Bolshevism. The ultimate clash between these two alternative versions of Socialism occurred in the Second World War. Whether any of this violence was in "the immemorial interests of civilization" remains to be seen, but we may very much doubt it after all we have been through.

However, it was not Sorel's proletarians but the First World War that struck the first major blow against civilization, as Furet so succinctly expressed it:

> World War I entirely transformed European life—its borders, its regimes, even its way of thinking and its mores. It plowed so deeply into the most brilliant of modern civilizations that it left nothing unchanged. It marked the beginning of Western civilization's decline as the center of world power, even as it ushered in the cruel century from which we are now emerging, filled with the suicidal violence of its nations and its regimes.[8]

The First World War was a cataclysmic event in European history, perhaps more destructive than any previous war. As its very name indicates, it was the first war that occurred throughout the whole of Europe, as well as many other parts of the world, particularly the Middle

East. Furet speaks of it as "the first episode of the European tragedy."[9] However, it was not as devastating as the Second World War, which, being so much more widespread and horrific, almost completed the destruction of civilization the First had begun. Western civilization in the Old World would never recover from the onslaught, though across the Atlantic in the New World, civilization seemed to gain a new lease on life. But was it any longer the same civilization? This is an issue we will take up in part II.

Above all, the Great War had a disastrous moral effect on civilization, quite apart from any political or material damage it caused, for it disillusioned and demoralized the people of Europe. This is the theme to which many of the great writers of the period addressed themselves, perhaps none more so than Thomas Mann with *The Magic Mountain*, written after the First World War and *Dr. Faustus*, during and after the Second. What Mann explores is how all the idealistic illusions that the long and prosperous period of bourgeois culture during the nineteenth century had fostered were shattered once and for all by these Events of the Twentieth Century. What could the idea of Progress mean in the face of such wholesale slaughter? What kind of a "civilizing process" could ensue after that? What moral improvement in civility, decency, or rationality could then be, when statesmen and generals colluded to send a whole generation of young men to their death or disfigurement? When the losses on both sides were so horrendous, what could distinguish winning from losing?

The anger and cynicism that pervaded Europe after the war prepared the ground for the reception of the totalitarian ideologies. Even in those countries where people did not act in their name, they had become sympathetic to such views, and some became ideological converts or fellow travelers, as they were called. Any desperate measure that promised salvation from the morass in which Europe found itself was eagerly sought and had ready supporters. In this way, not only the intellectuals and the educated classes but the masses themselves became politically radicalized, and many turned to the most extreme of the ideologies, such as Bolshevism and anti-Semitism. The latter, in particular, became more widespread, whereas it had only been marginal before the war. The former expanded throughout Europe and the world, whereas formerly it had been confined to Russia. The fact that Bolshevism was a Russian ideology, just as anti-Semitism was a German one, was lost sight of as it took on the aura of universalism. And something similar happened to anti-Semitism, as many became ideological anti-Semites though they bore no personal ill will to Jews themselves. The era of ideological warfare was initiated as what had been caviar for the general before the war became the staple food of the masses after it.

When totalitarianism first arose, it might easily have been contained. Neither Russia nor Italy was at the center of European affairs; both were on the periphery. In its original form it did not present much danger to the major powers, England, France, and Germany. However, in the last of these, Germany, a totalitarian regime emerged, largely as a result of the Great Depression, and that proved much more dangerous, for its leader, Hitler, harbored irredentist goals and was prepared to go to war to achieve them. From that point on, what became the Second World War became more or less inevitable.

The Second World War was a much greater disaster for European civilization than the First. Both the political and material damager it wrought was much more devastating. The whole of Central and Eastern Europe was almost completely ruined, with the exception of Moscow, Vienna, and Prague, which escaped destruction; all the other major cities were shelled or bombed into rubble. The loss of life was horrendous, and the tally now included not just the soldiers at the front but also much larger numbers of civilians. Many of these fell victim to a new kind of evil never before encountered in history—radical evil.

Immediately on the cessation of hostilities, the world was shocked with a new kind of horror: Auschwitz. An evil such as had never been seen before, a factory of death, had been exposed. This was the heart of darkness of the whole century of horrors, that which "neither heart nor tongue can conceive nor name." It was the "deed without a name" to which we now give the Kantian name of "radical evil" (*das radikal Böse*), even though Kant meant something else by this expression. Prior to it happening, nobody could have conceived that such a thing was possible, or that it could occur, as it were, in broad daylight in the very midst of European civilization. Similar things were happening in Russia, but the world did not yet know of these, for they took place far away and in total secrecy. When they were later exposed, few Europeans at first believed them, given the proclaimed humanitarian goals of Communism. But gradually the truth came out and was confirmed by Khrushchev himself in his speech of 1956. Even then, many would not accept the full extent of the evil, especially fellow travelers and Communists in France, until the work of Solzhenitsyn in the 1970s documented it in detail.

The effect of the exposure of Auschwitz and the disclosure of the Gulag was devastating; like a Medusa head, it blighted the moral vision of civilization. Who could any longer believe in a civilization that could lead to this kind of an outcome? Radical evil is the ultimate debasement of civilization for it is a denial of the humanity of groups and classes of human beings who are regarded as pests fit only for extermination. This is much worse than the age-old evils of slavery, for slaves might be conceived of as inferior human beings naturally fit for servitude—as, indeed, Aristotle argued—but they were human beings nonetheless. Those slated for extermination in the twentieth century were considered less than human, as *Untermenschen* or "human animals," as Himmler referred to them in his notorious speech of 1943 at Posen; or as social "parasites" and "blood-suckers," as the Bolsheviks declared.

These are the features that make "radical evil" a new type of evil never encountered before. It is the *"fleur du mal"* of the twentieth century, its most perfect expression in evil. For radical evil is not mere genocide, which can occur in a variety of circumstances for all kinds of reasons—ones we can understand because they make sense, even though they are morally wrong, such as the slaughter of manifest or hereditary enemies, or religious heretics or malefactors of one or another type. Radical evil is different in that the reasons for it make no such sense and are solely ideological: groups or classes of people are murdered solely because they fall into an ideologically designated category, they happen to be Jews or kulaks or whatever other category is slated for death. The fiction is elaborated that such people are "enemies" irrespective of what they might have said or done, as when Hitler declared the Jews the cause of the war and all, without exception, enemies of Germany. It is obvious that such presumed enemies are not real but purely imaginary, or perhaps they are scapegoats standing in for real enemies who are out of reach. How such categories of enemies are established has nothing to do with the victims themselves or their attributes and characteristics, and everything to do with the totalitarian need for enemies—namely, for victims to be sacrificed. As we shall show, this serves an important functional role in totalitarianism.

The identification of enemies usually follows a purely legalistic or fictitious casuistry. And once so identified, these categories of people can be exterminated with no qualms whatever, with a perfectly good conscience—that is, no conscience at all. Indeed, those who set about this task consider it a matter of duty, so-called, and any scruples that anyone displays are taken as weakness or sentimentality. No traditional moral sentiments are deemed to be relevant, neither pity nor sorrow; instead, complete ruthlessness is extolled, and deceit, where necessary to facilitate the job, is taken as perfectly proper. The executioners and killers traduce and betray every acceptable moral notion, so to speak of them as acting in accordance with an alternative ethic amounts almost to a self-contradiction. A pseudo-morality is not an alternative morality. Even the moral terms they invoke, like "duty" or "honor" or "virtue," mean something quite other than in their accepted sense, for they undergo a perversion of meaning for ideological ends.

These are the lessons of totalitarianism that took a long time to be properly appreciated and grasped. Even radical evil is still not fully understood, and confusion reigns when such facile expressions as Hannah Arendt's "banality of evil" are bandied about as if they explained anything. They are themselves the expression of a banal and even flippant attitude to the horrors. The idea that Eichmann and other such killers were just doing their job, or even that they did not know what they were doing, does them a great injustice. They were ideologically motivated and knew exactly, by reference to their ideology, what it was they were doing and why they had to do it. In Eichmann's case there is little sign that he changed his mind about that even long after the war. By all accounts he was proud of what he had done. Of course, he presented a different image of himself when on trial, as an insignificant and simple little bureaucrat, and took in and deceived such casual observers as Hannah Arendt.

What chance had ordinary people of understanding what Auschwitz meant when intellectuals and academics were so confused? In any case, once the war was over, the shock of Auschwitz quickly wore off as people returned to their ordinary lives and sought to resume some semblance of normality. They pushed the horrors aside as if they no longer mattered. A kind of amnesia descended over Europe, especially over Germany, where people were most intent on rebuilding and prospering. The economic miracle was at hand, and that helped people push the war out of their minds. Academic historians were not much better, and it took a long time for them to research what had happened. Later some simply saw this as a rich lode of materials to be mined, a veritable gold mine for advancement.

Thus, at the cost of partial oblivion, through the repression of painful memories, Europeans got on with the task at hand, and most people soon prospered. For many life had never been better; as British Prime Minister Macmillan told them, "You have never had it so good." In general, Western Europe attained unprecedented standards of living. The ruins had long disappeared, been either built over or restored, and in most cases the cities attained something approximating their original state.

However, the damage to civilization could not be so easily repaired. And in any case, the cultural and moral injury caused by the ideological civil war continued unabated as the Cold War grew in intensity. Europe was caught in a vise between the threat coming from Soviet totalitarianism, then at its worst during the last years of a paranoid Stalin, and the reaction of its American protectors who were ready to fight a war for Europe on European soil. In any case, the price that the Americans exacted for their aid and protection touched on the soul of Europe: they expected the Europeans to remake themselves in the image of America.

In West Germany the Americans could openly implement their policy of Americanization as part of an expiatory reeducation of a sinful nation that had to redeem itself from its past evils. And the Germans proved apt learners, in time to become America's closest allies in Europe. No such demands could be made on the other Europeans. But the overwhelming wealth, power, and prestige of America was so great in this period that no imposition was necessary; the Europeans were overawed by the influence America exerted and willingly adjusted to what they believe the Americans expect of them. With young people as always in the forefront, the masses came to adopt American ways in most respects, especially in cultural matters.

America was, of course, not a culture foreign to Europe; it was part of the same Western civilization, though a somewhat different version than that current in Europe, having developed itself in considerable isolation in the New World. For a while, during the first half or so of the twentieth century, it seemed as if America would take up the torch of civilization that Europe had abandoned during its time of troubles and carry it across the Atlantic. So many of Europe's best minds and creative talents had sought refuge in America during this time that it seemed as if European civilization could be recreated there unimpaired. The Americans seemed willing to play their part in this endeavor, for they welcomed the refugees with open arms and provided most of them with the positions and the facilities they required.

Unfortunately, this did not lead to the wholesale transplantation of the Old World civilization in the New World. The Americans could only absorb what was already familiar to them, mainly in the sciences, technologies, and popular arts. In many other respects what the Americans tried to take over they misunderstood and debased, as we shall show in part II. So Western civilization in its European mode did not experience a new lease on life in America. Instead, what arose there is what we have called in another work, *Beyond Civilization*, a postcivilizational condition about which we shall have more to say in this work as well.[10]

But before we turn to America, we must first study totalitarianism in greater depth, for that is the key to understanding the destruction of civilization in Europe. To that end we must first seek a definition of totalitarianism, which we shall attempt in this chapter; then in the next chapter we shall consider the ideologies that prepared the ground for totalitarianism in the pre-1914 period; and in the one following we shall study the actual emergence and evolution of the various kinds of totalitarian regimes during and after the First World War.

Section IV—The Definition of Totalitarianism

We must now address the simple question we have thus far avoided: What is totalitarianism? What does this word mean, and where does it come from? As is well known, totalitarianism is a much-contested concept, and there are many different definitions of it. The word was first coined and applied to Italian Fascism by its opponents almost as soon as the regime came to power. But, as is so often the case, what was meant derogatively was taken up in triumph by the Fascists themselves as describing the character of their movement. Mussolini himself gave it his imprimatur in an article he published in the *Encyclopedia Italiana*, edited by his resident philosopher, Giovanni Gentile, who most probably ghostwrote it for him; it closely reflects Gentile's philosophy of totality.

Later, it was taken up by refugees from Nazism and once more given negative connotations in the context of a critique of Hitler's regime. It was among these that the conceptual innovation arose of generalizing the concept also to Russian Bolshevism in order to show up the close analogies between Stalin's regime and those of Mussolini and Hitler. The first among these was Waldemar Gurian, a friend of Hannah Arendt, who presciently wrote in 1935, "both Bolshevisms, red and brown, were part of the political dissolution of European civilization."[11] Oddly enough, in the light of their later reputation, the members of the Frankfurt school avoided the term, perhaps seeing it as a slur on Communism, for which they still held out hopes despite their doubts about Stalin's regime. However, a number of other refugees, such as Franz Neumann, Franz Borkenau, and finally Hannah Arendt published works in which this term or its close cognates became the key concept in explaining the revolutionary developments taking place in Europe before the Second World War. In the period of the Cold War it was taken up by American political scientists and featured in a leading study by Carl Friedrich and Zbigniew Brzezinski. Most of those on the Left shied away from the term, denouncing it as Cold War propaganda, until close to the collapse of the Soviet Union, when they, too, came around to using it. Some did not object to it being applied to Stalin's regime, but not to that of Lenin, which again reveals how totalitarian politics infected theorizing about totalitarianism.

Even among those who accepted the concept, there was little agreement about what it applied to, and which regimes during what periods were actually totalitarian. There were those who applied it to far-right-wing dictatorships in general, calling them all Fascist totalitarianisms, but not to far-left-wing ones. Others applied it to both versions, but among the latter only to Stalinism, and with greater hesitancy also to Maoism. Still others insisted that Mussolini's Italy was not really totalitarian, despite the fact that it called itself by that name. The best known and most persuasive is Hannah Arendt's classification, according to which Italy was not totalitarian but Germany was, right from the start of Hitler's accession to power, and Russia was so only from the period of Stalin's supreme dominance. This is nearly right, except that there seems not much to distinguish Hitler's regime until 1939 from Mussolini's, but for the persecution of the Jews, which cannot be a decisive criterion in itself. Furthermore, Lenin's regime, about which Arendt is extremely lenient, was certainly more brutal than either of these in the prewar period, so how can it not be considered totalitarian? All these are problems with which we shall try to deal in what follows.

We still have not answered the question of what totalitarianism is, or attempted any definition of the concept. The account we shall proceed to offer differs from all standard definitions in that it does not attempt to specify any set or syndrome of features unique to totalitarianism. In contrast to such essentialist definitions, we shall provide a genetic or developmental one that is based on the assumption that totalitarianism is a changing historical formation that does not remain the same in any two of its transitional phases. How to capture the nature of such metamorphic changes becomes the task in formulating a definition.

The classic essentialist definition is the "morphological and operational" theory of Friedrich and Brzezinski. It postulates a syndrome of six systemic characteristics: a ruling ideology, a single party under the dominance of a Leader, a secret police apparatus, control of the media, monopoly of all weapons, and an economy that is state directed if not state controlled.[12] The problem with such a definition is that it cannot account for all the changes that totalitarian regimes undergo in the course of their transformative evolution, for the features that apply to some stages do not apply to others, and if they are invoked in a purely nominal sense to refer to all eventualities, then they become ambiguous, for the changes are too drastic to be covered by the same terms in the same sense. Those who try to overcome such problems inherent in historical transformation in a purely essentialist way insert more and more specifications to cover all possibilities. Following this method, one ends up with something like the definition provided by Emilio Gentile:

> By the term totalitarianism we mean an experiment in political domination implemented by a revolutionary movement that has been organized by a party with military discipline and an all-absorbing concept of politics aimed at the monopoly of power, which on taking power by legal or illegal means destroys or transforms the previous regime and builds a new state founded on a single-party regime with the principal objective of conquering society, that is, the subjugation, integration and homogenization of the ruled on the basis of the total political nature of existence, whether individual or collective, as interpreted by the categories, myths and values of an institutionalized ideology in the form of a political religion, with the intention of molding individuals and masses through an anthropological revolution, in order to regenerate the essence of humanity and create a new man devoted body and soul to the realization of the revolutionary, and imperialist project of the totalitarian party, and thus a new civilization of a supranational nature.[13]

Whether this formula finally does the trick and accounts for everything or whether it still needs to be further expanded is not an issue we will debate, for we are not seeking an essentialist definition. In any case, we shall criticize some of Gentile's specifications in the next chapter.

In his introduction to the 1965 edition of the book he authored jointly with Brzezinski, Friedrich makes it clear that they are not offering a genetic or developmental definition:

> In thus developing a morphological and operational theory of totalitarian regimes, I should like to make it clear that I still believe that

we are as yet unable to offer a genetic one. Some interesting further arguments have been advanced in the intervening years, and elements to such a theory are scattered throughout this book as they are through other writings on totalitarianism, but no one in my opinion has fully answered the question: why? Unforeseen and still unfolding, totalitarianism has shaped or, if one prefers, distorted the political and governmental scene of the twentieth century. It promises to continue to do so to the end of the century.[14]

Friedrich was off by only ten years; by 1990 the history of totalitarianism had almost concluded, at least in Europe; in Asia it persevered far longer and still is not over. By now we can view it in its totality as a historical phenomenon. Hence, we can now attempt a genetic definition from which Friedrich shied away in his time.

Totalitarianism is a historical formation that went through a number of transformations or metamorphic changes from stage to stage, somewhat on analogy with the life cycle of an insect, such as from egg to pupa to larva to chrysalis, finally to emerge as the adult moth or butterfly. Of course, one must not take this biological metaphor literally, for there is no natural force or developmental necessity driving the historical process from start to finish; quite other causes are at work, as we shall show. However, the metaphor brings out the fact that from one stage to another appearances can change completely, which is the reason that going by surface features or characteristics in order to arrive at an essentialist definition is such an endless task.

The metaphor also breaks down in that, unlike an insect, a totalitarian regime need not go through all its possible stages of development; it can remain stuck in an initial stage for a long time, though perhaps not indefinitely, without going on to the next one. Why it is that some totalitarian regimes go through all the phases of development and others do not becomes the key explanatory issue for us to resolve. As we shall see, the factors that determine this might have nothing to do with totalitarianism itself; they can be quite extraneous to it. We shall show, the First World War and the Great Depression played such a role, as did Hitler's initial victories in Europe, but these were in no way caused by totalitarianism, and at least the first two had nothing to do with it. Hence, there is no inner logic or necessity for totalitarianism to arise in the first place or to develop itself further; if it does so, then this is for extraneous historical or social or economic or cultural causes. Thus, to take one obvious example, totalitarianism in Italy under Mussolini became arrested in an initial phase for the whole of its history, discounting the final aberration of the Salo Republic, when Mussolini was no longer in control. It did so because the conditions in Italy were lacking for any further developments, in contrast to Germany and Russia.

In those countries where totalitarianism underwent a phase-transition from one stage to another, its complete character changed; as it were, its Gestalt switched from one aspect to another. There were continuities, of course, but the differences were enormous. There is no more resemblance between Lenin's regime and Stalin's, or between Hitler's regime at its beginning and at its end than there is between a grub and a butterfly. The organization was the same, but it transmogrified from a mere dictatorship following legal norms, no matter how ruthless these were to their victims and morally obnoxious, to a state machine of total terror at the behest of a megalomaniac monster. This is the reason that essentialist definitions of totalitarianism that focus on syndromes of features cannot work, for in the course of such a transition one syndrome gives way to another. Instead, what we must seek to characterize is what each of the constituent stages of totalitarianism is like in itself, and offer a number of partial definitions rather than a complete one that tries to combine them all, as Emilio Gentile attempts to do, ending up with a barely comprehensible sentence.

The key transition is from what we might call proto-totalitarianism to totalitarianism proper. This took place in Russian during the years 1929 to 1931 and in Germany between 1939 and 1941. It never took place in Italy, which, as long as Mussolini was at the helm, remained proto-totalitarian from start to finish. Hitler's regime was likewise merely proto-totalitarian at least until 1939. It might seem difficult to distinguish Lenin's regime from Stalin's given its ruthlessness, the sheer terror and murder that it perpetrated, but despite that, as we will argue in chapter 3, there was a fundamental difference between them, though both were totalitarian. What these differences between the two forms of totalitarianism amount to, we shall presently outline and go on to specify further in chapter 3.

There are three further distinctions that must also be made: firstly, that between proto-totalitarianism and a prior phase of pretotalitarianism; secondly, that between totalitarianism proper and a subsequent phase that usually follows it, which we will call subtotalitarianism; and thirdly, that between it and the complete end of totalitarianism altogether, which is posttotalitarianism. There are thus five stages altogether in the evolution of totalitarianism, provided it goes to its full term, which in fact it rarely does—the only known instance being Russia. Usually it is fixated at one or another stage or interrupted by outside interventions, as was the case in Italy and Germany. We must emphatically stress once again that there is no inner necessity or inevitability for any totalitarianism regime to pass through any of these stages; where this does happen, we must look for the causes that bring it about in the usual empirical manner. Totalitarianism does not simply develop itself in accord with its concept in any Hegelian way.

As we shall argue extensively in what follows, the main cause of totalitarianism was the First World War. But what made this possible was that prior to it, however, the condition of its occurring, the pre-totalitarian phase, had already been established. This pre-1914 period was that of warring ideologies that laid the basis for totalitarianism, because without a fully articulated ideology there can be no totalitarian movement or party, and, therefore, no totalitarian regime can arise. Such movements and parties were already current prior to 1914, but without the Great War and its consequences these would never have turned into proto-totalitarian regimes. Even the ideologies themselves were not yet in a fixed dogmatic state such as a totalitarian regime requires; they were still intellectually highly fluid and malleable, and there was still considerable interpenetration and fusion between them, as Norman Davies explains: "Before 1914, the main ingredients of the two movements [Communism and Fascism]—socialism, Marxism, nationalism, racism and autocracy—were washing around in various combinations all over Europe."[15] We shall take up Davies's suggestion and follow it up much further in the next chapter.

In the opposite position to pretotalitarianism is subtotalitarianism, which follows totalitarianism proper. This almost always happens when the godlike Leader dies, for he is never removed except by the hand of death. The sole exception to this has been the peculiar regime of North Korea, where the dynasty of the Kim family behaves as if it were a single person spanning a number of generations. In all other cases, when the Leader dies his followers do not battle it out to determine his successor; rather, they agree that there will not be another such overlord, and they settle amongst themselves to rule as a group and exercise collective leadership, with one of them acting as *primus inter pares* or figurehead. As a result, the whole nature of the regime changes, even though it maintains all the old totalitarian agencies intact. Thus, for example, the whole apparatus of repression remains, but it is subject to a considerable degree of legality, regardless of the draconian nature of the law. This is most important, because the pervasive fear throughout such a society in which nobody feels safe is much attenuated, though not completely removed. Similar changes occur in all other institutions. Hence, though this is still a totalitarian regime, it has undergone a metamorphic transformation to become subtotalitarian. It only becomes posttotalitarian when the Party is no longer in control and terror is completely dispensed with, which happened in Russia after Gorbachev and has not yet taken place in China, which remains subtotalitarian.

The full sequence of all five stages has so far only occurred once, in the case of Russia. Elsewhere the full development of totalitarianism was aborted by defeat in war, as happened in Germany; or it might not have gone any further even if the war had not intervened, which likely would have been the outcome in Italy. The outcome in those few countries where totalitarianism still exists, such as China, North Korea, and Vietnam, is yet inconclusive. It must not be assumed that they will inevitably progress to a posttotalitarian stage, for they might be permanently fixed in their present conditions. The one thing that seems certain—for it has never happened—is that they will not revert to earlier stages. The sequence of stages does not operate in reverse. However, this is theoretically possible if very unusual conditions prevail. While there is little danger at present of China returning to a Maoist-style totalitarianism of old, this possibility cannot be completely precluded if circumstances were to drastically change in the future.

As is clear from the previous sketch, which will be fully amplified in chapter 3, the theory outlined differs fundamentally from every other hitherto presented. We shall not expound and critically consider all the other theories, many of which are already well known, because the main differences separating them from our own account are all too apparent. Perhaps the crucial difference is that few of the recognized political philosophers or political scientists or sociological theoreticians took history seriously. They did not grasp the historically contingent nature of totalitarianism—for example, the fact that its origins are so closely bound up with the Great War. Some hardly mention this war in their accounts. It is a historian, François Furet, and not a theorist, who explicitly and thoroughly explored the connection between the war and totalitarianism, and we shall refer to him rather than the theorists in our own account.

Fully grasping the contingent historical nature of totalitarianism enables one to see its relation to Western civilization in a different light. It makes one realize that there was nothing inherently wrong with Western civilization prior to 1914 that necessitated the advent of totalitarianism, with all its disastrous consequences for the further course of that civilization. But for the historical "accident" of the Great War and the consequent onset of totalitarianism, Western civilization could have continued for an indefinite period. If that had been the case, we would now be living in a completely different world.

Notes

1. Arno J. Mayer, *The Furies: Violence and Terror in the French and Russian Revolutions* (Princeton University Press, Princeton, 2000), p. 72.
2. See Steven Pinker, *The Better Angels of Our Nature*, op.cit.
3. Irving Louis Horowitz, *Taking Lives: Genocide and State Power* (Transaction Publishers, Piscataway, NJ, 2002), p. 10.
4. Norman Davies, *Europe: A History* (Pimlico Press, London, 1997), p. 944.
5. Karl Polanyi, *Christianity and Social Revolution* (Victor Gollancz, London, 1935), p. 269.
6. Georges Sorel, *Reflections on Violence*, trans. T. E. Hulme and J. Roth (Collier-Macmillan, New York, 1961), p. 98.
7. Quoted by Edward A. Shils in his introduction to *Reflection on Violence*, op. cit., p. 24.
8. François Furet, *The Passing of an Illusion: The Cruel Century*, trans. Deborah Furet, (Cambridge University Press, Cambridge, 1999), p. 19.
9. Ibid. p. 37.
10. See Harry Redner, *Beyond Civilization*, op. cit.
11. Waldermar Gurian, *The Future of Bolshevism*, trans. E. F. Walker (Sheed and Ward, New York, 1936), p. 204.
12. Carl J. Friedrich and Zbigniew Brzezinski, *Totalitarian Dictatorship and Autocracy*, (Praeger Publishers, New York, 1972).
13. Emilio Gentile, *Politics as Religion*, trans. George Staunton (Princeton University Press, Princeton, 2006), p. 46.
14. Carl J. Friedrich and Zbigniew Brzezinski, *Totalitarian Dictatorship and Autocracy*, op. cit. Introduction.
15. Norman Davies, *Europe: A History*, op. cit., p. 948.

2

Ideology

Section I—Pretotalitarian Ideologies

Ideology is the *sinequanon* of totalitarianism. For no matter how dictatorial, harsh, or depraved a regime might be, it cannot be totalitarian without the right kind of ideology to justify its actions. Totalitarian ideology precedes totalitarianism. All the standard totalitarian ideologies were in circulation prior to 1914, before anyone could even imagine such a thing as a totalitarian regime. Bolshevism and anti-Semitism, out of which Nazism arose, already existed, as did all the elements out of which Fascism was later constituted. In fact, as we shall show, they had much in common, and the fierce animosity that they evinced later did not yet exist. It required the crucial event of the First World War to galvanize them and pit them against each other, and all of them together against the despised liberal-democratic order that prevailed before the war. All of them castigated it as bourgeois and called its democracy a sham. They felt they had more in common with each other, though as deadly rivals, than with the decrepit *Ancient Régime*. In this chapter we shall deal only with the prewar ideological preparations for totalitarianism, and in the next chapter we shall examine the effect of the Great War on these precursors.

Ideological politics in the modern sense started with the French Revolution. Fierce debates in the context of the revolution gave rise to all the ideologies that later pervaded nineteenth-century politics, its revolutionary movements, reform agitations, and the various defenses of the status quo, both conservative and reactionary. Ideological stirrings of all kinds were accepted as part of the normal run of politics, and would have continued in much the same perfervid fashion if the Great War had not occurred. Ideology was not, however, a major source of inspiration for the war, and only the prevailing nationalism current among all parties to the conflict influenced its conduct. Other types of ideologues were, in general, not involved; the political groups they formed were quite distinct from the warmongers who were the main instigators and prosecutors of the war. The former were parties and cliques of political activists, revolutionary agitators, intellectuals of all kinds, writers, artists, and journalistic riff-raff; the latter were people in established positions who wielded authority, such as monarchs, statesmen, generals, bankers, and industrialists, who would decide all the issues of war and peace. The two groups almost never encountered, save when some of the former assassinated some of the latter and were in turn executed by them. However, there were brief periods during the nineteenth century when the ideologues were in power: during the 1848 Revolution, for example, or the Paris Commune, or the 1905 upheavals in Russia, and other such events. No doubt this gave them a thirst for power and acted as an incentive for the institution of totalitarianism when the opportunity arose.

Modern ideologies of the kind we are concerned with in this work are systems of ideas and beliefs that act as motivations and guides for political action, frequently of a revolutionary type. Such ideologies incorporate worldviews or *Weltanschauungen* with theories about history, society, economics, politics, or anything else of importance, and provide plausible-seeming answers to all problems. Crucial to most of them were historical schemes covering the past, present, and inevitable future, focusing on all that mankind had accomplished, on what needed still to be achieved and where it would all end. They were particularly intent on what had been lost and urgently needed to be recovered. Motivated by resentment, as well as by idealism, they were determined to right what was wrong and to correct injustices. Though the extreme Left and extreme Right ideologies differed fundamentally on many issues, there were, nevertheless, close commonalities between them. In fact, they grew closer in the decade or so before the war. It is this peculiarity that explains the growth of Fascism and Nazism out of a common stock of Socialism, which was also the seedbed of Bolshevism.

A characteristic feature of the pretotalitarian period prior to 1914 was the extraordinary comingling of ideological currents from both the far Left and far Right. Ideas derived from both sources came together and produced unusual hybrids. Ideologies thus became extremely promiscuous, engendering works as idiosyncratic as those of Eugen Dühring and Georges Sorel. There was a general drift of socialist ideas from the Left to the Right, and nationalist ones in the reverse direction. The term "national socialism" might not yet have been devised, but there were many intimations of such a conjunction. The historian François Furet notes this unusual ideological phenomenon:

> In the nineteenth century, many European socialist thinkers, such as Buchez and Lassalle, were despising democracy and exalting the nation. Conversely, just before WWI, the widespread critique of liberalism brought even the most radical, that is, the most nationalist, members of the right closer to socialist ideas. . . . The idea of National Socialism was, then, not new in 1918 or 1920, but when the guns fell silent, it had shed its sophisticated intellectual robe, and appeared, in a certain popular version, as an instrument fit to galvanize the masses. Before the war the socialist-nationalist mix was but an esoteric cocktail for intellectuals. After it, it became a widely consumed beverage.[1]

Furet pinpoints the crucial differences separating the pre-1914 versions of ideologies from their post-1918 revisions: prior to the war they were debating topics for intellectuals; after the war they became weapons of attack, designed to arouse the masses. Propaganda warfare took the place of rational discussion. Once the proto-totalitarian regimes came into power, the ideologies were dogmatized and became articles of faith to be adhered to by everyone on pain of excommunication, followed by extermination.

In the pre-1914 open forum of political debate that obtained even in Czarist Russia, the most repressive regime in Europe, there was free interchange between all ideologies. Extremists had so much in common that they could argue about their remaining differences. Philosophers, historians, scientists, and littérateurs of all persuasions appealed to the same authorities. Hegel's philosophy, for example, variously interpreted and adapted, figured prominently on both the Right and the Left. On the one side, the Italian philosopher of Fascism, Giovanni Gentile, emphasized Hegel's worship of the state as the ultimate source of *Sittlichkeit*. On the other side, Lenin revered Hegel, and Georg Lukacs later showed how the ideas of the young Marx, whose early manuscripts were still unknown, derived from Hegel's philosophy. Marx himself was much appreciated by Gentile. And Nietzsche, Hitler's favorite though unread philosopher, found a ready ear in Lunacharsky and Trotsky, the later luminaries of Bolshevism. He was read by everybody on all ideological sides.

In the sciences, too, both Left and Right had common sources. The works of Charles Darwin and Carl Clausewitz were foremost among these, the former expounding the science of evolution and the latter the "science" of war. Both played a seminal role among intellectuals of the Left and Right, who utilized their theories in ways that suited their own causes. Science is always politically malleable in these ways.

When *The Origin of Species* appeared in 1856, Marx was at first very enthusiastic, for he believed, as he wrote in a letter to Engels, that it contained "the natural-history basis of our views"; later he somewhat modified this view, having come to the conclusion that Darwin was not sufficiently Hegelian for his purposes and was flawed because of what he called English "crudity."[2] Engels was much more taken with Darwin and incorporated his theory of evolution into his *Dialectics of Nature*, arguing that just as there are laws of nature, so there must be laws of human nature and history. This idea was taken over by Georgi Plekhanov, one of the founders of Marxism in Russia, and from him it was passed on to Lenin and Stalin. It became the basis of "dialectical materialism" and played a nefarious role as the official ideology of the Soviet Union. In the sciences, it enabled charlatans like Lysenko to flourish in the field of genetics.

On the Right, Darwin's ideas played an even more pernicious role. The first step in this direction seemed harmless: Herbert Spencer added a sociological dimension to Darwin's theory of nature and coined the term "the survival of the fittest." According to this version, the struggle for existence and the survival of the fittest in Nature continues in human society, in the form of war and economic competition. Such ideas became widespread in Germany, where they were popularized by Haeckel and also taken up by Nietzsche, reconceived as the "will to power." In retrospect it is clear that these ideas became dangerous when Social Darwinism was crossed with the equally pseudoscientific theorizing of racial science, which was also very common at the time. This combination made it possible to justify militarism—war was the hygiene of nations—colonialism, and the new ideology of anti-Semitism that arose at the same time as the establishment of the Reich. A leading expositor of all these trends a generation later was the eugenicist Eugen Fischer, who was to act as the unofficial "scientific" adviser to Hitler when he was writing *Mein Kampf*. He was rewarded by being appointed as rector of Berlin University, where his research institute sponsored the "medical" experiments in the concentration camps.

In his great study, *On War*, Clausewitz exerted an influence on both the Left and the Right that was complementary to Darwin's. As Gabriel Kolko writes:

> Clausewitz infused a new moral and pseudoscientific vision into thinking about war, providing the otherwise anti-intellectual warrior castes of Europe with a rationale for their power in an aggressively

empiricist industrializing era that the vast majority of officers deplored as crassly commercial and devoid of sufficient spirituality. The social thinkers that Darwin's work spawned rounded off Clausewitz's influence with their primitively conservative notions of struggle, survival-of-the-fittest and death for the weak. War now also had a positive scientific sanction and presumably could now he conducted in a rational fashion, and Clausewitz's stress on the importance of a military leader of genius further made it appear as an inevitable part of the natural order of things.[3]

It is easy to see why Clausewitz's "science of war" was favored by the Prussian officer caste, notably by Moltke the elder, who was instrumental in the publication of *On War*. But, surprising as it may seem, Clausewitz was also taken up by the Communists, who saw in his theories on the strategies of violence a guide to a possible science of revolutionary warfare. Engels—who took a great interest in military affairs and whose nickname in the Marx household was "the general"—was a keen reader of Clausewitz. Many later Marxists were as well. Lenin studied him at length in order to prepare his revolutionary plans. Trotsky and Stalin followed him in this—the former to good effect in founding the Red Army and winning the Civil War, while the latter only acquired the conceit of imagining himself a great commander. When he took it on himself to dictate strategy to the Soviet army at the opening of the Second World War, it only brought disaster. Unembarrassed by this, after the war he styled himself "Generalissimo."

His adversary in this war, Hitler, was an even greater disciple of Clausewitz. He claimed to understand him better than any of his Prussian generals did, and believed this gave him intellectual and moral superiority over them. He made himself the undisputed top commander of the *Wehrmacht* and devised the strategies that led it to defeat.

The resort to Clausewitz by Hitler and Stalin had the unfortunate consequence of steeling both to an amoral use of violence. Following his theories, they saw war as a normal and necessary means of achieving their respective political objectives. The allowance Clausewitz had made for total war, as a purely theoretical possibility, they actually put into practice. This meant that they saw no need for limits on violence; victory was all that mattered, and whatever level of violence was required to achieve it was justified. This facilitated their propensity to exterminism, which they rationalized as a matter of military necessity. Hence they recognized no restraints of any moral kind on killing people—as many as required. As Himmler declared: "Whether ten thousand

Russian females fall down from exhaustion while digging an anti-tank ditch interests me only in so far as the anti-tank ditch for Germany is finished." At the same time, he went on to reassure his listeners: "We Germans are the only people in the world who have a decent attitude toward these human animals." Clausewitz and Darwin are bizarrely echoed in these utterances: we hear that some people are no better than "human animals" and there are no limits on the uses to which "human animals" can be put when "military necessities" demand it. Apart from that, one ought to be kind to human animals—provided they are not Jews, for these are worse than animals, they are devils in human dress. All this is the intellectual background of radical evil.

At first, in the nineteenth century, none of this was apparent, for the work of Darwin and Clausewitz, as well as that of numerous other natural and social scientists between these two scientific poles, was interpreted to provide a basis for the ideas on which the ideals of the intellectuals were based. In itself this was harmless, even if it did lend many a spurious proposal the apparent ring of truth. It only became politically dangerous when such ideals were politicized and converted into ideologies, for then these ideologies were assumed to warrant certitude, like the sciences from which they were originally derived. Their exponents took them to be true and irrefutable. This was the first intellectual step toward radical evil.

In their pretotalitarian stage the ideologies of Left and Right did not just share authors and ideas; they also partook of common fundamental assumptions about history, society, and politics in general. In a recent publication Richard Shorten has explored this common ground between them and summed it up in three basic terms: scientism, utopianism, and violence.[4] These three assumptions separate the putative totalitarian ideologies from all other contemporary ideologies, whether of a liberal democratic, a conservative, or even a clerical reactionary cast. Whereas all the others accepted that the human condition is at best subject to gradual improvement, or really not capable of change at all, the extremist ideologies promised a fundamental alteration in the human condition that would resolve all of mankind's basic problems. A utopian resolution of the human tragedy would be achieved by violence, putting the scientific knowledge embodied in their ideology into practice with absolute certainty.

As we have already shown, scientism was inherent in the very idea that there are laws of human development that govern the future as well as the past and thus permit prediction of what is bound to happen.

Each of the ideologies relied on a science of society in which one key term explained everything: either class or race or nation. Once this is understood, everything else is accounted for, and all problems can be solved.

Utopia is the goal of all human endeavors and will be attained when the promise of progress inherent in the ideology is realized. Theodicy is the original religious model for such a secularized schema of salvation. Obviously, the utopias of the various ideologies differ fundamentally in content. Communist ideologies are universalist and in principle embrace the whole of mankind. By contrast, the utopia of the Right is exclusive and offers salvation only to the chosen people who are supposed to become a light unto the nations, the superior races having the duty to lead all others.

The way to attain the utopian goal can only be through violence, for refractory mankind will not see the light and move toward it; and besides, there will always be enemies of the good—the evil ones who must be put down by force. Revolution is the midwife of history, Marx famously declared, and if a little blood is shed, it is all to the good in giving birth to a new society. When some Marxists, the Revisionists who emerged toward the end of the nineteenth century, abandoned the need for revolutionary violence, their opponents within the movement became even more adamant that it was unavoidable. Lenin and the Bolsheviks insisted on it. Those on the other side of the political spectrum saw violence in a multitude of forms as necessary. Purging bad blood was essential to the health of the body politic, be that race or nation. Nietzsche was convinced that only through wars of titanic scope could the nihilism of the age be overcome. Those unfit to live had to be weeded out, whether they were inferior races to be eliminated through colonialism, or inferior individuals to be eradicated through eugenics.

In the decade prior to the Great War, ideological debate became more heated than ever, though this had no bearing on the war itself. In some ways it was an intellectual exercise that reflected a growing interest in ideas, thanks to the expansion of education, and broader political participation, due to the growth of parties and movements as democracy expanded. Intellectuals played a leading role in all these fervent and heated debates. And being intellectuals, who tend to lack a sense of responsibility for outcomes in practice, they pushed their ideas to extremes. It is hard for us, who have lived through the consequences, to realize that most of them did not really grasp what they were advocating. They were experimenting with all kinds of outlandish proposals, just as the artists of the time were experimenting with all kinds of styles. The scientists, too, in this period were propounding theories way beyond the bounds of common sense. All in all, it was an age of great creative ferment and excitement, perhaps the last in Western civilization.

The war put an end to it, interrupting the free flow of ideas. For just as the young men were mobilized for the front, so, too, the reserve armies of intellectuals, writers, academics, and even scientists were enlisted for the war of ideas, the propaganda battle that both sides waged relentlessly throughout the war period. Never before had so many men of culture so unhesitatingly and unthinkingly sprung to the defense of their cause and attacked foes from which, as fellow Europeans, they had scarcely distinguished themselves before the war.

They all claimed to be defending European civilization against the barbarians or the decadents on the other side. But in the name of defending their civilization, they were in effect destroying it. This mentality was even more grotesquely manifest during the Second World War when the radios blared out the "end of civilization" whenever it looked like their side would be defeated. The *trahison des clercs,* as Benda termed it after the Great War, was the beginning of the intellectual surrender that made it possible for totalitarian ideologies to triumph when hostilities ceased and the guns stopped firing at the enemy on the front, instead turning against the enemies within.

In what follows we shall concentrate on expounding the two major ideologies of Right and Left, anti-Semitism and Bolshevism. There were many others—above all, Italian-style Fascism—but all of these pale in importance, if we compare their impact with the damage done to civilization by anti-Semitism and Bolshevism. Only these two succeeded in constituting totalitarianism proper; all the others succeeded only in installing dictatorships that were at most proto-totalitarian.

Section II—Anti-Semitism, the German Ideology

The emergence of anti-Semitism as a major political ideology out of age-old and ordinary Judeophobia is a remarkable alchemical transmutation of the base metal of common ideas and emotions into the gold of a totalitarian cause. It could only have taken place in the modern period prior to the First World War. In any other age it would have been inconceivable. It required modern intellectuals of all kinds to carry it out, and a public willing to be influenced by their ideas.

Judeophobia—that is, hatred of Jews—does not by itself amount to anti-Semitism. The old joke that an anti-Semite is someone who hates Jews more than is necessary hides the awkward truth that no amount of sheer hatred of Jews can amount to anti-Semitism, because this is a political ideology. It requires much more than hatred of Jews to constitute an anti-Semitic ideology; it calls for a whole theory about the role that Jews supposedly play in human affairs. Someone who accepts the theoretical part of anti-Semitism might have very little personal hatred of Jews as individuals. There were Jews themselves, such as Otto Weininger in Vienna, who were in this sense anti-Semites. On the other hand, there were many who had a visceral hatred of Jews without having any idea of anti-Semitism as an ideology. Such were the ordinary Judeophobes to be encountered among the common people. Usually, of course, in the modern period Judeophobia and anti-Semitism go together.

That there should have been growing resentment and even hatred of Jews in many European countries during the nineteenth century is easily explicable in sociological terms. It arose out of ethnic rivalry, much like that provoked in our time among Malays and others by the Chinese minority in Southeast Asia, which at times has resulted in riots and even pogroms. The economic success of the Jews in Europe, like that the Chinese in Asia, was strongly resented, especially by those in direct competition with them. The circles of such competitors grew because the Jews, newly emancipated from their ghetto existence, were not only given to financial dealing, their tradition occupation, but were entering the professions and making their mark in the media and cultural life in general. That the social success of a previously despised pariah group should have aroused competitive envy is all too readily understandable.

All such contemporary social hatreds could draw on a wellspring of religious animosities, the traditional Judeophobia of the Christian churches. This had an age-old and well-established theological rationale that went back to the Gospels. The Jews were presented as God's enemies, who betrayed and rejected Christ. This story grew in the popular imagination and eventually gave rise to the charge that Jews were Christ-killers. It was the theological precursor of ideological anti-Semitism. The mutation from the one to the other has a complex history, which begins with the secular variants of Judeophobia that were already being elaborated by such intellectual luminaries as Voltaire and Fichte in the eighteenth century. The key to the transition is the gradual displacement of theology by science, so-called. There is no clear historical break between the two, nor can the one form be distinctly separated from the other in the minds of the anti-Semites.

It is not easy to explain how and why the transition from so-to-speak "normal" Judeophobia to the outlandish ideology of anti-Semitism took place. Why should a simple form of ethnic animus, even with theological overtones, have evolved into a highly sophisticated mode of theorizing about history, philosophy, culture, politics, and much else besides? Anti-Semitic historians saw the Jews as the key to the whole of human history. Anti-Semitic philosophers speculated about the Jewish *Geist* and how it could infuse itself into all realms of the mind. Anti-Semitic cultural theoreticians wondered what it was in the psychology of the Jews that made them want to dominate humanity and gave them power so malevolent that they constituted an overwhelming danger—unless they were stopped in time. The *Protocols of the Elders of Zion* was proof enough of their overwhelming ambition. Hence, it ought to be the primary task of politicians to deal with the Jewish threat.

Taken to its furthest intellectual reach, this is what anti-Semitism as an ideology amounted to. Horrifying as it might seem to us now after the Holocaust, some of the greatest minds were complicit in it to some extent—including not only the self-professed anti-Semites, but many others who displayed no particular hatred toward Jews. By far the greatest majority of these thinkers were Germans (though, as we shall see, a few French and English thinkers were also involved). Some surprising names must be listed among them. Certainly Nietzsche must be included, but so, too, must Marx, who saw Jews as the leading exponents of the worst aspects of the capitalism he so hated. We shall encounter many other such intellects in the course of our study of how anti-Semitism as an ideology was constituted.

It is essential to realize that it was primarily a German ideology, made by Germans for Germans, with but a few small contributions from others who were Germanophiles anyway. From Germany it was exported to the rest of Europe, though not to any great extent until Hitler came to power, and overwhelmingly so during the Second World War, when it became the staple of Nazi propaganda. Judeophobia existed throughout Europe, as it had done for ages. In fact, it was much more intense in Eastern Europe that it ever became in Germany itself until 1933. In the czarist domains, pogroms were instigated late in the nineteenth century; in Hungary, blood-libel charges were prosecuted; and in Rumania, there were also such manifestations. In France, Judeophobia was at its most intense during the Dreyfus affair; and some Judeophobia there was already tinged with anti-Semitism among right-wing intellectuals, such as Edouard-Adolphe Drumont. But nowhere was anti-Semitism as an ideology current except in Germany and Austria.

It arose in Germany as part of the general movement toward unification and nationhood, generating a new self-definition of what it meant to be German. To many nationalists, being a German was the opposite of being a Jew and vice-versa. This was usually expressed in terms of *Geist*, a favorite concept among German thinkers. Thus the Jewish Geist was defined as antithetical to the German Geist. Because it was expressed in such abstract intellectual terms, anti-Semitism could be perceived as an impersonal doctrine not necessarily direct against the Jews as people, for Germans who fell short could also be accused of falling prey to the Jewish Geist. Even some Jews themselves came to accept that there was such a thing as a Jewish Geist and either lauded it or condemned it when they identified with the aggressors. These would later discover to their cost that ideological condemnation is much worse than visceral hatred; the latter leads only to pogroms, but the former leads to mass extermination. As Yeats expressed it in another context, "intellectual hatred is the worst."

If we treat anti-Semitism metaphorically as a chemical compound of ideas, it can be analyzed and a large number of elementary ingredients separated out. At least the following are its active constituents: Aryanism and Semitism, nationalism and Judeophobia, racism and eugenics, both based on scientific premises. Each of these ingredients can be there in varying proportions, and not all might be present at once. In any given case of anti-Semitism, it is possible that only four or five are current; below that number it is doubtful whether we can any only longer speak of anti-Semitism. The reasons for this will become clear when we have examined them one by one.

Aryanism, a key factor, began with scholarly discoveries that had nothing to do with Jews and was remote from Judeophobia. It began in the recherché field of philology with a surprising finding made in 1788 by William Jones, an East India Company administrator in Bengal and an orientalist scholar by avocation. He found that the major European languages, such as Greek, Latin, Celtic, Slavic, and German, had a close kinship with some of the languages of Asia, such as Sanskrit and Persian, and that, consequently, they all belonged to the one language family, called Indo-Germanic or Aryan. On this basis he and subsequently many others, especially scholars in Germany, assumed that all these tongues derived from an original root source, an *ur*-Aryan language. And where there was the one language, they further assumed that there must have been the one racial group. This original racial group, it was argued, must have moved out from their original homeland—and much speculation followed as to where that might have been—and diverged in numerous directions to populate Europe and parts of Asia, above all Iran and India. It was assumed that they came as conquering invaders and became the main racial basis of the people who subsequently spoke these Aryan languages. Such assumptions about India seem to tally with what was recorded in the Vedas.

British colonialists in India were favorably disposed to such a theory, for it acted as an apologia for their rule over the Indians. Their supposed racial kinship with the Indians, especially with the lighter-skinned Brahmins of North India, whom they enlisted as assistants, gave them much greater legitimacy than the previous rulers whom they displaced, the Turkic-Mongol Mughals from Central Asia. The Mughals were foreign to India, whereas they prided themselves on being—as they imagined—long lost racial kin.

We now know that all this speculation about Aryans is an anthropological myth, which we can call the Aryan myth, for short. What is particularly dubious is the linking of language to race that the theory requires. The reason that this is a fallacy is set out by the Indian historian Romila Thapar:

> By the mid-twentieth century, the notion that language and race can be equated was found to be invalid and indeed the entire construction of unitary races was seriously doubted. The concept of an Aryan race fell apart. Race is essentially a social construct, although initially it was claimed to be based on biology. Recent genetic studies have further invalidated this claim. It is, therefore, more correct to refer to "the Indo-Aryan speaking peoples" than to the "Aryans," although the latter term can be used as shorthand. It is important to emphasize that it belongs to a language-group and not to a race, and language groups can incorporate a variety of people.[5]

Thapar goes on to argue that the old historical assumption of a supposed invasion and conquest of the dark-skinned people of India by white-skinned Aryans is probably also a myth, for there is little evidence of any such conquest.

The British did not make much of the Aryan myth; beyond invoking it as legitimation for their colonialism in India, it never formed part of their national consciousness. But this did happen in Germany, where being German and being Aryan were soon identified. The reason for this was the great enthusiasm with which German scholars, literati, and philosophers took up the Aryan myth. Philologists, such as Franz Bopp, were foremost among these, closely followed by littérateurs, such as Friedrich Schlegel, and philosophers, such as Arthur Schopenhauer. Except for Schopenhauer, none of the others in any way linked this nascent Aryanism to Judeophobia. In fact, Schlegel was married to the daughter of the German-Jewish philosopher Moses Mendelssohn. Thus the ground was being laid in all innocence for one of the most obnoxious conceptions of modern history.

The reason that Germans were so eager to seize on the Aryan myth was not that they wanted to establish a connection to the Indians, as the British did, but rather that it seemed to confirm their identification with the Greeks, which they based on both linguistics and racial grounds. The resurrection of ancient Greece in modern Germany was nowhere more fervently celebrated than in Weimar, the center of the German literary and cultural renaissance. It expressed itself in the Grecomania of the time, documented in E. M. Butler's scholarly classic *The Tyranny of Greece over Germany*.[6] In this spirit Schlegel declared: "To live according to the classical fashion and to realize Antiquity in oneself in a practical fashion – such was the summit and the goal of philology."[7] And much later Nietzsche boasted in no uncertain terms:

> From day to day we become more Greek, first, as is well understood, in our thoughts and our evaluations, as phantoms who play at being Greek; but one day, we may hope, also with our bodies! There resides (and has always resided) my hope for what is German![8]

Granted, of course, that the neoclassical or Attic style was common to all of cultured Europe, a huge distance separates the major nations in this respect. Keats, the poet of "Ode on a Grecian Urn," is very different from Hölderlin, the most fanatical of the neo-pagan exponents of German Grecomania.

As Hölderlin's poetry shows, part of the motivation for asserting that they were really Greeks was to deny that they were Christians—that is, children of Abraham, like the Jews. A covert way of doing this was to attack the Jews as surrogates for Christianity. Schopenhauer expressed this most clearly:

> We may hope that Europe will free itself some day from all Jewish mythology [i.e., Christianity]. Perhaps the century is approaching when the people of Japheth stock [i.e., Germans], originating in Asia [as Aryans], will find the sacred relics of their native land, because after going astray for so long, they have reached sufficient maturity for this.[9]

Richard Wagner, Schopenhauer's follower, learned from this and disguised his own rejection of Christianity in favor of Buddhism, at least as he interpreted it, by an attack on Judaism and the Jews. Wagner, as we shall go on to show, was one of the most important founders of anti-Semitism as an ideology.

Anti-Semitism was not yet prevalent in Weimar, though many of its ingredients already were. Aryanism was established together with Grecomania, its supporting foundation. So, too, was German nationalism and Judeophobia. The leading intellectual exponent of both was the philosopher Fichte, who wrote the famous "Address to the German Nation" to stir up nationalistic sentiment against Napoleon and the French. But he also dealt with the Jews as follows:

> A powerful, hostilely disposed nation is infiltrating almost every country in Europe. This nation is in a state of perpetual war with all these countries, severely afflicting their citizenry. I am referring to the Jewish Nation (*das Judentum*). I believe, and hope to demonstrate subsequently, that the Jewish Nation is so dreadful not because it is isolated and closely-knit, but rather because it is founded on the hatred of mankind.[10]

However, Fichte, who subsequently became one of Hitler's favorite philosophers, was not an anti-Semite, merely a secularized Judeophobe. At that time, there was still much lacking for fully ideological anti-Semitism to exist; in short, there was no "Semitism" as such, because there were no developed racial theories and as yet no advocacy of eugenics. The distance separating Weimar from Buchenwald, both in space and time, still had to be traversed, but it was rapidly being closed.

Semitism, the polar complement of Aryanism, the view that Jews and Arabs and other oriental people constitute a homogeneous race, was supplied not so much by German scholarship as by French. It was France, not Germany, that was involved with the Orient, having begun its colonialist ventures with Napoleon's expedition to Egypt, followed later by the conquest of Algeria. Hence, to begin with, Semitism had negative racial connotations only when applied to the Arabs, the supposedly decrepit underlings of the Ottoman Empire, not when referred to European Jews. On the contrary, the idea that Jews are racially Semites—which is also a myth, since it is doubtful that there is much genetic continuity between Jews in Europe and the original Hebrews—was made much of by Jews themselves in order to affirm their own distinctiveness. Benjamin Disraeli, both as novelist and prime minister, cultivated the mystique of himself as a Semite. But it was French orientalist scholars, above all Ernest Renan, who had first put Semitism on the map. Though Renan was also an exponent of Aryanism, he was not an anti-Semite. If anything, he, too, was biased against the Arabs, for he believed that Islam had become an intellectual and spiritual poison and he thought that it would not survive the twentieth century, as it was doomed to wither away in the face of scientific progress.[11]

Count Joseph-Arthur de Gobineau took up Renan's ideas of the fundamental distinction between Aryans and Semites, as reflected in the history of these races, in order to develop a general account of history in which human progress is based on the realities of race. But Gobineau, too, was no anti-Semite; on the contrary, as Poliakov writes: "as for Jews, to whom Gobineau attributed relatively unadulterated Semitic blood, his description of them might easily have been inspired by Disraeli. It ends with what is almost a panegyric to the Chosen Race."[12] Nevertheless, his and Renan's ideas on Semitism were obviously essential, since without Semitism there could be no anti-Semitism. But, paradoxically, as anti-Semitism developed into an ideology it came to be directed solely against Jews and not at all against Arabs. The Arabs and Turks were favored in Germany due to the pre–First World War alliance with the Ottoman Empire. When the Nazis came to power they carried on the same foreign policy and sought to stir up the Arabs to revolt against the British. During the Second World War many Arab leaders heeded this call and became open allies of the Nazis, who welcomed them with open arms. This is how far anti-Semitism had reversed itself.

The primary founder of anti-Semitism as an ideology was Gobineau's friend, the great German composer Richard Wagner. He was one of the very first to draw together all the diverse elements that constitute this compound: at once an Aryanist and Grecophile, a fervent nationalist, a secular Judeophobe, and a racist, he followed both Gobineau and the newly formulated "scientific" racial theories that derived from Social

Darwinism. According to Poliakov, he was one of the first to "invoke the image of the Jew as an agent of corruption, a 'ferment of decomposition' and also that of the tragic destiny of the nobler elements of humanity."[13] His music drama *The Ring* renders in mythological guise all these ideas about the nefarious and malevolent role of the Jew in bringing about the destruction of the noble Aryan. These same ideas were explicitly propounded and elaborated by Wagner's English son-in-law, Stuart Houston Chamberlain, in a book entitled *The Foundation of the Nineteenth Century*, which became an anti-Semitic bestseller and was one of Hitler's favorite books. This anti-Semitism was propagated not just from Bayreuth but also from the numerous Wagner societies that sprang up all over Germany, Austria, and adjacent countries.

The last links in the chain of anti-Semitism were scientific racism and eugenics, and these were forged more in Britain than in Germany, though it was in Germany that they attained their largest following and most lasting effectiveness. Both had a Darwinian source. As we have already seen, Social Darwinism was a sociological application of the theory of evolution and the idea of the survival of the fittest developed by Herbert Spencer. And eugenics was similarly devised by Darwin's cousin Francis Galton. Both of these so-called scientific departures were eagerly taken up in Germany. Social Darwinism became the justification for militarism, colonialism, aggressive nationalism, and eventually for Germany's *Drang nach Osten*. Eugenics became a quest for "racial purity," associated in Germany with Paul Lagarde and "racial hygiene," promoted by Walmann, Ploetz, Lenz, and Fischer. This was Hitler's favorite reading matter and the basis of his Nuremberg Race Laws.

Both racial theory and eugenic principles were invoked by the anti-Semites in their campaigns against the Jews. The Jews were seen as the enemies of Nature's favorite race, the Aryans, who in current times were represented by the Germans. They were inferior or degenerate forms of life that were out to debase the racial stock of noble humanity. They were counter to Nature itself, and if Nature was identified with God, an easy step for the neo-pagans, then they were against God, as Christianity had preached all along. Thus without any embarrassment and with complete conviction, Hitler could declare, "I do God's work in defending us from the Jews," and presumably also in exterminating them.

However, anti-Semitism as it was preached prior to the Great War was still a relatively innocent and harmless affair, compared with what came later. Although it had already gained a certain amount of political traction, and anti-Semitic movements and political parties were proliferating, nobody expected that these would ever come to power or put their policies into practice. Even the Jews themselves did not take this very seriously. The Jews of Vienna could live with the declaration by their Jew-hating lord mayor, Karl Lugger—who was by no means an anti-Semite in the sense defined here—in which he boasted: "I decide who is a Jew." Similarly, the Jews of Germany thought at first that they could put up with a Jew-hating chancellor. But Hitler was not just a traditional Judeophobe; he was a prime example of the new anti-Semitism. As they learned to their cost, a political ideology like anti-Semitism is not something to treat lightly.

The Great War had produced people who were ready to murder in the name of an ideology. The Bolsheviks under Lenin in Russia had demonstrated a ready propensity for mass killing. The Spartacists in Germany and Communists in many other parts of Europe, such as Béla Kun in Budapest, were also making a grab for power. It was not lost on the anti-Semites that many of these revolutionary activists were of Jewish origin, such as Trotsky and many others in Lenin's Bolshevik entourage. As a result, when the Nazis formed themselves as a movement under Hitler's leadership, they saw themselves as at war with these Judeo-Bolsheviks, whom they readily generalized to the Jews as a whole. If there were Jews in the Kremlin and Jews on Wall Street, then they were obviously confronting a worldwide Jewish communist-capitalist conspiracy for mastery of the world. This is how far the anti-Semitic ideology led its adherents from any reality or sense.

We now turn to Bolshevism, the contrary ideology, which made a fetish of class as opposed to race. It, too, led to absurdities for which its proponents were prepared to murder without compunction. How such a thing could arise out of the humanistic aspirations of Marxism and Socialism is a historical paradox we will endeavor to make comprehensible. For it is difficult to understand that the road that led to the Gulag was paved with good intentions.

Section III—Bolshevism, the Russian Ideology

How was it possible for so many rational people in Europe to become ideological anti-Semites? We have explained this in the previous section. In this section, we address a parallel, unfathomable mystery. How was it possible for comparable numbers to become Bolsheviks? We have shown that anti-Semitism was a German ideology inextricably tied to German self-definition and cultural history; we will now show that Bolshevism was a Russian ideology that arose out of the specific conditions of Czarist Russia. This is particularly puzzling, in view of the fact that Marxists in other parts of Europe, not to mention other Socialists, had no special affinity with or sympathy for Russia, yet many of them eventually became Bolsheviks or at least fellow travelers. How did the Russian ideology take root in left-wing movements everywhere?

First, it is essential to understand why Bolshevism arose in Russia and could not have done so elsewhere in Europe. It was uniquely Lenin's creation, so it should more properly be called Leninism. As we shall see, it was the first example of what might be considered national communism, other instances of which later arose in Asia, such as Maoism in China, Ho Chi Min thought in Vietnam, and Kim Il-Sung teaching in North Korea, though in Europe there were also other minor variants, such as Titoism in Yugoslavia. Though Bolshevism and all the other leftist revolutionary ideologies are based on Marxism, they deviate substantially from its basic premises, twisting these to meet the demands of revolutionary struggles in circumstances utterly unlike those in nineteenth-century Western Europe, where Marx intended his theories to apply. Bolshevism was the first of such adaptations and the model for all the others.

To understand the formation of Bolshevism, we must trace the vicissitudes of Marxism in Russia and explain how and why Lenin departed from Marxist orthodoxy. That he did so is not in question, for he was stridently criticized and attacked by orthodox Russian Marxists, such as Plekhanov and Martov, and equally by German Marxists like Kautsky and Luxembourg. Lenin took no notice of any of them and followed his own course, ignoring theoretical issues that had no bearing on his practical goal, which was to establish a subversive party, keep it under his control, and carry through a revolution to seize power. To this end, he shaped his theories as required and changed them as much and as often as necessary to suit his strategic ends, all the while protesting that he was a true Marxist. As Wittfogel attests, "Lenin abandoned cherished ideas when strategy demanded it."[14]

Was Lenin a Marxist? The question may seem absurd, like "Is the Pope a Catholic?," but in Lenin's case there is a point to it, since so many scholars have argued that Lenin and his Bolsheviks were Russian revolutionists far more than they were Marxists. He followed the tradition of Russian insurrectionist extremists and their writings more closely than the theories of Marx and Engels, as Robert Daniels states:

> Extremism in Russia was distinctive because it had already been active for decades beforehand, in a self-consciously revolutionary tradition of inflammatory rhetoric and terrorist action. The background was not originally Marxist, but lay rather in the tradition of Russian Jacobinism that extended from the Decembrist Revolt of 1825 through the Nihilists, the Populists, and the *Narodnaya Volya* to the Social Revolutionary Maximalists. All of these movements were based on belief in the conspiratorial seizure of power to remake the nation from above. Russian Jacobinism influenced Lenin and the Bolsheviks at least as much as Marxism did, and it generated the main distinction between Bolsheviks and Mensheviks.[15]

It has been generally also noted by commentators that Lenin was much influenced by his older brother, Alexander Ulyanov, who was executed on the capital charge of attempting to assassinate Czar Alexander III in February 1887. He had been a member of Narodnaya Volya (The People's Will), a secret revolutionary conspiracy. As a budding Marxist, Lenin was critical of the "unscientific" and purely moralistic doctrines of the Russian revolutionary tradition; nevertheless, he following many of its fundamental dictates, such as organizing a conspiratorial party, instigating a revolution, and utilizing it to establish a dictatorship.

The proclamation of Peter Zaichnevsky, written in prison in 1862, prefigures many of Lenin's own later ideas about organization and strategy:

> Remember when the time comes, whoever is not with us is against us! We are convinced that the revolutionary party which is to assume power must maintain its present centralized organization so that it may build the foundation for a new social-economic order in the shortest possible time. This organization must usurp government power through a dictatorship and must stop at nothing. Elections to the National Assembly must be directed by the government which shall immediately make certain that its members include none of those who are in favour of the present order, should any such person still be found alive.[16]

Lenin did more than live up to these admonitions when the Bolsheviks came to power; he exceeded them, for there was no question of allowing a National Assembly or an election to take place. As for those "in favor of the present order," none were left alive. That such ideas were quite common among the Russian revolutionists is shown by a missive in a similar vein penned by Peter Tkatchev in 1875, this time from the safety of Switzerland:

> A real revolution can be brought about only in one way: through the seizure of power by revolutionists. In other words, the immediate and most important task of revolution must be solely to overthrow the government and the transformation of the present conservative state into a revolutionary state. . . . The revolution is brought about by the revolutionary government, which, on the one hand, eradicates all the conservative and reactionary elements of society, eliminating all those institutions which hinder establishment of equality and brother-hood among men, and, on the other hand, introduces such institutions as favour the development of these principles. . . . The revolutionary minority, having freed the people from the yoke of fear and terror, provides an opportunity for the people to manifest their revolutionary destructive power. Supported by this power, and skillfully directing it towards the elimination of the enemies of the revolution, the minor-ity demolishes the bulwarks of the old government and deprives the latter of its means of defense and counter action.[17]

This is almost a blueprint for what the minority, the Bolsheviks, set about doing, not just to the old czarist regime, but also to the liberal-democratic republic of the February revolution in 1917.

The more Lenin developed his own ideology of Bolshevism, the further he departed from Marxism and the views of the founders of the Social Democratic party of Russia, such Marxists as Georgi Plekhanov, Paul Axelrod, Vera Zasulich, and Leo Deutsch. Increasingly, Lenin held them in contempt, as David Shub remarks:

> The tough core of his political lines had firmly set: despite his Marxist and European schooling, his philosophy was conditioned by power-ful ingredients of Russian revolutionary absolutism and a sense of his own unique mission. Arbitrary and dictatorial in the eyes of his former mentors and Social Democratic comrades, he regarded them with increasing disdain for their 'bourgeois' aversion to a monolithic party of revolutionary conspirators; for their constant preoccupa-tion with the moral aspects of revolution. . . . In his writings he was becoming more and more dogmatic, more intolerant of differences of opinion.[18]

The difference between Marxism and Bolshevism was precisely what was coming to the fore in these altercations between Lenin and the others.

Marxism as a social theory and a study of revolutions both past, present, and future was not formulated with Russian conditions in mind. It was only meant to apply to highly developed, capitalist economies, such as those of England, France, Germany, and America. In Czarist Russia the conditions were in most respects the converse of those in such societies. Marx dubbed it a semi-Asiatic Oriental Despotism, where masses of peasants were under the thrall of their landowning lords, who themselves were completely in the power of an autocratic ruler. Such a society, far from industrial capitalism, far from a proletariat, was, therefore, equally far from any Socialist revolution. The idea of basing such a revolution on rebellious peasants was anathema to Marx.

It is true that late in his life, when prospects of any revolution in the West looked dim, he was prepared to grasp at straws, so he wrote in private correspondence to Russian revolutionaries that the cause of revolution in Russia was not altogether forlorn. Such Russians were asking whether the peasant commune, the *obshchina*, might furnish the basis for a unique Russian path to Communism, bypassing the stage of private property altogether. In 1882, in a preface to the second Russian edition of the *Communist Manifesto*, Marx penned the following sibylline answer to this question, together with Engels:

> The Communist Manifesto had as its object the proclamation of the inevitably impending dissolution of modern bourgeois property. But in Russia we find, face to face with the rapidly developing capitalist swindle and bourgeois landed property, just beginning to develop, more than half the land is owned in common by the peasants. Now the question is: can the Russian *obshchina*, though greatly undermined, yet a form of primeval ownership of land, pass directly to the higher form of communist common ownership? Or, on the contrary, must it first pass through the same process of dissolution as constitutes the historical evolution of the West? The only answer to that possible today is this: If the Russian Revolution becomes the signal for a proletarian revolution in the West, so that both complement each other, the present Russian common ownership of land may serve as the starting point for a communist development.[19]

This so much as says that when the great Day of Judgment dawns and Socialism triumphs in the West and in Russia simultaneously, then the Russians will be granted a dispensation from the dialectics of historical development and will proceed in their own unique way to Communism. Like the Delphic oracle, Marx has told the Russians what they want to hear, but at the same time he has reserved for himself the right to disappoint them.

Lenin read Marx regarding Russia in both ways during the early and the late periods of his life. According to Wittfogel, in the first ten years of his mature life, from 1894 until 1904, Lenin insisted that Russia was not exempt from the dialectics of economic development: "starting as an orthodox Marxist, Lenin upheld the idea of a special 'Asiatic system.'" In his first important book, *The Development of Capitalism in Russia*, published in 1899, he began to designate his country's Asiatic condition as *Aziatchina*, the "Asiatic system." And he termed the Tsarist control over land and peasants as "fiscal land ownership."[20] Subsequently, however, Wittfogel goes on to argue, Lenin subtly modified his Marxist idea of Oriental Despotism in Russia by omitting all reference to its managerial function; and "by neglecting the managerial role of Tsarist Despotism, Lenin seriously falsified the picture of the Russian economic order."[21]

What pushed Lenin into this falsification was his insistence on a Socialist revolution in Russia, when theoretically no such revolution could occur under Oriental Despotism. But strategy triumphed over theoretical consistency in Lenin, as Plekhanov realized full well:

> Plekhanov, in harmony with the socialist teachings which Lenin also accepted, condemned Lenin's plan to seize power as "Utopian." . . . But Lenin was determined to take the Great Gamble. And it was for this reason that during and immediately after the Stockholm Congress [in 1906] he minimized and obscured Russia's Asian heritage.[22]

Plekhanov also warned that "revolution would lead to an Asian restoration." But the more determined Lenin became to launch a revolution, the further he retreated from any idea of Oriental Despotism, so that "World War I abruptly terminated Lenin's adherence to the Asiatic concept."[23] Wittfogel draws the obvious conclusion from this whole sequence of maneuverings and dodges:

> Observing these inconsistencies, we may wonder how a revolutionary leader whose ideas on the ruling class were blurred could seize power. But we have to recall Hitler's perverted interpretation of German conditions and his smashing victories over his internal enemies to realize that enormous political success can be won on the basis of ideals that are at best semi-rational.[24]

Lenin did not scruple to pervert any principle of Marxism, if it stood in the way of achieving his plan to seize power or to exercise it according to his needs, all the while protesting sanctimoniously that "Marxist theory is the objective truth. Following the path of the theory, we will approach the objective truth more and more closely, while if we follow any other path we cannot arrive at anything except, confusion and falsehood."[25] However, Lenin was in fact a revisionist who changed Marxist doctrine as much as Eduard Bernstein did, though when others did so Lenin excoriated and excommunicated them. He completely revised Marx's view of the rise of working-class consciousness as a spontaneous product of the industrial conditions under which they worked, to the opposite view that this consciousness had to be imparted to them by an avant-garde of intellectuals. He wrote:

> Socialist consciousness cannot exist among the workers. This can be introduced only from without. The history of all countries shows that by its unaided efforts the working class can only develop a trade-union consciousness, that is to say, a conviction of the necessity to form trade unions, struggle with employers, obtain from the government this or that law required by the workers, and so on.[26]

As Ulam comments, "Bernstein had frankly avowed that he was revising the doctrine, pruning it of its illogical and obsolete parts. Lenin, with the sure instincts of a theologian, was proclaiming his revision to be Marxian orthodoxy."[27]

What Lenin was advocating regarding workers' consciousness was not Marx but Pyotr Chaadaev, a Russian revolutionary philosopher:

> The masses are subject to certain forces located at the summit of society. They do not think for themselves; there are among them a certain number of thinkers, who think for them, who give impetus to the collective intelligence of the nation and make it go forward. Just as this small number think, the rest feel, and the general movement takes place.[28]

Other Russian revolutionists, such as Herzen and Chernyshevsky, voiced similar views. As Daniels states, "Lenin was a Russian revolutionary in heart and soul, though Marxism was on the tip of his tongue."[29]

By transferring the onus of making revolution from workers to intellectuals, Lenin was in effect preparing the blueprint for a dictatorship of intellectuals, which became the basis for all totalitarian dictatorships; Mussolini's Fascists and Hitler's Nazis proceeded on similar assumptions and, as we shall see, Hitler himself attests that he learned much from Communist methods of organization, undoubtedly those that Lenin initiated. In Russia, of course, there was no other way of proceeding for revolutionaries. Only political intellectuals, renegade members of the bourgeoisie, like Lenin himself and his fellow Bolsheviks, could make the revolution, because neither workers nor peasants were up to it. Lenin set out the mechanics of organization for such an event in *What Is to be Done?* The key to it is a highly disciplined party of cadres following directives from the top, unquestioningly obeying the ukase of a central committee presided over by a single leader, Lenin himself. This he later called "democratic centralism," though obviously it has nothing to do with democracy; perhaps collective dictatorship by committee is a much truer designation. The sole function of the lower rank-and-file revolutionaries was to act either as propagandists or agitators: the former expounded the received doctrine; the latter applied it in agitation to stir up trouble for the authorities and to enlist new recruits. Both types were bound by what was later termed "partinost"—that is, by the requirement to surrender their intellectual conscience according to whatever the party dictated.

As the Bolshevik Party became more organized and numerous, it assumed the aspect of an ecclesiastical establishment, a "church" modeled on the Russian Orthodox one. Debate degenerated to disputation about doctrines, which once authorized were presented as dogmas from which deviations to either right or left were regarded as heresy. For this purpose, congresses were called together to act as synods to affirm orthodoxy and expel dissidents, or to chastise them with demands for contrition in the form of self-criticism before they could be readmitted back into the fold. After the Revolution, discipline became ever more ferocious, and it could be enforced by all the new punitive means provided by the Cheka.

After the Revolution Lenin did not hesitate to pronounce the necessity of a dictatorship that rules by means of a terror far exceeding what the czars could even have contemplated, with the limited resources of the Okhrana. In 1920 he openly pronounced the "leadership principle" that became the basis of all the totalitarian regimes:

> Classes are led by parties and parties are led by individuals who are called leaders. . . . This is the ABC. The will of a class is sometimes fulfilled by a dictator. . . . Soviet socialist democracy is not in the least incompatible with individual rule. . . . All phrases about equal right are nonsense.[30]

Under Stalin, the rule of the individual turned into the cult of personality, which was more than even Lenin had bargained for, but it arose directly from his own prescription. And so, too, did the increase of Russification that Stalin carried out, "a far-reaching Russification of the already somewhat Russified earlier (Leninist) Soviet political culture," according to Robert Tucker.[31]

As well as being leader of the Party, Stalin also presented himself as a Russian autocrat on the model of the great czars who had built the Russian state, Ivan the Terrible and Peter the Great; he did not include Catherine. But all the heroes of old Russia were celebrated once again. The worship of holy relics and saints was resurrected in a secular form, beginning with Lenin's corpse, embalmed and placed on permanent exhibition for veneration by pilgrims to the Kremlin. To what extent, if at all, these can be treated as religious phenomena will be discussed next. However, all such features inaugurated by Stalin belong to totalitarianism proper; they go way beyond the proto-totalitarianism that Lenin instituted. There is no doubt that he would have been personally appalled by them.

Nevertheless, it was Lenin who inaugurated the first totalitarian regime, from which all the other dictators learned and which they sought to emulate each in his own way. Hitler was quite explicit about what he owed to Lenin, even though he does not mention him by name:

> I have learned a great deal from Marxism, as I do not hesitate to admit. I don't mean their tiresome social doctrine or the materialist conception of history . . . and so on. But I have learned from their method. The difference between them and myself is that I have really put into practice what the peddlers and pen-pushers have timidly begun. The whole of National Socialism is based on it. . . . National Socialism is what Marxism might have been if it would have broken its absurd and artificial ties with the democratic order.[32]

By Marxism, Hitler obviously means Bolshevism; and by "their method," he is referring to Lenin's techniques in organizing and running a revolutionary party, staging a revolution, and governing a one-party state. Mussolini might have said as much if he had expressed himself as frankly and freely. He also followed such "methods," though he did so employing far less violence than Lenin or Hitler.

Right from the start of the coup d'état that Lenin called the Revolution, it was obvious that he would have to rely on massive violence to keep himself and the Bolsheviks in power against such overwhelming opposition. Plekhanov had predicted as much already in 1918:

> Their dictatorship is not one of the laboring people, but the dictatorship of a clique. And precisely for this reason they will have to resort more and more to terroristic methods.[33]

Thus from the very start, terror became the mainstay of Lenin's regime. Trotsky later wrote: "That was the period when Lenin at every opportunity kept hammering into our heads that terror was unavoidable."[34] Terror vastly increased under Stalin and turned into the perpetration of radical evil.

As we have already noted, Stalin also sought to buttress his rule by seeking pseudo-legitimacy on a pseudo-religious and mock-moral basis. This ideological ploy raises the general question as to whether ideology can ever be considered some kind of religion or morality.

Section IV—Ideology and Religion

Ideology is both more and less than a religion. It is more than a religion in that it seeks to direct and control the whole of life, both public and private. No social act can be innocuous; everything should be supervised and made to contribute to the state and the collectivity. But it is less than a religion in that it does not meet the individual's deepest longing for meaning in life, nor answer any of the fundamental questions that religion addresses, such as where and how salvation can be sought, what life is worth in the face of death, where humans stand in relation to God or Nature, what sanctions the moral law or sustains fundamental values, and so on. Modern ideologies as secular creeds espouse a superficial atheism and have little to offer the meaning-seeking individual, though they can inspire the masses. Indeed, they deny any such search for meaning or individual worth, for they hold that individuals must submerge themselves in the masses or the collectivity and aspire to nothing higher than to fulfill a function. Hence, the individual must be ready to sacrifice everything, including life, for the sake of the goals of the ideological movement. All this is in direct contrast to religion.

During the modern period, ideologies and religions have been at odds with each other; even when they have coexisted, there has been an uneasy relation between them. It is true that religious leaders have often accommodated themselves to political realities, and some have even become collaborators of totalitarian regimes; nevertheless, the strain and tension between them always remains. And vice versa, totalitarian leaders have always been suspicious of the residual hold that religions retain over their followers. Most frequently there has been war, open or covert, between ideology and religion, with each trying to undermine and destroy the other.

Where a religion itself has taken on some of the features and functions of an ideology this invariably leads to its debasement as a religion. When under Nazi instigation Christians in Germany redefined their religion as a German version of Christianity that had nothing to do with Judaism, they were simply reenacting the Marcionite heresy of the early period of Christianity. This was no longer Christianity as it had been understood and practiced throughout the ages. Something analogous is taking place in Islam at present, as the Jihadist ideologues are reconceiving Muslim traditions to transform them into political ideologies. Invariably they have been influenced by secular Western ideologies, such as Fascism or Communism. This will no doubt harm their faith, as people become increasingly critical of clerics meddling in politics.

However, there are many thinkers and theorists who write as if ideology and religion were identical, or at least very similar. Some do so only in a *façon de parler* manner, without being theoretically serious about it, and that is understandable, for metaphors drawn from religion can offer illuminating insight into ideology and totalitarian practices. We have utilized them ourselves previously and will continue to do so. However, there are theorists who argue in all seriousness that ideologies are religions and that is another matter that must be critically addressed.

Certainly, there are close resemblances between the ideological battles of the twentieth century and the religious conflicts of earlier times, such as during the Reformation and in later wars of religion. Very similar phenomena occurred in both. There have been vatic leaders, apocalyptic doctrines, and chiliastic movements; churches and sects have arisen, heresies have been denounced, and opponents have been castigated as enemies of God or mankind or whatever else is held dear; Holy Scriptures or sacred texts have been invoked, and so on regarding countless features. It does no harm to draw attention to such similarities, and it can be useful in seeking common grounds of explanation for them. Religions clearly acted as preparatory forerunners of ideologies in the twentieth century, especially the Judeo-Christian ones. It is also the case that totalitarian leaders have deliberately drawn on the resources of religious practices, ritual and ceremonial, to create a form of liturgical life in totalitarian societies. There was hardly any aspect of organized religion that was not imitated: funerals of martyrs, dedicatory consecrations, parades, and oaths of devotion; pilgrimages, catechisms, sacraments, and rites of passage for children; and many more. Obviously, these leaders wanted to endow their ideological movements with the aura of religion and so make them more acceptable. It would not be wrong or misleading, therefore, to consider them pseudo-religions or *Erzatz* religions. But just as *Erzatz* coffee is not real coffee, so is ideology at best a poor substitute for religion.

To argue that because ideology serves the same function as religion, it is no different from religion is to take sociological functionalism to its reductio-ad-absurdum. The fact that masturbation fulfills some of the same biological function as sex does not mean that the two are the same kind of experience. Ideology is a poor substitute for religion, just as masturbation is for sex. In neither case is there the same sort of satisfaction. As we have already argued, religion satisfies needs that ideology does not even acknowledge.

Mutatis, mutandis, the same arguments apply to the relation between ideology and morality. There can be no such thing as a Bolshevik morality or Nazi ethic, for such notions belong to long-established traditions of thought and action, which both of these ideological movements transgressed and traduced or perverted through sham impersonation. Moral norms cannot be created from scratch, and certainly not by political means. Law and legal principles can be drastically changed, which the totalitarian regimes proceeded to do, but moral norms are either accepted or rejected. The totalitarians rejected them, because according to their ideologies everything is permitted for the sake of their highest goals, whether it be the Revolution or the *Volksgemeinschaft*. If there are no moral limits, then there is no morality. A single sentence in Vasily Grossman's novel *Life and Fate* expresses succinctly what might otherwise take a whole book to demonstrate, that ideology destroys morality just as it annihilates religion:

> It was the revolutionary cause itself that freed people from morality in the name of morality, that justified today's Pharisees, hypocrites and writers of denunciations in the name of the future, that explained why it was right to elbow the innocent into the ditch in the name of the happiness of the people.[35]

Of course, it takes the novel as a whole to spell out the full horrifying meaning of that one sentence.

It follows that expressions like "Bolshevik morality" or "Nazi ethics" are oxymorons, contradictions in terms. But as with religion, both the Bolsheviks and the Nazis played out the pretense that they had a morality or ethics. They utilized all the traditional terms but totally misused them and perverted their meanings. "Duty," "honor," "virtue," "conscience," and so on no longer meant anything that even approximated their traditional meanings; they were systematically debased to signify whatever the leaders wanted, or to signify nothing. This pretense worked for party faithful, bureaucrats, and the masses, especially children and youths, who were moralistically indoctrinated. The leaders themselves knew that this was nothing but sentimental window dressing, and they themselves were not in the least bound by any scruples in achieving their ends. This explains how they were able with apparent "good conscience"—but really no conscience at all–to commit radical evil: the wholesale extermination of predesignated categories of people.

The surest proof that the ideologies were neither religions nor moralities is that almost nothing survived of them after the death of their leaders and their military defeats or political failures. Nazism almost ceased to exist from one day to the next: as soon as Hitler was dead and the war was over, nobody was any longer a Nazi, though many still harbored secret sentimental feelings for Hitler. Allied fears to the contrary, the *Hitlerjugend* did not continue a guerilla campaign after hostilities ceased. They no longer believed in Hitler. It is true that a neo-Nazi movement among marginalized disaffected youth arose much later, especially among those deriving from East Germany, but this is more a manifestation of hooliganism than a serious ideological revival. Nazism is dead; it died with Hitler.

Much the same can be said of Bolshevism, which more or less died with Stalin. After 1953 there was less and less genuine credence given to the ideology in Russia, though people continued to pay lip service to it. It is much the same with Maoism in China at present. Certainly, in Russia there are Stalinist stalwarts, generally geriatrics by now, and in China there are ambitious politicians playing at a Maoist revival for popular effect, such as the disgraced local leader Bo Xilai. But in both examples, such pretenses will be dropped sooner or later, and there will be nothing left of the old ideologies but an historic memory, bitter or regretful, as the case may be.

In all such cases where ideologies are abandoned, their former adherents behave quite differently from the followers of a genuine religious prophet. When their leader is executed or dies in some other violent manner, and his worldly cause is defeated and crushed, people who are religiously motivated tend to adhere to the memory of their leader as a martyr, clinging to the truth of his gospel all the more tenaciously. There are innumerable examples of this phenomenon from many cultures and periods, both ancient and modern. In relatively more recent times there are such instances as Joseph Smith and the Mormons in America, and the Bab—precursor to Baha'ullah and the Bahai—in Persia; in ancient times there are such celebrated cases as Hussein, the grandson of Mohammed who was killed at Karbala, and Jesus, who died on the cross.

Religions do not disappear when they have suffered military or political defeats, even of the most catastrophic kind. The Jews did not give up the Law when the second Temple was destroyed or when their great revolt led by Bar-Kokhba was utterly crushed. Religious believers have shown at all times and places that they will maintain their faith, openly or in secret, in the face of extraordinary persecutions. It takes lengthy and sustained indoctrination and punitive measures to extirpate a religion. This has been demonstrated over and over again in the Church's battles against heresy. The Cathars and the Waldensians persevered for centuries despite the sternest measures of the Inquisition, established precisely for the purpose of eradicating them.

Nothing like this is evident with the now-defunct ideologies, which more than anything else proves that they were not religious phenomena. It is certainly true that while they were current they inspired extreme devotion, and masses of men were prepared to give their lives for them, as is the case with any great political cause or any charismatic leader. But that does not prove that the cause is a religion or the leader a prophet. Charismatic movements can take a huge variety of forms, according to Weber, only few of which are religious in character.

Among scholars of ideology there have been some surprising misunderstandings of the nature of charisma and its relation to politics. Some argue that since the totalitarian leaders were charismatic figures, their movements must have been religious; and others contend that since their movements were not religious, they could not have been charismatic figures. An example of the latter is this astonishing declaration from Friedrich and Brzezinski:

> Hitler has been described by a number of writers as a "charismatic" leader. Since Moses, Christ, and Mohammed were typical charismatic

leaders according to Weber, neither Stalin nor Hitler, nor any other totalitarian dictator fits the genuine type. Arguments to the effect that the factor common to Hitler and Moses—their inspirational and emotional appeal to their followers—are misleading in a twofold way. In the first place, Weber's conception of genuine charisma implies a transcendent faith in God, which was characteristically lacking in Hitler himself and in the typical follower of the National Socialist creed; the same applies to Mussolini and other Fascist leaders. In the second place, the believed-in charisma is not primarily an emotional appeal, but a faith of genuine religious content, meta-rational in its revealed source, rational in its theology. It is the gift (charisma) of God.[36]

This account involves a complete misreading of Weber's concept of "charisma." As a value-free sociologist, Weber did not believe in the original Christian concept of charisma, but he used it to construct a sociological category for a type of authority that is universally prevalent. Friedrich and Brzezinski have obviously confused the old religious concept and the new sociological ideal type, despite the fact that Weber makes it quite clear that all inspirational leaders, religious or otherwise, can be considered charismatic.

> For present purposes it will be necessary to treat a variety of different types as being endowed with charisma in this sense. It includes the state of the "berserk" whose spells of manic passion have, apparently wrongly, sometimes been attributed to the use of drugs. . . . It includes the "shaman." . . . Another type is Joseph Smith, the founder of Mormonism. . . . Finally, it includes the type of *littérateur*, such as Kurt Eisner, who is overwhelmed by his own demagogic success. Value-free sociological analysis will treat all these on the same level as it does the charisma of the men who are the "greatest" heroes, prophets, and Saviors according to conventional judgement.[37]

To suppose that this concept does not include Hitler and Mussolini is obviously absurd.

An equally astonishing misjudgment occurs in Hannah Arendt's work, when she peremptorily declares in a footnote that "it would be a serious error to interpret totalitarian leaders in terms of Weber's category of charismatic leadership."[38] Instead of charismatic leadership, Arendt believes, the real explanation for totalitarian movements lies in their similarity to secret societies like the Mafia:

> Perhaps the most striking similarity between the secret societies and the totalitarian movements lies in the role of the ritual. The marches around the Red Square in Moscow are in this respect no

less characteristic than the pompous formalities of the Nuremberg party days. In the center of the Nazi ritual was the so-called 'blood banner' and in the center of the Bolshevik ritual stands the mummified corpse of Lenin, both of which introduce a strong element of idolatry into the ceremony. Such idolatry hardly is proof—as is sometimes asserted—of pseudo-religious or heretical tendencies. The 'idols' are mere organization devises, which are also used to frighten their members into secretiveness by means of frightful, awe-inspiring symbols.[39]

This explanation borders on self-contradiction, for the symbols and rituals of totalitarian movements are not intended to "frighten their members into secretiveness," but on the contrary to elicit an open and public manifestation of what they believe. Her assertion that mass movements can be likened to secret societies of restricted membership is astounding. There can be little doubt that totalitarian movements evince "pseudo-religious or heretical tendencies" and that they are led by charismatic leaders.

However, according to Weber not all expressions of charisma are alike, and we must take this into account in comparing Hitler and Stalin. Hitler was a charismatic leader for the members of the Nazi Party and eventually for the majority of the German people who believed in him. But he was also the legally elected head of state. Hence, he combined rational-legal or constitutional authority with charismatic authority, and he was clever and adroit enough to use the one to make the most of the other—using his charismatic appeal with the people to disregard the whole spirit of the constitution, and using the constitution to buttress his legitimacy. Stalin, by contrast, did not become a charismatic leader in his own right, as Lenin had been. He presented himself as the inheritor of Lenin's charisma, wielding what Weber calls "the charisma of office."[40] He sought to bolster his authority by instituting the "cult of personality" and all the pseudo-religious paraphernalia surrounding it. But he could not inspire freely-given allegiance; rather, he demanded constrained obeisance—a response that bore no resemblance to genuine religious devotion.

There are overwhelming sociological reasons why in a modern period of secularism and disenchantment no genuine charismatic religious movement can arise among the masses. Weber had stated this with remarkable foresight just as the ideological movements were coming into being:

> The fate of our times is characterized by rationalization and intellectualization and, above all, by the 'disenchantment of the world'.

Precisely the ultimate and most sublime values have retreated from public life either into the transcendental realm of mystic life or into the brotherliness of direct and personal human relations. It is not accidental that our greatest art is intimate and not monumental, nor is it accidental that today only within the smallest and intimate circles, in personal human situations, in *pianissimo*, that something is pulsating that corresponds to the prophetic *pneuma*, which in former times swept through the great communities like a firebrand, welding them together. If we attempt by force to 'invent' a monumental style in art, such miserable monstrosities are produced as the many monuments of the last twenty years. If one tries intellectually to construct a new religion without a new and genuine prophecy, then, in an inner sense, something similar will result, but with still worse effects.[41]

The political demagogues who rose to power on the basis of intellectually constructed ideologies gave rise to "miserable monstrosities" whose results have been far in excess of Weber's worst imagining. They introduced a new "monumental style" in politics, and built monuments to their own glory that surpassed anything that the pharaohs or emperors or kaisers could have dreamt about. With the tools of the mass media and unlimited propaganda at their command, dispensing whatever lies and mass deceptions they wishes to purvey, they could present themselves in whatever roles they wished to play. The role of religious prophet was only one among many that they adopted.

There are now theorists who take their pseudo-religious posturing seriously as genuine religion expression. One such is Emilio Gentile, who states that "the features totalitarian regimes share with churches were considered by both opponents and supporters to be expressions of genuinely religious components to be found in the very nature of these political movements."[42] He goes on to quote a number of illustrious personalities who expressed themselves to this effect in the 1920s and '30s. Such notions may have been understandable at the time, especially in relation to the Bolsheviks, who were operating in the mysterious and to some even mystical realm of Russia. The differences between Lenin and Dostoevsky and even Jesus were none too apparent to Russophiles like Keynes and Wittgenstein, or many others to whom Gentile refers. But in our time it is clear that such views are not only theoretically mistaken but morally obnoxious and politically dangerous, for they can be invoked as ex post facto justifications and apologies for the totalitarian regimes.

Those who mistook ideologies for religions were deceived by their outward manifestations, for their leaders deliberately played with the trappings of organized religion, with Hitler borrowing from the ritual of the Catholic Church and Stalin from Russian Orthodoxy. This pretense of religion is sheer hypocrisy and must not be taken at face value. Gentile is quite right when he asserts that "the religious aspects of totalitarian movements and regimes were so manifest, invasive, and ponderous that it was impossible to ignore them or relegate them to the margins of any reflections on the nature of this new phenomenon,"[43] but he is quite wrong to conclude from this that totalitarianism "itself became a new kind of religion, it is true, without God, without ritual, and without life after death, but one which nevertheless, like Islam, flooded the earth with its soldiers, apostles and martyrs."[44] Islam has lasted fourteen centuries, some of the ideologies scarcely fourteen years; there is a world of difference between them. The pretense to religion does not amount to religion.

It is true that religion has embraced extremely varied phenomena in history. Not all religions call for a belief in God or in immortality; many of the Eastern ones do not require this. Religions are not necessarily based on any kind of truth; some are obviously pious frauds, and their scriptures can easily be discredited as impostures and deceits. But this is not what is at issue. What is important is that a genuine religion should play a role in providing believers with existential meaning in their lives and create cultural forms according to which they can order their lives. The proof of this lies in their longevity, the staying power that makes people adhere to them generation after generation. As the Gospel itself pronounces, "by their fruits ye shall judge them." It is impossible to predict in advance which of the many febrile enthusiasms, cultic frenzies, charismatic eruptions, or other movements of this type will become religions. We can be sure that very few, if any, at a particular time will do so, especially now in our irreligious epoch. Will Scientology, despite its own claim to being a religion, in fact become one, as Mormonism did in the nineteenth century, or will it disappear without trace? It is impossible to tell at present.

The ideologies have all disappeared almost without trace, except for those still alive who remember them. None of them developed into a religion. It serves little purpose to fudge the issue, as Gentile does, by calling them "political religions." This expression has some relevance when applied to premodern contexts, such as the Greek polis, or Emperor-worship in Rome, and even at a stretch to the Mikado cult in modern Japan. But in a modern European context religion and politics define themselves in opposition to each other in accordance with the precept "render unto Caesar what is Caesar's, and to God what is God's." The separation of church and state, though nowhere in Europe as complete as in America, became the accepted institutional arrangement.

Gentile argues the contrary case because he defines religion in an extremely loose fashion. He considers almost anything that arouses enthusiasm or calls forth self-sacrifice a religion. Thus he treats all revolutionary and nationalistic movements since the French Revolution as "secular religions" and speaks of an increasing "sacralization of politics." To this end he writes as follows: "nationalism was the new secular religion that became widespread . . . because of its ability to merge into different ideologies, institutions and regimes by subjecting them to the primacy of the nation as a sacred supreme being."[45] Used in a purely metaphorical sense, there is nothing objectionable to this kind of suggestive prose— though Gentile tends to overdo this kind of metaphor, overloading every political term with religious and moral expressions. Thus a "religious politics . . . *consecrates* the primacy of the secular collective entity . . ."; it "formalizes this concept in an ethical and social *code of commands*"; it "considers its followers to be a *community of the elect* and interprets its political action as a *messianic function* to fulfill a mission of benefit for all humanity"; and finally, it "creates a *political liturgy* for the cult of the person who embodies it. . . ."[46] He goes on in this vein for pages.

To interpret totalitarianism in such religious and moral terms is to grant its ideologues all that they have claimed for their movements and leaders. They were only too ready to clothe themselves in religious vestments. Did not Lukacs think of himself as the St Augustine of the new Bolshevik dispensation? Did not Giovanni Gentile present himself as the apostle of Fascism, which was to supplant Christianity? Did not Heidegger proclaim a "new Dawn of Being" with himself as its philosopher by the side of the *Führer*? But we now know that they grossly deceived themselves and all those who treat their writings with greater seriousness than they deserve. Emilio Gentile now informs us that these grand delusions were "imposing" attempts to found new religions that might well have lasted a thousand years. The fact that they did not was in his view merely "contingent," due to the bad luck of history.[47] Perhaps if Hitler and Mussolini had won the war, things might have turned out differently. But Stalin did win, and where did this get Bolshevism?

To examine such claims we need to make a more detailed study of what totalitarianism was all about in order to see whether it had hidden potentialities that were not historically realized. We proceed to do so in the next chapter.

Notes

1. Françoise Furet, *The Passing of an Illusion*, op. cit., p. 164.
2. Alvin Gouldner, *The Two Marxisms: Contradictions and Anomalies in the Development of Theory* (Macmillan, London, 1986), p. 10.
3. Gabriel Kolko, *Century of War: Politics, Conflict and Society since 1914* (The New Press, New York, 1994), p. 6.
4. Richard Shorten, *Modernism and Totalitarianism: Rethinking the Intellectual Sources of Nazism and Stalinism, 1945 to the Present* (Palgrave, Basingstoke, 2012).
5. Romila Thapar, *Early India: From the Origins to AD 1300* (California University Press, Berkeley, 2002), p. 15.
6. E. M. Butler, *The Tyranny of Greece over Germany* (Beacon Press, Boston, 1946).
7. Friedrich Schlegel *Athenäum Fragmente*, sec. 147.
8. Friedrich Nietzsche, *Will to Power*, W. Kaufmann (ed.) (Vintage, New York, 1968) section 419 (fragment August-September 1885), p. 226.
9. Arthur Schopenhauer, *Parerga and Paralipomena*, sec. 115, quoted in Léon Poliakov, *The Aryan Myth, A History of Racist and Nationalist Ideas in Europe* (New American Library, New York, 1971), p. 248.
10. Johann Gottlieb Fichte, "On the French Revolution", quoted in Paul Mendes-Flohr and Jehuda Reinharz (eds.), *The Jew in the Modern World: A Documentary History* (Oxford University Press, Oxford, 1986), p. 257.
11. Robert Erwin, *Dangerous Knowledge, Orientalism and its Discontents*, (The Overlook Press, New York, 2006), p. 168. It is noteworthy that Erwin completely discounts the celebrated, but highly dubious, work of Edward Said on this topic.
12. Léon Poliakov, *The Aryan Myth*, op. cit. p. 235.
13. Ibid., p. 198.
14. Karl August Wittfogel, *Oriental Despotism: A Comparative Study of total Power* (Yale University Press, New Haven, 1957), p. 407.
15. Robert Daniels, *The Rise and Fall of Communism in Russia* (Yale University Press, New Haven, 2009), p. 118.
16. Quoted in David Shub, *Lenin, A Biography* (Penguin, Harmondsworth, 1948).
17. Ibid., p. 26.
18. Ibid., p. 87.
19. Karl August Wittfogel, *Oriental Despotism*, op. cit., p. 378.
20. Ibid., p. 389.
21. Ibid., p. 343.
22. Ibid., p. 393.
23. Ibid., p. 395.
24. Ibid., p. 391.
25. Quoted in David Shub, *Lenin: A Biography*, op. cit.
26. Lenin, *Works*, Vol. V, p. 347.
27. Ibid., p. 232.
28. Quoted in Robert Daniels, *The Rise and Fall of Communism in Russia*, op.cit.
29. Ibid., p. 50.
30. Quoted in David Shub, *Lenin: A Biography*, op. cit., p. 88.

31. Robert Tucker (ed.), *Stalinism: Essays in Historical Interpretations* (Norton, New York, 1977), Introduction p. xviii.
32. Hermann Rauschning, *Hitler Speaks* (London, 1939, p. 185). Quoted in Richard Pipes, *Russia under the Bolshevik Regime* (Knopf, New York, 1993), p. 259.
33. Quoted in David Shub, *Lenin: A Biography*, op. cit., p. 328.
34. Quoted in Ibid. p. 344–5.
35. Vasily Grossman, *Life and Fate*, trans. Robert Chandler (Collins Harvill, London, 1985), p. 528.
36. Carl J. Friedrich and Zbigniev K. Brzezinski, *Totalitarian Dictatorship and Autocracy*, op. cit., p. 41.
37. Max Weber, *Economy and Society*, vol. I Gűnther Roth and Claus Wittich (eds.) (University of California Press, Berkeley, 1978), p. 242.
38. Hanna Arendt, *The Origins of Totalitarianism*, op. cit., p. 361.
39. Ibid., pp. 377–8.
40. Max Weber, *Economy and Society*, op. cit. vol. II, pp. 1139–43.
41. Max Weber, *From Max Weber: Essays in Sociology*, H.H. Gerth and C. Wright Mills (eds.) (Oxford University Press, New York, 1946), p. 155.
42. Emilio Gentile, *Politics as Religion*, op. cit. p. 45
43. Ibid., p. 48.
44. Ibid., p. 28.
45. Ibid., p. 30.
46. Ibid., pp. 148–9.
47. Ibid., p. 136.

3

The Metamorphoses of Totalitarianism

Section I—The Great War

A genetic or developmental conception of totalitarianism, such as we outlined in the last section of chapter 1, must begin with the First World War, for this was the main cause of the sequence of events that led to totalitarianism. None of the ideologies of the pre-1914 period, neither Bolshevism nor anti-Semitism, could have generated a totalitarianism regime if the Great War had never occurred. Even a revolution in Europe, namely in Czarist Russia where it was most likely, would not in itself have led to totalitarianism.

Totalitarianism owed everything to the Great War. It did far more than provide the opportunity to stage a revolution or a coup d'état: the war shaped the whole nature of totalitarianism by providing a precedent for mass mobilization and organized repression, without which no totalitarian regime can function. In this first section we shall examine how such wartime exigency measures became the permanent peacetime arrangements of totalitarian regimes. Thus we will look on totalitarianism as a state of permanent war preparation without fighting, but one bound to issue in real war sooner or later.

At first mobilization and repression took the mild and somewhat ineffectual form of the proto-totalitarianism of Mussolini's Italy. Both of these organizational measures were much more rigorously and savagely adopted in Lenin's Russia, but this was largely due to the bitter civil war and Lenin's own ruthless character as leader. Once the Bolsheviks emerged victorious, the severities eased off as the New Economic Policy initiated by Lenin (NEP) came into effect, and after Lenin's death there was a brief period of thaw and relative normality. All that came to an end with Stalin's elimination of the other *diadochi*, Lenin's warring successors, and his emergence as sole autocrat. Mobilization and repression then embraced the whole of society, thus assuming the total character associated with totalitarianism proper. We shall examine how this differed from proto-totalitarianism in the next section. Then, in the third section, we will briefly outline the subtotalitarianism that supervened in Russia after Stalin's death—as it would in China also, after Mao's demise. These are examples of the penultimate stage in the genetic evolution of totalitarianism and its various mutations, which can be followed by a final stage, which we describe as posttotalitarianism, like that which ensued in Russia after 1989 but has not yet reached China, if it ever will. We will have something to say about this in chapter 8, which deals specifically with China.

In the present study, we can only discuss the causes of the First World War in very general terms. We must stress once again that incipient totalitarianism or the ideologies circulating in the prewar period played no role in causing the war. For the Bolsheviks, the Fascists and the anti-Semites, the war was a piece of good fortune without which they would never have succeeded. None of those responsible for the war had any intention of furthering the plans of such extremist groups, but they inadvertently brought about a situation where they were no longer in control, and power passed to others. They were the heads of state, such as emperors, kings, presidents, and prime ministers; all the other political and administrative leaders; the generals and military officers; the industrialists, especially the arms manufacturers; writers, journalists, intellectuals, and academics of a nationalist persuasion; and finally, though to a much lesser extent, the church dignitaries and clerics who blessed and condoned the war-making endeavors of all the others. They all regarded war as simply another tool of policy and were willing to wage it if it should prove favorable for attaining their nation's ends.

They had all engaged in the balance of power politics that dominated European foreign policy throughout the nineteenth century. Alliances and alignments changed, but the balance of deterrence had been maintained for such a long time that people had forgotten what a major war was like, the last one having been the Napoleonic war. Few people could even imagine what a modern war would be like, least of all the generals.

Almost inevitably, when the balance of power was threatened by new developments, or it seemed to be tilting against one side, then one or the other side would resort to war. This was happening in the decade prior to the actual war, when German generals feared Germany would be caught in a two-front war between the French and the Russians, because they could not compete in numbers of men, and the weight of arms was moving against them. They were ready to strike first when the opportunity offered itself. This was bound to occur, for the reasons that David Stevenson gives:

> ... between 1905 and 1914 the bases of deterrence crumbled as the two great alliances moved closer to military equality while armaments competition between them intensified and political antagonisms—fuelled through a succession of diplomatic crises around the Mediterranean and the Balkans—mounted. Although neither side saw the war as inevitable, both were increasingly willing to contemplate it.[1]

The incident at Sarajevo and a series of diplomatic blunders that followed was all that was necessary to set the mobilization timetables in motion—and inevitably war ensued.

Once the war started, "the new factors of globalization, popular involvement, industrialization, and scientific armaments would then make conflict all the more devastating."[2] These were the unforeseen factors that led to four years of mechanical slaughter of millions of men and the utter exhaustion of nations, with the populations of those on the losing side reduced to famine. As the fortunes of war would have it, on the winning side were the West European democracies, Britain and France, together with the United States, who imposed their conditions of peace on the losing sides at Versailles; these included the three imperial dynasties—the Hohenzollerns, Hapsburgs, and Romanovs—together with the Ottoman Caliphate. Though Russia started the war as France's and Britain's ally, it lost the war in 1917, in fact, and large parts of it were under German occupation. The fact that all these powers were on the losing side proved extremely propitious for totalitarianism, for had the Central Powers won it would have been a different story altogether.

It so happened that the countries on the losing side, as well as one on the winning side, Italy, fell within what might be called the arc of instability in Europe. This largely concerned all those countries on the peripheries of Western Europe, to the east, southeast, and south, which were not as well developed as those on or close to the Atlantic seaboard. For all kinds of reasons these countries had lagged behind in all the crucial aspects of the Forces of Modernity: in industrial capitalism, in a rational-legal state authority, in science and technology. Their societies were backward in all the key criteria of modernization: serfdom had just barely been abolished, in some as recently as half a century ago;

literacy levels were low; political participation was either limited or a sham or nonexistent; traditional, highly reactionary, religious authorities prevailed; women were in an inferior position; and so on. Russia, Austro-Hungary, the Balkans, the Ottoman Empire, and to a considerable extent Spain and Italy, at least as far as its southern regions were concerned, were all within the arc of instability. This meant that they were precarious in every respect, apt to suffer revolutions or revolts, to have their government overthrown or even to be broken up territorially. Russia had already experienced a minor revolution in 1905, and the others had also gone through unrests of various kinds.

It is true that Germany was exceptional compared with all the others. It was certainly a much more modern state and society where the Forces of Modernity were as well developed as anywhere in Europe and in some respects, such as science and technology, superior to all others. Yet Germany, too, had serious weaknesses. It had only existed as a unified state for less than fifty years before the war. Its unification had resulted in the dominance of Prussia and the Junkers, as far as its monarchy, court and the whole military establishment were concerned. The Kaiser had the last word on all issues of foreign policy, and the generals were a power unto themselves. When Bismarck ran the show, none of this mattered, but once Wilhelm II was in the saddle, German foreign policy lurched from one confrontation to another.

All this was bound to cause instabilities, but not of a kind so severe they could not be overcome; and in fact prior to 1914 Germany was moving toward a liberal democratic polity in which the Marxist Socialist party, the largest in the Reichstag, was bound to play a major role. The unevenness of development and the consequent instabilities were very much worse in Austro-Hungary and were greatly aggravated by the problem of different nationalities across the far-flung Empire, but even there the situation might have stabilized but for the war. In Russia, the situation was almost beyond repair, as indeed the partial revolution of 1905 had demonstrated; czarism would have been overthrown sooner or later, but even such a generally expected occurrence need not have been followed by totalitarianism. A similar fate awaited the Turkish Empire, with an unpredictable outcome.

Totalitarianism arose in Europe because of the remarkable confluence of a large number of factors, some of which were long-festering structural imbalances, such as the inroads of the Forces of Modernity into the backward arc of instability; others were purely contingent historical events, such as which countries would come out on the winning and losing sides in the war. Such conjunctures are neither inevitable nor predictable, which does not mean that they cannot be given ex post facto adequate explanations in terms of casual interactions. To give such an account is not easy, since it raises very difficult methodological questions of how structures relate to events and vice versa; that is, how large-scale sociological forces generate specific historical occurrences, and how the actions of people that constitute historical events can impact on the forces that generate social structures. In Kantian terms, the difficulty consists in mediating between the realm of freedom and the realm of necessity, an issue we discussed in *Beyond Civilization.*

After the war, there was a good chance that Germany would succeed in establishing a stable democracy, but for the Depression, an event that opened the way to totalitarianism. In the other countries of the arc of instability there was no such possibility; they all fell into some form of dictatorship, with the exception of Czechoslovakia. The combined effect of losing the war and the suffering, pain, and humiliation that this caused, together with long-established social and political problems, was more than enough to push them over the edge into chaos, from which only a dictatorship of the Left or the Right could save them. It seemed that only an iron fist could hold such countries together or prevent them from tearing themselves apart.

Russia was the first to fall into the abyss with the Revolution of 1917, which Lenin exploited with a gambler's recklessness and a revolutionary's desperation to win the game of power and establish the first proto-totalitarian regime. Attempts to repeat his success by the Bolsheviks in Germany, Austria, and Hungary predictably failed and led to right-wing reactions that established dictatorship in Hungary and later Austria, but failed to do so in Germany until 1933. In Italy a similar Bolshevik grab for power caused great instability during the *"bieno rosso"* of 1919–1920, but it did not succeed in gaining anything and also provoked a counter-reaction, this time from Mussolini's *squadristi* and other *Fascisti* who, with the connivance of the established authorities of monarchy, army, and church, seized power to form the second proto-totalitarian regime. What gave the Fascists such a great advantage over the Bolsheviks was that Italians emerged from the war very disgruntled, almost as if they had been on the losing side. Few of their irredentist claims were recognized at Versailles. Italy had sustained huge loses in the war, as if for nothing. Mussolini played up to these feelings of resentment and promised to satisfy nationalist yearnings to see Italy great once more, perhaps for the first time since the Romans. And so the totalitarian era in Europe was born.

The war was the cradle of totalitarianism in that it nursed the very people who would become totalitarian personalities and constitute the postwar totalitarian regimes in Russia, Italy, and Germany. As we have already mentioned, there were two types of deviant Socialists: those on the far Left who advocated social revolution and a total state-tyranny, such as the Bolsheviks under Lenin; and those on the far Right who wished to capture state power so as to harness it for nationalistic or racist ends, such as the Fascists under Mussolini or the Nazis under Hitler. Both sides differed fundamentally in their attitude to the war. The Bolsheviks, Spartacists, and Communists had irrevocably opposed the war and refused to take part in it, much to the chagrin of the established Socialist parties, who went along with the war policies of their governments, albeit often reluctantly so. But the socialists also numbered among them individuals who were nationalistically minded and who would later become Fascists and Nazis. These men had ardently supported the war—seeing it as a battle for national salvation—and after the war, unable to adjust to peacetime existence as mere civilians, they formed groups of militant right-wing ex-servicemen, who now turned their backs on Socialism and were contemptuous of the new postwar Social Democratic or Liberal governments. They were particularly enraged with the Bolsheviks, Spartacists, and Communists, who had tried to seize power immediately after the war was over in all the defeated states as well as Italy.

In this way, through a confused tangle of adventitious circumstances, the two proto-totalitarian regimes were installed in Russia and Italy, and a third followed not much later in Germany. These were the early forms of proto-totalitarianism that had to undergo a further metamorphosis before they could emerge as totalitarianism proper. Proto-totalitarian regimes derived their essential features and main organizational arrangements from the course the war took when it became, in Ludendorff's words, a "total war." The key to waging a total war, as all the main warring powers realized, was total mobilization; not only the manpower, but all the resources of a nation had to be mobilized for the war effort, and those nations that mobilized most efficiently emerged as victors.

Section II—Proto-totalitarianism

Apart from ideology, the constitution of a proto-totalitarian regime is based on two factors: mobilization and repression, both of which emerged directly out of the war. The two go together, for the one is impossible without the other. The exercise of both together was made mandatory for all the warring nations during the Great War. Those who did so best won the war; those who could not manage it so well lost. Mobilization meant the enlistment of all people and resources and their utilization for the sole purpose of winning the war, for which supreme end all was sacrificed. Repression meant the elimination of any opposition, or even criticism of this program. Nobody could refuse being drafted, nobody could resist the authorities, nobody could voice any objections; not only the official bodies, but public opinion itself was at one in enforcing these strictures. Anyone found wanting was accused of unpatriotic behavior, cowardice, or even treason. After Ludendorff, the chief of staff and de facto dictator of Germany, declared a "total war" policy and took complete control of the nation's resources, Germany plunged toward totalitarianism. By that point Britain had already been on a total war footing for some time. France followed suit.

> This was a war waged by industrial societies able to mobilize all their men and all their factories. Every citizen contributed to the joint effort, either as worker or as soldier. The *levée en masse* decreed by the Convention had become a reality. The effort of organization, including the 'organization of enthusiasm' [Elie Halévy], for which the survivors of the massacre later reproached the old men, was incomparable.[3]

Raymond Aron's account of total mobilization is not equally applicable to all the warring nations. Britain was ahead of all the others; the idea of a "home front" to complement the fighting front was conceived there; censorship was severe, and women were enlisted for work in factories and farms. France also organized to a large extent. At first Germany failed to do so for sentimental reasons; Germany was late in mobilizing all its resources, but did so finally with great thoroughness. Austro-Hungary was in no position to mobilize efficiently. Russia soon descended into disorganization and indiscipline. This gives a clear indication in itself of why Britain and France won and the latter three combatants lost the war. Success in modern warfare requires central rational control of all the Forces of Modernity: industrial production, state bureaucratic enforcement, scientific capacity, and technology must all be devoted to the fight on the battlefront. It also calls for what Aron refers to as the "organization of enthusiasm": the burdens to be borne and the sacrifices to be made should be equalized, so that the population will be willing to participate and embrace the national cause with utmost enthusiasm. In all these respects the democratic powers were more advanced than the others. Oddly enough, Germany did not apply this lesson of 1914–18 in the Second World War: Hitler refused to mobilize women, and Goebbels called for total war only in 1943.

These wartime conditions provided the blueprint for totalitarianism, which paradoxically emerged not among the winners, who quickly restored prewar liberties, but among the losers. This was already noted by Horkheimer in 1939 on the eve of the Second World War:

> The German war economy in the First World War was a forerunner of modern 'five year plans': the compulsory conscription used in modern warfare between nations is a major constituent of totalitarian social engineering. Mass mobilization brings the columns of workers who have been assigned to the armament industry and the construction of ever more motorways, underground railways and blocks of flats, little that is new, except that is, for a mass grave.[4]

For reasons of prudence or ideological propriety, Horkheimer fails to point out that Stalin had already provided the mass graves that Hitler would soon emulate. Hitler had not yet achieved the total terror that Stalin exercised. Russia was already a fully totalitarian society before the Second World War, whereas until this point Germany was still proto-totalitarian, involving a much lesser form of repression.

The First World War also pioneered state repression in the European liberal democracies. Draconian punishments were meted out to any opposition to the war or criticism of its conduct by the generals. Conscription was universal, and conscientious objection was only allowed in rare cases in Britain, and prohibited elsewhere. The press was censored heavily, and publications regarding peace overtures were banned; in other words, the war could not be freely discussed, so to that extent thought controls were being imposed. This was a clear foretaste of totalitarianism. Oddly enough, such censorship was more stringent in Britain than in Germany: Bertrand Russell was sent to jail for opposing the war, whereas Max Weber was able to publish a strongly worded attack on Wilhelm II. Terror, however, was not yet invoked anywhere, except at the front: during the battle of Verdun, for example, French regiments were decimated in the old Roman style—with randomly selected soldiers being executed because morale was dangerously low—in order to "*encourager les autres.*" With the coming of totalitarianism, civilians were similarly treated.

All these practices of mobilization and repression pioneered during the war were ardently advocated by the theoreticians of totalitarianism as new methods of rule, considered to be vastly superior to democracy and capitalism. Rational planning and discipline were the new watchwords both on the far Left and far Right, both sides advancing such proposals under the old rubric of Socialism. On the Bolshevik side the most lucid and theoretically acute expositor of such ideas was Leo Trotsky; on the Nazi side a no less able intellectual was Ernst Jünger. Both were highly cultured men who set about destroying the culture that nurtured them, thereby both contributed to the negation of the humanist ethos of Western civilization.

Trotsky was the principal exponent of the militarization of labor; he expressed these ideas clearly and eloquently at the Ninth Party Congress in March 1920. Workers would be mobilized just like soldiers and would unquestioningly obey the orders of their superior managers on pain of condign punishment. Striking and slacking were outlawed, just as in wartime. Everybody had to work or be declared a social parasite, which could be a sentence of death. Mobilization and repression were the two sides of the one coin. According to Donald Rayfield:

> From the start, Lenin and Trotsky secretly planned the totalitarian organization of labor, with mobile labor armies and cooperatives of peasants on state land. In the summer of 1918 Trotsky organized the first concentration camps. Nothing could shake Trotsky's belief that the 'unproductive nature of compulsory labor is a liberal myth', but it took a decade for Cheka labor camps to make any perceptible contribution to the economy.[5]

That was the decade of NEP, the New Economic Policy, which allowed some private enterprise and was opposed by Trotsky, who favored rapid industrialization and collectivization, which necessitated total central control of labor. Stalin opposed Trotsky's ideas for tactical reasons at first, but then implemented them when he had eliminated all his rivals and come out on top. Rayfield argues that "the differences between Trotsky and Stalin were in style not substance,"[6] but his view can be questioned. Trotsky still represented the proto-totalitarianism of Bolshevik rule in its initial phase, and perhaps under his direction such policies would have been implemented very differently from the brutal way that Stalin imposed them as part of his inauguration of totalitarianism proper, or at least that is what his supporters contend.

Jünger was an admirer of the new Soviet Union and of Trotsky's ideas; what appealed to him most was the "militarization of labor." This fitted in very well with his own concept of *"totale Mobilmachung"* or total mobilization, which the war had first unleashed on the world. Jŭnger, unlike Trotsky, who sat out the war in America, was a war veteran who gloried in his war experiences and believed that these had made him and his fellow comrades at the front into a new type of Man of the Future. These were the kinds of ex-servicemen who flocked to the Nazis and the other Right wing associations of returned soldiers. According to Jŭnger, such people marked a new epoch in human history, as Jeffrey Herf reports:

> The really distinguishing feature of the twentieth century in Jŭnger's eyes was the process of total mobilization of social and technological resources by the State. The nineteenth century, by way of contrast, had still been an era of limited war, of firm distinctions between soldiers and civilians, and of "partial mobilization," a partiality that corresponded to the "essence of monarchy." The era of partial mobilization imposed limits on the extent to which technology would be placed in the service of armaments and popular mobilization in war times.[7]

It is clear that the Jŭnger's *"totale Mobilmachung"* was a rearmament program that could only lead to war. This is, in fact, what happened under Hitler, whom Jŭnger at first supported. He certainly did not approve of Hitler's lurch into complete totalitarianism at the start of the Second World War, but by then he had already served his purpose.

Jŭnger was a highly cultured individual and a writer of considerable prowess; he was one of many such intellectuals who prepared the ground for the destruction of civilization. He did so, in particular, by extolling the saving virtue of violence in identifying it with labor. The workman and the warrior were one, as he writes in his essay *"Unsere Kampfstellung"*: "Thus labor has within it a value directed outward, that is at the same time its warlike nature. Every hand gripped on the machine suggests a shot will be fired, every completed work day is like a marching day of an individual in an army unit."[8] Could Trotsky, despite his militarization of labor theory, have expressed himself in this way? This is doubtful, since creation and destruction were still distinct for him. But for the proto-Nazis they were not. However, after the Second World War, many intellectuals who had fought Nazism, such as Sartre, Fanon, and others, took up the theme of violence as a virtue in itself. These were so many nails hammered into the coffin of Western civilization, which most of them abhorred anyway for they considered it bourgeois, colonialist, imperialist, and so on.

The relationship between civilization and intellectuals is a vast topic, to which we cannot do justice in this work. However, we have already partly adumbrated it in *Beyond Civilization*, and a few points made there are worth repeating in this context. As we showed in the previous chapter, totalitarianism would have been literally inconceivable without the work of intellectuals in the widest sense, including artists such as Richard Wagner, the key founder of anti-Semitism. In other words, intellectuals gave the ideas of totalitarianisms of all varieties their necessary start and grounding. These ideas, applied in practice, largely through the exigencies of the Great War, would lead to the ruination of the civilization from which they derived. This is the way in which European culture was complicit in its own suicide.

Prior to the Great War, in the period starting with the French Revolution and continuing through the whole nineteenth century, intellectuals had played the leading role in sustaining European culture and, therefore, also Western civilization. They had become literally its *Kulturträger*. Without their efforts, this culture could have fallen into decadence, regurgitating the stale repetitions of a civilization in decline, such as we find in China, India, and Islam—as we shall show in part III. The West did not slowly decay and go to seed; it suddenly exploded, going with a bang, not a whimper. The intellectuals who had given it a new life for well over a century had initiated many new revolutionary departures in the last phase before 1914: innovations in the natural sciences, such as relativity and quantum theory; the new sociology of Weber, Simmel, Durkheim, and others in the social sciences; departures in all fields of philosophy, such as positivism, phenomenology, and existentialism. The list of achievements in this climactic period goes on, yet among these very intellectuals were those who actively or passively, knowingly or unknowingly, were implicated or involved in the foundation of totalitarianism. This is the great tragedy of European civilization that intellectuals brought about. But for this to happen there had to be a transition from proto-totalitarianism to totalitarianism proper.

Section III—Totalitarianism Proper

The difference between proto-totalitarianism and totalitarianism proper is one of kind, not merely one of degree. This is an instance of the so-called dialectical jump from quantity to quality so beloved of Hegelians: when something is extremely enlarged and intensified it becomes a different thing altogether. The same consideration applies to whole systems. Proto-totalitarianism arose when the imposition of mobilization and repression, the temporary emergency measures of wartime, were continued into peacetime as a permanent state of affairs. Totalitarianism proper arises when these partial and still lax measures of early totalitarianism are driven to an extreme and become total mobilization and total repression. As a result they completely change their character. Thus, for example, in proto-totalitarianism repression is applied selectively, and no matter how heinous it may be, it still accords with legal norms; under full totalitarianism it becomes total terror, which is tantamount to radical evil. Radical evil does not exist as yet within proto-totalitarianism; it is one of the hallmarks of full totalitarianism. The leader's power in proto-totalitarianism is still limited, and there are other forces that can curb or even gainsay it. In totalitarianism proper the leader has unrestricted and unchecked power; it is total. Ideological aims in proto-totalitarian states, furthermore, tend to be limited or only entertained as an ideal or ultimate fulfillment; in fully totalitarian states, by contrast, ideological aims are embraced as goals capable of immediate practical realization. The method of realization is war, and this inevitably entails a global war for world supremacy, since totalitarian ideologies make universalist claims.

The transition to what we might call simply totalitarianism, for short, occurred in Russia under Stalin between the years 1929 to 1931, when he embarked on the first Five-Year Plan, implementing rapid industrialization and collectivization, and at the same time ordered the amalgamation of all the penal camps into the one Gulag system. The ostensible purpose of these changes was to arm the Soviet Union against the capitalist encirclement that Stalin claimed was about to strangle the nascent Bolshevik regime, the first Socialist state in the world. But these purportedly defensive preparations against a nonexistent enemy—for no country had any intention of attacking the Soviet Union—can be seen as a cover for aggressive preparations to wage a revolutionary war if circumstances should ever become propitious. World revolution would then become a realizable goal.

Hitler launched Germany into totalitarianism ten years later, in the heady years when National Socialist domination of the most important part of the world seemed within easy reach. The whole of Europe, with the sole exception of Britain, had fallen into his hands, and Russia was there for the taking; all it required, as he said at the time, was to kick in the door and the whole rotten structure would crumble. He was in sole authority, having total sway over all the agencies of state and society, including the army itself, which he had finally brought to heel.

His one key mistake, the one that led to the defeat of Germany and his own downfall, was not to totally mobilize German society for the long conflict that the Second World War became. He thought he could get all he needed by plundering the conquered countries of Europe and utilizing their people as slave labor. At the same time, given the opportunity of wartime, he embarked on radical evil in murdering the Jews of Europe and many others, such as the three million Russian prisoners of war—which, if nothing else, was wasteful from an economic point of view.

Mao's chance to inaugurate full totalitarianism came in 1949 after his victory over Chiang Kai-shek and the Kuomintang in the civil war. Prior to that, Mao as leader of the Chinese Communist Party (CCP) had practiced a kind of proto-totalitarianism, following the Long March and his establishment in the relative safety of Yan'an. His leadership was still far from absolute, as it became after1949; he could still be challenged. He had to win over the peasants, and he put reform policies of land distribution into effect, just as Lenin did after 1918. However, once he was totally in control and all such obstacles were overcome, he launched himself into radical evil with the mass murder of landlords and others who were active in the former regime, and he forced the people themselves to be complicit in this by participating in the kangaroo trials he set up. His attempt at total mobilization followed with the collectivization campaign and the Great Leap Forward, which achieved the militarization of labor by creating one vast slave labor camp. He completed his career with the further radical evils of the Cultural Revolution.

The transition from proto-totalitarianism to full totalitarianism is by no means inevitable, nor is it driven by an inner logic or propulsion. It happens for reasons that are peculiar and particular to each case. As we know, in most cases it does not happen: Mussolini in Italy, Franco in Spain, Tito in Yugoslavia, Castro in Cuba, Ho Chi Min in Vietnam, and other possible candidates never became fully totalitarian leaders or attempted to set up such a system. They were content to be dictators in proto-totalitarian regimes or authoritarian rulers of some kind. Personality is decisive in this regard. Such leaders as Mussolini were not, like Stalin, Hitler, and Mao, power-driven megalomaniac personalities, displaying the *"deformation professionnelle"* typical of great dictators, especially those dominating large states.

Obviously the "profession" they were plying did not exist prior to 1914; it only arose as a result of the Great War, at the conclusion of which talented demagogues could gain a mass following and build up parties on this basis. Thus Lenin developed a small conspiratorial band of professional revolutionaries into the Bolshevik party; Mussolini developed a new party of his own, the Fascist Party, almost from scratch; Hitler took over a small rabble of National Socialists in Munich and built them up to become the Nazi Party; and in China Mao gained ascendancy over the CCP in the course of the civil war. Thus, complete control over his party gave each of them the possibility of leading it from a mere proto-totalitarian dictatorship to a truly totalitarian one. Mussolini did not press his advantage any further because he was content with his role, and also because circumstances in Italy did not favor such a move. Had Lenin lived longer, he might have gone further, we cannot tell; but Stalin, once he had eliminated all opposition within the Party and was in sole charge, used it as the instrument of power to achieve totalitarian domination and press forward with his plans for Russia. Hitler, too, eliminated all intra-party opposition, culminating in the murder of Röhm and many others, thus acquiring the means to impose totalitarianism once he had gained ascendancy over the army in the heady days of victory at the start of the Second World War. Mao followed in Stalin's footsteps almost to the letter. Thus in each of these cases the prescription for the step from proto-totalitarianism to totalitarianism is the same: first achieve total control of the party, and then use it to acquire total domination of the country.

When and how such a move would occur depended on historical circumstances that gave the Leader the chance to push forward in his quest for power. For Stalin it was the economic crisis that had arisen toward the end of the NEP period when the peasants were loath to produce more wheat, there being nothing much they could buy with excess earnings as industry was not geared to producing consumer goods; for a while it looked as if the cities might starve. Stalin stepped into this critical juncture and first expropriated produce by force, then he embarked on the plan Trotsky had first proposed: collectivize the peasants and squeeze them for the surplus capital necessary to build up heavy industry. To achieve this total mobilization and militarization of labor, maximum repression would need to be applied, as force was the only way of achieving it. Stalin did so with particular ruthlessness, as usual: "for once Stalin embarked on war against the peasantry, the massive machinery of repression opened the way to a particularly fero-cious, despotic autocracy and mass terror," as Ronald Suny remarks.[9]

Was this inevitable, the only course that the Soviet Union under Bolshevism could have taken? Or were there other ways of resolving the immediate crisis and going forward? There has been much dispute on this issue among sociologists and historians, and the general consensus, apart from apologists for Stalin, is that there was an alternative: in fact, the one proposed at the time by Bukharin.[10] Bukharin argued for giving greater incentives to peasants to produce more food and industrializing more slowly. However, within the Party at the time there was considerable support for the Stalin policies among radical Bolsheviks, and great enthusiasm was whipped up for it among the workers. It was the way, they believed, that "Socialism in one country" would turn into Revolution throughout the capitals of the world—*urbi et orbi* in accordance with the universalism of Bolshevism.

Hitler's opportunity to become the Great Dictator that Chaplin parodied came with his stunning and overwhelming victories in continental Europe. Suddenly he became supreme master over the whole German military machine, having already achieved mastery over his Nazi Party and the state apparatus of Germany. It was his decision and his alone to embark on the conquest of the Soviet Union, and at this point there was hardly a dissenting voice in the whole of Germany: the generals went along eagerly, the administrators had already prepared plans for conquest and occupation, the whole populace cheered in anticipation of victories. After all, this was in accord with long-standing dreams to fulfill the "*Drang nach Osten*," the destiny of Germany.

This was the fatal step into totalitarianism, one that was neither preordained nor inevitable; it could have been avoided. In fact, Göring advised against it. But once it was taken, the further course of Nazi totalitarianism was set; for, in accord with its dominant ideology of anti-Semitism and racism in general, the war was conducted as a campaign of extermination of the Judeo-Bolshevik enemy and the enslavement of the Slav *Untermenschen* to serve as hewers of wood and drawers of water for the future German colonists. Russia was to become Germany's India, Hitler said, and a staging post on the way of further world conquest, perhaps of India itself, where the German armies were heading. Apart from some grumbling among the more morally squeamish of the officers, there was little opposition to Hitler's way of carrying out these visionary plans, until defeat started to pile on defeat; and only then were there attempts to remove him by assassination—the only possible way, given that totalitarianism was by then firmly established. In Italy Mussolini was dethroned by his own Fascist Party, at the behest of the monarchy, army, and Church. In Germany such a thing was inconceivable, which marks the differences between proto-totalitarianism and totalitarianism proper.

In China, as in Russia, totalitarianism arose out of victory in a long, bitter, and closely fought civil war of over twenty years. By the end of it, Mao had achieved mastery over the Chinese Communist Party as proto-totalitarian ruler, and with victory he proceeded to establish himself as a fully totalitarian dictator in emulation of Stalin. Like Stalin, he eliminated everyone who stood in his way or appeared as a potential rival. Those who survived, such as Chou En-lai, were those who went along with him. He even adopted measures far in excess of Stalin's, in carrying out total mobilization and the militarization of labor, which were taken to a degree of irrationality that Stalin would not have countenanced, for he had not completely lost his sanity. Mao led China into disaster in every way, nearly provoking a nuclear attack by the Soviet Union that only the Americans, his other enemies, managed to deter for reasons of realpolitik. Was any of this necessary or inevitable? Did China have to have to go through totalitarianism to reach its present position? Only apologists for Mao would dare to say so.

A common feature in all these cases of totalitarianism, as opposed to all those of proto-totalitarianism, was that the former aspired to world domination in accordance with the basic premises of their ideologies. This is what distinguishes Fascism from Nazism. Bolshevism, however, aimed for world revolution in its Leninist, Stalinist, and Maoist varieties. Fascism was a limited ideology of national revival and greatness, and its aim was to elevate Italy to a great power status on par with the other European powers. With that end in view, Mussolini embarked on an imperialist policy of conquest in Africa and on the shores of the Adriatic. He entertained dreams of a new Roman empire throughout the Mediterranean and preached the cultural values of *romanita*, but did not seriously attempt to realize this.

It was another matter with Hitler and the Nazis, for whom European conquest was an accomplished reality and world domination seemingly only a step away. The presumed superiority of the Aryan races over all others gave them the confident assurance that it was all achievable, indeed predestined. The Bolsheviks, too, saw the triumph of Communism throughout the world as the inevitable working out of the logic of Progress, for, as Marx predicted, capitalism was doomed due to its inherent contradictions, and Socialism was its only possible successor, to be followed by Communism in some utopian future. Both types of totalitarianisms were convinced that the liberal democracies were fated to disappear into the dustbins of history and that one or the other of them would take over the world. Thus in the clash with each other, they saw a battle for the domination of the world. Both Stalin and Hitler held each other in great regard as worthy enemies, each recognizing the other as a fellow totalitarian—namely, as the exponent of the opposite ideology.

It is not only the Leaders and the Parties and propitious historical circumstances, such as we have thus far outlined, that make it possible for proto-totalitarianism to be converted into totalitarianism proper; there are also further background factors to be taken into account. Such a transition took place in the three major societies of Germany, Russia, and China, and this fact prompts a consideration of what, if anything, these societies had in common that make them prone to such a move. Hence we must unavoidably venture into the nebulous territory known as "national character," a notion often misused for nefarious purposes. Nevertheless, the concept can be useful if nationality is clearly distinguished from racial or ethnic identity, related prejudices are avoided, and no attempt is made to identify innate qualities that supposedly define a people's essential character. In contradistinction to any of this, by national character we simply mean the mentality of a people as shaped by its collective historical experiences and embedded in its cultural predispositions, prejudices, and assumptions—especially if they are unified as members of a nation-state with which they identify as Englishmen, Frenchmen, or Germans. The national character, once so formed, governs what a given nation will expect, approve, and condone when acting collectively, and what it will be willing to suffer and sacrifice for the national good as dictated by its rulers. What one nation will accept and enthusiastically endorse, another will do so only very unwillingly or not at all. Certainly, under modern conditions of communication, propaganda and indoctrination can make a considerable difference, but there are limits to what even the most skillful utilization of these means can achieve. There will always be some claims or demands that go against the grain, which no amount of media manipulation will persuade a people to accept. This is particularly evident in the different ways nations behave in wartime.

With this definition of national character in mind, we might describe some nations as authoritarian and others as less so or not at all. An authoritarian nation is one in which people willingly accept all their rulers' demands, do not, in general, question authority, and frequently hold it in awe. In such cases, long-established historical experiences and institutional arrangements have habituated people to obedience without question or argument. It is in this respect that a sharp contrast can be drawn throughout much of modern history between Germans and Italians. Starting with the Prussians from the early eighteenth century onward, Germans became habituated to military discipline and *Gehorsamkeit*. Prussia was defined not as a state that has an army, but as an army that has a state. It was under Prussian domination that Germany was unified and the Reich formed, so it was Prussian authoritarian structures that were imposed on all other Germans. This was the human material that the Kaisers molded and Hitler could work on so successfully once he turned himself into a Führer, to whom obedience was owing as a moral duty, as even Kant had prescribed.

Mussolini had quite other human material to work with, which would have made it difficult for him to become an absolute dictator, like Hitler, even if he had wanted to do so. If Italians extended unquestioning obedience to any institution at all, they did so to the pope and the Catholic Church on matters of faith, to which many in fact no longer fully subscribed. Otherwise they generally took an extremely blasé attitude to their rulers. Even the cries of *Duce! Duce!* that were uttered enthusiastically during Mussolini's bombastic harangues can be taken more as effusions of crowd excitement than as genuine commitments. Italy, like Germany, was also a young nation-state, driven by nationalistic ardor, but its *Risorgimento* was quite different from Germany's *Vereinigung*; it carried none of the latter's aggression, especially toward France and Russia, though it did harbor irredentist pretensions that Mussolini could exploit.

The transition to full totalitarianism was much easier to achieve in Russia and China than even in Germany, for these were largely peasant societies that had hardly known any liberalism or democracy and had been autocratically ruled for many centuries past, its people having known no other form of government. They were in fact what Wittfogel calls "Oriental Despotisms" in the famous book by that name, which we shall study in chapter 7. Russia owed its form of despotism to the Mongol yoke imposed in the Middle Ages; this left an indelible mark on Russia's national character even though it had undergone a process of Europeanization and almost become a European society before the Revolution. China had only just abandoned its imperial government and traditional mandarinate, early in the twentieth century. In both, once a totalitarian regime was installed the national character of its people made it almost impregnable, short of outright rebellion, impossible under modern conditions of domination. Once a ruler was firmly in the saddle he could assert his authority almost without limit. Hence, it was easy for Stalin, once he was in power, to become the supreme autocrat on the model of Ivan the Terrible and to carry out the same types of purge that the latter undertook, though on a much greater scale. He was obeyed in all things; there was no stirring of rebellion or any kind of opposition until his dying day. Mao, too, could similarly model himself on Shih Huang-ti, the first emperor, and undertake the same types of monumental mass project, meant to redound to his own glory, without the least resistance, even though tens of millions starved.

This last point indicates that one more crucial determinant must be added to all the factors that promote the transition from the one type of totalitarianism to the other, such as the nature of the Leader, the Party, the historical circumstances, and the national character: this last factor is readiness to perpetrate radical evil. Radical evil does not occur in proto-totalitarianism, but it is an essential feature of totalitarianism, without which it could not function. Why radical evil should be necessary for any political regime is very difficult to understand since it challenges everything we know about human nature and how society functions. Unless we postulate a Freudian Thanatos or drive to destruction or Canetti's survival instinct, both involving implausible assumptions that psychology now considers false, it becomes very difficult to explain why some rulers should require masses of corpses and why their followers should oblige them in this respect. This goes totally against most moral beliefs and also against any notions of rational conduct, given the massive economic waste that such evil causes. Radical evil is a mystery of human behavior. Some have sought a theological explanation. If Auschwitz was considered to be the *anus mundi*, then it was God showing his backside to the world, as George Steiner put it. But what kind of a God would do a shameless thing like that?

Perhaps we can shed a little light on the mystery of radical evil by noting that totalitarianism needs enemies; without enemies to strive and battle against, it cannot justify itself or gain the unquestioning support of its followers. Where it no longer has any real enemies, it tends to form imaginary enemies or finds scapegoats to stand in for them; for enemies are to totalitarianism as God is to religion: if they do not exist they must be invented, as Voltaire's witticism has it. Without enemies the whole fight would go out of a totalitarian movement; it would lose its drive and anger, the energy by which it moves forward. And it must always be driving forward; this is its inner dynamic. If it were to come to rest, it would cease to be. Hence there must be constant campaigns, purges, and inquisitions to hunt out the malefactors and exterminate them and when these give out, wars are prosecuted in order to find more of them.

Who are the enemies? They are usually identified according to preestablished categories set down in the ideology. For Nazism they are racial enemies of Germany and mankind, primarily Jews and other *Untermenschen*, however arbitrarily these are designated. For the Bolsheviks they are class enemies, primarily bourgeois and others like them who can also be specified at will. And where for proto-totalitarians it was enough to defeat the enemies and keep them in check, for the real totalitarians it is necessary to expose them and exterminate them, a difficult and potentially endless task since the enemies are camouflaged and well hidden, devils cunning enough to pass themselves off as real people. Who knows whether someone who looks a German and acts like a German and is otherwise indistinguishable from a German might not be really a Jew? Who can tell which Germans harbor a Jewish *Geist* within their Aryan bodies? And the same problems arise with bourgeoisie for the Stalinists. Hence, constant vigilance and unmasking is called for.

All this exertion in identifying, segregating, incarcerating, concentrating, and finally exterminating enemies serves an extremely useful, indeed, necessary function for the totalitarians themselves. It helps to unify them and bind them to each other: it seals in blood the bond between the Leader and his followers in the Party and between the movement as a whole and its people. Extermination or murder is the transgressive act in which they are all complicit, and thereby it constitutes their community in crime. No matter how much they might tell themselves that the Final Solution or the Great Purge is not mass murder but merely an act of racial hygiene or social cleansing of bad elements, implicitly and instinctively they know that it is morally wrong and this common knowledge, unspoken and never admitted, cements their solidarity. Himmler hinted at this in his notorious speech to the

SS functionaries at Posen at the height of the Holocaust in 1943—what they were doing was a noble and heroic thing, but they must take the secret of it to their graves.

Radical evil is, in fact, an open secret that sooner or later everyone knows about, and all who know it, except for the victims themselves, are to some degree complicit in it. The executioners, such as the SS death squads and the NKVD guards, know all about it, but so do all the numerous others who deliver their prey to them. The bystanders—a considerable proportion of the population—who witness the arrests, the round-ups, the forced marches, and so on but do nothing about it are also implicated, though not guilty of anything. In the occupied territories a large part of the German army was in one way or another involved. In Russia all those who were promoted to the positions left vacant by those purged, or who occupied their apartments were involved. Radical evil radiates like an invisible ray throughout a society. All who know about it are terrified that such a fate could befall them as well, if they happen to slip up. This generates total terror in a whole population.

Total terror operates outside any law, apart from any formal procedures; people are arrested in the night and vanish into the prisons or concentration camps that everyone knows about, though nobody knows exactly what goes on in them. This is how totalitarianism ensures complete compliance from everybody, believers and nonbelievers in the ideology alike. Compliance with the will of the Leader and the Party on this level and to this degree could not be accomplished without radical evil. It serves a multitude of functions within a totalitarian regime, none of which could be achieved in any other way. Thus, as long as the totalitarian regime lasts—that is, as long as the Leader is alive—it cannot dispense with or abandon radical evil. But as soon as the Leader dies, radical evil ceases, and then the whole nature of the regime changes, entering into its subtotalitarian phase, which we shall presently examine. However, before we do so there is one difficult issue to settle.

We have shown that Hitler's regime was not totalitarian in the full sense until the exterminations had started. Whether one dates this phase from the gassing of the mentally deficient, or from the extermination of the Jews or from the cold-blooded shooting of commissars is not a real issue. It is more difficult to establish the point at which the Bolshevik regime became fully totalitarian. We now know that acts of murder were taking place from the very start of the Bolshevik seizure of power. So how do we classify Lenin's regime? Was it not a full totalitarianism from its very beginnings?

This is an extremely difficult matter to resolve. The Cheka under Dzerzhinsky was established by Lenin almost as soon as the Bolsheviks seized power, and within its first year, according to Yuli Martov, the Menshevik leader, its tally of victims was already "in excess of 10,000."[11] According to Nicolas Werth:

> The change of scale went well beyond the figures. The introduction of new categories such as "suspect," "enemy of the people," "hostage," "concentration camps" and "revolutionary court," and of previously unknown practices such as "prophylactic measures," summary execution without judicial process of hundreds of thousands of people, and arrest by a new kind of political police who were above the law, might be said to have constituted a new sort of Copernican revolution.[12]

Is this any different to what Stalin and Hitler were later to do? Donald Rayfield believes that it is not:

> The Holocaust that took place between 1918–1922 seems less horrific than Hitler's or Stalin's only because it was directed more at a class than a race, because most survivors remained cut off from the Western world, because the paper trail has been destroyed and because, as Stalin liked to say, "Victors are not put on trial."[13]

But is this altogether correct? Now, long after the event, when we can no longer pretend ignorance, when the bare facts have mostly been established, can we, nevertheless, draw a distinction between Lenin and Trotsky and Stalin and Hitler?

Lenin's and Trotsky's crimes are not so very different from those of Robespierre and the Jacobins during the period of Terror in the French Revolution. The French regime was certainly not totalitarian in any sense and not even a dictatorship, for the Assemblée National still held power. Their crimes, for undoubtedly these were crimes, also did not amount to radical evil, even though the numbers were very large, as in the massacres in the Vendée. And something similar can be said of Lenin and Trotsky, though their regime was a proto-totalitarian dictatorship.

We cannot debate here the morality or wisdom of the Bolshevik coup d'état during the Revolution in Russia. It would have been much better for Russia and the world if there had been no coup; whoever had come to power instead could not have done as much harm as the Bolsheviks went on to do. Once having grasped power, however, they had to defend their hold by bloody means, for they were surrounded on all sides by real enemies, not imaginary or invented ones, as was the case with Stalin and

Hitler. Their killings served a rational purpose at a time of intensified civil war when their enemies, the Whites, were doing much the same. This does not mean that such killings are not murders or that they are morally justified. Far from it. But, we do need to understand that such killings do not amount to radical evil in spirit or motivation. They serve a different purpose altogether, a much more pragmatic one in the circumstances. Did Lenin murder more than was necessary to wage a brutal civil war? Undoubtedly he did, for he always erred on the side of excess, given his ruthless nature. He was no doubt a bloody dictator, like so many others in history, but once the civil war was over, the killings almost stopped. He was not addicted to murder, and neither was Trotsky.

Stalin became addicted to murder, as did Hitler. Hitler gloated when the conspirators were strangled in agony on meat hooks. Stalin enjoyed signing off on lists of death warrants. He could not stop: just before his own death he embarked on a new campaign of murders with the so-called "doctors' plot." Had Hitler lived and remained in power, he would have indulged in further killings. But even if Germany had won the war, once Hitler was dead totalitarianism would not have continued in full pitch under a new Leader. Similarly, after Stalin's demise a new form of rule arose, which we have called subtotalitarianism.

Section IV—Subtotalitarianism

No sooner was Stalin dead than the totalitarianism he created changed, but it did not disappear. And the same thing happened in China after Mao's death. Totalitarianism could not continue once the Leader was gone, which proves how much it depends on the Leader as the lynch-pin to hold it together. The fears of such writers as George Orwell that totalitarianism was a self-perpetuating system that might last indefinitely were not realistic. Totalitarianism depends on what Khrushchev, one of Stalin's successors, but not himself a Leader, called "the cult of personality" surrounding a specific person. Once he departs, a new cult of personality does not arise, except in the mysterious kingdom of North Korea, where one Kim steps into the shoes of another in a kind of dynastic "cult of the family personality."

This is an ironic outcome in light of what Communist ideology proclaims. As Furet notes, "the death of the Leader reemphasizes the paradox of a system allegedly inscribed in the laws of social development, yet so dependent on a single person, that when he dies, the system loses something essential."[14] What it lost was the single commanding will that was driving the system toward the extremes and never letting up, so that one campaign was followed by another, for the Leader could never rest on his laurels; he always had to be setting new schemes in motion, like the rider of a bicycle who can never sit still but must always keeps his machine going forward, for if he were to stop he would overbalance and fall. When there is nobody in the saddle, the machine does stop or slow to a crawl. All the machinery and all its gears and chains remain in place, but they are no longer propelled with full thrust, as totalitarianism degenerates to subtotalitarianism.

The first thing to go is radical evil, for total terror is no longer necessary to keep everyone in place. In particular, the rulers themselves wish to be free of the terror that hung over their heads like a sword of Damocles while the Leader was alive. In Russia, immediately on Stalin's death, and whether he was killed or allowed to die remains an open question, it was Beria, head of the KGB, who oddly enough made the first moves to remove terror by exonerating the Kremlin doctors and declaring an amnesty for millions of Gulag prisoners.[15] Despite this show of clemency, Beria paid with his life because of the fear he had aroused in the other members of the Politburo. They had agreed amongst themselves that no new Leader could ever be allowed to emerge and that totalitarianism proper would not be reestablished. Instead, they would embark on a new system of collective leadership or rule by committee in which one of them, answerable to the others, would be chosen by them to act as front man and chief executive. In Russia, after some initial maneuvering this position was allotted to Khrushchev, formerly the clown in Stalin's court. When he slipped up over Cuba later, he was dismissed, but not executed, by his colleagues, and a new chief, Brezhnev, was chosen. This marked a huge change in the way that issues of succession were decided, which altered the whole system.

It was clear that no supreme Leader would emerge again when Khrushchev gave his speech to the Twentieth Party Congress in 1956. He denounced Stalin and exposed the cult of personality on which Stalin's rule depended. He did this to consolidate the new arrangement of collective leadership, with himself as top man. He went even further than this: he abolished arbitrary terror and introduced a measure of the rule of law. He even introduced a cultural thaw that permitted writers, artists, and intellectuals to express themselves with greater freedom than at any time since the Revolution. This was when Pasternak published his work abroad without "disappearing" and Solzhenitsyn found his voice. But this is not to say that repression was completely lifted.

Far from it; it was only eased and regularized. Later under Brezhnev, new means of punishment were invented to silence dissident writers, such as consigning them to lunatic asylums.

What happened in Russia after Stalin more or less repeated itself in China after Mao. Under a new paramount chief, Deng Xiaoping, the Chinese went much further in liberalization than the Russian dared to go until Gorbachev assumed the leadership. The Chinese reintroduced private ownership, a free market, foreign investment, and altogether a large measure of capitalism. They saw their whole economy sprint ahead, whereas the Russian economy went into a period of stagnation from which it has still not recovered. The Chinese collective leaderships also devised an orderly system of succession in the top positions. Since Deng, there have been three such peaceful transitions. Nevertheless, repression has not been completely lifted, though the Chinese people enjoy more freedoms than they ever did in their history. Dissidents are still harshly dealt with, and the apparatus for doing so is fully in place. China is still far from being in a posttotalitarian condition.

It might be surmised as a speculative hypothesis that if Hitler had won the war and died soon after, he would not have been succeeded by another Führer but by a Nazi version of collective leadership. The Nazi paladins would never have allowed one of themselves to have power over them like that which Hitler held; the animosity between them was too great for this to happen. It would have entailed a retreat from totalitarianism to something approaching subtotalitarianism. Total terror and radical evil would have ceased and a more normal tenor of life resumed. Beyond this point one dare not speculate on such a hypothetical situation.

One might also speculate as to whether a retrograde move from subtotalitarianism back to full totalitarianism could ever occur. It has never happened in reality, but it cannot be ruled out as a theoretical possibility. However, it would require extremely improbable circumstances for this to occur. It is conceivable that if Russia or China were faced with complete chaos, due to some unforeseeable social disruption and economic failure, then someone might arise to take up Stalin's or Mao's mantle. But this could never happen under present circumstances.

Nothing in social or political life is impossible, and nothing is inevitable. Things happen in the way they do because of the force of circumstances; causal conjunctions push them in a given direction. These general considerations also hold for totalitarianism. It is not inevitable that once a Leader dies there must be a fundamental change.

North Korea is the exception. But it is the exception that confirms the rule. Under more normal circumstances than those now confronting North Korea—one-half of a divided country perpetually at odds with its severed twin and its powerful protector, and so on—it is highly likely that the Leader's death would bring a drastic change. It is in the interest of the new leadership to make such a change, so as to give themselves some legitimacy. But they have no interest in overthrowing the system completely. The resultant compromise works itself out as a subtotalitarianism of some kind.

Such a subtotalitarian system can be relatively stable, much more so than totalitarianism; it can persist for a long time and need not necessarily devolve into posttotalitarianism. The Chinese have found a way of maintaining it that could go on into the foreseeable future. At present, most of the people seem content with it, as it provides the stability on which their rising prosperity is based. Most of them do not have any high expectations of political freedom; that is part of their "national character," which could at some point change. What will happen when a large and wealthy middle and upper class arises, which is quite familiar with the culture and politics of the West? This is impossible to predict. But one must not assume that they will prefer freedom to security.

In Russia things turned out very differently, for its subtotalitarian system provided neither freedom nor security. It became sclerotic, just as its leaders became geriatrics. It so happened that a new young leader, Gorbachev, arose who was fired with enthusiasm for major reforms, in order to bring the system back to life, but not to abrogate it. But in the course of introducing his reforms of glasnost and perestroika he unintentionally did succeed in killing it. The Soviet Union broke up under the pressure of long-repressed nationalities, and a new posttotalitarian phase of democracy and chaos under Yeltsin began. Since then, under Putin, both the democracy and the chaos have been much reduced. Most Russians seem not too dissatisfied with that compromise; their "national character" is more attuned to security rather than freedom. When that might change is not predictable.

The world is now developing differently from the way many Americans expected in their triumphalist period, following victory in the Cold War and the demise of totalitarianism. Not every country is following their political lead into liberal democracy, though all have accepted that for economic reasons a large measure of free-market capitalism is essential. Globalization makes it mandatory, and no country can opt out of that system. But where it leaves civilization is still unanswered.

In fact, in the rush to get ahead in the global competition, it is not a question that is even asked. Who cares for civilization if globalization is providing all that can be asked for?

At the end of the Second World War, which was so much worse than the First World War because it was the conclusion of the great battle between the two totalitarianisms, the call to save civilization was more loudly heard than now. There were still many Europeans who had not succumbed to the idea that their civilization was close to an end. Despite the moral and material damage they had suffered, they still felt that there was much that could be saved of their cultural traditions. At this, one of the darkest moments of European history, when the shadow of Stalinism arose from the East and loomed over the rest of the continent, they nonetheless were undaunted and persevered in rising from the ruins to rebuild civilization anew. What came of their endeavor; what did they in fact achieve?

Notes

1. David Stevenson, *1914–1918: The History of a First World War* (Penguin, London 2004), p.10.
2. Ibid., p. 9.
3. Raymond Aron, *The Dawn of Universal History* (Weidenfeld and Nicolson, London, 1961), p. 41.
4. Max Horkheimer, "Die Juden und Europa" in *Zeitschrift für Sozialforschung*, 8 (1939), quoted in Roger Griffin, *Fascism* (Oxford University Press, Oxford 2009), p. 272.
5. Donald Rayfield, *Stalin and His Hangmen* (Penguin, London, 2004), p. 74.
6. Ibid., p. 131.
7. Jeffrey Herf, *Reactionary Modernism: Technology, Culture and politics in Weimar and the Third Reich* (Cambridge University Press, New York, 1984), p. 93
8. Quoted in Ibid, p. 8.
9. Ronald Gregor Suny, "Reading Russia and the Soviet Union in the twentieth century," in R. G. Suny (ed.) *Cambridge History of Russia*, Vol.II (Cambridge University Press, Cambridge, 2006), p. 37.
10. See Moshe Lewin, *Russia's Twentieth Century: The Collapse of the Soviet Union* (Verso, London, 2005).
11. Nicolas Werth, "A State against Its People: Violence, Repression and Terror in the Soviet Union", in Stéphane Courtois, Nicolas Werth et al. *The Black Book of Communism: Crimes, Terror, Repression*, trans. Jonathon Murphy and Mark Kramer, (Harvard University Press, Cambridge/Mass., 1977), p. 78.
12. Ibid., p. 83.
13. Donald Rayfield, *Stalin and his Hangmen*, op. cit., p. 81.
14. François Furet, *The Passing of an Illusion*, op. cit., p. 438.
15. Ibid., p. 433.

4

The State and Fate of Europe

Section I—In the Aftermath of Totalitarianism

At the end of the Second World War, immediately after Auschwitz, Europe had reached the nadir of its fortunes. This is the time Germans call *Stunde Null,* zero hour. Europe was in ruins, divided in two halves, dominated by the Soviet Union and America, the one totalitarian, the other free and democratic. For most Europeans the latter was preferable to the former, but there was strong support for the former as well in both parts; in some countries, notably France and Italy, the democratic process itself had almost played into the hands of the powerful Communist parties, which had emerged from the war with great prestige as the parties of the resistance. Western Europe was spared this fate by timely American intervention, in the form of the Truman Doctrine and the Marshall Plan, the latter a massive infusion of dollars that relaunched the destroyed West European economies; it was the most enlightened move of American foreign policy ever undertaken.

However, it came with some invisible strings attached: Europeans had to reshape their societies along American lines, which had consequences for their cultures and their character as Europeans. In short, West Europeans had to Americanize, which they did voluntarily enough, unlike the East Europeans, who were forcibly compelled to Sovietize. Eventually even the East Europeans acquired some aspects of American popular culture, for these were everywhere irresistible. As we now know, Sovietization or the imposition of the Bolshevik system of totalitarianism proved a failure in the long run and annulled itself, but at the time nobody could have predicted this outcome with any assurance. The two mutually antagonistic systems seemed well matched as opponents.

Americanization and Sovietization are both outgrowths of Western civilization that arose in the two regions peripheral to

97

Europe, North America, and Russia. Ever since Hegel there had been speculation to the effect that eventually these two powers would prove to be the successors of Europe, inheriting the torch of civilization. But at the end of the Second World War this is not how it seemed to Europeans themselves. They saw both as extreme versions of what we have called the Forces of Modernity: America cultivated a rampant capitalism, a liberal democratic state, and a pragmatic attitude to science and technology; Russia, its polar opposite, imposed a centrally planned economy, a totalitarian state and a controlled program of scientific and technological development. Both differed substantially from the European versions. Even more important for civilization was the fact that their assumptions about society, culture, and the individual were contrary to those that had hitherto been cultivated in Europe. A civilizational break had occurred, and neither of the two contending powers would carry on Western civilization in its European form.

Thus, as Furet maintains, "the Second World War confirmed what the First had announced—the decline of Europe."[1] Europe became the cockpit of the battle between the two world systems. At the same time a fierce ideological "civil war" raged within Western Europe that, as we showed previously, proved inimical to civilization for it debased thinking about politics and society and discourse in general. Ideological Bolshevism gained great sway over the minds of many Europeans, among them some of the finest intellectuals, especially so in France and Italy. As Furet points out:

> The collapse of Nazism did not spell the end of the great secular religions of the twentieth century. On the contrary, its disappearance left Marxist-Leninism as the sole master, or sole beneficiary, in the religious investment in the battles of the City. The theological-political realm, far from being reduced by the war, had increased its hold over Europeans.[2]

We have already discussed the question of whether these are "religions" in any real sense, and have come to the conclusion that they are not, and that therefore this term should always be placed in quotation marks. However, it is true that what gave Bolshevism its hold over people's sense of themselves was its capacity to mimic religion and hold out promises of salvation similar to those held out to religious believers. Its prestige in the postwar period was particularly high because it was able to present itself as the doctrine of the forces that had defeated

Fascism, which it tendentiously interpreted as the outgrowth of capitalism. As Furet puts it,

> Liberal democracy offered no such simple and powerful interpretation of the war as the pairing of capitalism and of Fascism on the one hand and of anti-Fascism and Communism on the other, pairings that formed part of the mental arsenal of the first Comintern and Cominform.[3]

According to Furet, "This was the great illusion of the age . . . from which we are only just emerging, thanks more to the force of circumstance than to intellectual virtue."[4]

The Americans and their supporters had their own "mental arsenal" of intellectual weapons with which they sought to counter the illusions of Communism, among which was the concept of "totalitarianism" and the "end-of-ideology thesis." As Furet intimates, none of this was ideologically successful until events themselves decided the issue. However, where the Americans succeeded way beyond anything the Soviets could rival was in the sphere of ordinary life activities and so-called popular culture. As Norman Davies writes:

> American influence was felt in almost every sphere, especially in Hollywood films, dance, music, and popular dress. Youth fashion and 'pop' culture, where adolescents dressed in unisex jeans and jived and minced in imitation of film idols or rock stars, became entirely transatlantic and cosmopolitan.[5]

There was high-minded resistance to this lowbrow Americanization, but it was to no avail:

> Mindless materialism, however, came to be regarded as the most insidious of American imports. It may have been unfair to blame the USA for reducing Europeans to the level of economic animals; but Willy Brandt was expressing widespread feelings in this regard when he asked, "Do you want to be Americans?"[6]

At the time when this challenge was made, most Europeans would have replied that they wished to remain European. Now the answer is not so certain. Americanization has proceeded so far that most Europeans might want to be Americans, especially now after they have been hit by the global financial crisis.

Americanization is a process that had been going on throughout the twentieth century, ever since America had developed and displayed its huge economic resources. It took an upward turn after the First World War when America first came to the rescue of an ailing Europe, and even much more so after the Second World War when Europe was destitute. It was America that enabled Europe to rise like a phoenix from the ashes; it was behind the German *Wirtschaftswunder*, the Italian *miraculo* and the French *trente année glorieuses*, as well as rescuing Britain from bankruptcy. But it was a Europe remade in the image of America. Europeans became Americans, whether they knew it or not.

Prior to 1914 Europe was altogether different, and the Americans looked to it for almost everything they valued. They were then proud to call themselves Europeans. The richest among them were only too glad to procure aristocratic titles for their daughters in exchange for large dowries. The poorer ones eagerly bought themselves the cultural products of Europe, above all the latest novels by British writers, whose main market became America. Politically and militarily the balance of power was still all in Europe's favor. The British navy ruled the waves when the American White Fleet made its first appearance. European colonialism was complete when America acquired its first colonies. Yet within less than half a century the advantage had been completely reversed. This is how quickly civilizations can fall from grace. Need it have happened like that?

Prior to 1914, European civilization was still fully intact. There was no intimation that anything could go wrong with it. The prospects of revolutionary upheavals had long dissipated. Social conditions were improving, and standards of living were rising for everybody, even in faraway Russia. Except perhaps to some degree in Russia under czarism, the basic freedoms and rights were upheld everywhere else in Europe, though women were still excluded. Democratic suffrage was becoming universal—except for women—and all states had parliaments. In Germany, the largest party in the *Reichstag* was the Socialist. Even Marxists recognized these facts and were moving away from orthodox Marxism toward revisionism— except, of course, for Lenin and his Bolsheviks, who still preached revolution. This was still likely in Russia and perhaps possible in the arc of instability to the east, southeast, and south of Europe, where uneven developments had taken place in the Forces of Modernity, and social conditions for many, especially the peasants, were still very difficult. But it was generally assumed that over time progress would reach even these backward areas with their benighted rulers.

Culturally, Europe was experiencing a new flowering, as Modernist movements came into being in all the spheres of science, art, and intellect. The intellectuals were an extremely strong presence, especially in the countries of the arc of instability, where later, as we know, some of them would cause most damage. In Russia they constituted a whole status group, the intelligentsia. They were prominent in the main capitals of the Austro-Hungarian Empire and the big cities of the German Reich. Many among them were Jews who made remarkable contributions to all fields of cultural endeavor. They would become the main victims of both forms of totalitarianism: Stalin slaughtered large numbers, though not as many as Hitler. Only those who fled to America or Britain survived. This might seem but a minor aspect of the Holocaust and the general European carnage, but it was one that was devastating for European civilization.

This new flowering was nipped in the bud by the icy winter winds of the Events of the Twentieth Century. Despite all the prosperity that Europe has since attained, there could be no recovery. Europe's spirit was broken. The intellectual flurry of ideological disputation was no substitute for cultural discourse. The "*trahison des clercs*" about which Benda complained after the First World War became a wholesale betrayal of the intellect after the Second. Genuine intellectuals became scarce, as academics multiplied to fill the burgeoning chairs catering to mass education that came with the growing need for professionals and certification for every type of employment. As in everything else, the European university was giving way to the American multiversity, which had something of everything for everyone. European academics themselves began to commute across the Atlantic in seasonal postings. They became a new breed of global intellectuals who have little in common with the old variety.

By the time travel across the Atlantic became commonplace, the world had shrunk, and every country was within reach. It marked a new epoch in the world when global relations between people had reached a new level of complexity and when consciousness of a common planetary unity grew. Europe now found its place as part of the one world enmeshed in a process called globalization.

Section II—Globalization

Globalization in general is the manifestation of a world in which communication from any one part to any other is instantaneous, and travel between any two such points is rapid and cheap. It is the third of our major themes, after totalitarianism and colonialism, and we shall treat it further in the next two parts on the New World and the

Third World. Here we are only concerned with it insofar as it touches on the Old World.

Globalization in its broadest sense is complementary to European colonialism, for it began as soon as Europe reached out to the rest of the world in voyages of discovery, trade, and ultimately conquest. The interconnection of the world through European-devised systems of economic exploitation and political domination proceeded apace as colonialism expanded and all the countries of the world, many by force of arms, were opened up to European influence.

However, in its more recent, twentieth-century manifestations, globalization has been driven forward more by America than by Europe. In fact, in this mode it arose precisely from the failure of Europe to be able to maintain its colonial possessions. As a consequence of the Second World War and the debilitated state in which Europe was left, as well as the defeats that the colonial powers suffered in Asia, colonialism was no longer sustainable. Both the Russians and the Americans, the two superpowers, were pressing the Europeans to abandon and liberate their colonies. Once freed, most of these went on to try to organize themselves as a bloc, called the Third World, that would be neutral as between the two superpowers, though most of these countries leaned toward some form or other of Socialism.

However, the institutional machinery of globalization that would bring together the Old World, the New World, and the Third World was set up by the Americans soon after the end of the Second World War. As one American author, Thomas Barnett, states: "globalization—our historical gift to the world."[7] It was the Roosevelt administration that was most intent on establishing the United Nations as a more embracing and effective successor to the European-run League of Nations. And the same administration hosted the meeting of statesmen and economists, most notably Keynes, that negotiated the Bretton Woods Agreements that oversaw the creation of the International Monetary Fund, the World Bank, and also the General Agreement on Tariffs and Trade, out of which the World Trade Organization grew.

Soon after the end of the war, the OECD was established under American sponsorship; it joined the main industrial nations of the so-called Free World in partnership. Because of its unrivalled economic wealth—at the end of the war, America had a productive capacity that equaled that of the rest of the world—America was able to create a free-trade zone among its close allies and also to extend most favored nation treatment to many other friendly nations. Thus under American aegis a global trading system was built up that more and more countries joined because of its obvious economic benefits. China joined when the new leader Deng Xiaoping opened up the closed state-owned and -managed system to private enterprise and foreign investment. India joined when Manmohan Singh became finance minister and abandoned the licensing raj of state controls and restrictions practiced by all previous administrations. After the collapse of the Soviet Union, Russia joined the OEDC and many of its East European satellites amalgamated with a united Europe.

Europe's contribution to globalization was to create the Common Market and then the European Union. This brought into being a new economic entity that could equal America—and also China, when that country became the second biggest single economy in the world. At the same time, it moved in gradual stages toward political union, something that is still work in progress and far from complete, having recently suffered a serious setback due to the Global Financial Crisis. Its history is well known and need not be expounded at length. It began as an across-the-Rhine alliance between France and Germany, intended to ensure that a war in Europe due to national rivalries could never break out again. It was sealed by the personal rapport between de Gaulle and Adenauer, who also intended to provide a counter to what de Gaulle called Anglo-Saxon dominance. For that reason, Britain was at first excluded by de Gaulle's veto, but was admitted into the Common Market eventually after his death. The next step in economic integration, the creation of a eurozone, has been rejected by Britain and a number of other members of the European Union. Politically, the European Union, with its European Parliament and executive machinery of administration, is meant to be the precursor to federation, the creation of a United States of Europe. This is what the Germans intended it to be, on the model of their own nineteenth-century unification as a state. However, they might no longer be so keen on the idea, considering the huge financial burden it would impose on them in bailing out many of the other states that are now close to bankruptcy.

Europe is one node in a network of trading and manufacturing arrangements that connect it with China, Japan, many of the other Asian countries, such as South Korea, Taiwan, and India, and the United States, which is still central to the whole world economic system and whose currency, the US dollar, is the main medium of exchange and the reserve currency of the world. American-owned companies comprise the bulk of the multinational corporations that trade and manufacture throughout the world. Their affiliates are to be found in most countries, and their brand names are household words in most languages. There are other major firms that have a presence throughout the world. Many of these are European, so Europe, too, has a hold on the world, but it shares this with Japan, and increasingly also with China. Around five hundred multinational corporations dominate most of world trade and production; most of these are American owned.

A new global system of capitalism has come into operation. Goods are no longer produced within the one country, as used to be the case in the European-style capitalism of national enterprises. Now the production process of a single commodity is distributed throughout many countries in different parts of the world. This has been made possible by instant communication and bulk transportation. Thus one country might provide the raw materials, another the processing, a third the design and development work, a fourth the manufacturing facilities of components, a fifth the assembly of the final product, and a sixth the marketing, advertising, insurance, and other ancillary services. Thus the product has become a global commodity. Many of the above phases in this process are located outside Europe, in countries where labor is cheap, land is available and labor regulations and environmental laws lax. This puts European workers at a great disadvantage and has led to unemployment and de-industrialization in many of the older industrial zones of Europe. Some European countries, generally those in northern Europe, have coped well with such problems, but many others, generally those in southern Europe, have not managed at all. This threatens to create a two-tier Europe that will militate against any unification.

Globalization also creates cultural problems for Europe that it has never previously had to face. In a global capitalist system culture, too, has become a commodity, manufactured and traded like any other. A new form of culture fit for global consumption was developed, which we can dub global culture. Global culture is different from the previous popular culture current in Europe during the belle époque prior to 1914, as well as the national mass culture that flourished between the two wars. Global culture came to Europe as part the process of Americanization; television shows, Hollywood films, and rock-and-roll music were its earliest manifestations. This became youth culture throughout Europe and eventually throughout the world.

The great bulk of global culture is manufactured by media companies or the so-called culture industry in America, both for the home market and for export, much of it to Europe. At present, as Richard Pells reports: "Eighty percent of all movies and television programs that anyone, anywhere might see were either made in the United States or were financed by American studios and production companies."[8] Pells ascribes this extraordinary success to the talents of American producers, both their creativity and marketing nous:

> The ascendancy of American mass culture did not happen by accident. But neither was it the result of a conspiracy by Hollywood, the television networks, and the American government. To explain how figures as disparate as Madonna and Mickey Mouse, J. W. Ewing and Woody Allen, became international icons, one has to understand both the economics of the American entertainment industry and why the industry was so successful at marketing precisely the movies and television programs audiences everywhere wanted to see.[9]

However, it is more than just a matter of America's skill at making and selling its cultural wares. To understand this we have to trace the history of how America gained such a stranglehold on cultural consumption in Europe.

It happened as part of the general Americanization of European society, beginning after the First World War, when American fashions and styles first made their mark. For Europeans these represented all that was new about the New World. They were particularly impressed by new American technologies, such as the motorcar and the habits surrounding driving as a leisure activity. They were also attracted to American music and dance, such as Broadway melodies, crooners, jazz, the Charleston, and, later, jive. But this was only a small start, since there were strong European competitors in all these respects. Hollywood could not capture all movie audiences, as each major European country had its own film industry and produced what its people wanted to see.

A bigger breakthrough in Americanization came with the Second World War when American troops were stationed in large numbers for long periods in European countries. The English could not but be overcome by American influences, because, as the old joke has it, their soldiers were "overpaid, oversexed and over here." They were, in effect, the advance guard of American cultural imperialism, if one puts it at its most cynical. In the case of West Germany this was openly expressed policy; the Germans had to be reeducated in the ways of liberal democracy—which, in effect, meant American ways. And without force or compulsion, the Americans were very successful at this, for after the years of Nazi totalitarianism, Americanism came as a great relief, and what's more, it was fun. The Germans took to it with glee. It is not surprising that they came to prefer American movies to their own, especially as Germany produced mainly saccharine sentimental *Heimatfilme* in the 1950s and '60s. The British maintained their preference for BBC radio and television until privatization brought in the commercial channels, and cheap imports of American programs flooded the market. The fact that they shared a common language meant that there were no barriers or costs to releasing shows that had already paid for themselves in America.

The French resisted most and are still doing so now. The difference in language and in general cultural attitudes made it impossible for the American producers to dump their wares on the French market. The French government, ever since de Gaulle, has taken the lead in erecting barriers to American importation in the name of protecting national culture. Such ideas are strenuously opposed by the American trade negotiators, who argue that this amounts to obstruction of free trade, and they threaten retaliatory measures. This quarrel has exposed a fundamental difference in attitude to culture: to the Americans culture is simply a type of commodity, basically no different from any other; to the French and older-style Europeans the commodification of culture is to be resisted because higher values than monetary ones inhere in cultural goods. They accuse the Americans of cynicism, in accordance to Oscar Wilde's witticism that the cynic is one who knows the price of everything but the value of nothing.

It is clear from the way globalization is spreading that the Americans are bound to win this battle. In trade relations Europe will not be able to attain any special concessions to protect its native culture, especially at present, when so many European countries are in deep financial trouble and will look to America for help. At present, a transatlantic free trade treaty is being negotiated, and it is unlikely that American negotiators will agree to give away their advantage in cultural exports.

It is likely that much of European culture will be forfeited for the sake of establishing closer relations with the United States. Thus the nations on both sides of the North Atlantic will come to constitute one economic bloc, which they hope can counter the challenge posed by the much more populous and much harder-working society of China. Otherwise, many authors see little hope for Europe, and some already speak of the "fall of Europe," as Walter Laqueur puts it:

> The Europe I have known, I wrote five years ago, is in the process of disappearing. What will take its place? The importance of Europe in the world has been shrinking, but it probably still has a future, albeit

apparently a modest one, something between a regional power and indeed a valuable museum.[10]

He expresses the second possibility more precisely when he states,

> I was merely predicting that one of the possible fates of Europe was to turn into a museum or cultural theme park for the well-to-do tourists of East Asia.[11]

Something like this could happen to the countries of Europe bordering the Mediterranean, with the exception of France, but not to those of northern Europe, which have proven highly productive and will be able to ride out the financial storm.

Laqueur is aware of such differences between the regions of Europe, but he does not believe that this will make any difference to the ultimate fate of Europe:

> The euro and the Eurozone may be saved in years to come, but this would not necessarily bring stability, for the next crisis or the one after could cause their downfall. But this, resulting in a European split, would not necessarily mean the end of a united Europe, for a new initiative would probably be made after a decent interval. The same seems likely if the Eurozone should dissolve earlier rather than later.[12]

Thus Europe is bound to stumble from disrupted unity to breakup, followed by new alignments and so on—an altogether sorry prospect for the future. Perhaps the decisive blow will be the end of the welfare state, Europe's major achievement since its recovery from the Second World War:

> What will be the political consequences of gradual disintegration of the welfare state? The social programs were based on a social contract, and if the contract ceases to exist, political conflict seems inevitable.. . . Depriving citizens of services that were taken for granted could lead sooner or later to a political earthquake, and even a lethargic Europe could witness violence. No one can predict what form protests will take—probably a populist reaction that could turn left as well as toward the authoritarian right and that could see the end of political parties and the parliamentary system as Europe has known it since the Second War War.[13]

Events in Greece certainly seem to be bearing out this prediction. But can the situation in Greece be generalized to the rest of Europe, or is it a special case?

According to Laqueur, the coup de grace to an ailing Europe will be delivered by migrants from Third World countries:

> Uncontrolled migration was, to repeat again, not the only and not the main reason for the decline of Europe. Its threat is not immediate, but long-term. But taken together with its other misfortunes, it is leading to a profound crisis. A miracle might be needed to extract Europe from these predicaments.[14]

A demographic time-bomb known as the "youth bulge" is waiting to explode in the Muslim countries to the south of Europe: over a hundred million young people with no job prospects in their own countries are expected to head north and flood the European labor market. Adding to Europe's own youth unemployment, this will cause intolerable strains that may give way to racist and neo-Fascist manifestations. Little wonder that Laqueur judges the present crisis "to be considerably deeper than those Europe passed through after the Second World War.[15]

Are such obsequies for Europe premature, or somewhat exaggerated in Mark Twain's sense? If Europe found its way out of totalitarianism and the aftermath of the Second World War, then might it not also find a solution to what at present at least seem much lesser problems? Of course, what such solutions might be, we cannot tell, though America will probably play a leading part in the rescue of Europe once more. Perhaps a new transatlantic alliance and economic integration will be the answer to some of Europe's present woes. Beyond that point no further predictions can be made with any confidence. The future of Europe is still undecided; there are no inevitable outcomes to be expected.

Section III—Contingency and Necessity

The future of Europe is still open, but what of its past—was that also contingent, or was it determined? Did Europe necessarily have to undergo the torments of totalitarianism? Was its agony its destiny, or merely a chance quirk of fate? Were there any fatal turnings that might have been averted and so led to a very different outcome? Such questions open up the theoretical issues of contingency and necessity that we have already debated in *Beyond Civilization* in relation to Western civilization in general. Here we raise them once again by reference to the much more specific issues of the Events of the Twentieth Century. In *nuce*, were they contingent or necessary?

Raymond Aron raised much the same questions half a century ago in the course of his discussion of industrial society, then the fashionable term for considering Modernity.

> The spread of industrial societies and the unification of the human race are two happenings which were either brought about or speeded up by the thirty years' war, but were they not in any case inevitable? And are they not in accordance with the law of necessity? And is not this dramatic change merely the method of achieving the very result predicted by Auguste Comte, namely the creation of a single industrial society, uniting, for the first time, the entire human race?[16]

The "single industrial society" is, of course, our current globalization, which in terms of production, communication, transportation, and the circulation of knowledge and technology does operate like a single society, though it does not do so yet in any other terms, and certainly not politically or culturally. This new global condition was most surely not brought about by the "thirty years war" (1914–1945) or what we have called the Events of the Twentieth Century, but it was undeniably accelerated by it, as we have already established by our study of totalitarianism and de-colonialization. What brought it about were, in the first place, the Forces of Modernity, which arose uniquely in the West, and, in the second place, it was the agencies of de-civilization, namely, colonialism, totalitarianism, and globalization and the respective forms of modernization that each of these promulgated: Europeanization, Sovietization, and Americanization.

But was the end result inevitable, regardless of the specific means by which it came about? Was humanity destined to be brought together on the basis of the Forces of Modernity, and were these the ineluctable outcomes of human development? What might have been the fate of the world, if the agencies of de-civilization had not been operative? Were they also inevitable, or were they the result of sequences of events set in motion by the actions of individuals and groups and hence the contingent outcomes of willed decisions? How do necessity and contingency or freedom mutually interlock in the causation of historical eventualities? All these questions were already raised and partially answered in *Beyond Civilization*. Here we will approach them once again from another direction.

It was certainly not inevitable that Western European civilization would be the one in which the Forces of Modernity would come to fruition. Indeed, for most of its medieval period this looked most unlikely, as Europe was then no more than a warring swarm of petty principalities on the edge of the Eurasian landmass, poor in population and backward in many aspects of economic and political development. At its start, before AD 1000, it could hardly be compared with the ebullience of its coeval civilizations, the Abbasid Caliphate of Islam, the Sung dynasty in China, and even the Byzantine Empire of the Macedonian emperors. Yet for reasons we briefly spelt out elsewhere—and which have been intensively explored by many authors, notably by William McNeill and in a more specialized way Rémi Brague—it was the West that made the next crucial step in human development by pioneering the Forces of Modernity. This, as we have said, was of course not inevitable. It might have been accomplished by one of the other civilizations. The reasons that they, in fact, failed to do so is also an intensive area of study first fully adumbrated by Weber.

However, had the West not done so first, one of the other civilizations would have managed it in due course, for it was inevitable in terms of the evolution of history that sooner or later humanity would have attained to something approximating our Forces of Modernity and became unified on that basis. Advanced production methods based on industrialization and a system of efficient investment would have arisen sooner or later. A way of organizing societies through political domination and the monopoly of the means of violence would also have had to emerge. Knowledge of the natural and human environment and its systematic elaboration through theorization and experimentation could be temporarily stifled, as it so often was, but not permanently halted if humans remained as inquisitive and acquisitive as they undoubtedly are. And finally, techniques, instruments, and machines are the inescapable means for mastering that environment, so humans are bound to develop them, given their inventiveness and intelligence. All in all, then, the Forces of Modernity arise out of tendencies inherent in the human mind and of the human social development we call history.

Given, therefore, that the Forces of Modernity were inevitable, the next question that arises is this: did this have to operate through the agencies of de-civilization in order to bring about the unification of humanity that Aron contends Comte prophesied? Were colonialism, totalitarianism, and globalization and their modernization correlatives of Europeanization, Sovietization, and Americanization also necessary, or were they contingent aberrations of Western civilization? Could the nations of the world have been brought together without these tragic misfortunes? Anyone with a humanistic predisposition is strongly tempted to reply that these were not necessary and might have been avoided. But we have no way of conceiving how this unification would then have taken place. The vision of a peaceful coming-together of all people on earth is only the secularized vision of the fulfillment of the prophecy that swords will turned to plowshares and the lion will lie down with the lamb. It might have happened in some other way, but perhaps one just as bloody, lasting longer and thereby extending the agony of humanity.

As Aron suggested, the "thirty years war," or indeed the whole period of colonialism totalitarianism and globalization, "speeded up" the process. At its very worst it has taken just one century, the fatal twentieth century, to be nearly accomplished. How this speeding-up of an inevitable outcome occurred—how, indeed, in theory it could occur—still remains to be explained. However, it can easily be illustrated by a few salient examples, showing how the agencies of de-civilization worked to promote the rapid growth of the Forces of Modernity.

Colonialism, which was itself the partial outcome of capitalism, worked back on it to increase its scope and intensity. Britain, the leading industrialized colonialist power in the eighteenth and most of the nineteenth centuries, utilized its colonial possession to further the growth of its economy and its productive potential. Though it is simplistic, as argued by doctrinaire Marxists and Asianists, to see colonialism as the main cause of industrial capitalism, it is not wrong to see it as having a decisive effect on it. However, colonialism did not arise only from an inner necessity in capitalism, as Hobson first argued and Lenin maintained when he saw imperialism as the highest stage of capitalism. For in its late stages there was no longer any economic imperative for colonialism. German capitalism, which overtook British capitalism toward the end of the nineteenth century, did not need colonies, and Germany entered the colonialist race purely for purposes of national prestige and little else. There is some truth in the contention that the British acquired their Indian colonial possessions in a fit of absentmindedness, which is to say that the British government did not notice what the East Indian Company officials were up to so far away. There is thus a certain element of historical contingency in this and many other colonial acquisitions by European powers. Colonialism was certainly not inevitable. Eventually it became more of a political than economic process. Nevertheless, the main point holds: colonialism did accelerate the evolution of capitalism.

We have extensively explored the contingent nature of totalitarianism, which was also far from inevitable. If not for the numerous accidents that precipitated the First World War, there would have been no such thing as totalitarianism. As we have also shown, the precipitating thoughts and actions of a few individuals, above all Lenin, were also essential for its occurrence. Yet once totalitarianism arose, it had a decisive effect on the Forces of Modernity, on economic development, on the state, on science and technology, and, more indirectly, also on colonialism and globalization, the other agencies of de-civilization. Totalitarianism and the battle against it led to a huge surge in industrial capacity in all the major powers, nowhere more so than in the United States, and eventually this became the basis of American-led globalization. In many respects, totalitarianism furthered the welfare state, in totalitarian states themselves as well as their opponents. Finally, totalitarianism and the battle fought against it released the inventive powers of engineers and scientists to create new war technologies of every imaginable kind, nearly all of which were usable in peacetime as well and had a great impact on the production capacities of all nations. This development also quickened and transformed science, especially in its American incarnation as Big Science.

Totalitarianism had another decisive effect on world history, in that it made de-colonialization virtually inevitable, because the struggles over totalitarianism so weakened and exhausted the colonial powers that they were in no position to defend their colonial possessions after the Second World War. This in turn opened the way to globalization under the aegis of America. But for totalitarianism, the liberation of the colonial people might have taken much longer or perhaps might not have taken place at all, for they might have been completely Europeanized.

This last consideration prompts the question of what might have happened if totalitarianism had never occurred at all, if all the wars caused by it were not fought, and if Europe was not depleted and devastated. This is, of course, a "what if" question, a purely hypothetical matter we have no way of answering with any certainty. Yet we can fruitfully speculate about it in a number of ways. If Europe had continued as it was proceeding prior to 1914, Western civilization would certainly have lasted for much longer. The Forces of Modernity would not have exercised the rapid catalytic effect on European society and culture. Until 1914 the traditional institutions in Europe and its class system had succeeded in keeping the civilization intact and preventing capitalism, the state, science, and technology from becoming completely dominant. If this situation had continued, these Forces of Modernity would have developed at a much slower pace, with the possible exception of science, which was following a purely theoretical and intellectual trajectory, was still immersed in its own traditional culture, and had not yet been co-opted by industrial technology. But it would have been worth sacrificing the speed of material growth for the security of civilized life. The affluent lifestyle and all its creature comforts might not have been attained so soon. It is true that America, with its size and expansiveness in these respects, was looming on the horizon and nothing that happened in Europe would have prevented it from having an impact on Europe and other parts of the world. The mechanization of life would have proceeded along American lines; yet it need not have been as devastating as it in fact was, because there would have been cultural resources, both ethical and aesthetic, to counter it, even in America itself. Americans would have remained more respectful of European civilizational values as part of their own heritage, as they still were prior to 1914, and less intent on Americanizing everything they encountered.

For the colonized peoples, however, it would perhaps have been a sadder story. Their Europeanization would have gone on apace. They would have lost much more of their native customs and traditions, indeed, of their religions and the living remnants of their old civilizations. Many of them would have become second-rate Europeans—*babus*, as they were known in India. The battle for independence might have been long and bloody, and it could have failed if the Europeans had been able to devote all their resources to it, as Winston Churchill was urging the British to do before and after World War II. The British Empire could have survived; the French might have incorporated Algeria into metropolitan France; the Dutch might have hung on to the East Indies. But none of this happened, because Europe virtually destroyed itself. Was the destruction of Europe worth the speedier liberation of its colonies? Did the lowering of the Union Jack in New Delhi and Jerusalem make some amends for Auschwitz?

Our explanation of the ongoing destruction of civilization in the twentieth century is based on the interaction between two sets of factors: the Forces of Modernity, long-term sociological trends that were almost certainly inevitable in human historical development; and the agencies of de-civilization, colonialism, totalitarianism, and globalization that were contingent events in European history that need not have happened. How it is possible for such necessities and contingencies to interact is the most puzzling theoretical problem of historical explanation. That it is possible is undeniable, because such necessary and contingent factors as we have studied do undeniably exist. It would be theoretical folly to deny that some aspects of human historical development are inevitable and insist that all is a matter of choice and chance. And conversely, it would be equally foolish to maintain that everything is predetermined and that human will and fortuitous coincidences play no part—namely, that events do not matter. The difficulty is in determining what is to be ascribed to each of these categories. We have argued that there is good reason to ascribe the Forces of Modernity to the former and the agencies of de-civilization to the latter, which leaves us with the aforesaid problem of how they related to each other.

We can clarify this issue by once more retracing the key steps we have taken in the above account. As previously stated, the Forces of Modernity began during the civilizational eruption we call Modernity within the Western European civilization starting around AD 1500. Had they not arisen then and there, they would have done so elsewhere at another time, and have taken a somewhat altered form, though one in keeping with the inevitability of this trend. The Forces of Modernity constitute the causal background and compelling force for all the shorter-term contingent events that occurred in European history and through European influence in the history of the world. The agencies of de-civilization were molded by these background conditions, though not completely determined by them. They follow their own autonomous courses, as do other such contingencies.

Though they were constrained by the causal parameters established by the Forces of Modernity, the agencies of de-civilization were also shaped by all the contingent events that were influencing them, including, as we have amply demonstrated, the thoughts and actions of single individuals. A battle won or lost, a book published or unpublished, falling into the right or wrong hands, the chance death of a great leader or king, the birth of an heir or his premature death—these and an infinite number of other events or chance exigencies can make a huge difference in history. The history they affect is not merely that which falls on the contingent side but also that which lies on the necessary one as well. But how can necessity be touched by contingency? How can chance or willed events disturb inevitable trends? This is the nub of the paradox we are seeking to resolve.

The solution lies in the realization that not everything about the way a predetermined trend takes place is equally determined. There is an indefinite possible variability in any such trend, and each such variation can itself be contingent or subject to contingent influences. Only in its most general form is a trend inevitable; in all its other specific features it can be indeterminate. Thus, for example, it can most certainly be supposed that humanity would develop high technologies sooner or later. But the form in which this in fact took place within the Modern period in the West was characterized by all kinds of features that were the peculiar outcomes of Western civilization, and many of these were prompted by contingent events governing their origins within the historical period that produced them.

The chance occurrence of inventors of genius at decisive moments was not without its impact, at least on the speed and intensity with which technological change occurred, even if not on its eventual occurrence or its specific character. James Watt's invention of the steam engine certainly speeded up the Industrial Revolution and prompted all kinds of other technological inventions in rapid succession, even if it can be argued that if Watt had not done it, someone else would have produced much the same machine somewhat later. However, it is quite plausible to argue hypothetically that if technology had developed at another time in another civilization, it would have had a very different character. Thus Needham supposes that if the Chinese had had the time and opportunity to develop their own technologies in their own way, these would not have been as ecologically damaging as Western technologies. A hypothetical Chinese technological revolution might have been more in keeping with Taoist philosophy and developed devices and uses that did not exert such overwhelming brute force on Nature, but rather utilized Nature's own subtle powers to achieve human ends. Such speculations cannot be proven; however, they do serve to illustrate that the technology that we now possess and deploy was not the only one that an industrial revolution might have developed and utilized.

This kind of hypothetical argument can be speculatively extended to all the Forces of Modernity. They were inevitable, but not necessarily so in the form they actually assumed in the West. They could have been otherwise in all kinds of respects. For such variations contingent factors can often be adduced. Thus human volition and chance conjunctures are events that can also play a role in shaping what is inevitably bound to come about.

This consideration brings us back to the topic we have already amply explored in the previous chapters, namely the role of the individual in history, such as Lenin's part in bringing about the Revolution. This enables us also to begin to understand how it is possible for individuals to play crucial roles in eventualities that were otherwise inexorable. Thus it was possible for Plato and St. Paul to decisively shape Western civilization by means of works that only each of them with his unique genius could have written. Had they not existed, Western civilization would inevitably have continued anyway, but it would have had a vastly different character. Speaking evaluatively from our point of view, it would have been much the poorer. Conversely, if Stalin and Hitler had not lived, totalitarianism might not have taken its ultimately fatal turning; Auschwitz and the Great Purge would not have occurred; and, therefore, its effect on the course of Western Civilization would not have been as drastic. History might also have been spared World War II with all its disastrous consequences. It is possible that all these events are part of some inevitable process that is still working itself out. But we cannot know what it is, for, as we argued at length in *Beyond Civilization*, inevitabilities cannot in principle be predicted, they can only be retrospectively arrived at through historical interpretation. Hence, we cannot now predict what will be the future fate of Western civilization or civilization in general.

However, that does not preclude us from making some short-term prognostications about where things in the world seem to be heading. In particular, we can make some tentative predictions about globalization, a process driven by America, the most potent and inventive country in the world. To do so we must embark on a study of America, to examine its past so as to be able to say something about its likely future.

Notes

1. François Furet, *The Passing of an Illusion*, p. 363.
2. Ibid., p. 59.
3. Ibid., p. 359.
4. Ibid., p. 360.
5. Norman Davies, *Europe: A History*, op. cit., p. 1077.
6. Ibid.
7. Thomas P. M. Barnett, *Great Powers: America and the World After Bush* (Putnam's, New York, 2009), p. 182.
8. Richard Pells, *Not Like Us: How the Europeans Have Loved, Hated and Transformed American Culture since World War II* (Basic Books, New York, 1997), p. 211.
9. Ibid., p. 205.

10. Walter Laqueur, *After the Fall: The End of the European Dream and the Decline of a Continent* (St Martin's Press, New York, 2011), p. xii.
11. Ibid., p. x.
12. Ibid., p. x.
13. Ibid., p. 242.
14. Ibid., p. 230.
15. Ibid., p. ix.
16. Raymond Aron, *The Dawn of Universal History* op. cit., p. 44.

II

The New World

5

America Comes of Age

Section I—The Rise of America

Amerika, du hast es besser
Als unser Kontinent der alte
Goethe

America has, indeed, got the better of the old continent; the New World
has outdone the Old World. How can we account for the remarkable
success of America, especially in the twentieth century? As we will
argue, it has much to do with the self-inflicted disasters of Europe, but
that, clearly, cannot be the whole explanation. In its times of trouble,
Europe undoubtedly gave America the opportunity to extend its reach,
but America would not have achieved dominance without developing
its own capacities and powers. The Americanization of the world at the
start of the twentieth century, even before Europe's woes had begun,
was not a foregone conclusion, but to some astute observers, such as
the journalist W. T. Stead, it already looked inevitable, as he wrote in
a book by that very title.[1] He based himself mainly on the remarkable
technical progress that America had already achieved by then, progress
that revolutionized everyday life. The telephone, typewriter, electric
light, sewing machine, gramophone, elevator, airplane, cinema, radio,
and eventually—after Stead's time—television, computer, nuclear
power, pharmaceuticals, and much more—all these have transformed
the lives of people all over the world. These were not all American
inventions, but American companies succeeded in patenting them,
marketing them, and gaining world dominance in their distribution.
A leading example is the motorcar; it was not invented in America, but
once mass-produced by Henry Ford, it became the basis of the complete restructuring of living arrangements all over the world, which we
now call car-culture. And, as John Lukacs, notes, "during the 1920s the
automobilization of the world moved apace with its Americanization."[2]

The Americanization of the world was based on the superiority America had already achieved on so many fronts of Modernity at the start of the twentieth century; it was further consolidated by its victory in the First World War and the state of Europe after the war, as Lukacs comments:

> After World War I she was not only the most productive but the richest state of the world; she changed from a relative debtor to a creditor among nations. Before 1914 the most renowned international currency was the British pound, and the financial capital city of the world was London, by 1918 the dollar replaced the pound, and New York, London.[3]

But America had come to the fore not only in economics, but in culture as well—at least as far as mass culture (often mistaken for popular culture) was concerned, thanks to the Hollywood film industry and Tin Pan Alley in music and dance. The Europeans were still able to hold their own only in high culture. For a while it also seemed as if the liberal democratic politics that President Wilson sought to impose on Europe would prevail, but unfortunately this was not to be; Europe soon reverted to old political habits. Many of the new states established at Versailles became dictatorships, and totalitarianism emerged in Russia and Italy. It was not until after the Second World War that America could embark on its project of making the world safe for democracy, and this is still a work in progress.

The Americanization of the world brought about a new kind of globalization, different from that which was formerly based on Europeanization and tied to colonialism. Colonialism was phased out after the Second World War, and the Third World that emerged eventually became susceptible to American influence. American globalization now prevails, for any country that wishes to participate in world affairs must join one or another of the global arrangements instituted and dominated by America, whether economic, political, military, technological, scientific, cultural, or intellectual. Just as all roads once led to Rome, so do all global connections now lead back to America. America sits like a spider in the center of the World Wide Web, the network that connects it to every other country and each country to every other. Directly or indirectly, it all goes through America. But that does not mean that America governs a world empire in the Roman or colonialist sense, for it does not conquer and rule territories. Any country that so chooses can defy the United States—whether it is as small and weak as North Korea or Cuba—but only at huge cost to itself, for it then remains poor, lonely, and isolated. America is not an imperialist power, but it maintains a hegemonic presence throughout the world.

America's overwhelming success was undoubtedly due to its achievements; this was greatly assisted, however, by the demise of its main rivals. Europe ruined itself in two World Wars of increasing intensity and destructive power. In both cases the New World had to be called on to restore the balance of the Old. In the First World War only American economic might enabled the Western powers to win, but in doing so they became heavily indebted to America. In the Second World War America had to step in and give aid gratis, for Europe would never have recovered without help and would have fallen into the totalitarian orbit of the Soviet Union. One of America's greatest achievements was to rescue its two most bitter enemies, Germany and Japan, from utter ruination and enlist them as its closest allies from then on. But in the process they became heavily Americanized. Something analogous happened to its two Cold War enemies, Russia and China; the latter in particular was coaxed into an ever-closer partnership with America, to the point where their economies are now interdependent and their educational and scientific establishments are closely integrated. Though it has established good relations with most members of the former Soviet Bloc, America has not succeeded particularly well with Russia, which indicates a degree of failure in American foreign policy.

Totalitarianism, which was an unmitigated disaster for Europe, Russia, China, and other parts of the world, actually gave America an opportunity to expand its influence. Far-sighted thinkers in the nineteenth century, such as Hegel and de Tocqueville, predicted that Russia and America would eventually take over the leadership of the world from Europe. Before the First World War it certainly looked as if this would happen in the course of the twentieth or twenty-first centuries. But it did not eventuate, because Russia was devastated by Bolshevism and its totalitarian system. Something similar happened in all the other cases where totalitarianism was at work. The failure of totalitarianism was America's greatest gain, for it meant that its rivals were doomed to destruction by their own hand. America gained world leadership without having to fight for it. It was said that Britain acquired India in a fit of absentmindedness; America, we might say, acquired the world more by default than design.

This is not to deny America's own resources, which enabled it to take easy advantage of the weaknesses of rival powers and rise to a position of world hegemony. Already prior to 1914, before totalitarianism was thought of, America was superior to any single European power in the crucial dimensions of the Forces of Modernity: an industrial capitalist economy, a rational-legal state and technology. It was not yet proficient in science, which was to come a little later. The American economy, as we have seen, was already second to none and with its enormous productive capacity in both agriculture and manufacture could out-compete any other. The American political system, as enshrined in the constitution and in the practical arrangements that followed from it, was America's greatest invention of all and perhaps also its greatest contribution to civilization. American technology, as we have already discussed, was its trump card until our own time and will probably remain so well into the future. American science, somewhat backward before 1914, caught up rapidly with the major European scientific establishments of Germany, Britain, and France, surpassing them easily after the Second World War—for reasons we shall examine in chapter 6, section III.

What was it about civilization as this developed in the New World that enabled it, in respect of the Forces of Modernity, to outperform that of the Old World? There are many reasons for this, which will become clear as we explain the rise of America in the next section. In a brief preliminary way we can specify here that America had enormous advantages over Europe in these respects. American industrial capitalism had at its disposal the almost unlimited resources of a great continent, together with cheap immigrant labor coming from all parts of Europe. It had the ingenuity of its inventors and engineers, and the daring of its entrepreneurs and speculative investors. It was not restrained by a class system, establishments, and political movements, like those that hampered the capitalists of Europe. It was favored by a political system that safeguarded private property and the free market. The new system of liberal democracy also ensured stability and lack of conflict, except for the one time that it broke down and led to the Civil War, the only real all-out war America has ever known. Behind all these economic, social, and political developments there stood the culture and mentality of American individualism that Europeans, such as de Tocqueville, so admired. This was the individualism of self-made men who recognized no binding ties to party, class, or even family in any extended sense, and whose origins were of no concern. Such were the people who built America.

It was this homegrown version of the Forces of Modernity that Americans have sought to spread throughout the world. This is, as we saw previously, what they mean by "modernization." In Americanizing the world, they have at the same time achieved its globalization. This, they believe, is their greatest gift to the world, as Thomas Barnett expresses it:

> The American System blossomed into an international liberal trade order, which in turn gave birth to the globalization we enjoy today. These are the United States' most powerful acts of creation. This world-transforming legacy created the twenty-first-century environment, one marked by more pervasive poverty reduction, wealth creation, technological advance, and—most important—stabilizing peace than any previous era in human history. This legacy is worth preserving, defending, and expanding to its ultimate heights—a globalization made truly global.[4]

All this is no doubt true, but what is left unsaid is that in defending these achievements what is also being defended is America's dominant position in the world. What will it take to defend that, and what dangers will it incur?

There is, furthermore, a dark side to American triumphalism, proclaimed so loudly at the end of the Cold War, and that is the issue of the effect of globalization on civilization. We addressed this question at great length in *Beyond Civilization* and cannot repeat all its arguments here. However, some doubts as to this matter can be raised by noting how all the world's local cultures are rapidly being swallowed up by the global culture generated by America, which is an integral part of its capitalism. Even the culture of Europe, Western civilization itself, is not safe from this invasion.

America also represents Western civilization, but in a variant somewhat different from that of Europe. It seems that in crossing the Atlantic Western civilization had undergone something of a sea change. In what follows, we examine how it differs from its original European form, that current prior to 1914. The form of civilization that has developed in Europe since 1945 is clearly very different from earlier versions, for when Western Civilization returned to Europe after all the catastrophic disruptions, it returned in its American version. The attempt by some traditionalist Europeans, such as de Gaulle and Adenauer, to retain their national cultures has clearly not succeeded.

But Europe is not our concern here. We must return to America and study historically how it evolved gradually out of its European origins to become what we now see as a distinctive American civilization. How and why this happened will be of primary interest in our account.

Section II—The Development of America

As every schoolchild knows, America as it is at present is overwhelmingly a product of Europe. Apart from the genes of some of its people, little else is left of the cultures and civilizations that predated the European arrival. The Spanish settlers came first to South America and destroyed as much as they were able of the pre-Columbian civilizations they found there. Somewhat later, the French, Dutch, and British came to North America and were equally rapacious in dispossessing the natives and eradicating their cultures. Eventually it was the American-born descendants of the British who established the United States of America and set their stamp on the whole northern part of the continent, and eventually they dominated the southern. Why they were so successful in establishing a society that did so well in all the measures of Modernity, while their southern counterparts did so poorly, is a much-debated topic that we can only briefly consider.

The settlement of the Americas by two distinct European peoples at different times, the Iberians in the sixteenth century and the British and others in the seventeenth, had profound consequences for American civilization. It led to a division into two civilizational spheres, which for most of their history were almost hermetically sealed off from each other. European civilization in the Americas was from the start bifurcated and could not reproduce itself in complete integrity. Each half inherited a part of the European original, but neither could regenerate the whole of it. Latin America was Iberian, Catholic, and plagued by the Inquisition until well into the nineteenth century; its economy was feudal in keeping with its sixteenth-century origins; its politics was for the whole colonial period paternalistic authoritarian, directed by a distant court, and later revolutionary, with dictatorial rule by juntas; its society was racially stratified in a complex hierarchy ranging from white to black, with all kinds of mixtures in between. By contrast, British America was predominantly Protestant, inclined toward Puritanism in places; its economy was nascent capitalism, in keeping with its seventeenth-century origins; its politics was based on self-government in both church and state, with a tendency toward liberalism and individualism; its society was linguistically and racially homogenous, except for a small minority of blacks bound in slavery and, even when emancipated, still not socially accepted until the later part of the twentieth century. Thus British America was constitutionally geared to movement in the direction of the Forces of Modernity, whereas Latin America was constituted in a way that made any such movement very difficult. In fact, it was not until the later part of the twentieth century that any real progress was made in that respect, and even then it was uneven, with huge barriers still to be overcome.

It is true that Europe itself was divided by the Reformation into a largely Catholic south and a largely Protestant north, but that separation was not as watertight as it became in the Americas, except for the Iberian Peninsula, from which Protestantism was rigidly and violently excluded. In most other parts of Europe, Catholics and Protestants mingled, interacted, and even intermarried. This meant that as well as sporadic warfare between them there was continuous intercourse and collaboration. We can see this clearly in the sciences: it cannot be established whether Copernicus was a Polish Catholic or a German Lutheran, nor does it matter which he was; Galileo, a Catholic, corresponded with Kepler, a Lutheran who worked for the Catholic emperor in Prague; Descartes, a Catholic, lived in Calvinist Holland and died in Lutheran Sweden, and so on. It is not conceivable that any British American of comparable stature could have had dealings with someone in Latin America until the twentieth century. Could Benjamin Franklin have corresponded with anybody in one of the universities in Peru or Mexico? What could they have talked about, and in what language?

British Americans had little Latin and less Greek. They were divorced from the Latin civilization of medieval Europe and from the Greek culture of the Renaissance, from which classicism derived. They were further removed from these sources of European civilization than the British in Britain, for the Church of England and the ancient English and Scottish universities maintained continuity with these pre-Reformation traditions. There was nothing comparable in America; those who sailed to the New World, such as the Pilgrim Fathers, deliberately rejected and shunned such quasi-papist remnants of their homeland and sought to establish a New Jerusalem on the basis of the Bible alone. They had no desire to reproduce European civilization as a whole even in its British form, retaining only that part they felt was untainted by idol worship. In fact, as we shall see, what they kept was precisely suited for developing the Forces of Modernity.

Thus America's extraordinary success story in the modern world can to some extent be explained by its origins. It is not just the favorable objective conditions they encountered in America—so much virgin land thus far unexploited and very sparsely settled by the Indians—but even more so what they brought with them from the Old World and what they left behind, that together account for its success. They were making a new beginning in a new land. It is a feeling that immigrants to America have experienced ever since. A new start, a fresh start—this is what Americans think is possible for every individual at all times. For if one part of America became too settled and crowded, there was always the frontier to which a man could escape, like Huck Finn clearing out to the territory to get away from the civilizing influence of Widow Douglas. That, of course, was only possible as long as there was a frontier; when there was no more land to settle, Americans went in search of new frontiers elsewhere, even dreaming about outer space.

A new society required a new kind of government, so the Founding Fathers devised a new political order, a *Novus Ordos Terrarium,* according to Thomas Jefferson. It was based on first principles established by political philosophers in Europe, but brought to practical realization in America, as Allan Bloom explains:

> The expositions of Hobbes, Locke and Rousseau of the origins [i.e., the state of nature] made possible a new beginning in theory, a project for the reconstruction of politics, just as the exploration and discovery of the New World promised a new beginning in practice. The two beginnings coincided and produced, among other wonders, the United States.[5]

This relationship of Old World theory and New World practice was to reproduce itself over and over again. Anyone with a new theory or crackpot idea in Europe always believed that America was the place where he would be given the opportunity to test it. The latest among these were the nuclear physicists who gave America the Bomb and the mathematical logicians who gave it the computer. For all others as well, America was the land of opportunity.

It was this sense of innovation and renewal—that everything could be done better by starting from scratch, that traditions and the old ways of doing things could always be set aside and discounted—that gave Americans such an edge over Europeans in developing the Forces of Modernity. Yankee ingenuity was already a byword from Benjamin

Franklin onward, and it still resonates. It culminated in Thomas Edison's factory of invention, which was the precursor of the research and development laboratories and think-tank institutes of today. America still attracts the bulk of the world's inventive brainpower from all parts of the globe.

But perhaps the greatest invention of all was neither technological nor scientific, but political—the Constitution. The American Founding Fathers collectively invented liberal representative democracy almost from scratch. They combined three utterly distinct and historically diverse principles of government into one highly workable and durable whole, which has since become the preferred form of government for almost the whole world. They took Democracy from the ancient Greeks; they inherited Representation from the English parliamentary tradition, which they recreated during the colonial period; Liberalism they learned from Locke, who based it on the tolerance and freedom of Holland and England. To all this they added the system of federalism that had precursors in Holland and Switzerland as well as in ancient Greek leagues; this was then coupled with a division of powers separating the executive, legislative, and judicial arms of government, which had precedents both in Roman law and English common law practice. The division of the legislature into two chambers, Senate and House of Representatives, also went back in principle to Rome, but in practice to the English houses of Lords and Commons. Finally, in establishing a president as chief executive officer as well as head of the armed forces, they obviously had an elected emperor in mind. What an amazing collocation this is—and yet it works and has lasted until now, and looks like it will continue well into the future. Little wonder that Americans consider it their greatest gift to the world and that the chief aim of their foreign policy has been to "make the world safe for democracy." It is true that their basic power instincts have often got the better of their high-minded idealism; nevertheless, it has been the polar star by which they steer their ship of state.

Economically, American capitalism did not come into its own until after the Civil War, for then the whole of the continent was opened up by the railways for exploitation. As William Chafe states, "America's industrial expansion in the years after the Civil War knew no precedent. With the technological and industrial innovations of war itself as a catalyst, America swiftly became the leading industrial power in the world."[6] This war set a precedent for what America was to gain from the next two major ones, the First and Second World Wars. It was this enormous economic power that drove the Americanization of the world, which Stead had already registered in 1902. However, this had begun a little earlier, soon after the Civil War was over, as Lukacs notes:

> It was then [in 1876] that the Americanization of the world began—a process that was social, cultural and political and goes on in full force even now. In the history of mankind the twentieth century has been the American century. Tocqueville was one of the few who one hundred and fifty years ago foresaw that the United States and Russia would become the two main powers of the world sooner or later; but even he did not foresee how American habits, institutions, and forms, ranging from American techniques to American speech and manners, would be adopted, sometimes thoughtlessly but always eagerly, in the strangest places, and by the strangest people all around the world, including Russians, Asians, Africans.[7]

The Americanization of the world recounted by Lukacs and many other authors went on apace, irresistibly so, because—as we do not tire of repeating—of the enormous success America had made of the Forces of Modernity by the start of the twentieth century. Only in respect of the sciences were they still backward, but they were catching up very fast. They were sending their best students to the great universities and research schools in Germany, then the most advanced in the world, and were themselves establishing new universities with schools of postgraduate research on the German model. However, as we shall see later, it took the huge influx of refugee scientists and scholars fleeing from the totalitarianism of Europe, especially Jews escaping Hitler, to bring American science to the preeminent position it attained after the Second World War and which it has more or less kept, despite a renewed European challenge. Most Nobel prizes still go to Americans themselves, or to those working in American institutions, or to those scientists who were trained in America.

Americanization is, however, not the same as American civilization. In fact, as we shall go on to argue in the next chapter, there is a contradictory relation between them—simply put, Americanization is destroying American civilization, just as it is every other. American civilization is not just the Forces of Modernity, it is much more and other than that. It mainly concerns cultural life, rather than material and organizational matters. American culture is European culture as this developed in the New World. Differences between them gradually evolved as both went their own ways, though they were always in mutual communication. Americans read what Europeans wrote, and some Europeans read what Americans wrote.

Both in literature and other modes of writing, as well as in all cultural respects, Americans developed their own forms, which were somewhat distinct from those current in Europe. When he came to America during the presidency of Andrew Jackson, de Tocqueville was fully aware of how American culture had already departed from that of Europe. American social relations, manners and morals, tastes and predilections, and, above all, its individualistic propensities had no counterparts in Europe. Americans had attained higher levels of literacy than Europeans and were starting to develop a literature that was equal to that of any in Europe, though de Tocqueville might not yet have been aware of that fact. But a little later, Baudelaire certainly was, and ever since then American literature has exercised an influence on Europe. In fact, one of the great themes of American literature has been the portrayal of the differences between American and European civilization. Henry James was the great master of this genre. In a similar way the differences between American and European philosophy were explored by his brother William James, one of the founders of Pragmatism, the quintessentially American philosophy. All in all, though of lesser scope, American civilization could stand unabashed next to that of Europe as a second wing of Western civilization.

Unfortunately, in the twentieth century American civilization has not fared all that much better than European. In the next chapter we will go on to study what was responsible for this de-civilizing downturn, which certainly cannot be ascribed to totalitarianism, as in Europe. Obviously, there were other forces at work. But before we go into that, we must first search for theories that explain the rise of America and account for its character as a civilization.

Section III—The Origin of America

In what follows we shall adopt a sociological framework in attempting to explain America's rise to world dominance, and try to locate those factors that gave it a head start over Europe, almost from its very origins. To do so we turn to the classic theories of Max Weber and Louis Hartz. They are now sometimes discounted or neglected, as in a recent work by Stephen Mennell, *The American Civilizing Process*. In our view, these classic theories still offer the best available explanation of America, much better so than the theories of Elias on which Mennell relies.

In developing his theory of the Protestant Ethic and the Spirit of Capitalism, Weber turned to America for conclusive proof. He travelled there in1904 and gathered material for his book by that title, some of which he also wrote up in an essay devoted specifically to the relationship between religious sects and capitalist business ethics. He concluded that "not a few (one may say the majority of the older generation) of the American 'promoters', 'captains of industry', of the multi-millionaires and trust magnates belonged formally to sects, especially to the Baptists."[8] It is little wonder that the representative figure in his account of the derivation of modern capitalism is the archetypical American, Benjamin Franklin, a man of all trades, businessman printer, technical wizard and man of science, aphorist of capitalist wisdom, politician and statesman, one of the Founding Fathers. The fact that he was no Quaker or Puritan, but a libertine and free thinking Deist, a child of the Enlightenment, is in keeping with Weber's thesis.

Toward the end of his life, at the end of the First World War, he felt relieved that America would dominate the world rather than Russia, even though he still had no inkling of the nature of the Bolshevism to come. According to his wife, Marianne, he said that "America's world rule was as inevitable as that of Rome after the Punic Wars in ancient times."[9]

Though Weber predicted the success of America and anticipated what we now call Americanization, he had some qualms about it. In his great speech "Science as a Vocation," delivered to students in 1918, he distinguishes between the spirit of learning that motivates Americans and that which motivates Germans, or Europeans in general:

> The American boy learns unspeakably less that the German boy. In spite of an incredible number of examinations, his school life has not had the significance of turning him into an absolute creature of examinations, such as the German. For in America, bureaucracy, which presupposes the examination diploma as a ticket of admission to the realm of office-prebends, is only in its beginnings. The young American has no respect for anything or anybody, for tradition or for public office—unless it is for the personal achievement of individual men. This is what the American calls 'democracy'. This is the meaning of democracy, however distorted its intent may in reality be, and this intent is what matters here. The American's conception of the teacher who faces him is: he sells me his knowledge and his methods for my father's money, just as the greengrocer sells my mother cabbage. And that is all. To be sure, if the teacher happens to be a football coach, then, in this field, he is a leader. But if he is not this (or something similar in a different field of sports), he is simply a teacher and nothing

more. And no young American would think of having the teacher sell him a *Weltanschauung* or a code of conduct.[10]

Commenting further, Weber says that "when formulated in this manner, we should reject this," for as a German professor he does not approve of a purely pragmatic attitude to knowledge; he would have been dismayed to know that one day the American approach would prevail in Germany itself. Yet he has some sneaking sympathy for it and wonders "whether there is not a grain of salt contained in this feeling." It is important to keep the historical circumstances in mind; when he said this, young Germans were hankering for a *Weltanschauung* and looking for great personalities as leaders. This made them highly susceptible to ideological politics. At about this time, the young Georg Lukacs, Weber's student, then living in Budapest, converted almost overnight to Bolshevism and took part in the revolutionary government of Bela Kun. A little later, another student, Carl Schmitt, would become a Nazi. American students were spared such *crises de conscience* experiences because they did not think of themselves as intellectuals. In this one fact lies much of the contrast between American and European civilization.

According to John Lukacs—a Hungarian expatriate who spent most of his life in the United States—the reason that American civilization did not attain the depth and scope of European civilization is that it lost touch with the intellectual traditions that predate the Enlightenment:

> The United States was created in the middle of the Modern Age [circa 1500 to 2000], about 250 years ago. At least in some sense, its revolution, its war of independence, and its constitution belong to the Enlightenment. (In some sense only: because the American revolution was very different from the French revolution; because the Founders depended much more on English and Scottish experiences, institutions, laws, education and ideas than on French ones.) Still: for the United States, having been the creation of the Modern Age was a great advantage—at least for some time. But it was—increasingly—also a handicap. That handicap was the absence of intellectual traditions older than those of the so-called Enlightenment—together with the persistence of the most dangerous idea and illusion of the Enlightenment, whether Parisian or Scottish: the limitless belief in Progress, resting on a shallow and mistaken view of human nature, the "*homme machine*" of the eighteenth century, with its jaunty and unthinking denial of complexity and sinfulness.[11]

This might sound like the fulmination of an old-style European conservative with theological leanings. Yet it is a view with which many would agree, particularly like-minded people, such as the American poet T. S. Eliot. He would have appreciated the point about "complexity and sinfulness," for it was a perceived lack of such complexity in the American Congregationalism into which he was born that prompted him to convert to the Church of England. But theology apart, there is much in Lukacs' critique of American civilization that must be taken seriously. Certainly, the American preoccupation with the computer and the cognitivist information processing approach to the human mind is of a piece with the "homme machine" notion of some Enlightenment philosophers.

But beyond such specific points of criticism, there is Lukacs' general charge that America has lost any connection to the deeper traditions of Europe preceding the Enlightenment. This fits in with our view that the Americas were settled by two distinct fragments of Europe: the southern fragment, which absorbed a limited version of the Latinity of the Catholic Church and feudal Spain, and the northern fragment, which brought over from its British sources some of the extreme tendencies of the Reformation, such as those of the Puritans and other sects. These two variants of Europe were no longer in touch with each other, each was almost oblivious of the other, and each shunned what it knew of the other. Rémi Brague considers Latinity to be the Roman basis of Western civilization and credits it with mediating the heritage of the Greeks, yet North America had little sense of it.[12] American civilization was therefore somewhat limited from the start: it could not develop into a fully autonomous civilization because it could not overcome the above shortcomings.

This view is backed up by Louis Hartz's theory of the origins and developing nature of colonial societies. According to this theory, these societies "are fragments of a larger whole of Europe struck off in the course of the revolution which brought the West into the modern world."[13] Each of the colonies was constituted by a "fragment" that carried over from its land of origin a specific sociohistorical inheritance acquired at the point of its departure: those who would eventually become Latin Americans brought with them feudalism; those who would form the United States, British Canada (but not French Canada, which was feudal), and Dutch South Africa brought bourgeois liberalism; while those who settled in Australia and British South Africa brought the worker agitation of the Industrial Revolution. When the "fragment" of the Old World arrives in the New World, or wherever else it settles, it develops itself in isolation from all the antagonists it had to confront in its place of origin. It no longer has to contend with its former rivals and foes and behaves like a species freed from its natural predators:

> Once a fragment has escaped the European challenges past and future, once it has achieved its curiously timeless place in Western history, an unfolding within it takes place which would have been inconceivable in the constricted atmosphere of Europe.... Jacksonian democracy burgeons, the New Deal flowers, because the right and left are missing. The fixity of the fragment liberates in the end a rich interior development.[14]

The "fixity of the fragment" results from the fact that "when a part of a European nation is detached from the whole of it, and hurled outward onto new soil, it loses its stimulus toward change that the whole provides. It lapses into a kind of immobility."[15]

According to Hartz, "the fixity of the fragment" frees it not only from much of the past of its land of origin but also from its future as well. Thus the United States not only left behind many of the past traditions of Britain, but it also no longer shared in Britain's future development. For example, it did not follow Britain in developing a Labour Party or any such socialist movements, but remained fixed in the liberalism of its two alternating parties, Democrat and Republican, Tweedledum and Tweedledee. This also explains why the United States never abandoned its Enlightenment origins and never gave rise to counter-Enlightenment movements, either of the Right or Left, as Europe did in the course of the nineteenth century. Thus America never absorbed any of the totalitarian ideologies that Europe spawned—except for small deviant minorities who imported them or were themselves immigrants. Totalitarianism could not take root in America. America remained so to speak, politically innocent and never knew radical evil.

Hartz's theory of the "fragment" has considerable force; it enables him to give a comprehensive reading of the whole history of the United States, the colonial period, the formation of the republic, and the later evolution of democratic government. Hartz maintains that democratic self-government in America did not have to be fought for and won by means of revolution, as it did in Latin America and most of Europe, with the notable exception of Britain, for "in a Protestant individual-ist culture the institutions of self-government immediately take root, and by the time of the Republic a tradition of popular assemblies had been evolved which made Locke quite a common matter of fact."[16]

At this point Hartz's thesis joins hands with that of Weber as he argues that "the Puritan ethic becomes all the more vividly 'independent,' all the more vividly a nation in itself, as the American colonies overtly break with the mother country. Since the ethic itself is used to justify the break, the continuity between ideological and national separations is practically perfect."[17] When the separation came, it "flowed from the political institutionalization of a liberal spirit which had shaped every phase of colonial society as well. And this was why the doctrinal articulation of that spirit was a matter of intoning tradition, not shattering it."[18] Even the new institutional forms that arose were, according to Hartz, not revolutionary:

> There were reforms, some of them vivid, as in the case of the Pennsylvania constitution, which adopted not only manhood suffrage, but a single-house legislature as well. But at no point did the current of change produce anything like a break with tradition that republicanism produced in Latin America.[19]

Hartz is surely overplaying his basic idea of traditional continuities deriving from the nature of the original "fragment." The Constitution of the United States might not have emerged out of revolution in the European or Latin American sense, but it was nevertheless revolutionary for all that, for it was something utterly novel in politics that had to be fought for.

Hartz is more correct when he insists that once the United States is established, democracy in America follows its own trajectory, one quite distinct from any of those taken in Europe. As he has stated, Jacksonian populism and the New Deal were indigenous American developments because democracy in America did not have to contend with either conservatism or socialism: "the American democratic movement did not have to become involved in significant anti-clerical crusades,"[20] nor deal with an organized working-class party. "What replaced socialism—if 'replaced' is the word to use in such a situation—was the tradition of Liberal Reform as manifested by Populism and Progressivism. No one could confuse this movement with socialism."[21] At the opposite pole to socialism, "America stands out as the purest form of 'capitalist democracy.'"[22] And having achieved its own political salvation, America was intent on converting the whole world:

> Nothing betrays more vividly the interior psychic life of the American fragment than the Wilsonian demand that other cultures instantly

behave along American lines. The American cannot grasp the relativity of the form in which his historical substance has been cast.[23]

To this day, making the world safe for democracy has been the main plank of American foreign policy. And it has succeeded to an extent that would have surprised Hartz, for this form of government obviously suits the modern world better than any other. In Churchill's words, it might be the worst government, except for all the others.

As in any experimental test, Latin America acts as the control group in Hartz's study. In all the crucial respects in which the North Americans flourished—those mainly dealing with the Forces of Modernity—the Latins failed. Neither industrial capitalism, nor a rational-legal state, nor science and technology could properly develop in Latin America until late in the twentieth century. Only now are Brazil, Chile, and Mexico catching up, with most of the others still way behind. According to Hartz, the main reason for this poor outcome is that the "fragment" from which they were constituted was antithetical to the Forces of Modernity. The Iberian fragment was feudal with no freehold land tenure; it was monarchical with an autocratic centralized authority structure; it was clerical with the Catholic Church in sole spiritual control; it was obscurantist with the Inquisition repressing free thought, which made modern science impossible. In every such respect it was the contrary to British America where, according to Weber, an "elective affinity" between Protestantism and capitalism, liberalism, science, and individualism came fully into play.

Where Hartz's thesis of the "fragment" coheres with Weber's theories, he has a strong case. But he overplays his hand and ascribes much more to the "fragment" than it can possibly support. According to Hartz everything comes from the "fragment" itself, detached from the whole and its inhibiting repressions, once it is free to develop itself according to its own inner dynamic in a virgin land of limitless opportunities. This theory has some of the features of Darwinian evolution, with the "fragment" reproducing itself free of predators, like the finches on the Galapagos Islands or the rabbits in Australia. Hartz alludes to Darwin, perhaps unconsciously, when he states that "on the world scene today this 'sport' of European culture, bred in isolation from Europe itself, has become a familiar matter." But America is no "sport" or genetic mutation of European culture, and it did not assume its own form of development merely because it was free of natural predators. It is far from the case that it was "bred in isolation," as we shall presently show.

Hartz makes it seem as if being detached from its European whole is all that the "fragment" needed to become America:

> For the greatest agitations of the eighteenth century were in the seventeenth, when the "Mayflower" came; and they were resolved not by self-controlled revolt or fabulous constitutional invention, but through migration, through leaving the "old world" behind. It is obvious, from the standpoint of Europe and the "fragments," that what steered the Americans through the vicissitudes of the Revolution and the Constitutional Convention was a liberal cohesiveness which had been established from the outset of colonial life.[24]

It seems from this that all that mattered was "leaving the old world behind." The Enlightenment, in its Scottish or French versions, did not count for much. The Founding Fathers did not read and study the works of European philosophers and *philosophes*. All contact between the New World and the Old World had been lost. But, of course, we know this was not so.

Hartz makes it seem as if the Americans were stranded on the new continent like Robinson Crusoe on his desert island. All Crusoe could rely on was what he had brought with him, either lodged in his mind or salvaged from the wreck of his ship. So, too, it seems, all the Americans had was what they brought with them in their minds and ships. But this was far from being the case; contact with England and even with continental Europe was never lost or even interrupted, as happened to the Icelanders. There was continual coming and going in both directions. Everything that was available in England was also available in America. Americans read the books that Englishmen and Scotsmen wrote, and even most of those that Frenchmen wrote as well. According to Mennell, as late as 1820 70 percent of titles were by British writers and only 30 percent by Americans.[25] There was continuous movement of people from the British Isles to America; these were not only impoverished immigrants, but also government officials, teachers, preachers, and even writers and thinkers. George Whitefield, for example, came from England to preach in New England and the South between 1730 and 1740, which initiated the first so-called Great Awakening in religion.

What Hartz has presented is a kind of Robinsonade, as if a Swiss Family Robinson had settled America. His thesis works much better for the Quebecois in Canada or the Boers in South Africa, for these settlers had in fact largely lost touch with their home countries and had become isolated. As a consequence, they became crabbed and morbid, obsessed with their religions, Catholicism and Calvinism respectively, which became ingrown and stunted; they were fixated at their point of origin and unable to develop. Such a fate never overtook the Americans, though there were tendencies in that direction, especially inland, away from the Eastern Seaboard and along the frontier.

Hence, Hartz's theory needs to be complemented by a study of the contacts and influences continually exercised by the Old World on the New Word—to the point where eventually that relation was reversed and the Americanization of the world began. But it was always to some extent a two-way matter. America's development must, therefore, be seen in terms of the interplay been the indigenous tendencies displayed by the "fragment" and the outside influences coming across the Atlantic. The one without the other is only half the story of American civilization, which is both a homegrown and an imported product.

The one thing the Americans did not import from Europe was totalitarianism. As we have argued, the indigenous forces of liberal democracy were too strong to give it an opening, despite the efforts of small groups of intellectuals and others to bring in Bolshevism and Nazism or at least anti-Semitism. Such efforts were doomed to fail in the face of American traditions. And so the difficult question arises: How could it be that despite the absence of totalitarianism American civilization was, nevertheless, so badly damaged in the twentieth century?

Notes

1. W. T. Stead, *The Americanization of the World: On the Trend of the Twentieth Century* (Horace Mackley, New York, 1902).
2. John Lukacs, *A New Republic: A History of the United States in the Twentieth Century* (Yale University Press, New Haven, 2004), p. 105.
3. Ibid., p. 97.
4. Thomas P. M. Barnett, *Great Powers* op. cit.
5. Allan Bloom, *The Closing of the American Mind: How Higher Education Has Failed Democracy* (Simon and Schuster, New York, 1987), p. 163.
6. William H. Chafe, *The Rise and Fall of the American Century: The United States from 1890–2009* (Oxford University Press, New York, 2009), p. 2.
7. John Lukacs, *A New Republic*, op. cit., p. 4.
8. Max Weber, "The Protestant Sects and the Spirit of Capitalism," in *From Max Weber*, H. H. Gerth and C. Wright Mills (eds.), op. cit., p. 308.
9. Marianne Weber, *Max Weber: ein Lebensbild* (Tübingen, 1926), p. 301.
10. Max Weber, "Sciences as Vocation", in *From Max Weber*, op. cit., p. 143.
11. John Lukacs, *A New Republic*, op. cit., p. 435.
12. Rémi Brague, *Eccentric Culture: A Theory of Western Civilization*, trans. Samuel Lester (St. Augustine's Press, South Bend, IN, 2002).

13. Louis Hartz (ed.), *The Founding of New Societies: Studies in the History of the United States, Latin America, South Africa, Canada and Australia* (Harcourt, Brace, New York, 1964), p. 3.
14. Ibid., p. 6.
15. Ibid., p. 3.
16. Ibid., p. 75.
17. Ibid., p. 80.
18. Ibid., p. 76.
19. Ibid., p. 76.
20. Ibid., p. 87.
21. Ibid., p. 107.
22. Ibid., p. 119.
23. Ibid., p. 118.
24. Ibid., p. 73.
25. Stephen Mennell, *The American Civilizing Process* (Polity Press, Cambridge, 2007), p. 55.

6

The Destruction of American Civilization

Section I—Political and Social Failures

America never knew totalitarianism. Thus it can act as a control group in an experimental demonstration of the destruction of civilization, which in the case of Europe we have primarily ascribed to totalitarianism. There is no doubt that in Europe totalitarianism was the main culprit, just as colonialism was the villain in Asia, as we shall show. So we might well ask: What is it that accounts for de-civilizing propensities in America? Who or what is to blame?

We can only ascribe responsibility for such an outcome to the main factors of modernization, the Forces of Modernity: industrial capitalism, the rational-legal bureaucratic state, and science and technology. In a previous work, *Beyond Civilization*, we have expounded a theory concerning the catalytic working of the Forces of Modernity in breaking down the complex civilizational fabric of society, culture, and individualism to cruder and more elementary manifestations. In America we can study these catalytic workings as it were in their purity, without disturbance from any complicating factors.

In developing the Forces of Modernity to such a high degree, frequently ahead of the Europeans, American civilization became the victim of its own success. Its very economic, organizational, political, and technical achievements militated against it. What we now call Americanization, exemplifying the modernization characteristic of the Forces of Modernity, stands in a contradictory relation to American civilization; as the former grew the latter shriveled. We will briefly sketch out how this took place before proceeding with more detailed studies.

As American capitalism grew and developed into the huge industrial, financial, and marketing complex that it has now become, it generated an affluent lifestyle for most Americans—but at the cost of concentrating them in the suburbs of big cities, away from the small-town traditions of their ancestors in which they had been brought up; as a result they lost the morality, manners, and civility on which they had formerly prided themselves. The rise of big corporations and the bureaucratization of work meant that most became office employees or so-called organization men (and later organization women as well). This imposed on them all kinds of pressures for conformity and made it difficult for most of them to realize themselves as individuals, except in an egocentric form. Thus the individualism that de Tocqueville described now survives only in dysfunctional relics, such as objection to gun control laws.

The huge expansion of the state and all its bureaucratic agencies, now employing up to a third of the labor force, had a similar effect. And besides its civilian roles, it also exercises a vastly enlarged military function. The military-industrial complex, against which President Eisenhower warned in his valedictory address, has had a disturbing effect on civilization. It infiltrates many aspects of life and distorts them for purposes of waging wars of every variety. It is said that truth is the first casualty of war, and it is also that of Cold War as well, for propaganda gets the better of truth whenever the two are in competition. Research funded by the military has become the lifeblood of the universities, but at the same time it diverts scientific and scholarly effort away from its proper intellectual functions. It shrouds truth in secrecy and buries it in an unmarked grave.

Science and technology, as these are now carried out at the behest of the state and the big corporations, have an even more insidious effect in that they technify all human activities. Working together in tandem with each other as techno-science, they reduce all human ways of proceeding to technical procedures. Everything becomes a matter of routines frequently carried out at least partly by machines, of systematic processes and best-practice methods. The advent of the computer has greatly accelerated the pace of technification, leaving little scope for individual judgment, for creativity, and for inventiveness and adaptation to new circumstances at which humans excel but machines, even the most powerful computers, prove to be incompetent. In the fast-approaching technical world, what room is left for civilization?

All these very general considerations have a bearing on America's greatest civilizational achievement, its liberal democracy. Ever since de Tocqueville's report on politics in the Jacksonian era, there has been appreciation and even admiration for America's vibrant political culture, the formation of public opinion, and its formulation through debates and oratory. The recent film on Lincoln by Stephen Spielberg is a sentimental reminder to Americans of what it was like in those days of yore, because it certainly ain't so no more.

Now a small proportion of Americans take part in the most basic rite of citizenship, the mere minimal act of participation—the casting of a ballot on Election Day. During the presidential election of 1996, only 49 percent of eligible voters bothered to vote; in 2000 it was 50 percent. In elections for the House of Representatives the participation rate is around 35 percent, or close to a third. Clearly most Americans have no wish to vote because it no longer matters to them who wins elections; all politicians are alike as far as they are concerned. Cynicism about politicians and politics in general has never been higher or more corrosive.

It was very different a century ago when the formation of public opinion could not be manipulated by a few media conglomerates and their mogul owners. Once, there were a number of newspapers in every major city, catering to an intelligent and still very literate public. Now the number of papers in the whole country is rapidly diminishing, and the circulation of the few remaining quality ones is shrinking. Those that still garner a mass readership do so by pandering to a semiliterate public by dumbing down their content with pictures and large headlines. But even these might not survive much longer given the competition from television news that is really infotainment.

In the age of electronic media, money buys votes—not through the direct transfer of cash into the pockets of voters, as so often happens in Third World democracies—but through the procurement of advertising space and time in the media. Money also buys media gurus, spin doctors, and other expert advisers who can craft a convincing media image for any politician who employs them; they ghostwrite speeches, arrange media and photographic opportunities, stage mock debates to coach the politician in delivering preprepared one-line repartees. As a result, most electors have no idea who it is they are voting into office, for the media illusion is all pervasive. Only years later does the truth emerge at the hands of discerning historians.

Thus it has taken all this time until now for an eminent scholar, Stephen Graubart, to reveal to us what kind of men have acceded to the purple after the Second World War, and how the office of the imperial presidency was created in this period. He explains how "a presidency that once enjoyed great dignity, relying on its republican simplicity, became increasingly royal—some prefer to see it as imperial—and this created vulnerabilities that those who crafted the presidency in the eighteenth century had failed to anticipate."[1] The greatest vulnerability revealed itself in the fact that as the office became more powerful, so the men who occupied it became more puny. "Theodore Roosevelt... Woodrow Wilson, Franklin Roosevelt and Harry Truman, these were giants of an extinct era, political dinosaurs in a late-twentieth century America dominated by very different kinds of men."[2] Those who came later were not mere dwarves perched on the shoulders of giants, but cripples who could not even climb so high.

> To describe all these transformations, to understand how a presidency that once attracted men of learning has lost that distinction, calls for a consideration of more than the craftiness of political entrepreneurs who understand the rules of the primary election game. A critical gaze must be cast on an electorate that has tolerated and at times seemed positively beguiled by the men they have chosen. . . . For what one acerbic critic has described as the 'post-literate generation,' historical knowledge is discounted and hyperbole rules. The far greater hazards once posed by Hitler's Nazism and Stalin's Communism are made to appear almost inconsequential besides the threat of contemporary terrorism, where patriotism is imagined to be the American solution to a problem that calls for intelligence and invention in their traditional meanings.[3]

Graubart and other political scientists, such as Elizabeth Drew, have focused on a basic flaw that has arisen in recent times due to the system for selecting candidates through primaries, which has given rise to a contradiction between the attributes required to secure preselection and win the election and those necessary to exercise presidential rule once in office.[4]

> The proposition that the new system gave an advantage to skilled politicians who knew how to use it to advance themselves and that it simply created the potential for new mediocrity in the White House, would have been thought irreverent, offensive to those who believed in the virtues of popular choice. Pulchritude and pleasing TV presence, recognized as crucial in the Kennedy-Nixon encounter, became even more critical as the capacity to raise funds from all who imagined they would be advantaged by the victory of their candidate.[5]

Nixon, who lost out to Kennedy but became president later, was perhaps the last man who had some competence to manage the office and wield its powers, though sometimes for dubious and once for criminal ends. All his successors had no such capacity. None, except for George Bush, had any executive experience, all were novices who had to learn their craft on the job, and some managed to do so provided they were granted two terms. Clinton, "a superb political campaigner, once installed in the White House fumbled badly and constantly."[6] Obama, also a great campaigner with a moving personal story to tell, once in office proved himself weak and ineffectual, unable to deal with any of the major problems confronting America.[7] It is to be hoped that he has learned something in his first term and will improve in the second.

Under a weak president and with the mutual blocking powers of the two houses of Congress when they are under the control of different parties, the United States threatens to become paralyzed and ungovernable. Even the most urgent business becomes impossible to resolve. Climate change legislation cannot pass both houses and can only be dealt with by presidential decree in a partial fashion. Action to reduce the budget deficit and halt the growth of the national debt to unsustainable levels seems beyond the capacity of the political system. There are numerous other major matters where nothing can be done by legislative means. Often the only way to resolve such a logjam is by means of a Supreme Court ruling, which means that it has in effect become an unelected and unacknowledged legislative body.

One major cause for the political impasse into which the United States is falling is its division into what Disraeli called "two nations," and their growing mutual animosity. On the one side are the so-called liberals: all those who espouse political correctness—that is, libertarian views on race and ethnicity, sex and gender, and personal relations—and who evince strong environmentalist concerns. Totally antithetical to them are the traditionalists who identify themselves as born again Christians and who constitute between 35 to 40 percent of the population. For such people the Bible is literally the word of God, and they also believe in miracles. Apart from such traditional beliefs, a staggering proportion of Americans also hold to views about angels and demons, UFOs and aliens who supposedly regularly visit the earth.[8] Koch and Smith comment that "the polls indicate a revival of belief in magic that has no precedent since the Middle Ages."[9] All this is taking place in a nation that is the leading scientific power on earth. It is also in stark contrast to public attitudes in Europe. Is America abandoning its Enlightenment legacy and sinking into a new obscurantism?

In both of these "nations" of America there are symptoms of a failure of rationality, and this bodes ill for American civilization. According to Koch and Smith this is due to "the growth in the last half-century of anti-intellectualism. Influenced by television and the fashionable doctrine of relativism—that one view is as good as another—we are witnessing the elevation of emotion over reason, of personal 'relevance' and conviction over hard thinking."[10]

All such problems are aggravated, if not caused, by the multiple failures of American education. Measures that were meant to solve problems have only made them worse. Much hope was held out for what computers would do for learning among children. Not only was this not realized, but computers seem to have made things worse. So-called computer literacy makes for illiteracy, as it has been shown to have pernicious effects on the capacity to concentrate, to take in an extended text, to evaluate an argument, or to follow a theory, for the information processing of knowledge breaks up everything into discrete facts or disconnected fragments of information.[11] The incapacity of the current generation of university students, even from the most prestigious places, to pen a coherent essay in the way their grandparents used to do is at least partly attributable to such developments. Even worse, among elementary school children the very ability to handle a pen is lapsing. Apart from such educational difficulties children are experiencing social problems from the "virtual" nature of their relationships due to reliance on the social media.

The poor quality of education in America can be accurately assessed by the fall in SAT scores over the years. Increasing years of schooling make little difference. John Lukacs has noted this curious paradox: "that the progress of universal education has proceeded together with the decline of culture and even with the decline of literate civilization during the twentieth century is a sorry fact at the time of the passing of the Modern Age."[12] He adds further that "this has been happening in many nations," which indicates that it is a general civilizational failing and not merely an idiosyncratic fault of America alone. It means that literacy in a cultural sense is faltering and could degenerate still further.

The combined effect of poor education and intellectually impoverished media leads to a general stupefaction where people cease to want to know much about their own society or the outside world. Such people become less and less competent to make any decisions on political issues. John Lukacs comments on this condition:

> But we ought to be aware of an attendant contemporary condition, which is the American people's general lack of interest and considerable

ignorance of world events. This had, and still has, much to do with the continuous decline of education in the schools and with the obvious deterioration of their information in the television age (notwithstanding slogans about the Information Revolution and the Internet World).[13]

This benighted condition of so many of the American people is not only of concern to American leaders but to those of the world as a whole, given that so many of the crucial decisions concerning the world are made in America.

Section II—Middle-class Hopes and Delusions

What was it that brought America to this parlous state at the end of the twentieth century, when it had such promising prospects at the start of that century? Just when it seemed that America might be able to take over from a devastated Europe ravaged by the Events of the Twentieth Century, America proved itself not up to the task. Western civilization did not get a new lease of life across the Atlantic.

According to John Lukacs, America did experience an ephemeral "bourgeois interlude" during the first half of the twentieth century, when it looked as if it might be able to advance Western civilization by continuing the great bourgeois age of Europe in the nineteenth century, up to the First World War. Unfortunately, it proved not to be. Whether this failure presages the "end of civilization as we know it" is the question Lukacs asks, and replies that "it is not yet answerable!" We have dealt with many similar questions in *Beyond Civilization* and shown that there are many possibilities still left open, ranging from the end of the world as we know it, at worst, to a preservation of what is still left of civilization, at best. We discussed how the best outcome might be achieved under a number of general policy headings, such as the restoration of society, the conservation of culture, and the recovery of individualism.[14]

To assess whether there are any such prospects for America in the next half-century, we must consider what went wrong in the last half-century, hoping thereby to avoid repeating the same mistakes. Why did Lukacs's so-called "bourgeois interlude" prove so ephemeral? Why could America not make better use of the cultural resources flowing in from Europe? American society showed itself highly receptive to the large number of talented people seeking refuge, yet their influence was soon attenuated. As we shall see, the situation in the sciences was different from that in the arts and other spheres of cultural endeavor. In general, however, the refugees and immigrants arriving before the

Second World War made significant but limited and only short-term contributions. America simply could not absorb all that Europe in its desperate state made available to it. What explains this apparent failure?

Part of the explanation lies in the fact that what John Lukacs calls "the embourgoisement of the American people"[15] was, in fact, not that at all, but merely a vast expansion of the middle classes due to rising standards of living. Lukacs took it that the American social system was evolving into a European bourgeois one, and he believed that it would have the same civilizational consequence as in Europe.

> Between 1895 and 1955 the standards of a large number of American people—of their material comforts, their families and their manners, their social civilities as well as their cultural and educational aspirations—came to resemble (and even, on occasion, to supersede) in many ways, though not in all, the standards of the lives of European and English bourgeois families. By the early twentieth century important strata of the American people were living interior lives that, while admittedly not identical with those in Europe, marked a civilization that may be called urban and urbane and bourgeois.[16]

What is at issue with this account, as Lukacs himself realizes, is whether this was culturally a bourgeoisie in the European sense or merely an affluent middle class. It is now apparent that it was the latter rather than the former.

Whatever aspirations Americans had toward bourgeois cultural standards in the first half of the twentieth century, they disappeared rapidly in the second half. As Lukacs notes, "while the embourgoisement of the American people had been faster than that of many of the peoples of Europe, so has been its dissolution."[17] What brought this dissolution about were the new styles of life and living arrangements that rapidly came into effect after the Second World War—material affluence and suburbanization. The two went together, but we shall concentrate on the second first.

American civilization was founded on farming communities, small rural towns, and major cities of trade and commerce. During the period of industrialization and large-scale immigration after the Civil War, the bulk of the population shifted into the big metropolitan centers. The mechanization of farming meant that very few people were left on the land. After the Second World War a further dislocation of population took place, as those who could afford it—and thanks to rising salaries many now could—left the city centers for the bourgeoning suburbs springing up on their peripheries. Thus mass suburban living spread, based on motorcar transportation and home amenities, and this became the preferred way of life of most Americans, despite its cultural shortcomings and de-civilizing propensities. The city centers suffered an even worse fate as they were left for those too poor to be able to escape, and rapidly degenerated into slums, creating urban blight or uninhabited commercial enclaves heavily policed for protection, in the so-called downtown areas.

The effects on civilized forms of life of these population shifts was disastrous, for anything previously associated with city life, such as civility and urbanity, soon disappeared. As cities themselves became human jungles, where a struggle for survival was fought, any thought of civilization at all was stifled by the prevailing savagery. The suburbs, too, soon lost their cultural veneer, for, as Lukacs remarks, "it is still an open question whether a suburban people can develop something resembling a high level of culture."[18] But even a low level of culture becomes more difficult as people become socially isolated in their detached dwellings and totally dependent for any culture at all on the mass media.

We can follow the demise of American culture step by step via the decline of newspapers, the printed medium that had carried so much weight in the period 1880 to 1940. Lukacs calls this the "Golden Age of the Press"; yet he grants that it "carried the seeds of its own demise."[19] In a capitalist system, the press is vulnerable not only because of competition from new electronic technologies, but also because newspapers must be financed. They depend to an ever-growing extent on advertising, and have to compete with the new media of radio and television and the Internet, which are more amendable than newspapers to advertising sponsorship. After the Second World War, newspapers gradually had to resort to more pictures with fewer articles, and utilize bigger headlines and shorter sentences to retain readers who were less and less literate, due to the educational shortcomings we previously discussed. Now even the readership of such dumbed-down productions is declining. The competition from the Internet will most probably prove fatal, as most of the advertising revenue is shifting online. Thus the combination of capitalism and new technology has almost destroyed whatever common knowledge and public intelligence was maintained by the press.

The same combination of capitalism and technology brought about what Adorno and Horkheimer called the Culture Industry, which

149

had consequences for popular culture that are similar to those out-lined above for the press. True popular culture is always local, as it is addressed to a specific community of aficionados. It has gradually been displaced by mass culture, created for a broad public of anonymous consumers. This process occurred first in America and is now sweep-ing the world. Global culture, produced largely in America, is having the same effect on local popular cultures everywhere; both inside and outside America there is less and less of it left.

During the first half of the twentieth century, even the growth of mass culture seemed somewhat promising. Hollywood produced many cinematic masterpieces in this period and cannot be sneeringly written-off from an elitist European vantage point, as Adorno and Horkheimer tend to do. The Broadway musical developed as a quintes-sentially American operetta form not inferior to European operettas. Jazz was a unique musical expression of American blacks that found favor around the world. However, the Tin Pan Alley songs, pleasing as they are, cannot be considered examples of genuine popular culture, because they cater to a mass public. Nevertheless, they are superior to later pop-musical forms, because at least they can be memorized and sung. During the second half of the twentieth century, all of these vital cultural expressions petered out. Hollywood had to meet the competi-tion of free-to-air television and so resorted to big-budget technical innovations and spectacular effects to woo viewers, eventually coming to rely on blockbuster productions for a largely juvenile audience, who constituted the only regular cinemagoers. After Sondheim, the Broad-way musical more or less ceased, to be replaced by global stage shows, like those produced by Lloyd Webber. Pop music succumbed first to juvenile rock and roll and finally to rap and hip-hop; the latter can be neither memorized nor sung, and though they seem to be popular expressions of ghetto culture, are actually ghetto-chic, manufactured for white middle-class consumption.

The final death knell of culture, even in its popular forms, has probably been sounded by the advent of the computer and the Inter-net. Americans took to the computer with great avidity, especially adolescents and children, who see in it a wonderful toy they can play with. Americans have always been keen on gadgets of all kinds, and the computer is simply the last in a long line of devices. But as far as culture and the intellect are concerned, it is the most dangerous of all, for it invades the mind and shapes it according to its own mechanical specifications. A process we might call the mechanization of the mind is taking place in all spheres of intelligence, whether it is secretarial work or higher learning; everything is being transformed to make it compatible with information processing. Information has become the new coin of all intellectual transactions, and every exchange is mediated by it. The damage to thinking and learning is literally incalculable; it cannot be measured by quantifiable criteria, but it can be judged by the qualitative loss of standards in respect of work skills, learning abilities, and literacy in general.

As we have stated previously, civilization in America is declining due to the catalytic action of the Forces of Modernity. We have just examined what the combined impact of capitalism and technology has been to popular culture and public intelligence. We can show analogous trends in the effects on mass education of a vastly expanded state bureaucracy. The military-industrial complex also had a damaging effect on scientific research because most postwar research was funded by the military; even scholarship in the higher reaches of academia was affected, since obtaining a research grant became the substitute for having an idea or a theory to test. Obviously, the competition for these was fierce. *Bildung* in the bourgeois European sense could not develop in America, at least not after the Second World War.

In what follows we shall examine in somewhat greater detail the development of the sciences and arts in America during the twentieth century. Obviously, they have had very different histories, in some ways the opposites of each other. America emerged from the nineteenth century with very high standards in literature, not inferior to any in Europe. It maintained these for roughly the first half of the twentieth century, perhaps until well into the 1960s. But from then on there has been a steady decline. In the sciences, it was just the converse, for American science in the nineteenth century was backward compared to that of Europe. It had steadily been catching up during the first half of the century, and during the second half it came into its own and surpassed Europe. We shall next examine the significance for American civilization of these two different trajectories of high culture.

Section III—Science in America

Science has undoubtedly been the great success story of culture in America during the twentieth century. By science we mean here only the natural sciences, for the social sciences have not done so well at all, despite some exceptional achievements, and the humanities are by comparison almost failures. American natural sciences have triumphed, of that there can be little doubt. Since the end of the Second World War, a disproportionate number of Nobel prizes have gone to Americans, around 58 percent, though many of these scientists came originally from Europe. Now they might come from anywhere in the world, as America draws the best scientific talents to its universities and research laboratories. This process began soon after the First World War and has continued ever since.

American science was transformed by the huge influx of refugees, especially around the time of the Second World War, and particularly Jews from Germany. But there were many others as well, all fleeing totalitarianism: Russians escaping the Bolshevik regime, Italians fleeing from Fascism and Germans from Nazism. But there were also many British and some French and Italians who sought temporary refuge in the United States during the war and stayed on to make their careers there. They came from all over Europe, for it was in America that both safety and opportunity beckoned.

To their great credit, the Americans received them all with open arms. As Ulmen states, the "history of virtually all these immigrants is witness to the openness of American Society."[20] America could employ them and make good use of them because it was rapidly expanding its institutions of higher learning and research, universities were multiplying, new institutes of technology were being founded, and all leading companies that were dependent on scientific research had laboratories, some devoted to pure research, such as Bell Labs. American institutions had the finances and resources, both human and material, to undertake every kind of investigation into the natural world.

Thus the Americans together with the European refugees were able to build on the European discoveries of the early part of the twentieth century and carry them further in the subsequent period. In no science was this more evident than in physics, where it led to great achievements. It was not merely the practical application of nuclear physics in building the A-bomb—a world-shaking event in itself—that mattered in science, there was a steady stream of theoretical findings in what became known as high-energy physics, which uncovered the constitution of the nucleus and discovered the fundamental constituents of matter, or quarks. What is now known as the Standard Model was established and has remained.

America made one field in particular its own, that of information theory and information processing, centered on the application of the computer, a wartime invention made in Britain and America, which

America more or less appropriated because the British were too poor and too opinionated to carry it further, after the very promising start made by Turing. In America, von Neumann, a refugee mathematician collaborating with American engineers, established the basic architecture of computers and the computer science that governed computer operations. From then on, bigger and faster computers were built in America and given a vast array of functions, to the point where no scientific work could be done that was not computer assisted; much of this work was, unfortunately, focused on weapons research.

In some cases the Americans developed new sciences on the basis of the computer, the most important being cognitive sciences, such as cognitive psychology; the computer also had its uses in linguistics, anthropology, neuroscience, and others.[21] A start in this direction was already made before the advent of the computer in the theory of cybernetics, which was developed by Wiener and Rosenblueth in the context of a series of meetings of scientists called the Macy Conferences. These were attended by such luminaries as von Neumann, McCulloch, Pitts, Shannon, Licklider, Bateson, Mead, and von Foerster, as well as Savage, Wiener, Rosenblueth, and many others. Most of these were or came to be associated with MIT, which became the nursery of cognitive science, artificial intelligence, and allied activities directed at the mechanization of mind.[22] Such people as Chomsky, Miller, Pinker, Minsky, Papert, Marr, Simon and Newell (Simon and Newell we are not at MIT, but an allied technical institution, Carnegie Mellon) were jointly or individually involved in the pursuit of this scientific project. There were allied developments in other sciences that went along parallel lines of mathematization and systematization of human behavior, such as mathematical economics (associated at MIT with Samuelson), game theory (the invention of von Neumann and Morgenstern), operations theory, decision theory, rational choice theory, and others.

Philosophers, too, played their part in all this at MIT, where the young Putnam, Fodor, Pylyshyn and Katz developed the functional theory of mind, arguing that the mind is simply the software component of the hardware that is the brain. Fodor took a modular approach to the mind, arguing that it was composed of semiautonomous faculties or modules quite distinct from each other. The answer to the question as to whether the mind or the brain is a machine was already preordained by this whole approach. All these researchers took for granted that the mind/brain was a machine or information processing device like a computer, only more powerful.

The close association with MIT of most of the scientists and philosophers involved in the project for the mechanization of the mind is reason enough to dub the resultant image of the mind the MIT-Mind. The fact that this institution, as well as many of the others similarly aligned, are institutes of technology is, of course, highly significant. It reveals the leading role that technology plays and exposes the strengths and weaknesses of American science. The contrary approach to the MIT-Mind was also technologically generated; it arose at the California Institute of Technology where connectionism was revived after a long hiatus by the rediscovery of so-called Hopfield nets in the early 1980s. In honor that it might be dubbed the Caltech-Mind. However, its further development was spread throughout California, especially in San Diego where Rumelhart, McClelland, the Churchills, and Sejnowski were resident. They had an outpost in New Mexico at the Santa Fe Institute. The Caltech-Mind is in most respects the opposite of the MIT-Mind, being wholly associationist, but it is also mechanically generated based on connectionist nets.

The project to mechanize the mind, out of which the MIT-Mind and Caltech- Mind arose, clearly developed from traditions in philosophy and science that were native to America, such as pragmatism and behaviorism, even though it went beyond them. But it received a huge boost from the triumphs of technology that emerged out of the Second World War—the Manhattan Project and, of course, the invention and development of the computer for military purposes at the same time—and all the subsequent technological achievements, many of them connected to Cold War research. In fact, much of the funding for all those involved in developing the MIT-Mind came from military sources—Licklider was the leading conduit in this at MIT. This funding, almost without limit, produced a tremendous amount of scientific activity. Much was accomplished, but still far more was promised to secure grants. What was promised was in effect the solution of the age-old mystery of the problem of the mind, to be achieved by science alone without recourse to any metaphysics or philosophy. The solution always seemed just around the corner, but it never came. It is still nowhere in sight.

Humanist critics of the MIT-Mind, as well as the Caltech- Mind, generally Europeans, such as Jean-Pierre Dupuy and Jean-Pierre Chageux, but also some disenchanted Americans, such as Hilary Putnam in his old age, have long observed that it is nothing but an updated version of the Enlightenment "homme machine," as expounded by La Mettrie.

Such people, averse to reductive materialism, mechanization, computational functionalism, pragmatism, and other technology-minded approaches reject such conceptions of the mind. Another reason to reject the MIT-Mind in particular is that in the sciences of man it tends to favor innateness and modules rather than learning and culture. It relies on geneticist approaches that see most human capacities as the products of evolution that, so-to-speak, nature has hardwired in the brain and endowed it with inbuilt capacities that require no learning. Chomsky was a pioneer in this regard, considering universal grammar to be simply an innate mechanism peculiar to the human brain. Something analogous for many other capabilities is proposed in evolutionary anthropology by Cosmides and Tooby and their European ally, Sperber, according to what is known as massive modularity. Obviously, such views tend to negate the role that society, culture, and history play in human development and are fundamentally anti-humanistic.

Unfortunately, critics of the MIT-Mind or the Caltech-Mind or other cognate scientific approaches have, as yet, no alternative scientifically respectable model to offer. Something along the lines of the Maturana-Varela *autopoesis* theorizing in biology has not yet proved itself. But the field is still open and waiting for new developments, for the mystery of the mind has not been resolved.

When we turn from the natural sciences to the social sciences, a quite different picture of American achievements presents itself. The social sciences have done neither as well as the natural sciences nor as badly as the humanities. To some extent the social sciences have suffered from the formalistic and mathematicizing approaches that have been encouraged by similar developments in the natural sciences. The urge to make the social sciences genuinely scientific—that is, to model them on the natural sciences (for example, to make them quantifiable and experimentally demonstrable)—has generally had poor results and led to the neglect of methods more germane to the study of human thought and action. Hence, systems theory, rational choice theory, and game theory have tended to produce scant results of no great significance; sometimes their misuse in contexts where they should not be applied has had dangerous consequences. The application of game theory to nuclear deterrence, for example, encouraged such risky ventures as plans for limited nuclear warfare.

Setting such theories aside, we might look at the state of the more classic social sciences in America, such as sociology, political science, and anthropology; economics in its neoclassical mathematical version has entered such a technical state that no discussion by someone who is not an expert is possible, yet the failure of the mass of economists to either foresee the global financial crisis or to have much to offer once it came, says something about the inadequacies of this kind of economics. In the social sciences, as in the natural sciences, we must consider the influence of refugees from Europe and their impact on the pursuit of these disciplines in America. But here a big difference emerges, for while the natural scientists could easily take up the European theories and develop them further, but this was not so simple in the social sciences. We shall consider the fate of two major European theorists in America—Marx and Weber.

Both Marx and Weber came to America in the baggage of the refugees. But once they were planted in the inhospitable American soil they did not take root properly and produced only stunted growths. The aversion to Marx is partly explicable by the strong American hostility to Communism and by the difficulties Marxists had in separating Marx the social theorist from Marx the revolutionary socialist. But there were no such problems with Weber; why should he have been so poorly understood in America? That he was so badly misunderstood is evident from examples such as the deplorable conception of charisma entertained by Friedrich and Brzezinski, highly acclaimed professors at Harvard, or Hannah Arendt's misconception which we criticized in chapter 3. Despite valiant efforts by some Americans, such as Talcott Parsons and C. Wright Mills, Weber did not effectively transform American social science; it went on much as before. Ulmen provides some of the reasons:

> Incorporation of some of Marx's and Weber's concepts and perspectives into the American social sciences never fundamentally transformed their character. . . . There is no denying the profound influence of Marx and Weber on the American intellectual milieu, or the profound impact of the intellectual immigrants in the universities and beyond. But neither this influence nor the impact succeeded in making history and theory at home in America. . . . Weber's works, which were translated piecemeal, were never fully appreciated. His methodology is stressed but not his historical approach. . . . [This] has led to the ignoring of Weber's more significant contributions to the science of society and history.[23]

The nub of Ulmen's explanation for the failure of European theory to catch on in America—and he is mostly concerned with the work of Wittfogel, which we shall examine in chapter 7—is the cultural difference that separates an European intellectual milieu from an American academic environment. We have already alluded to this difference in quoting Weber's caricature of the differences in attitude to studies that separates the American student from the European (see chapter 5). Writ large, it is the difference between the old German professor and his current American academic counterpart. Many of the German professors or intellectuals who came to America as refugees could successfully negotiate this difference, but some, such as Wittfogel, could not. As Ulmen explains:

> For intellectuals, however, it is the character of the intellectual milieu and university life that is decisive. The character of university life in America was radically different from that of Germany, the country from which many of the refugees came. . . . Yet transition from membership in an elitist group primarily concerned with research to membership in a broad-based democratic system of education with an emphasis on teaching was not as difficult as the transition to an American intellectual milieu. . . . But coming from a tradition grounded in history and theory, they found adjustment to the essentially a-historical pragmatic American tradition difficult, in some cases impossible.[24]

Wittfogel, who combines Marx and Weber in an unusual fashion, was one of these who found it impossible.

What made it impossible was largely the typical American segregation of university teaching and research into departments, which in effect functioned as compartments hermetically sealed off from each other. To what department could such a man as Wittfogel belong, not to speak of Marx or Weber? In fact, there were as many Marxes and Webers in America as there were departments that touched on single aspects of their work. The Weber of American sociology is not the same as the Weber of political science or economics or law or religious studies, et cetera, and it becomes very difficult to reconcile these Webers with one another. And some Webers, such as those of music or ethics or philosophy, are not represented in America at all. And what student can cope with even one of these Webers when he or she knows so little history or theory, far less even than their predecessors? As Allan Bloom reports: "Today's select students know so much less, are so much more cut off from traditions, are so much slacker intellectually, that they make their predecessors look like prodigies of cultures."[25] If anything, the situation is even worse at present than when Bloom wrote.

Despite the fact that Weber was so poorly understood, his technical vocabulary became part of the social theory jargon that perme-
ated everyday discourse. Bloom asks, "Who in 1920 would have
believed that Max Weber's technical sociological terminology would
someday be the very language of the United States, the land of the
Philistines, itself in the meantime become the most powerful nation
in the world?"[26] Weber would not have been surprised by this latter
outcome, but he would have been astonished had he known that
something similar would be done to Nietzsche and Freud, the other
great German thinkers whom the refugee intellectuals had brought
with them to America. Their translation and transplantation across
the Atlantic was highly influential, though superficial, because what
they stood for was so much against the prevailing liberal temper of
American culture, with its roots in the Enlightenment. Such counter-
Enlightenment thinkers, with their sophisticated intellectuality, held
out to American students tantalizing prospects of an alternative to
their own culture, but they could not make much headway in America.
Bloom laments the passing of the brief era in American education
when such hopes were entertained:

> Obviously, then, the glory days of social science from the point of view
> of liberal education are over. Gone is the time when Marx, Freud and
> Weber, philosophers and interpreters of the world, were just precur-
> sors of what was to be America's intellectual coming of age, when
> youngsters could join the charms of science and self-knowledge, when
> there was the expectation of a universal theory of man that would
> unite the university and contribute to progress, harnessing Europe's
> intellectual depth and heritage with our vitality.[27]

At present, as Bloom goes on, "the hopes for unity of the social science
have faded; it cannot present a common front. It is a series of discrete
disciplines and sub-disciplines."[28]

As for the humanities, Bloom's verdict is even more damning, and,
if anything, they have greatly deteriorated since his time. There is now
a real possibility that they will vanish from the educational scene in all
but name, except perhaps in a few traditional universities and colleges.
The reasons for this are those that Bloom has already given:

> The professors of humanities are in an impossible situation and do
> not believe in themselves or what they do. Like it or not, they are
> essentially involved in interpreting and transmitting old books, pre-
> serving what we call tradition, in a democratic order where tradition

is not privileged. They are partisans of the leisured and the beautiful in a place where evident utility is the only passport.[29]

In our time only a few humanities professors are any longer engaged in "interpreting and transmitting old books"; most of the others concern themselves with newly minted disciplines such as culture studies, gender studies, ethnic studies, eco-cultural studies, and numerous others. Not only old books, but books in general are being replaced by so-called texts that might have nothing bookish about them, consisting largely of information and illustration. How did this disaster come about?

A century ago the humanities in America were in a promising state. Philosophy flourished, with a number of outstanding thinkers, such as Peirce, James, and Dewey of the Pragmatist school native to America, together with many others. Leading Europeans, such as Whitehead and Russell, taught in America, and major European schools were represented. Today, so-called Continental philosophy is a minority interest, while the great majority of philosophy departments have hardened into analytic philosophy, frequently in close collusion with the cognitive sciences. The MIT-Mind is as prevalent among philosophers as among scientists. How this situation has arisen is a long story that cannot be told here. The refugee philosophers played a part in it, especially members of the so-called Vienna circle who espoused logical positivism, and also immigrants from England who expounded linguistic philosophy; both groups played a positive and negative role at once that is difficult to untangle. Other philosophical refugees had far less influence and did not really catch on in America. It is a similar story in psychology, where the Gestaltists, for example, could make no headway against the prevailing behaviorism.

The story of literary criticism in this period is in many ways also similar. At the start of the twentieth century there were some outstanding literary critics, such as Babbitt, T. S. Eliot's teacher, and Eliot himself, though all his critical work was done in England. Later, under the influence of Richards, who taught at Harvard, and Empson and Leavis in England, there arose the school of New Critics, mainly based in the South and allied to the Southern Agrarian literary movement. Criticism and literature had not yet parted ways. During the Second World War period, America was filled with refugee critics and litterateurs, many of whom remained there permanently. Among these were Auerbach, Poulet, and Jakobson, the latter a leading exponent of linguistics as well as a critic. They had no marked influence on literary studies in America. It was only much later, beginning with the 1970s, that French avant-garde intellectuals, led by Derrida at Yale, inaugurated the so-called turning to theory known as deconstruction. It is difficult to explain why this particularly arcane approach became so entrenched in many American humanistic disciplines. It has left the affected disciplines, in particular specialist fields that are intent on cultural studies, struggling with a theoretical jargon that many fellow scholars, not to mention students, find incomprehensible and some ridicule its pretensions. The humanities in the American university are thus in a sorry state at present.

The great age of the American university more or less coincided with what John Lukacs termed the "bourgeois interlude," roughly the period from 1890 till 1960. The newly remodeled universities, with Johns Hopkins in the lead, combined the best features of undergraduate studies derived from the British universities with the best of postgraduate research based on German practice. This university system easily absorbed the large number of refugees from the Continent, as well as other academic immigrants, mainly from Britain. The first signs that something was going wrong occurred in the late 1950s as a result of the Sputnik scare, when it was wrongly believed that America had fallen behind the Soviet Union in scientific education, just as it had supposedly fallen behind in missile numbers. This led to a surge of funding to the technical faculties, including those intent on developing the MIT-Mind. The result was the rise of the multiversity, a huge congeries of faculties and departments, seen as a corporation to be run on business principles.

From then on, like the inland American rivers, the universities have been getting ever wider and shallower. The student movement from the mid-1960s onward certainly did not improve standards; in fact, affirmative action programs and other such methods of using the universities to ameliorate social ills have had the effect of lowering standards still further. In the subsequent era of "greed is good," the universities became gateways to Wall Street and other such money-making destinations.

All in all, in summing up the achievements and failures of the American universities in the natural sciences, social sciences, and humanities the words of George Friedman ring true:

> American culture does not deal easily with the true and the beautiful. It values getting things done and not worrying too much about why whatever thing you are doing is important.[30]

160

According to Friedman, "American culture is an uneasy melding of the Bible and the computer, of traditional values and radical innovation."[31] This corresponds approximately to the two "nations" that we previously identified as inhabiting America, the born-again Christians and other religious fundamentalists on one side, and the tech-savvy libertarians on the other. However, the latter are more important than the former, for "it is the computer that is reshaping American culture and is the real foundation of American cultural hegemony."[32]

The computer, as Friedman stresses, is more than just a machine or useful tool; "the computer represents both a radical departure from previous technology, and a new way of looking at reason . . . since it reduces all information—music, film and the written word—to a number."[33] This, as we have seen, is the basis of the project for the mechanization of mind and the constitution of the MIT-Mind. All this has profound cultural consequences that are de-civilizing, for the computer acts as a catalyst in breaking down complex cultural forms, the products of centuries and even millennia of historical development, into the elemental quasi-primitive manifestations of global culture. Friedman seconds this view:

> Computing culture is also, by definition, barbaric. The essence of barbarism is the reduction of culture to a simple, driving force that will tolerate no diversion or competition. The way the computer is designed, the manner in which it is programmed and the way it has evolved represents a powerful reductionist force. It constitutes not reason contemplating its complexity, but reason reducing itself to its simplest expression and justifying itself through practical achievement.[34]

A full and complete study of what this means calls for a Kantian critique that might be entitled *Critique of Mechanical Reason.* Such a work has yet to be written.

In assessing why "American culture does not deal easily with the true and the beautiful," as Friedman puts it, we have so far dealt only with the true. In the next section we go on to consider the beautiful. Keats declared that "beauty is truth, truth beauty," but in America beauty has fared much worse than truth.

Section IV—Art in America

The contrast between the history of science and the history of art in America could not be starker. Science started very poorly and did very well, while art started very well and did very poorly. At the start of the twentieth century, high art in America was full of promise; by the end of the century this had almost completely evaporated. At the start, in most fields of artistic endeavor Americans were on a par with the best European masters. In the field of literature Americans were particularly distinguished. Some of the best writers, such as Henry James, T. S. Eliot, and Ezra Pound were expatriates, but there were still many great writers who remained in America: Fitzgerald, Faulkner, Hemingway, and later Saul Bellow. American dramatists were particularly talented: the sequences of plays by O'Neil, Williams, and Miller were as good as anything produced at the time in Europe. A similar story can be told in some of the other arts. In architecture, among the outstanding world masters were Sullivan, Wright, and Kahn. America was less well endowed with painters, but the late-nineteenth-century realist tradition, starting with Homer and Eakins and continuing with Bellows and Hopper, produced works equal to any of the great European realist paintings of the period. Music was not so well developed; Gershwin, Copeland and Bernstein, to mention the most well-known, produced fine but minor works. Unfortunately, the great Modernist masters—Bartok, Schoenberg, and Stravinsky, who had been in America since they fled Europe in the 1930s—seem to have inspired only minor imitators and thus had little effect on the quality of American composition.

With such promising beginnings, what can account for the artistic decline that followed? One explanation lies in the futile and self-defeating attempt to take over and outdo the radical avant-garde of European Modernism, which had begun to blaze such a triumphant path into the future in the period prior to 1914, and which continued sporadically to shine in the 1920s and 1930s and sometimes even into the 1940s among the older artists. But these Modernist achievements were not continued in America; they were merely repeated in an exaggerated fashion that ultimately rendered them absurd.

We can study the way this process of reductio-ad-absurdum, literally a reduction to nothing, unfolded in painting. To begin with, American artists made a sincere and honest effort to absorb the lessons of European Modernism, to which they were first exposed by the Armory show of 1913. After the First World War a quartet of painters arose who initiated abstract art in America: Graham, Davis, Gorky, and de Kooning, who, apart from Davis, were immigrants to America from various quarters.[35] They were active from the mid-1920s to the mid-1940s without having much to show for their efforts by way of acknowledgement or success, which they certainly deserved.

Then the Second World War intervened, and New York was filled with refugee painters; the Surrealists were there in force: Ernst, Dali, Masson; there were a few German expressionists, Gross and Beckmann; and there were many abstractionists, most notably Mondrian. The Dadaist, Duchamp, had already settled in America much earlier. Many of these were closely associated with Peggy Guggenheim and the forthcoming Guggenheim museum. The effect of all these personalities on American artists was to make them want to surpass what the Europeans were doing. Foremost among these was Jackson Pollock, who together with others founded the New York school of abstract expressionists or "action painters." They pushed abstraction to its limit and made nonsense of it.

However, they enjoyed great success because they had the backing of extremely authoritative supporters: Alfred Barr, director of MOMA; Leo Castelli, a wealthy gallery owner; and influential art critics, such as Clement Greenberg and Harold Rosenberg. They attracted the attention of journals, such as *Life Magazine*, which in April 1949 presented Pollock as perhaps the greatest artist in America. As we shall see, the Cold War played a role in this presentation, for it enabled Americans to contrast their freedom of self-expression with the rigidities of Soviet socialist realism. Hence all realism came to be damned by the critics. Greenberg, a critic who was—according to Didier Ottinger— "authoritarian to the point of dogmatism," refused to recognize any painting except abstractionism. He was particularly down on Hopper, the outstanding American realist, stating in 1946, "He is not a painter in the full sense; his means are second hand, shabby, and impersonal. . . . Hopper simply happens to be a bad painter."[36] Other critics echoed this view and compared Hopper unfavorably with Pollock. Thus, "Jackson Pollock epitomized the abstract formalism that gradually dominated collections and museums."[37] The fate of American painting was sealed from that point on, with each new wonder painter celebrated in the media, painting went a step further into inanity. Finally, with the arrival of Warhol and his factory-line production of art objects, painting became a high-priced fashion accessory for millionaires.

Architecture, too, failed to fulfill its earlier promise. Driven by commercial interests, this time to maximize the square footage of commercially available space in the downtown areas of large American cities, the functionalist orthodoxy was established. As Douglas Tallack states, "socially conscious European architecture became the abode of corporate capitalism."[38] The so-called international style, as developed by the Bauhaus architects Gropius, Mies van der Rohe, and Neutra, was admirably suited to meet commercial requirements and the demand for corporate status. Suitably modified and simplified by American architectural firms, such as Owings, Skidmore, and Merrill, this style came to predominate: glass boxes filled the square grids of American cities, in row upon row, with the occasional glass skyscraper as the signature building of a major corporation. This has now extended throughout the world. Even worse results ensued, beyond the confines of aesthetics, when the slum-clearance schemes of politicians led to architects building multistory apartment blocks, vaguely inspired by Le Corbusier, which were repeated identically over acres of otherwise waste ground. The poor were confined in these with no chance of escape—unaware they were experiencing salvation according to the Modernist aesthetic credo.

Why did the artistic avant-garde fail so abysmally in America, when at least for some time in Europe it flourished? Stuart Hobbs provides some of the answers in listing four crucial factors:

> . . . the appropriation of the avant garde by the Cold Warriors; the movement of intellectuals into the university and other institutions; the rise of consumer culture and the transformation of art and ideas into commodities, the avant garde's loss of faith in the future.[39]

The irony is that the very same factors that explain the aesthetic failure of the American avant-garde also account for its extraordinary worldly success. Indeed, failure and success are of a piece: the more cynically corrupt and outrageous an artist became, the more he was rewarded in celebrity and money; the more recognition and praise he gained, the more his art grew empty and defunct.

The American avant-garde began as a series of artistic movements of revolt against conventional society, especially against market capitalism; but it ended up in thrall to the market and the seats of power, serving to decorate the boardrooms of major corporations, offices of government bureaucracies, and university administrations. According to Hobbs, this is true not only of painters and architects but also of avant-garde writers and poets, such as the Beats, the Black Mountain College artists, the San Francisco Renaissance group and others. In his view, all these artists were only too glad to take up paid university appointments to designated residency programs and to occupy permanent chairs, where their work stagnated. He believes that this is also true to a lesser extent of composers, musicians and dancers, whose output declined after they accepted positions in the newly built performance spaces, studios, and classrooms.

These migrations of artists coincided with the movement of intellectuals into the universities as well, which is Hobbs's second point. Intellectuals in America were killed with kindness; they were showered with research grants, appropriations, and chairs, but at the same time were smothered and silenced. Very few of them lived up to the promise with which they began. As there were few American intellectuals to start with, the devastation of intellectual life in America was easily accomplished. American society had never been welcoming or appreciative of intellectuals. Rather than being honored as representatives of *reine Intelligenz* or the cultured intelligentsia, American intellectuals were more likely to be disparaged as unwashed bohemians whom society shunned. Many of them came from immigrant strata, such as the Jews of New York, and espoused left-wing views, which made them doubly suspect. These, in fact, were the ones who were most successful in the universities, once they became anti-Communists.

This brings us to Hobbs's first main point, the role of the Cold War in the perversion of avant-garde art and intellect. There is no doubt that American Abstract Expressionist painters and American intellectuals were used as propaganda tools by the CIA and other agencies of government. The CIA surreptitiously funded a number of exhibitions exclusively featuring works of the painters of the New York school, which were exhibited worldwide, especially in the Western European capitals. This was touted as an expression of American freedom. At the same time it influenced the Europeans to ape the American avant-garde and raised American art to world leadership. Commercially it also served the purpose of shifting the art market from Paris to New York.

In the same secret way, the CIA promoted the Congress of Cultural Freedom in West Berlin in 1950, which became the American Committee of Cultural Freedom, whose members were numerous prominent intellectuals and writers, some of whom became neoconservatives much later. The CIA also funded the publication of a number of intellectual journals in the major European languages, such as *Encounter* in English, *Die Monat* in German, and *Preuves* in French. At the time, the few people in the know believed all this was in the service of a good cause; perhaps it was, but it led to the presumption that in intellectual matters, too, the ends justify the means. When the means are deception and propaganda, this is a betrayal of the intellect and leads to the forfeit of a far higher end than those for which the Cold War was fought, namely the forfeit of civilization.

Apart from all the institutional and political traps we previously listed in which American avant-gardists were ensnared, they were also subject to their own illusions. As Americans, they shared in the universal American belief that they could remake the world anew; that they were not bound by history and the past and could start from scratch and make of themselves whatever they wished. Applied to art and thought, this led to the presumption that traditions and precedents did not count, especially as most of these were European. Art in America could start from the bare elements—color and line in painting, tones and rhythms, or better still, sounds and noises in music, textures and materials in building, and even bare words in poetry; nothing more was necessary. All that mattered was the self-expressive capacities of the individuals, and the less these were rationally, even consciously controlled, the more they were allowed to run free, the better and more authentically original their art would become. The view that there was no need for schooling and discipline, for craft or experience supervened; and it seemed self-evident that in a conformist society, the less the artist or thinker conformed to anything at all, the less inhibited he would be and the more his true inner self would emerge.

Such ideas about expression and alienation "also freed cultural radicals from conformity to critical expectations and the weight of art and literary history," as Hobbs states.[40] Thus the Beats induced in themselves extreme states of consciousness, frequently with the aid of jazz, alcohol, and drugs, and also sought to evacuate any thought content from consciousness, in accordance with their Zen Buddhist beliefs. They were either unaware or did not want to know that Rimbaud had already tried something like this, with very unfortunate consequences. The precedents of history and culture were of no interest to them. Composers like John Cage and his disciples also disavowed history and tradition, for they evinced a "complete antipathy to the idea that there are any connections between past and present music."[41] And so, too, during the 1960s "for a new generation of intellectuals, ideas about civilization, culture and the future became meaningless," according to Hobbs.[42]

The more the American avant-gardists sought to alienate themselves from the society of media celebrity and the culture of consumption, the more they fell into it. The Beats became stars in a publicity circus;

Cage became a campus feature and in Italy a quiz celebrity; as for Pollock, his violent death made him a tragic hero next to James Dean and other Hollywood actors who also killed themselves—a wise career move, as the cynics say, which certainly paid off in Pollock's case. The avant-garde lived and died in a blaze of publicity, for "advertisers and editors of mass-market magazines denuded the American avant-garde of cultural concerns and reduced the movement to celebrity, lifestyles, status and fashion."[43] No better fate awaited intellectuals in the universities, even though they occupied privileged positions and pontificated *ex cathedra*, for "the main thrust of American [humanist] higher education in the postwar world was to train the managers of consumer culture. Art galleries sold style to affluent consumers. Avant-garde innovations became commodities in a culture of consumption."[44]

Thus American civilization was traduced and betrayed. It could not continue the cultural traditions that Europe had so willfully and wantonly destroyed. There was to be no new flowering of Western civilization on the other shore of the Atlantic. There the Forces of Modernity consummated their catalytic processes and now threaten to reduce all cultural resources right around the world to their simplest and most primitive manifestations. Whether there is any way of averting this outcome is at present unknown.

Much will depend on America itself, for at the moment it holds the fate of the world in its hands. Where America goes, the rest of the world follows. Hence, it is to America we must look for any signs of a civilizational recovery, or at least some movement toward the conservation of civilization equivalent to the other conservation movements. America cannot just allow its civilization to go by default. And if such a turning should arise in American, the rest of the world would follow.

Section V—The American Caesar

America bestrides the narrow world like a colossus, and all the petty countries walk under its huge legs and peep about to find themselves dishonorable graves. There are countries in the world that are clearly envious of America's stature and secretly scheme to bring it down. Russia is one example, for it is seething with resentment at the role the United States played in the defeat and breakup of the Soviet Union. An open conspiracy has formed itself against America, with Iran in the lead and many smaller hostile countries aiding and abetting it. Where China stands in relation to America is hidden behind impenetrable screens; China is at once friend and enemy: America's biggest trading partner, its creditor and mainstay of its economy, but also its most dangerous rival, contending with it for influence throughout the world. America still has many old allies, especially the European nations. But can these be altogether trusted if they too come to depend on China economically? France has crossed America before and could do so again. How will America manage all these tensions and keep the world at peace?

America is indisputably the Caesar in the world, but that does not mean that it is the *Kaiser*—the emperor of the world. Strictly speaking, America does not have an empire; the term applies to another epoch and another kind of politics, and it is not relevant to a globalized world. America does not occupy and rule other countries, as Rome did. Perhaps a better word for its role in the world is the term the Greeks used for what they called the Great King (of Persia)—hegemon. It meant that the Great King was involved with everything that went on in the Greek world. In an analogous manner, America is involved with everything that goes on in the world. Whenever any country contemplates a major step, it is done with one eye on America and the unspoken question, "How will the Americans take this?" As Fareed Zakaria states, "for every country—from Russia and China to South Africa and India—its most important relationship in the world has been its relationship with the United States."[45] It is always possible, and has often occurred, that a country, even a very minor player, can act counter to American wishes: North Korea has done so consistently for some time, as have Cuba and Iran. But there is always a high price to pay for incurring American displeasure; trade embargoes, loan restrictions, diplomatic isolation, and sometimes in extreme circumstances even UN sanctions. Even friendly little New Zealand was punished for banning nuclear-powered ships from its harbors. Hence not many have dared to confront the Americans openly, and to affront them is next to suicidal. Even China, the next biggest power in the world, deals circumspectly with America.

It is in this way that America acts as the world coordinator, keeping the peace and managing common global affairs. It took over this pivotal role from Great Britain, also a naval power, after the Second World War. It is unpredictable how long it will go on playing this role in the twenty-first century. But at present, as Zakaria notes, "for all its abuses of power, the United States has been the creator and sustainer of the current order of open trade and democratic government—an order that has been benign and beneficial for the vast majority of mankind."[46] Whether and for how long America continues in such a role will at least partly depend on the quality of its statesmanship. Hillary Clinton has recently stated:

> In twenty-first century statecraft, the general understanding, which cuts across both parties, is that the United States can't solve all the problems in the world. But the problems in the world can't be solved without the United States, and, therefore, we have to husband our resources, among which is this incredibly valuable asset of global leadership, and figure out how we can best deploy it.[47]

If Mrs Clinton wins the 2016 presidential election, it will be interesting to see how far she lives up to her own words.

However, America itself faces tremendous problems, which, if unresolved, could bring it down from the position of Caesar in the world. After the end of the Cold War and the collapse of the Soviet Union, it seemed as if America was bound to lead the world for most of the twenty-first century, for no challenger appeared on the horizon. But the recent global financial crisis has revealed unexpected difficulties for America and its European allies. Can America somehow save itself from drowning in its own sea of troubles?

America is actually drowning in debt. Ben Bernanke, the Federal Reserve chairman, has admitted as much:

> It is not something that is 10 years away. It affects the markets currently. It is possible that the bond market will become worried about the sustainability [of deficits over $US one trillion] and we may find ourselves facing higher interest rates even today.[48]

How can the United States bring down its budget deficit and reduce its debt level without causing a recession, thus further aggravating the deficit and debt, as is currently happening in Greece and other European countries? Certainly, the United States is not Greece or any such minor economy; it is the country of the dollar, the global reserve currency, the axis on which the financial world turns, since money makes the world go round. Thus it has many other ways of meeting its financial problems than other countries. Yet its financial situation is still very troubling, as Henry Ergas, an Australian economist, explains:

> The fundamental problem is simple; the US is living beyond its means. With government debt equal to 107 percent of gross domestic product, its indebtedness is 14 percent higher than the Eurozone's. And even taking account of cyclical positions, its budget deficit is

substantially larger than the Eurozone's and is projected to decline more slowly. Given the scale of accumulated shortfalls, the International Monetary Fund estimates reducing the US government debt to 60 percent of GDP by 2030 would require tax rises and spending cuts equivalent to nearly 20 percent to GDP. There is no painless way of achieving an adjustment of that magnitude.[49]

But how can any adjustment be possible at all given the unfunded liabilities that will be incurred by Medicare, Medicaid, and Social Security? Will the American welfare state wither away? How will the people take that? All of these are unanswerable questions, just as the problems that raise them are insoluble.

Certainly, there has been of late an upsurge in the US economy, which provides at least a stopgap solution. This has largely been brought about by the availability of new sources of energy, cheap gas and oil produced by fracking, which has lifted production. But America still relies far more on its financial than its productive sector, and especially on the export of global culture, which is so dependent on global taste and therefore not secure. It is true that in many high-tech industries the US is still in the lead, such as the defense industries, data transmission, microelectronics, aeronautics, pharmaceuticals, biotechnology, nanotechnology, and others. The agricultural sector is still highly productive. Going by such indices, the French futurologist Jacques Attali predicts that American preeminence will continue until 2030, after which he foresees the end of what he calls the American empire:

> My prediction is that at least until 2030 it [the US] will succeed in keeping its agriculture going, protecting its cutting-edge industries, perfecting new technologies, increasing the productivity of its services, modernizing its weapons systems, defending its commercial zones, guaranteeing its access to raw materials and maintaining its strategic influence. Thus California will remain the core, and the United States will keep its technological lead through massive public investments aimed at its strategic businesses, particularly in the military field, financed by a budget whose now yawning deficit will remain covered by international borrowing.[50]

However, after 2030 the "American empire" will fall:

> Facing increasing competition in numerous sectors from enterprises and research centres located elsewhere, US strategic industries will exile their production and research . . . these firms will realize that

their commercial interests are no longer in step with those of their government, whose increasingly degraded image will hamper sale of their products.[51]

Whether or not such long-term forecasts are sound—and we know from experience that they are usually falsified by events—Attali's comments raise some troubling prospects. America has come to depend more and more on foreigners, rather than on its own people. Its deficit and debt burden is no longer financed by its own investors, but by foreigners and foreign governments, principally China. But for how long will they continue buying US bonds and other treasury instruments? There is a similar situation in research and development, which is also coming to depend on foreigners. At present a large proportion of its entrepreneurs and innovators, scientists and technologists come from overseas, though they are usually trained in America, as Zakaria reports:

> Foreign students and immigrants account for 50 percent of science researchers in the country and, in 2000, received 40 percent of doctorates in science and engineering and 65 percent of doctorates in computer science. Experts estimate that in 2010 foreign students received more than 50 percent of PhDs awarded in every subject in the United States. In the sciences, the figure is closer to 76 percent.[52]

What will happen if all these foreigners eventually decide to set up research establishments, universities, and training institutions in their own countries and offer their products at far cheaper prices than the United States? China is already well on the way to doing this, and no doubt India will follow.

As we have already argued at length, America cannot make full use of its own human resources, because its whole education system is in crisis. American schools and universities are failing their students by passing them all too easily. Consequently, there has been a general miseducation, caused by the constant lowering of standards and expectations, by catering to the lowest common denominator. This is the main reason why America must import foreigners to do much of its brain-work. This corruption of education is part and parcel of a general erosion of civilization that manifests itself firstly in culture but then has social and ultimately economic consequences.

We have already written extensively about this in *Beyond Civilization*, so here only a few salient points need reiterating. The prevalence of the computer, the electronic media, and the global culture they purvey is having a long-term stupefying effect on the American people, especially the young. The very media products that America exports so profitably are creating a cultural loss among its own people. People brought up on a diet of juvenile movies and comics, on television and video games, rock music and drugs are doing to their brains what fast-food is doing to their bodies: both become fat, gross, and lazy. Authors such as Benjamin Barber and others have written extensively on both kinds of degeneration, which are now well substantiated.[53] Barber, in particular, stresses the dangers that this represents to democracy, given an electorate that can no longer judge crucial political issues or assess the politicians who are standing for office. As we saw previously, the outcome is a series of weak and incompetent presidents.

Great danger to American democracy is also generated by fact that many Americans who wish to escape from the Sodom and Gomorrah of the permissive society are turning to fundamentalism. These are mainly the born-again Christians who believe that the devil is a real presence lurking at home and abroad to entrap the unwary. Conservative politicians cater to such naive fears that are easily aroused by anything foreign or strange. The so-called Tea Party is an early intimation of where such politics can lead. Excessive overreaction to the terrorism threat, often at the expense of civil liberties, is another result of such popular pressures.

America is losing the Enlightenment liberalism in whose name the Republic was founded. There is not much left of any of its other traditions. The individualism of the self-made man, so astonishing to de Tocqueville, has given way to the go-getter generation, whose slogan is "greed is good." The global financial crisis has amply demonstrated the harm of which such people are capable. Now there is no way of shaming or stopping them; we can only wait in anticipation for the next scandal and hope that it does not prove too damaging.

Can America cope with its own internal weaknesses and at the same time confront the external challenges facing it? Unfortunately, so much of its energies and resources have been misdirected and wasted. For over a decade, since the horrific events of September 11, outrageous provocations from Islamic terrorists have distracted America from recognizing more significant, real long-term threats. Terrorist threats dominate because they seem immediate and have become daily news. But actually, they are more of an annoyance than a mortal danger. As we shall see, China represents such a danger.

Yet, so much treasure has been devoted to the ragtag Jihadis that not much is left for coping with the real problem of buttressing America's position in the world.

Cracks are appearing in the American colossus. Will it crumble and fall with an almighty crash or slowly subside into dust? Internal weaknesses will inevitably invite external aggression. Will the conspirators of the world eventually turn on the American Caesar? Britain will not play Brutus in any such assassination attempt, but another country may take up this role. Will it be China? If so, how might it deliver the killing blow? Will it simply withdraw its dollar holdings? Or subtly and stealthily undermine America's position throughout the world? Nobody can answer such questions now, and only a futurologist like Attali, who calls himself "brave and controversial," but who might be considered bold and brash, dares even to speculate about them. China has a long way to go before it dare mount such a challenge. It has its own problems that seem almost insuperable. India and Islam are even in deeper trouble. We turn next to the Third World to examine how and why it has come to its present predicament.

Notes

1. Stephen Graubart, *The Presidents: The Transformation of the American Presidency from Theodore Roosevelt to George W. Bush* (Penguin, New York, 2004), p. xiv.
2. Ibid., p. xiv.
3. Ibid., p. xv.
4. Elizabeth Drew, *The Corruption of American politics: What Went Wrong and Why* (Overlook Press, New York, 2000).
5. Stephen Graubart, *The Presidents*, op. cit., p. 63.
6. Ibid., p. 643.
7. See Bob Woodward, *The Price of Politics* (Simon and Schuster, New York, 2012).
8. Richard Koch and Chris Smith, *Suicide of the West* (Continuum Press, London, 2006), p. 84.
9. Ibid., p. 84.
10. Ibid., p. 84.
11. See Nicholas Carr, *The Shallows: How the internet is changing the way we think, read and remember* (Atlantic Books, London, 2010).
12. John Lukacs, *A New Republic*, op. cit., p. 91.
13. Ibid., p. 410.
14. See Harry Redner, *Beyond Civilization*, op. cit., chap. 10.
15. John Lukacs, *A New Republic*, op. cit., p. 170.
16. Ibid., p. 162.
17. Ibid., p. 170.
18. Ibid., p. 162.
19. Ibid., p. 189.

20. G. L. Ulmen, *The Science of Society: Toward an Understanding of the Life and Work of Karl August Wittfogel* (Mouton, the Hague, 1978), p. 207.
21. See Howard Gardner, *The Mind's New Sciences* (Basic Books, New York, 1985). See also R. A. Wilson and F. C. Keil (eds.), *The MIT Encyclopedia of Cognitive Sciences* (The MIT Press, Cambridge, MA, 1999).
22. See Jean-Pierre, Dupuy, *The Mechanization of Mind: On the Origins of Cognitive Science,* trans. M. B. De Bevoise (Princeton University Press, Princeton, 2000).
23. G. L. Ulmen, *The Science of Society,* op. cit., p. 207.
24. Ibid., p. 207.
25. Allan Bloom, *The Closing of the American Mind: How Higher Education Has Failed Democracy* (Simon and Schuster, New York, 1987), p. 5.
26. Ibid., p. 147.
27. Ibid., p. 367.
28. Ibid., p. 368.
29. Ibid., p. 353.
30. George Friedman, *The Next 100 years: The Dawn of the American Age* (Doubleday, New York, 2009), p. 63.
31. Ibid., p. 61.
32. Ibid., p. 61.
33. Ibid., p. 61.
34. Ibid., p. 63.
35. See William C. Agee, Irving Sandler, and Karen Wilkin, *American Vanguards: Graham, Davis, Gorky, de Kooning, and Their Circle, 1927–1942* (Yale University Press, New Haven, 2011).
36. Quoted in Didier Ottinger, *Hopper* (Grand Palais, Paris, 2013), p. 43.
37. Ibid., p. 43.
38. Douglas Tallack, *Twentieth Century America: The Intellectual and Cultural Context* (Longman, London, 1991), p. 118.
39. Stuart D. Hobbs, *The End of the American Avant Garde* (New York University Press, New York, 1997), p. 15.
40. Ibid., p. 55.
41. Catherine Cameron quoted in Ibid., p. 66.
42. Ibid., p. 16.
43. Ibid., p. 150.
44. Ibid., p. 138.
45. Fareed Zakaria, *The Post-American World: And the Rise of the Rest* (Penguin, New York, 2011), p. 52.
46. Ibid., p. 57.
47. Quoted by Steven Lee Myers, *The Australian Weekend Magazine,* 21–22 July 2012.
48. Quoted by Satyagit Das, *The Australian,* 29 November, 2012.
49. Henry Ergas, *The Australian,* 5 November, 2012.
50. Jacques Attali, *A Brief History of the Future: A Brave and Controversial Look at the Twenty-First Century* (Allen and Unwin, Sydney, 2011), p. 150.
51. Ibid., p. 152.
52. Fareed Zakaria, *The Post-American World,* op. cit., p. 211.
53. Benjamin Barber, *Consumed: How Markets Corrupt Children, Infantilize Adults, and Swallow Citizens Whole* (Norton, New York, 2007).

III

The Third World

7

East and West

Oh, East is East, and West is West, and never the twain shall meet.
Rudyard Kipling

Section I—The Third World in the Twentieth Century

In this work we have already dealt with the Old World and the New World; now only the Third World remains. The Third World concerns the three old civilizations of China, Islam, and India, known collectively as the East, which together with the West constitute the four main surviving civilizations of the world. It is, of course, difficult to define civilization and even more difficult to specify autonomous civilizations. This is a problem of taxonomy, which we do not intend to tackle. There is, for example, long-standing debate as to whether Japan is an integral civilization in itself or whether it is part of a Sinic civilization deriving from China, and similar questions have been raised about Russia and its relation to Europe, Byzantium, and even the Mongols. Unfortunately, we have neither the space nor the specialized knowledge to discuss such issues. In any case, we cannot deal with every culture in the world. Hence, somewhat arbitrarily, we propose to restrict ourselves to the three so-called Third World civilizations of China, Islam, and India. Where do these civilizations stand at present, and how much is still left of them? Indeed, where does civilization in the world stand at present?

In the aftermath of the twentieth century, with its wholesale destruction of civilization, the world is entering into a new state of collective being which elsewhere we called postcivilization as we explained in *Beyond Civilization*.[1] This does not mean that civilization is at an end, for considerable portions of former civilizations, above all our own Western one, are still current and play an important role in cultural life. But they are no longer the dominant aspect of society, which has now been usurped by the Forces of Modernity in their globalized manifestations, now largely determined by America. Civilization has

177

become recessive and plays a secondary role to globalization, which is in essence anticultural and so destructive of civilization. Whether or not civilization will eventually wither away is the great unanswerable question for the future to determine. At present we know that the passing of civilization is a possibility fraught with great danger, perhaps threatening the very existence of humanity; hence we must not allow it happen.

The four main extant civilizations are in different states of preservation; in some respects some are better preserved than others, but none is fully intact. The West, represented by America and Europe, has maintained its high culture better than any of the others despite the depredations of totalitarianism and now of globalization. China's civilization has suffered much from colonialism, Japanese aggression, Maoist totalitarianism, and now globalization initiated by Deng Xiaoping's dictum that to get rich is glorious. The best-preserved aspect of Islam is its religion, but its civilization is otherwise severely depleted. India is in the anomalous situation of trying to recover something of an almost forgotten civilization that was virtually destroyed by Muslim invasions over nearly a millennium, and it, too, mostly survives in religious form.

The historical relation between the West and the three other civilizations, sometimes referred to as the Rest, has been very varied, depending on particular factors. China, the most distant from Europe, occupying a unified landmass under an emperor, never became a colonial possession, though the major European powers and Japan had already divided it up into spheres of influence. India became the first great European colony, easily conquered by the British because it was so internally divided and split between Muslims and Hindus. Islam was an extremely heterogeneous sphere; nevertheless, most of Islamic civilization was contained within three empires: the Ottoman, the Qajar in Persia, and the Mughal in India. As these empires weakened and broke up, various parts of them fell under European overlordship of one kind or another, ranging from outright colonial occupation, as in India, Algeria, central Asia, and Indonesia; to protectorates, as in Egypt; to spheres of influence, as in Persia; to mandated territories, as in the Middle East after the First World War; and other types of dependency arrangements.

Due to the varied nature of their historical relation to the West, the three civilizations took up quite different stances regarding the three Western-induced forms of modernization: Europeanization,

Sovietization, and Americanization—or globalization, as it has now become known. Each of them, at different times, displayed varying attitudes to the West, ranging from complete rejection to complete acquiescence, with all kinds of variants in between. Where the West came to establish complete dominance and impose Europeanization on the native people, much less tended to remain of the original civilization than where a measure of independence was retained. The degree of resistance to modernization also reveals how much of their original civilization people were willing to surrender in return for the benefits of power and prosperity, and what they were determined to retain, despite all the inducements to give up part of their culture. The three non-Western civilizations displayed great variety in these respects.

China resisted modernization far longer and more doggedly than any other major power, in marked contrast to its near neighbor Japan, which surrendered extremely rapidly to Europeanization once it was forced to drop its guard. The Chinese held Europeanization at bay until the twentieth century. The reason for their apparent obduracy—which seemed to Europeans so irrational and averse to progress at the time—was the crucial fact that the unity of China depended on its imperial system and that this was also the heart and soul of its civilization. To weaken the imperial system and its traditions was tantamount to undermining the civilization as a whole, something that the Chinese were not prepared to do for a long time. Thus, for example, Western science and knowledge could not have been introduced into Chinese education without abandoning the examination system and the classic literature on which it was based—an impossibility because mandarin officials were selected on the basis of results at these examinations, and imperial rule depended on them. However, once the emperor had been overthrown and the court and its ministers disbanded, and the period of the Republic dominated by the Nationalists under Chiang Kai-shek followed, rapid Europeanization took place. This was followed after the civil war by extreme Sovietization under Mao, to be replaced by an equally extreme Americanization under Deng and his successors once Mao was dead. In the twentieth century, China has reeled from one revolutionary change to another. We will assess what is still left of its ancient civilization in the next chapter.

India presents a very different pattern of modernization by gradual stages. The Europeanization that followed colonialism was barely resisted and even warmly embraced by the elite strata of both Brahmins and Muslims. Having their boys educated in English schools, or better still in England itself, became the overriding ambition of wealthy parents. Such Europeanized elites, quasi-English gentlemen, led the struggle for independence; among them were Gandhi, Nehru, and Jinnah. After independence, the ways of India and Pakistan parted: whereas Pakistan moved steadily into the Muslim sphere and based itself increasingly on Islam, India followed the secularist path set by the Congress party under the Nehru dynasty. After a period of Socialism— really a mixed economy—India took to globalization, following on China's heels but falling behind China in the rate of development. Throughout all these gradual changes, Hinduism as a religion and as a social system prevailed; despite all the official legislation, the caste system endured and in some respects was becoming more ingrained as a wealthy middle class developed. The paradox of modernization leading to a stronger affirmation of tradition is one that Europe had already experienced from nationalism and Romanticism onward, especially in the eastern and southern parts, and India is now undergoing similar developments, with a reaffirmation of Hinduism in modern political terms as an organized movement mobilizing to seize power.

In the Islamic sphere there has been enormous variety in the way modernization took place or failed to do so, depending on how the West encroached and how it was received and perceived. Where the struggle was fiercest and had been going on for a long time, as in the Ottoman Empire, Europeanization was strongly resisted until the twentieth century. Once what remained of the empire had collapsed and only Turkey was left, isolated after its defeat in the First World War, a social revolution occurred under Kemal Pasha, the self-styled Atatürk, and complete Europeanization and secularization was imposed, on the model of Peter the Great in Russia. Persia under Reza Khan followed a similar course, but less intensely so. Iran has now reversed direction and become an Islamic theocracy, and Turkey, too, has a moderate Islamist party in government. At the other end of the Muslim ecumene, Indonesia and Malaysia, which became colonial possessions, have conformed more to the Indian pattern of modernization. As for the Arab peoples, most of these countries, after a long or short period of complete or partial colonialism, emerged into independence as military dictatorships that proclaimed a Socialist credo and embarked to some extent on Sovietization, with the military and economic support of the Soviet Union. Hence globalization could not ensue, and modernization faltered. At present many of them are undergoing a process of Islamization as a result of the so-called Arab Spring, but this is also being fiercely contested by secularists and others. The outcome cannot be predicted.

A noteworthy feature in nearly all cases of non-Western, so-called Third World countries is that after they threw off the European yoke of colonialism they almost invariably embarked on a period of Sovietization euphemistically called Socialism, but in reality heavily influenced by the Marxist-Leninist ideology and state-managed economy of the Soviet Union. Some, such as China, North Korea, Vietnam, Cuba, and a number of African and Arab countries, such as Iraq and Syria, became totalitarian or authoritarian dictatorships; others assumed milder forms of dictatorship, such as Indonesia and Egypt; still others retained democratic institutions but perverted them through one party domination, such as Singapore, Malaysia, Kenya, and for one brief period even India under Indira Gandhi.

What was it that made Sovietization so appealing to the former colonial countries and for so long made them resist American-inspired globalization? Clearly, the Cold War played a key role in this, for despite their official stand of neutrality, by far the great majority of these were more drawn to the Soviet Union than to Europe or America. The explanation lies in the extreme reaction against the West, both Europe and America, and the illusion that the Soviet Union represented something different, a new path to the future that would bypass the decadent and dying West. As François Furet puts it, "In our century, no European doctrinal corpus would be so avidly adopted outside Europe than Marxist-Leninism—that post-Hegelian philosophy harnessed to a totalitarian ideology."[2]

Socialism seemed to promise a shortcut to the Forces of Modernity that all these countries wanted to harness, once they had gained their independence or settled down after the upheavals of the Second World War. These were the countries that eventually became the Third World. What they undertook was modernization of a different kind from the previous attempts at Europeanization. They were no longer interested in the cultural side of European civilization, its codes of dress and manners, its morals and religion, its arts, pure sciences, and so on. What they wanted above all was to acquire the Forces of Modernity, for it was on these that power and productivity depended. Thus they no longer looked to Europe or to America, but to the Soviet Union instead. Hence, they undertook a process of modernization based on Sovietization.

In the initial phase, Sovietization appealed to them much more than its ideological rival, Americanization. It is for this reason that they invariably declared themselves Socialist. The imagination of Third World statesmen was fired by the myth of the Russian Revolution and the illusion of what Stalin had achieved with his Five-Year Plans; they were also inspired by Russia's apparent military and economic strength and its scientific prowess, as exemplified by the launching of Sputnik, and in general by the fact that the Soviet Union had emerged as the main victor of the Second World War. Even such a liberal and democratic leader as Nehru in India, a man schooled by the British, was very impressed with what the Soviets had achieved; he directed India through a partial Sovietization program based on electrification and heavy industry, in alliance with the Russians. Mao emulated Stalin, of course, and Sovietization in China was a carbon copy of what had taken place in Russia, on a still grander scale and leading to even greater disaster. Other Third World leaders followed suit in a minor and more measured way only because they lacked the resources to give their ambitions full scope. Such were Nasser in Egypt, Sukarno in Indonesia, Nkrumah in Ghana, Nyere in Tanzania, and many lesser fry. Their failures were catastrophic for their countries.

With the collapse of the Soviet Union, there was a general realization that Sovietization, the way modernization was carried out in the Soviet Union, was not the path of development. Frustrated in this, Third World countries all turned to the alternative approach of capitalism and free-market economics advocated by America. Americanization ensued throughout the Third World, in many places even before this culminating event: Deng in China had turned away from Mao's system, Sadat in Egypt broke with the Russians, Suharto in Indonesia turned to the Americans, and after much delay Singh in India steered the economy away from autarchy and state control toward the international free market.

Modernization in the American style is very different both from the older Europeanization and the newer Sovietization. Unlike Europeanization, it has no longer much to do with civilization; as American theorists of modernization make amply apparent, it has only to do with the Forces of Modernity in their American version: with a free-market capitalist economy, with a bureaucratic state based on elections, with useful science and technology in all its varied applications. Cultural or social matters play little role. A characteristic example of this view of modernization is to be found in a volume devoted to China by nine American scholars under the general editorship of Gilbert Rozman, where in answer to the question "What is modernization?" the following answer is given:

> We view modernization as the process by which societies have been and are being transformed under the impact of the scientific and technological revolution. . . . Throughout this volume we refer to the elements of social change commonly associated with modernization and often regarded as essential features or events, as defining elements of the process: such things as increased international dependence; relative growth in non-agricultural production, especially manufactures and services; the movement from high birth and death rates to low ones; sustained economic growth; more even distribution of income; specialization and the proliferation of organizations and skills; bureaucratization; mass political participation (whether democratic or not); and an expansion of education at all levels.[3]

It is obvious that these factors all concern the Forces of Modernity and their consequences. None of them has anything to do with civilization in a cultural sense.

Americanization mutates into globalization when it becomes a general worldwide condition. The world becomes integrated, but only on the basis of the Forces of Modernity and nothing else. Civilization in any cultural sense plays no role in it. It is clear, therefore, that globalization has a de-civilizing effect and that the world is moving beyond civilization into a postcivilizational condition. This is the conclusion we came to in *Beyond Civilization.*

Globalization in its present American form is thus the culmination of a globalizing process that the Europeans first undertook when they launched themselves into colonization and colonialism. Their project to Europeanize the whole world and give European civilization the monopoly of all civilizing endeavors failed because Europe was itself defeated by the Events of the Twentieth Century and by the totalitarianism that it spawned. Europe lost its influence over the Third World of de-colonized countries, and it ceased to count as a global power. In its stead arose the two superpowers, America and Russia, who fought for sway over the rest of the world. At first, Sovietization seemed the answer to the world's problems, but that proved the god that failed. Now the world has turned to America on the assumption that American-style globalization is the only possible model.

It is impossible to predict what the future holds in the long term for the Third World in general. That has not prevented some analysts from making such predictions. Futurologists prophesy, for example, that

China will become the top country in the world in a few years, having overtaken America in this and that respect by this or that specific date, or that Europe will become an historical museum for Asian tourists before the end of the century, and so on. Such people seem to know the future, but they have little idea of the past. They are a little like historians in the former Soviet Union who were certain of the future, since that was "scientifically" predictable, but very unsure about the past—since that kept changing with every new Party dictate, or, as at present, with the vagaries of fashion in academia. In order not to succumb to such soothsaying we must study the past, for that alone will enable us to say anything about the future at all.

The rest of this chapter is therefore addressed to the past, to the historical background of the three Third World civilizations: China, Islam, and India. We are intent on establishing what these civilizations were like before the onset of Modernity—that is, before Western colonialism disrupted them. How did these civilizations differ from that in Europe? This inevitably also raises the issue of whether there is any fundamental difference between what is conventionally known as the East and the West. Can any such distinction be made at all? We will begin on the assumption that such a distinction is valid and can be justified on historical and sociological grounds.

We shall utilize Wittfogel's concept of Oriental Despotism as one of the key criteria for distinguishing East and West, or the main civilizations of Asia from those of Europe. But by itself it does not provide the full justification for any such separation. It focuses on the material, organizational, and political aspects of the societies of the East. To it we must add the religious and general cultural aspects—distinguishing, that is, between Eastern and Western religions. As we shall see, this causes a serious conceptual difficulty in relation to Islam. And, finally, we must also add a third criterion to the previous two, concerning the nature of the civic and civil character of social life, which involves distinguishing between the types of cities that people in the East and West inhabit. This is a crucial factor generally, for it, more than anything else, marks the difference between two types of civilizations: court civilizations and city civilizations, but it has unfortunately been neglected.

The three criteria, which we shall discuss separately in the following three sections, do not neatly overlap. Hence, no sharp separation between East and West can emerge. But they overlap to some extent, enough to make such a distinction possible. The boundary between these concepts is fuzzy rather than neat, as East and West interpenetrate and fuse in many respects. East and West do meet. Nevertheless, this distinction remains not only conceptually and theoretically useful for historical study, but also important for understanding the present alignment of Third World countries in relation to those of the New World and Old World.

Section II—Oriental Despotism

Oriental Despotism is the much-disputed term that has traditionally been used to distinguish the West from the East. According to Hegel, Oriental Despotism is where only the one, the ruler, is free and all the rest are slaves; whereas in the West some are free, as in the ancient world of slavery, or all are free, as in modern states. This assumes that one standard of freedom is applicable to all societies and that history is the progress toward greater freedom, both of which are extremely dubious assumptions. However, freed from such Eurocentric prejudices, Oriental Despotism remains a useful concept once it has been detached from such value assumptions and treated in purely descriptive sociological terms.

It has an extended ancestry going back to Machiavelli, who contrasts the absolute rule of the sultan over all his subjects to the limited rule of the king of France, whose power is checked by the other high dignitaries of his realm. For Machiavelli, the former case, which was later called Oriental Despotism, is to be preferred to the latter, later called feudalism. Much later Voltaire, impressed by the Jesuits' reports of the role of the emperor in China, also contrasted it favorably to the rule of kings in the West. However, he was contradicted by Montesquieu, who considered Oriental Despotism an arbitrary and unmediated exercise of power. Such criticisms were seconded by the early British colonial administrators of India, such as Richard Jones, James Mill, and his son John Stuart Mill.

Marx derived the term from all of these sources. But he endows it with much more of an economic than the purely political meaning of earlier authors. Oriental Despotism is the political expression of what Marx calls the Asiatic mode of production, which, according to him, differs fundamentally from the Western. The Western mode of production proceeds dialectically from stage to stage, from the ancient slave mode of production to the feudal, and from that to capitalism, eventually to culminate in socialism. By contrast, the Asian mode of production remains fixated and stagnant; it cannot progress. Going on such assumptions, Marx went on to ascribe all kinds of failings to Asiatic societies, such as the lack of classes and class conflict, one of the main motors of social change; the lack of trade and developed cities, the basis of a mercantile economy; the complete regimentation of social life by bureaucratic state officials; and so on. Most of this has since been disproven by greater knowledge and better scholarship. There was considerable urban life in the East, sometimes exceeding that of Europe; manufacture and mercantile trade was flourishing, there were guilds and other free associations, and finally, far from being stagnant, the East displayed great technical and intellectual inventiveness, especially China.

Most of the criticism of Oriental Despotism has been directed at the Marxist version of the concept, and as such it is amply justified. Unfortunately, few of these critics have realized that Wittfogel's version is very different, both theoretically and empirically. Theoretically it combines Marx and Weber, and empirically it accommodates the relevant research made in more recent times. Certainly, Wittfogel starts off with Marx's account of the Asian mode of production as based on hydraulic water-management or irrigation, rather than rainfall. This form of agriculture led to an agro-managerial system that issued politically in Oriental Despotism. However, he enlarges on this basic idea and considerably modifies it, so that it is no longer mono-causal, and other factors, above all cultural ones, are also brought into play. Hydraulic works do not necessarily give rise to Oriental Despotism, and not every case of Oriental Despotism depends on hydraulic works; there are numerous exceptions in both directions.[4]

Why it is that Wittfogel's work has been generally shunned by scholars is a complex, multifaceted question. The answer is largely political. Leftist scholars were hostile to him because of the strong anti-Communist stand he took during the McCarthyite era in America. Right-wing scholars were put off by his closeness to Marx, not noticing that he was equally close to Weber. Thus we get the situation where Ira Lapidus, one of the foremost authorities on Islam, never mentions Wittfogel and places the term Oriental Despotism in scare quotes, yet what he describes fits perfectly Wittfogel's theory. Asian scholars are understandably resentful of anything that seems to demean their civilizations, so they are more openly critical of Wittfogel and any mention of Oriental Despotism. A recent example of this is Romila Thapar, who writes as follows:

> The theory was widely discussed by Asian Marxist historians, who pointed out that there was little evidence to support it. The question of technologies, such as irrigation, and their impact on Indian history, is in any case far more complex than the simplistic notion of bureaucracies controlling water management and thereby the entire economy.[5]

We are not told who these "Asian Marxist historians" were by name, but whoever they might have been, they have a lot to answer for How anyone can brush aside five hundred pages of closely argued theory based on factual data as "little evidence" is hard to credit.

This does not mean that Wittfogel's views must be uncritically accepted, as his disciple Ulmen tends to do. The main criticism we shall direct at Wittfogel is his contention that Oriental societies were historically stagnant as compared to Western societies. As he put it, "in the Orient the socio-economic system reproduces itself instead of developing itself."[6] This is obviously wrong and shows that Wittfogel has not completely freed himself from the Marxism view of the dialectic of development as going through the stages of ancient society, feudalism, and bourgeois capitalism, so that any society where there are no such stages does not develop. It is, of course, a view of development that only suits the West and thereby makes it seem as if the East was frozen fast in immobility. This takes no account of the extraordinary achievements that took place in China, India, and Islam in so many respects, often way ahead of anything comparable in the West, as so many authors from Needham onward have revealed. Hence, it follows that Oriental Despotism is no bar to development. It is true, however, that once the major empires were established between the sixteenth and seventeenth centuries–the Ottoman, Safavid, Mughal, Ming, and later the Tokugawa—then a marked stagnation did ensue. But other causes must be sought for that apart from Oriental Despotism in itself, as we will show in what follows.

The historical importance of Oriental Despotism is indisputable, as Wittfogel states: "hydraulic society surpasses all other stratified pre-industrial societies in duration, extent, and the number of persons dominated."[7] Once established, which always takes place under conditions of irrigation farming, this type of sociopolitical structure can reproduce itself under all kinds of ecological conditions and in very many historical contexts. It can take a primitive or extremely developed form. In this respect, as a basic structure, Oriental Despotism can be treated as a Weberian ideal-type, or given its variety, as a whole constellation of such types. Hence it cannot be refuted by pointing to anomalous cases or exceptions to the basic form. The ideal-type methodology is precisely intended to allow departures from the model, for which special explanations must then be sought.

The ideal-type of what Wittfogel calls "hydraulic society" is also to be found in Weber, as this quotation reveals:

> Throughout Mesopotamia and Arabia it was not rain that was the creator of the harvest, but artificial irrigation alone. In Mesopotamia, irrigation was the sole source of the absolute power of the monarch, who derived his income by compelling his conquered subjects to build canals and cities adjoining them, just as the regulation of the Nile was the source of the Egyptian monarch's strength. In the desert and semiarid regions of the New East this control of irrigation waters was probably the source of the conception of a god who had created the earth and man out of nothing, and not procreated them, as was elsewhere believed. A riparian economy of this kind did actually produce a harvest out of nothing from the desert sands.[8]

Weber embraces this type of social structure within his still more general conception of patrimonialism. He defines this as follows:

> We shall speak of a patrimonial state when the prince organizes his political power over patrimonial areas and political subjects—which is not discretionary and not enforced by physical coercion—just like the exercise of his patriarchal power.[9]

This means that "all power, economic as well as political is considered the ruler's personal property."[10]

Lapidus provides an account of patrimonial rule in Islamic society in much the same terms:

> The patrimonial authority of the Ottoman Sultan was foremost. The state was his household; the subjects his personal retainers. The soldiers were his slaves, loyal to him personally. The territory of the empire was his personal property, but much of it was given to members of the ruling class in the form of iqta's.[11]

Lapidus shuns the odious term "oriental despotism" and uses the more technical term "patrimonialism," but it is clear that it means the same thing. He also applies it to "the Abbasid and later Persian empires," or Muslim rule in general. Weber extends it much further, also to pharaonic rule in Ancient Egypt, the Chinese imperial rule, the late Roman Empire after Diocletian, Byzantine Caesaro-papism, and even in some respects also Russian czarism. Obviously, some of these depart from the ideal-type of Oriental Despotism in various ways by combining it with other forms of rule.

Under pure Oriental Despotism the will of the ruler is absolute. As Wittfogel puts it, "the ruler who exercises complete administrative, managerial, judicial, military, and fiscal authority may use his power to make whatever laws he and his aides deem fit."[12] And he goes on to point out that "in China all legislative, executive and judicial powers belonged to [the emperor]. In Byzantium there was no organ in the state that had the right to control [the emperor]."[13] This legal situation in China existed from the foundation of the empire onward, as Zhengyuan Fu writes:

> The Chinese imperial legal tradition was from its very inception dominated by the autocratic principle of the Legalists. The emperor, as the embodiment of the highest legal authority, was above and beyond the law. All legislative, judicial, and executive powers were concentrated in his hands. The emperor was the sole law giver, and he alone could make or disclaim any law arbitrarily. He was also the supreme judge whose decision was the ultimate court ruling; in fact, his ruling could override the existing law. He could at will create, change, override, abolish, suspend, and interpret the law.[14]

Zhengyuan Fu obviously agrees with Wittfogel, and he is one of the few recent authors who quote him approvingly.

It may be thought that Islamic rule is an exception in respect of law, since it is supposedly based on the Koran and the accepted interpretation of it. But in practice what this has meant, almost from the very start, was that interpretations were devised that enabled the ruler to exercise complete legal sway, as Weber shows:

> Officially, however, the entire corpus of private law was claimed to be an interpretation of the Koran, or its elaboration through customary law. This took place when, after the fall of the Omayyad Caliphate and the establishment of the rule of the Abbasids, the Caesaro-papist principles of the Zoroastrian Sassanids were transplanted into Islam in the name of a return to the sacred tradition.[15]

Thus Muslim rulers, though in principle bound by sacred law, were in practice not at all limited or restrained by this, as Wittfogel explains:

> In Islamic Society the caliph, like all other believers, was expected to submit to Sacred Law and generally he was quite ready to uphold it as part of the dominant religious order. But he asserted his power whenever he thought it desirable by establishing (administrative) secular courts or by directing them through special decrees (*qanum* or *siyasa*). And the religious judges, the *kadis*, were eager to support a government that appointed and deposed them at will. Thus the theoretical absence of legislature modified the appearance but not the substance of Islamic absolutism.[16]

Wittfogel is, consequently, impatient with those who argue that "regimes of this type were limited by institutional and moral checks which made them bearable and at times even benevolent."[17] If there were any such checks, they would only have occurred under a weak ruler, in the form of army insubordination, or city riots, or assassinations. Otherwise, he insists, "the Caliphate . . . was a despotism which placed unrestricted power in the hands of the ruler."[18]

The capacity of the 'ulama, the clerics, to influence the ruler differed somewhat as between the Sunni Empire of the Ottomans and the Shia Empire of Iran. In the former the 'ulama could exercise very little sway over the rulers because they were recruited directly by the sultan, as Charles Lindholm explains:

> Only the 'ulama, of the state employees, were recruited from the free population, the rest were *kul*, slaves of the Sultan whose whole regime was conceptualized as an extension of his own household, with himself and his immediate entourage cared for by a slave army set off from the rest of the people by background and practice.[19]

Thus, "Ottoman clergy became paid government functionaries, absorbed completely into the state, and lost their connection with the people. When the Empire fell, so did they."[20] But it was different in Iran, where the Shia clergy maintained its contact with the people and were able to rouse them in popular revolts and uprisings against the Shah through the nineteenth and early twentieth centuries. The most recent such insurrection against Shah Reza Mohammad installed the ayatollahs themselves as the rulers in a theocracy they have maintained to this day. Lindholm explains the theological reasons for this as follows:

> Due to their capacity for independent judgment [in legal-theological matters], their reliance on personal charisma, their powerful hierarchical ecclesiastical organization, their millenarian eschatology, and their high degree of financial and political independence, the twelve 'ulama had sufficient organizational independence and popular support to stand up against the state.[21]

Thus it is clear that for these special reasons Iran constitutes a special case of Oriental Despotism. Originally, of course, it was the Persian Achaemenid emperors who established one of the greatest and most efficient despotic systems on record.[22] This was the precursor of the Sasanian, on which in turn the Abbasid Caliphate was based.

Patrimonial empires such as these had specific administrative arrangements, which Weber has made one of his major topics. He speaks of "patrimonial bureaucracy" and distinguishes a number of different types, thus once again emphasizing that not all Oriental Despotisms are cut from the same cloth. He begins with Ancient Egypt, "the first consistent patrimonial-bureaucratic administration known to us," which "originally was staffed with royal clients—servants attached to the pharaoh's court."[23] By contrast, the Chinese administrative apparatus was quite different because "the patrimonial bureaucracy benefited from the even more complete absence of a landed nobility than was the case in Egypt."[24] In an insight that prefigures Wittfogel in all essentials, Weber goes on to make the following observation about China:

> Here, too, [as in Egypt] the power of officialdom was bound to river regulation, especially canal construction—but primarily for transportation, at least in northern and central China, and on tremendous military fortification; again these projects were only possible through the intensive use of compulsory labour [corvée] and through the use of magazines for storing payments in kind, from which officials drew their benefices and the army its equipment and pensions.[25]

Once instituted, a sociopolitical system of this kind can persevere for centuries—indeed, for millennia—for it will always reconstitute itself after every disruption. Even modern China has in a way recreated it through the agency of totalitarianism, which but thinly disguises the traditional forms, as Zhengyuan Fu insists.

One of the key ways in which a traditional Oriental Despotism legitimates itself is through the resort to religious sanctions, which are always at the disposal of the ruler. This takes very different forms depending on the nature of the religion. At its most primitive and simple, the ruler has himself declared a god; but in later more sophisticated variants the ruler is depicted as descended from the gods, or as representing a god, or as becoming a god after death (apotheosis), or at the very least as ruling by the god's favor, and there are many other such variations. In Oriental Despotism, politics and religion are always closely intertwined; the one depends on the other. But whether the king is also high priest, or whether these roles are divided between two individuals, or even whether there are a number of high ecclesiastical officials—all such variants also depend on the religion being invoked. At its most archaic the ruler was treated as a god, as Lindholm explains:

> The rulers of ancient China and India, as well as Mesoamerica, were indeed considered by their subjects and by themselves to be manifestations of gods of nature and these leaders did actually spend much of their lives playing roles in highly elaborate public ritual performances in which they exemplified and embodied their statures as demiurges.[26]

However, the Persian monarchy, first established by Cyrus, was a later variant, for "although Persian theory saw the king as representative of the divine, nonetheless the king was not divine himself; as in Arabia, he was conceptualized as a mediator balancing the relationships between the various social segments." A functional separation between the religion and the political also occurred in Persia: "temple and palace were clearly distinguished—the priest was protected by the king but was not the king, nor was the palace a microcosm of the universe, though it was definitely a center of power and justice."[27] This conception of kingship was reinstated by the Sasanian dynasty, and from this source it passed over to the Abbasid Caliphate and later Muslim rulers. As Lindholm explains, "after the downfall of the Persian Empire, the Sasanid model was appropriated by many Muslim secular kings and princes seeking to legitimatize their power, who adopted the customs and luxuries of the Sasanian court and portrayed themselves as ideal rulers according to Persian political theory."[28] They introduced the courtly practices of *adab*, "the elaborate Persian protocol mandating a courtier's proper manners and bearing."[29]

The caliph was the deputy of God and in no way divine himself. He was "the human instrument who guarded the community and executed the law, which being divine, could not be changed."[30] This was, of course, the theory; the practice, as we have already seen, was very different: the caliph or any other sultan could manipulate the law to suit his purposes. The gap between theory and practice yawns very wide in Muslim rule. In theory the ruler is a mere Muslim whose "office is contracted by a handshake with fellow Muslims who were coequal brothers in the faith; in theory his power could be cancelled if he were unfit."[31] However, in practice this was almost never so. From the Umayyads onward, rulers gained their power through military might and retained it for as long as they could sustain their armies. Since from the time of the Abbasids these armies were frequently recruited from Turkish tribes, it was only a matter of time before they took over the ruling function themselves. The Seljuks and others who became Sunni rulers called themselves sultans and made no pretense to any religious status whatever. But this was always claimed by Shiite rulers, such as the Fatimids, who were installed as imams or even mahdis (redeemers).

The political-religious alignment was very similar in Byzantium for the simple reason that initially, under the Umayyad dynasty, the Muslims had followed the Byzantine model. This was the Caesaro-papist style of state and church relations: the emperor's role was distinct from that of the ecclesiastical dignitaries, the bishops, but he maintained firm control over them, including the patriarch of Constantinople. As Weber puts it, "Caesaro-papist government treats ecclesiastical affairs simply as a branch of political administration."[32] Religion was thus an integral part of the state system; the state controlled what was worshipped and how. In Byzantium saints, "dogmas and cults are accepted or rejected at the ruler's discretion."[33] However, Weber notes that "these powers are everywhere limited by autonomous ecclesiastical charisma":[34]

> The Byzantine *basileus*, like the pharaoh, Indian and Chinese monarchs, also the Protestant *summi episcopi*, attempted repeatedly, and mostly without success, to impose religious beliefs and norms of their own making. Such attempts were always extremely dangerous for them.[35]

A similar conclusion applies to Muslim rulers as well, including the most powerful, such as Mehmed II, the conqueror of Constantinople, and Akbar the Mughal emperor in India, both of whom made attempts to introduce heretical religious innovations, but without success.

Hence Wittfogel's view that under Oriental Despotism religion is under the complete control of the ruler is not strictly correct. The ruler can certainly manipulate it to his own advantage, but he cannot change it at will. The power of the ruler in this, as in other respects, is not unlimited. The mere fact that these states were current in preindustrial societies also introduces numerous other limitations that were only overcome with modern forms of communication and transport. The problem of controlling officials in distant provinces could never be completely overcome by traditional methods, though all such rulers strove to do so by all the means available to them, such as maintaining roads, sending out emissaries, and separating civilian from army command. But none of them had the means or resources of a modern totalitarian state.

It is clear from the previous account that the East and West distinction by no means coincides with what is meant by the Orient and Occident in geographical terms. The late Roman Empire and Byzantine Empire were Oriental Despotisms on many counts, yet they were located in Europe. And so, too, was their successor, the Ottoman Empire. Geographically considered, the boundary between East and West shifts depending on the historical situation and how this determines economy, society, politics, and religion. Hence, the East can at certain times reach deep into Europe or alternatively recede into Asia. Metternich's witticism that Asia begins at the bottom of Bergstrasse in Vienna has a certain ring of truth to it.

Section III—Religion in the East and the West

If we take religion as the main criterion, the East-West boundary shifts deep into Asia, for by all accounts Islam is a Western religion. It is a monotheistic faith, one of the Abrahamic creeds, and shares this patrimony with both Judaism and Christianity. According to Islamic doctrine, both of these are religions of the Book, based on prophets who preceded Mohammad, but he is the ultimate and final prophet who supersedes them all and whose message takes precedence over all the others. All other religions are considered idolatrous and treated quite differently; this is particularly so in regard to the religions of Asia.

Sociology more or less upholds this theological distinction. According to Weber, the presence or absence of what he calls a "personal transcendent and ethical god"—namely, the God of the Old Testament—marks the difference between Western and Eastern religions. Belief in such a god is the *sine qua non* of Western faiths, which he calls "religions of belief":

> Every religion of belief assumes the existence of a personal god, as well as his intermediates and prophets, in whose favour there must be renunciation of self-righteousness and individual knowledge at

some point or other. Consequently religiosity based on this form of faith is characteristically absent in the Asiatic regions.[36]

By contrast to this conception, Eastern religions that do not entertain such a God appear "godless" and "atheistic" despite the proliferation of lesser gods and demons in Eastern religions, and despite the Hindu conception of Brahma as the substance of the universe, which to Westerners appears merely pantheistic rather than monotheistic.

The practical upshot of this religious schism between East and West is that each expounds a very different type of ethics, carried by quite distinct prophetic figures and social strata that most readily take up their message. Thus in the East there were "distinctive strata who were the bearers of the Hindu and Chinese ethics, and who created the 'godless' religious ethics in those countries," and these were quite different from the ones who subscribed to monotheistic religious ethics in the West.[37] This brings Weber to his crucial distinction between exemplary prophets and ethical prophets, who were characteristic of the East and the West respectively:

> Thus there remain two kinds of prophets in our sense, one represented most clearly by the Buddha, the other with special clarity by Zoroaster and Muhammad. The prophet may be primarily, as in the last case, an instrument for the proclamation of a god and his will, be this a concrete command or an abstract norm. Preaching as one who has received a commission from a god, he demands obedience as an ethical duty. This type we shall term "ethical prophet." On the other hand, the prophet may be an exemplary man who, by his personal example, demonstrates to others the way to religious salvation, as is the case of the Buddha. The preaching of this type of prophet says nothing about a divine mission or an ethical duty of obedience, but rather directs itself to the self-interest of those who crave salvation, recommending to them the same path as he himself travelled. Our designation for this second type is that of the "exemplary prophet."[38]

Weber makes it clear that the ethical type of prophecy is closely bound up with monotheism and is impossible where such a God is absent: "the absence of a personal, transcendent and ethical god . . . makes it not appear at all probable that prophecy of the ethical type, such as developed in the Near East and Iran, could ever have arisen in India or China."[39]

Weber relates the emergence of a transcendent God to the rise of empires in the Near East—that is, to the consolidation of Oriental Despotism on a vast scale, such as culminated in the near universal sway of the Persian Empire. As he states, "a personal, transcendent and ethical god is a Near Eastern concept. It corresponds so closely to that of an all-powerful mundane king with his rational bureaucratic regime that a causal connection can scarcely be denied."[40] Weber suggests that the rise of new and unprecedented ethical systems is also closely bound up with the formation of empires, a case we have extensively argued in *Beyond Civilization*:[41]

> The period of the older Israelite prophecy at about the time of Elijah was an epoch of strong prophetic propaganda throughout the near East and Greece. Perhaps prophecy in all its forms arose, especially in the Near East, in connection with the reconstitution of the great world empire of Asia, and the resumption and intensification of international commerce after long interruption.[42]

This means, of course, the so-called pre-Homeric Dark Age in Greece and the turmoil caused by the so-called Sea People in the Near East.

In such passages Weber comes close to asserting the thesis of an Axial Age now associated solely with his friend Carl Jaspers, who, unfortunately, does not acknowledge Weber's precedence in this respect or even advert to Weber's work on the subject. But statements such as the following make it clear that Weber had already said most of what Jaspers went on to say:

> It is not necessary to detail here these developments of the eighth and seventh centuries, so brilliantly analyzed by Erwin Rhode [*Psyche: The Cult of Souls and Belief in Immortality among the Greeks*] some of which reached into the sixth and even fifth century. They were contemporary with Jewish, Persian and Hindu prophetic movements and probably also the achievements of Chinese ethics in the pre-Confucian period, although we have only scant knowledge of the latter.[43]

One can only regret that Weber had not taken the trouble to "detail here these developments of the eighth and seventh centuries" across the Eurasian landmass, for that would have dealt with the Axial Age in a properly sociological fashion, which Jaspers is unable to do.

Weber goes to great length to distinguish Eastern from Western religions. He lists altogether five salient points of fundamental difference, which we do not need to specify any further here.[44] His main intent is to account for the economic consequences of the various attitudes to the world that follow from different religious orientations, for it is in relation to this that Weber seeks to explain the emergence of capitalism in the West and not in the East. In this respect he stresses the following consideration:

> The decisive historical difference between the predominantly oriental and Asiatic type of salvation religion and those found primarily in the Occident is that the former usually culminate in contemplation and the latter in asceticism. The great importance of this distinction for our empirical consideration of religion is in no way diminished by the fact that the distinction is a fluid one, recurrent combination of mystical and ascetic characteristics demonstrating that these heterogeneous elements may combine, as in the monastic religiosity of the Occident.[45]

As we know from his previous work, it is inner-worldly asceticism as practiced by the Protestants that constitutes the crucial religious predisposition for what Weber calls the "spirit of capitalism."

In the context of his investigations of the origins of capitalism, Weber goes on to distinguish between the three Western forms of religion: Judaism, Christianity, and Islam. He is particularly intent on demonstrating that capitalism could not have come from the Jews, despite their extensive trade activities during the early middle ages and especially their sophisticated financial arrangements, which had led his colleague Sombart to postulate the Jewish origins of capitalism. How Weber would have reacted to the recent findings of S. D. Goitein, published in his five-volume study, *A Mediterranean Society: The Jewish Communities of the Arab World as Portrayed in the Documents of the Cairo Geniza (1967–88)*, is, of course, impossible to tell. But this is of no particular interest in this context.

What does interest us is the distinction that Weber draws between Islam and Christianity, for this marks another way of separating an Eastern from a Western sphere within the monotheistic faiths themselves. The boundary between East and West, which had shifted deep into Asia on the basis of monotheism, moves back into Europe on the basis of the rift between Islam and Christianity. However, it is not the actual conflict between the two warring camps that matters but the nature of the religious differences.

According to Weber, "Islam was never really a religion of salvation," in total contradistinction to Christianity:

> There was nothing in ancient Islam like an individual quest for salvation, nor was there any mysticism. The religious promises in the earliest period of Islam pertain to this world. Wealth, power, and glory

were the martial promises, and even the world beyond is pictured in Islam as a soldier's sensual paradise.[46]

Such rewards in the afterlife are still held out to the soldiers of Islam at present, as when the suicide-bomber Jihadis are promised seventy-seven virgins in paradise. In this world, it was wealth—initially as booty and spoils, and later as regular tribute (jizyah) leveled on the unbelievers—that served as an incentive for the ghazi, the warriors of Islam, to expand the bounds of conquest, the dar al-Islam, even further. Weber draws a sharp contrast between the attitude to wealth and gain as between Muslims and Protestants:

> The role played by wealth accruing from spoils of war and from political aggrandizement in Islam is diametrically opposed to the role played by wealth in the Puritan religion. The Muslim tradition depicts with pleasure the luxurious raiment, perfume, and meticulous beard-coiffure of the pious. The saying that "when god blesses a man with prosperity, he likes to see the sign thereof visible upon him"—made by Mohammed, according to tradition, to well-circumstanced people who appeared before him in ragged attire—stands in extreme opposition to any Puritan economic ethic and consequently corresponds with a feudal conception of status.[47]

The conclusion that Weber draws from this is that Islam "accommodated itself to the world in a sense very different to Judaism" and antithetical to Christianity.[48] And the world to which Islam accommodate itself was precisely that of Oriental Despotism, which it encountered in the Near East in its Byzantine and Sasanian forms. The Muslims were tribal conquerors who usurped the place of the two former types of imperial rulers and joined their warring empires into a single Islamic one.

As conquerors in their new dispensation, the Muslim rulers were less interested in converting their unbelieving subjects than in extracting tax revenue from them. This continued to be the practice of Muslim conquerors from then on, whether in the Balkans or in India. Hence from the start they shaped their religion to suit what Weber, following Nietzsche, calls "a religion of masters."[49] They were particularly intent on not mixing with their infidel subjects, though they were forced to live among them; above all they sought to avoid the assimilation that was invariably the fate of conquering warriors in such situations, whether in India, China, or Europe.

198

The Muslims achieved the feat of living amongst their subjects but not becoming part of them by devising consumption prohibitions that made fellowship impossible. No doubt they had learned this from the Jews and their laws of kashrut and all such other Talmudic prohibitions, which serve a similar purpose, though the Jews devised these rules for themselves as political underlings, not as conquerors. The Muslim prohibitions on pork and their insistence on *halal* meat are similar to Jewish *kashrut*, but they add the Ramadan fast and ban on alcohol, which separates them from both Jews and Christians, who drink wine on ritual occasions. Very likely all such rules were devised during the early period of conquest in Mesopotamia in close proximity to the great Talmudic academies at Sura and Pumpedita.

It is important to note in this context that all religions distinguish themselves from each other by the prohibitions they devise and the functional purposes these serve. Christianity separated itself from Judaism by abandoning consumption laws, according to Jesus's stipulation that it is not what goes into a man's mouth that matters but what comes out of it, and instead concentrated on regulating sex. Sex is the other major human need after eating and drinking, but it can be totally avoided, unlike the latter, hence it is the favorite domain for ascetic practices, and corresponds closest to Freud's idea of repression. Such practices are only mandatory for monks or renouncers in the Eastern religions, not for laity. The Hindu Brahmins are bound by the quite different laws of pollution, especially with respect to the lowest castes, the untouchables, and otherwise only by the ban on the consumption of beef, which seems to have been a much later innovation, possibly modeled on the Muslim taboo on pork. This is, of course, the way in which the caste order is maintained and the superiority of the Brahmins affirmed.

The Christian focus on sex went through many different stages that have to be seen in relation to the Church's position in society, particularly its place within the ruling power elite. The extolling of celibacy and virginity originated when Christians were living in a pagan society, where sex was a routine matter, and it served their need for social segregation. Later, sex regulation was not simply limited to the asceticism of monks and nuns but made to serve the Church's control over reproduction, which gave it power over family life. The laws of licit and illicit marriage and the rules of forbidden consanguinity, as well as the ban on divorce except by dispensation, evolved during the Middle

Ages. At the time marriage functioned to consolidate landholdings at all levels of society, even for the rulers themselves, so sexual regulation gave the Church an enormous hold over the mundane affairs of society. Confronted by the feudal aristocracy, who settled issues of war and peace by means of marriage alliances, such complex rules at the Church's disposal gave it a hold over the kings themselves.

The Islamic attitude to sex and marriage is almost diametrically the opposite of the Christian. It reflects the status of the Muslims as a ruling elite in a society into which they did not wish to sink; their principal need was to separate themselves and to reproduce themselves as quickly as possible. To that end, polygamy with up to four wives and an unlimited number of concubines, usually slave girls, was permitted to Muslim men. These could be selected from among the womenfolk of the subject people and subjected to facile conversion on the principle that women have no religion. This assured both unlimited progeny and sensual satisfaction for Muslim men even in this world, provided they were rich or powerful enough. For Muslim women there were no such delights or choices; they were obliged to marry, for monasticism of any kind was shunned, and compelled to do so to Muslim men only on pain of death. Within marriage they had no security, for they could be divorced almost at will, and their children belonged to the fathers. This religiously sanctioned disparity between men and women in Islam is a major problem in the modern world.

The history of Islam shaped itself very differently to that of Christianity. Both these religions split into many distinct denominations, but they did so in different ways and for very different reasons. In Islam the prophetic tradition was over because there could be no further prophets after Mohammed, the last and final messenger of God. All religious disputes were about the succession—basically whether the companions of the Prophet or his relatives should rule. In Christianity the main dividing factors concerned orthodoxy and heresy, for theological differences went on endlessly at all times. In Islam such disputes were almost nonexistent, apart from differences over legal interpretation. The prevalence of theology in Christianity meant that quasi-prophetic figures propounding new doctrines were always bound to arise. Eventually these would give rise to the Reformation, something impossible in Islam. In a secularized version, chiliastic movements would also give rise to revolutions, which before the modern period were also absent in Islam.

Thus, inherent in the basic differences between the two religions there is a whole civilizational disparity. Islamic civilization and Western civilization are fundamentally different, with differences that stem from religious premises but go way beyond them. This has been well studied in a work by Rémi Brague, who separates the civilizations on the basis of two fundamental grounds: their diverse reception and attitude to the Bible, and their quite different evocation and incorporation of the heritage of Greco-Roman civilization and culture.[50]

Christianity and Judaism share the Bible—that is, the Old Testament—in common, whereas Islam displaces the Bible with its holy book, the Koran. The Bible is honored in Islam but left unread; as Brague notes, "the texts of the Old and New Testaments are in fact read in the Islamic world only exceptionally. The examples of direct consultation of Jewish and Christian sources, as with Ibn Qutaybah, remain rare."[51] Indeed, for the Muslims the Bible is not an authoritative text because the Jews and Christians have supposedly tampered with it, and as a corrupt text it is unreliable and cannot be a basis for religious doctrine. Such accusations are almost never exchanged between Christians and Jews, who both accept the authenticity of the revelation of the Old Testament. Hence, Brague warns that one must not take the unity of the three religions based on their general monotheism at face value:

> Islam is not to Christianity (not even to Christianity and Judaism) what Christianity is to Judaism.... While Islam rejects the authenticity of the documents on which Judaism and Christianity are founded, Christianity, in the worst case, recognizes at least that the Jews are the faithful guardians of a text that it considers as sacred, as the text that is properly its own.[52]

Hence the Bible plays almost no role in the history of Islam, whereas the history of Christianity—that is, Western civilization—is inconceivable without it. The role that the Bible has played in the West is incalculable. It legitimated all consecrated kings who were anointed at coronation ceremonies, just as Samuel anointed Saul. But at the same time it justified all manner of rebellion and revolution according to the prophetic tradition of speaking truth to power. The ethics of the West, especially the morality of love, derives directly from it; and so, too, does the promise of salvation. Translations of the Bible, or lack of them, have played a crucial role in the language and literature of all European nations throughout the ages. In short, Western civilization is based on the Bible. All this is absent from Islam, where the Koran plays a very different role.

In their relation and attitude to Classical Greco-Roman civilization Islam and the West also differ fundamentally, in ways that Brague brings out with great acumen. In this respect Judaism has more in common with Islam than it does with Christianity. Ancient philosophies and sciences were certainly translated into Arabic, though almost always from the Syriac and Persian, not the original Greek, and were absorbed into the body of accepted learning. But ancient literature and general culture were shunned, as Brague shows:

> Ancient literature, in what it had of the truly "literary," that is, epic, tragic and lyric poetry, never reached the Arab world—unlike, as we have seen, philosophy and the ancient sciences. Now, it is just this literature that carried something of the ancient conception of man, with the models of his possible excellence and his difficulties in relation to the gods, to nature, to the city, etc. The Arab world has not therefore had to confront in its full force a global conception of man anterior of the Islamic religion. . . . The Christian world, on the other hand, had to measure itself against a more vigorous paganism: that of the anti-Christian Neo-Platonism of Porphyry and of Proclus that had not been adapted as the texts of Plotinus or Proclus translated into Arabic had been . . . and especially against the Greek tragedians, "the true adversaries of Christian sanctity."[53]

The Christians maintained an unbroken continuity with ancient culture both in literature and art. The Church Fathers had absorbed the pagan literary classics, even though some felt guilty about this, as when Jerome accused himself of being a Ciceronian rather than a Christian. The monasteries maintained these texts throughout the Dark Ages. Also the ancient artistic heritage was passed on to the West through Byzantium, and this the Muslims shunned completely.

Hence, according to Brague, the West could initiate constant renaissances of the ancient Greco-Roman culture, while Islam could not do so. "In the lands of Islamic faith, there were some attempts to restore a knowledge perceived as having come from outside, and moreover, very explicitly and technically identified under the name of 'external science,'"[54] but beyond that any other reception of outside influences from the ancients was impossible. By contrast, in Western Christendom, though not in Byzantium, there was a whole sequence of "renaissances" that would resurrect ancient culture and learning: the Carolingian renaissance, the twelfth-century renaissance, the Italian renaissance, the

Great European Renaissance, the Augustan age, the eighteenth-century Hellenic revival, and so on. In the Arab world there were awakenings or revivals, but no renaissance. The difference is crucial for Brague:

> In one case, that of religious awakenings, it is a matter of going back to the sources while remaining in the interior of the tradition that originated it. In the other case, that of renaissances properly said, the source one proposes to draw on is found beyond a solution of continuity, or even has never been in continuity with us. It is then a matter of *appropriating an origin in relation to which one feels foreign, and even alienated*—and in particular, the ancient sources.[55]

It is on the basis of its capacity to appropriate the foreign into itself that Brague develops his theory of Western Civilization. He believes that "no culture was ever so little centered on itself and so interested in the other ones as Europe. China saw itself as the 'Middle Kingdom.' Europe never did."[56] He believes this trait was inherited from the Romans, who saw themselves as secondary in relation to the Greeks. We cannot pursue this idea any further, however, as we must go on to consider in what other ways the West can be distinguished from the East, wherever the boundary between the two might lie.

Section IV—City Civilizations and Court Civilizations

In distinguishing the civilizations of the Occident from those of the Orient, perhaps the most crucial feature of all is the nature of the city and its relation to the court, the abode of the rulers. In the East, as might be expected from the prevalence of Oriental Despotism, it is the court that is of crucial importance to the civilization, whereas the city plays a secondary role, unless it is the city where the court is located, the capital city. Hence, such civilizations might be called court civilizations. In the West it is just the opposite; it is the cities that are the loci of civilization, and the courts, if these exist at all, play an auxiliary role. Here civilization is defined by what transpires in the city: city life, not courtly life, is the model of what it means to be civilized. Such civilizations can, therefore, be called city civilizations.

City civilizations were founded by the Greeks and were initially based on the autonomous and self-governing community of citizens constituting a polis. In most cases there was no court, for kingly rule was abolished early on throughout the Greek world and in areas influenced by it, such as in Rome. Only in some relatively backward places, such as Macedonia, was a court maintained. But it was the Macedonians who conquered Greece and deprived the poleis of their political independence. Nevertheless, city life followed the established civilized pattern of self-government in internal matters. When, under Alexander, the Macedonians extended their conquests through the Middle East and Persia, it was Greek-style cities they founded everywhere they went and sought to civilize the natives by introducing them to Greek city life. Hence the numerous Alexandrias scattered throughout Asia. However, during the Hellenistic age of the diadochi, Eastern-style courts reestablished themselves, and so a mixed civilization of cities and courts arose.

The Romans in their turn continued this pattern of extending civilization by founding cities wherever they conquered, be it in North Africa, Spain, Gaul, or Britain. But at the same time one court—that of the emperor in Rome and later in Constantinople—became the center of the civilization as a whole. Classical civilization persisted for as long as the cities throughout the empire retained their internal autonomy. This only began to wane in the late Roman period when the Diocletian reforms imposed a bureaucratic stranglehold over the cities. This brought about a flight from the cities by the wealthy to escape the enforced liturgies that the state imposed on them. The resultant decline of the cities marked the start of the downfall of the civilization. The fact that Christians opted out of civic life, considering it pagan, contributed to this decline of cities. With the barbarian invasions and the consequent depopulation of the cities, civilization went into retreat and did not recover for many centuries.

The real recovery of civilization in the West came with the revival of cities in Europe and not with the establishment of courts. Charlemagne's attempt to found a courtly civilization based on Aachen failed. A new civilization only arose when the city communes, first in Northern Italy, then in Flanders, achieved a measure of autonomy and developed a new city economy, political organization, and culture. This is basically the celebrated thesis of Pirenne, which was also asserted by Weber before him.[57]

This is not to say that courts did not matter in the West, but such royal residences, frequently located in castles outside the cities, were secondary in the civilizing process, which once again tells against Elias's thesis: even if he widened its focus to include more than the mere cultivation of aristocratic manners, he locates civilizing influences in the wrong place, the court. The kings knew that in order to rule they had to establish their overlordship over the cities, for it was there that most of what mattered—socially, culturally, or politically—occurred.

Henri Quatre rightly decided that Paris was worth a mass. And even though his grandson Louis XIV withdrew from Paris to Versailles and took with him the high nobility as courtiers, it was nevertheless in Paris that he had to establish his legitimacy. The Revolution was a purely Parisian affair that ensued once that legitimacy was lost.

The picture presented by the role of the cities in the East is just the opposite of the one we have depicted in the West. Civilization centered on the courts. Cities mattered less, unless it was the capital city where the court was located. From the earliest Oriental Despotisms to the latest, the court was always the center of civilization, and it established the standards of civilized living. From the earliest period of Egyptian civilization until Alexander's invasion, it was the pharaoh's court that defined the civilization; only when Alexandria was founded did a city begin to play a major role, but then it was no longer an Egyptian civilization. It was very similar in Indian civilization, where the palace was often presented as the center of the universe, its refulgence radiating in all directions. A glimpse of such a model of the universe could be had in the Hindu kingdom of Bali, in present-day Indonesia, until late in the nineteenth century, as Clifford Geertz recounts:

> By the mere act of providing a model, a paradigm, a faultless image of civilized existence, the court shapes the world around it into at least a rough approximation of its own excellence. The ritual of the court, and in fact the life of the court, is thus paradigmatic, not merely reflective of social life.[58]

Much the same comment could be made of the role of the imperial court in China in relation to Chinese civilization during all periods until the end of imperial rule early in the twentieth century, though its cultural and political organization was much more complex than anything to be found in Bali, for it also involved a court-certified bureaucracy, the mandarinate.

As for Islamic civilization, its height was attained during the Abbasid dynasty at the court of the caliph in Baghdad, a city specially built to house the court. What this type of civilized life involved is set out by Charles Lindholm:

> In this milieu nobility was experienced and ratified in what Ira Lapidus calls "aristocratic self-cultivation," as expressed in the practice of *adab*, the elaborate Persian protocol mandating a courtier's proper manners and bearing. Those wishing to be recognized as aristocratic could not rely on their bloodlines: they had to demonstrate knowledge of poetry,

horsemanship, letter-writing, literature, finance, history and the sciences, along with a background in the subtleties of religious debate.[59]

It was much the same at the other end of the Islamic world, in Spain, where a scion of the Umayyad dynasty reigned as caliph in Cordova. It was similarly the case in all subsequent Muslim courts, such as that of Mahmud of Ghazni (988–1030), a great patron of the arts and sciences, as well as subsequently in the court of the sultanate of Delhi and that of the Mughals, Ottomans, Safavids, and all the others. When the court was brilliant, so was the civilization; when the court faded, the civilization declined. Islamic civilization could never overcome its dependence on the court. Hence there was no way it could transform itself when faced with the modern challenge of the West. One by one the Muslim courts disappeared, starting with the Mughals in India, and once all the courts were gone, round about the First World War, the civilization went down with them.

In a court civilization the cities are dependencies administered by officials from the court or appointed by the ruler for this purpose. They are usually garrisoned by his troops. This was so from the earliest Oriental Despotisms, as Weber attests:

> The Asian city was a princely fortress; hence it was administered by officials (in Israel: *sarim*) and military officers of the prince, who held all judicial powers. The dualism of the officials and the elders can be clearly observed in Israel at the Time of Kings. The royal official always gained the upper hand in the bureaucratic monarchies. To be sure, he was not all-powerful; in fact, he often had to take account of popular opinion to an amazing degree. The Chinese official, in particular, was quite powerless viz-á-viz the local organizations, the sibs and occupational associations; whenever they seriously combined in opposition, he lost his office.[60]

Thus it was only rarely a matter of tyrannical rule over cities, though there was always military force to back up the ruling power, for the Asian city "was usually the seat of the high officials or of the prince himself and thus under the cudgel of their military bodyguards."[61]

Thus, though Asian city dwellers could react in various ways against officialdom and even royal authority, they were not citizens in any sense whatever. The contrast between the Oriental and Occidental city could not be starker in this respect, as Weber asserts:

> In contrast to the Occident, the cities in China and throughout the Orient lacked political autonomy. The oriental city was not a "polis"

in the sense of Antiquity, and knew nothing of the "city law" of the Middle Ages, for it was not a "commune" with political privileges of its own. Nor was there a citizenry in the sense of a self-equipping military estate such as existed in the occident . . . the fetters of the sib were never shattered. The new citizen, above all the newly rich one, retained his relations to the native place of his sib, its ancestral land and temple. Hence all ritually and personally important relations with the native village were maintained.[62]

Thus no sharp separation between town and country or even between town and village, such as obtained in the West, could occur in Asia. As we shall see, this is also the case with the Muslim city. In China, "in sharp contrast with the Occident, but in harmony with Indian conditions, the city as an imperial fortress actually had fewer formal guarantees of self-government than the village. Legally the city consisted of 'village districts' under particular *tipau* (elders)."[63]

There is no question that extensive urbanization took place in China and other parts of Asia, at times exceeding that of Europe. Marx's idea that cities failed to develop or that they lacked commercial activity is clearly wrong. In China there were more cities than in Europe, and many of them were much larger than contemporaneous European cities. Cho-yun Hsu writes that "the urbanization of the Song and Yuan dynasties represents a major milestone in Chinese history."[64] He goes on to elaborate further:

> Chang-an, Luoyang and Yangzhou during the Tang; Bianliang (Kaifeng), Hungzhou, Guangzhou and Quangzhou (Zaytun) during the Song and Yuan dynasties; Nanjing and Beijing during the Ming and Qing dynasties—all these can be considered world-class cities for their time. They had large populations and flourishing trade and industries that compared with the major contemporary cities of Europe and the Middle East. Most of the major cities in Chinese history were either centres of government or involved in world trade. Most cities that served as regional centres were primarily concerned with military government while also carrying out some commercial functions.[65]

The last point, in effect, gives away the real situation of cities in China: they were garrisoned and under military occupation; they had no autonomy whatever.

What matters in city development is not size or wealth or even the degree of urbanization of the population as a whole, but the institutional structure. As Mark Elvin comments, in China "the great cities, so much larger than their European counterparts, never developed the distinctive institutions and autonomy only possible within the looser feudal matrix."[66] As Elvin goes on to make clear, cities in China did not have the civilizational function that those in Europe fulfilled:

> Yet Chinese cities did not play the same historic role as their much smaller counterparts in medieval Europe. They were not centers of political or personal freedom, nor did they possess distinctive legal institutions. Their inhabitants developed no civil consciousness (as opposed to a certain regional pride), nor served many autonomous citizen armies. They were not communities of merchants at odds with an alien countryside and its rulers. Manor did not conflict with market.[67]

In other words, Chinese cities had none of the features of European cities that made the latter the basis of Western civilization. Civilization in China was of the opposite type; it was court dominated through the agency of an Oriental Despotism. As Elvin acknowledges, "the basic reason for the divergence between China and Europe was rather the continuing existence of a unified imperial structure . . . [that] made urban development in China as impossible as the development of a true feudal political and military structure."[68]

The situation regarding cities in ancient India was much the same as that in China, for it, too, was a court civilization overseen by an Oriental Despotism. In the period before 200 BC and after AD 300, at the height of Indian civilization, there were many large cities in existence: Taxila, Mathura, Kaverpattinam, Mahasthan, Nagarjunakonda, and Shishupalgarth. But as Romila Thapar makes clear, these were bureaucratically managed, for "a centralized bureaucratic state [is] the standard description of virtually every large kingdom in India."[69] Cities were under the direct authority of the court; "in the Ganges Plain, under the direct control of the Guptas, the king was the focus of administration, assisted by princes, ministers and advisers."[70] In fact the whole tenor of a resurgent Hindu religiosity was against cities: "Brahmanical sources remain dubious about or even hostile to urban life, particularly when it was a commercial center, and viewed the city as acceptable primarily as the location of a court."[71] In other words, courts were given a dispensation from what was otherwise an anti-urban attitude. Once the Muslims conquered India, such Brahmanical rulings no longer mattered, and cities developed in the Islamic pattern.

Islam, too, was a sphere rich in cities, both the cities they had conquered from the Byzantine and Persian Empires and ones that the

Muslim rulers had founded. Urban life was central to Islam, as John Tolan writes:

> In the cities, where peoples and traditions mingled, a Muslim culture and civilization developed. The Umayyad caliphs (680–750) were the first to make urban culture and urban movements central to Islam and to caliphal authority. This was apparent in Palestine, where the Dome of the Rock was built in 692 and al-Aqsa Mosque some twenty years later, and Damascus, which turned into a major capital befitting caliphal ambitions. A dense urban network emerged linking Roman and Persian cities to the new cities arising from Arab military encampments.[72]

However, a city civilization did not develop for the obvious reason that the military encampments, frequently housed in a citadel, controlled the cities on behalf of rulers who were oriental despots. As Ira Lapidus recounts:

> The first principle of 'Umar settlement entailed the transformation of the Arab conquerors into an elite military caste that garrisoned and subdued areas and carried on further conquests. To prevent the Bedouins from raiding indiscriminately, to forestall the destruction of the productive agricultural lands, and to segregate the Arabs from the conquered people, the Bedouin were settled in garrison cities (*amsar*, sing. *misr*). The three most important were now founded in Iraq and Egypt [namely, Basra, Kufa on the Euphrates, and Fustat the new capital of Egypt, to which many others were added later].[73]

This is the political and social background to the strict consumption prohibitions and the lax sexual mores for men of Muslim religion, which we discussed in the last section.

Lapidus has done his utmost to break down the dichotomy of "self-governing commune and bureaucratically administered city" and to argue that cities are not completely the one or the other. And he is right in practice, but wrong in theory, for these are theoretically constructed ideal-types that in practice are almost never fully instantiated. It is true that there are some cities in both categories that do not conform completely to the ideal-type. Nevertheless, the vast majority of European cities are of the self-governing commune type, whereas Muslim cities correspond far better to the bureaucratically administered city type. And we can categorize them because their defining features are given by comparison with the ideal-types. Thus we can grant Lapidus his point when he insists that "the difference between European and

Muslim towns cannot be summed up in the dichotomy of communes versus bureaucracy," without conceding his main point which is to maintain that this is not a real difference.[74] It is true that "communes did not embrace all the public life of European cities any more than the Mamluk state excluded all vocational life,"[75] but it does not follow from this that both were alike or that fundamental differences did not remain. Lapidus is right to maintain that "communes should not conjure up images of democratic harmony, nor should the term "oriental despotism" evoke images of spiritless and prostrate towns."[76] This does not mean, however, that it is irrelevant whether cities were the one or the other. On the contrary, this mattered crucially, as Lapidus implicitly concedes:

> Muslim cities were not ordinarily independent political bodies. They were subject to state regimes which embraced a much larger territory. They were composed of Muslim religious associations which were not territorial at all. They did not have self-contained economies for they depended on regional agricultural production and international trade. Nor did they have an exclusive local culture. They have been indispensable to the organization of more complex societies, but were not themselves a defining institution of Islamic or Middle Eastern societies.[77]

In the Occident, by contrast, at most times the city was a defining institution of society, that is, of Western civilization.

Nevertheless, by attempting to break down the dichotomy of self-governing commune and bureaucratically administered city, Lapidus does show that forces within the latter are much more complex than is commonly supposed. For one thing, military rulers had to take the influence of religious bodies into account, at least during the Mamluk period with which Lapidus deals—though this may not still have been so under the Ottomans. However, for the earlier Middle Ages it is true that the military elite could not completely dominate:

> The 'ulama, or religious leaders had emerged as effective spokesmen and representatives of urban communities. The development of factional movements among the common people and the proliferation of convents and monasteries for Muslim mystics or Sufis also lent the cities cohesiveness, not equal to the alien political regimes, but not a wholly ineffectual counterpoise.[78]

This might well be so, but it still does not lead to the conclusion that "more recent insights and discoveries suggest similarities behind the apparent differences between the European and Muslim towns."[79] When we are dealing with civilizational differences then these cannot be considered merely apparent, for they are very real.

Inherent in this difference was the basic fact, as expressed by John Toland, that "in a large number of European cities, especially in Italy, merchants would ultimately take (that is buy) power, whereas in Muslim countries power remained in the hands of the politico- military elite."[80] To this must be added the social structure, inner articulation and lay-out of the Muslim city which in all these respects is different from the European city, as Lindholm brings out at length:

> The typical Middle Eastern city was in actual fact not so very much different from the tribal world surrounding it. The Muslim town was defined by the mosque, market and bathhouse (all independent of civic rule) and by the variety of persons who lived within it: merchants, craftsmen, scholars, administrators, warriors. Yet the city itself hardly had a civic identity: there was no mayor, no town council. As Ira Lapidus puts it, Middle Eastern cities "were simply the geographical locus of groups whose membership and activities were either larger or smaller than themselves." This fragmentation of the city was indicated by its structure. It was divided into walled squares, which, as in rural areas, were generally inhabited by members of the same patrilineal kin groups, often composed of immigrants from the surrounding hinterlands, who maintained their relationships of alliance and factionalism in the urban environment. Although there were exceptions, in general, the whole city was overseen and exploited by formerly tribal military rulers who lived in a garrison-palace complex nearby, and who also kept their own tribal values.[81]

It is surprising how this whole pattern of city life has maintained itself in many parts of the Muslim world right into the modern period up to the present day. The Americans discovered this, to their surprise, when they conquered Iraq and tried to rule its cities. Only when they realized what they were dealing with could they put down the insurrection. Of course, there are other cities in the Muslim world which have been to some extent Europeanized, but none completely so.

What confirms the nature of the Asian city in general and its role in court civilization is the capital city, that in which the court is situated. In Europe capital cities are fixed and permanent; the capital city is where the court has to be located, or at least in close proximity to it. The only suitable location for a papal court in Italy, for example, was the established city of Rome; this was also the case with Constantinople, where the Byzantine emperors set up their courts. Local rulers established courts in capital cities, such as Palermo, Naples, or Milan. This happened all over Europe: cities like Paris, London, Vienna, and others became the local capitals of the new kingdoms and dynasties. The court had to move to the city, the city did not move with the court—extended palaces outside the cities, like Versailles, notwithstanding.

In Asia it was the other way round: wherever the court was located, this place became the capital city, even if a new city had to be built for the purpose. Thus, almost invariably in Asia with every new dynasty a new capital city arose. This held true for China, India, and the Islamic world. Many of the most important cities in this whole domain were literally court creations, built either from scratch, like Baghdad, or on minor ancient foundations, such as Nanjing, where the Ming dynasty established its court. Frequently the capital changed at the mere wish of the emperor or for good strategic reasons, as when the court shifted back from Nanjing to Beijing at the behest of the Yongle emperor. A decision about court location can sometimes appear to have been made on the basis of a whim, as when Emperor Akbar changed capitals so often that it finally became a moving court caravan, able to shift from day to day. J. F. Richardson explains how this happened:

> One of Akbar's earliest public expressions of his intended autonomy emerged from the decision not to make Delhi his imperial capital. . . . [H]e selected a site for a new imperial capital at Sikri, a village located some 20 miles from Agra. Renamed Fatepur Sikri, the new capital, despite its characteristics and sandstone battlements, was primarily a court city—essentially dependent upon the proximity of Agra for economic and military support. . . . [T]he city was a firm political statement and symbol of the new order.[82]

But no sooner was Fatepur Sikri built than it was abandoned, and "Akbar's camp, after his departure from Sikri, in 1585, became a mobile version of that capital."[83] Obviously, this is an extreme case, but it shows that it is the emperor and his court that is all-important, and the city in itself does not count for much.

There is almost always a capital city, however, that becomes the center of the universe, for all the power emanates from it. The emperor radiates power from the center of his court, which is housed in a palace or citadel, which is situated in the center of the capital city. From there his authority descends by means of his officials and military commanders to all the other major cities of the empire. From there it flows down to all the towns and townships, and from these to every village headman and then on to every peasant hut. Thus the whole society is at least in principle held in a tight grip, though in practice this does not prevent disobedience, insubordination, and outright rebellion. This is the classical pattern of Oriental Despotism from which, of course, there are all sorts of departures.

To what extent did Oriental Despotism and the subordination of cities in the East prove a bar to the development of Modernity, and to what extent did the free cities of the West facilitate this process? These questions have long been subjects of scholarly debate. Most of the classical authors hold that the origins of the Forces of Modernity—capitalism, the rational-legal state, and science and technology—had much to do with the status of its cities, and, by contrast, that the lack of such cities in the East had an inhibiting effect on such developments. But a recent author, the distinguished anthropologist Jack Goody, has sought to refute any such ideas by arguing that there is nothing much to distinguish Western from Eastern cities in any of the respects adduced by the major theorists we have invoked, such as Marx, Weber, Pirenne, and others; he does not even bother mentioning Wittfogel.

He states that "the process of modernization in the West has been seen by European scholars as being linked to the emergence of the city and of its corporate political body, guaranteeing certain freedoms for its inhabitants and separating the private from the public." He goes on to say that "both Pirenne, by implication, and Weber, quite explicitly, exclude the towns of Asia from this category of city."[84] Goody believes he can refute this case by reference to two exceptions, one in India, studied by Gillion, and one in China, studied by Rowe:

> For India Gillion's analysis of the Gujarati city of Ahmedabad shows it as having had many if not all of the features thought to be exclusively European.[85]

For China, "Rowe's detailed study of Hankow demonstrates that guarantees were provided by the administration and that Chinese firms used 'principles of rational capital accounting' in a 'rational, orderly market.'"[86] He shows the importance of guilds as "proto-capitalist corporations" as well as that of other voluntary associations that helped Hankow to escape "heavy handed bureaucratic domination." In other words, at least some Indian and Chinese cities were not as monolithic as has been supposed, leaving ample opportunity for "trade-commercial relations as well as providing a window for the later adoption of factory production and knowledge from the West."[87]

There can be no doubt that Ahmedabad and Hankow were exceptional cities, but they were the exceptions that confirm the rule. This becomes evident when one looks more closely into the unusual circumstances that made such cities possible in otherwise very hostile environments. Both were very late developments, occurring on the cusp of colonial incursion, which tells one something about their unusual nature.

An implicit critique of Goody on Ahmedabad is provided by Sunil Khilnani when he states that "this is perhaps the only example of an Indian city modernizing on its own terms, without being dragooned through a phase of colonial modernity."[88] This reveals its exceptional nature that contrasts with all other Indian cities. Unlike Europe, cities in India were specialized in their activities:

> ...besides commercial and economic centres like Ahmedabad, Surat and Cochin, there were destinations of religious pilgrimages like Benares, Puri and Madurai whose size expanded and contracted in line with the religious calendar; and political and administrative cities like Delhi or Agra, their ascendency or decline hitched to the fate of dynasties. The conjunction of commercial and economic wealth with political and administrative power, typical of major European cities, was rare in pre-colonial India: colonial ports like Calcutta were the first such examples.[89]

Khilnani states explicitly that no Indian city, including Ahmedabad, had any of the major features of European cities:

> These cities were not governed by known rules that applied uniformly to all their residents, and that a single authority could enforce; they had no municipal government, no state power with definite territorial jurisdiction. Above all, the city itself did not appear as a single cohesive space, an 'anonymous subject' which could be rationally administered, ordered or improved.[90]

Ahmedabad was exceptional when compared to other Indian cities, and Khilnani makes clear the reasons for this unusual development as a commercial and manufacturing center. It was founded early in the fifteenth century based on textile manufacturing; hence it was "reliant neither on the patronage of a court or the exploitation of the surrounding countryside."[91] Early on, it developed powerful mercantile and artisanal corporations and guilds, and it used these through the threat of work stoppage "to constrain interference by external political authorities in the management of its affairs."[92] It maintained civic order and peace between the three main religious groups of Hindus, Jains, and Muslims and erected public buildings for all these faiths. All this is a far cry from the situation in Ahmedabad at present, where communal riots are common.

Hankow, as depicted by William Rowe, had a similar exceptional status in China due to unusual circumstances that could rarely be duplicated elsewhere. Rowe states explicitly that "the study is designed to portray a locality that reflected the highest state of indigenous development of Chinese urbanism before wholesale imitation of Western models deflected this process into a new era of pan-cultural urban history."[93] This is as much as to say that Hankow came closest in China to a European city, though was still far removed from becoming one. In any case it was not at all typical of Chinese cities "due to its unusual commanding commercial position and the other peculiarities of its history, such as its late founding."[94] Legally speaking, Hankow was no more than an overgrown suburb of the much smaller city Hangyang, which together with the larger Wuchang made up the city complex of Wuhan. Hence, "until the end of the Ch'ing, then, Wuchang served as vice-regal, provincial, prefecture, and country capital; Hanyang served as seat of its own prefecture and county; Hankow remained legally no more than a suburb of Hanyang city, which it dwarfed."[95]

Wuchang, which was part of the same complex, was "a city totally dominated by officialdom."[96] It was the residence of provincial officers, the Manchu garrison, and "a literary population of influence";[97] and besides it was "the site of the triennial provincial examination."[98] Thus it was strongly controlled by the authorities. However, Hankow, its close neighbor, "despite its many officials, . . . was able to escape the heavy-handed bureaucratic domination posited by Weber."[99] Why this was so is the burden of Rowe's study. He ascribes this to its late founding during the period of the White Lotus Rebellion, late in the eighteenth century when administrative oversight was much weakened due to financial difficulties. The other main reason is that "guilds and other voluntary associations (such as benevolent halls) became progressively more powerful . . . [and] devised broad, bureaucratic coordination to achieve communal goals."[100]

Thus, given the exceptional nature of Ahmedabad and Hankow, it is clear that Goody's case falls to the ground. We can thus maintain that there is a fundamental difference between cities in the East and West on which we can base a distinction between court civilizations and city civilizations. This distinction largely overlaps with the others that we previously established. It coincides more or less with the separation of religions into different types, provided one treats Islam as exemplifying non-Western characteristics, for its cities correspond to the Eastern sphere. This in turn overlaps with the Oriental Despotism of Muslim government as well as that of the rest of Asia.

However, in Europe curious anomalies arise if one applies all three criteria together. Byzantium was Orthodox Christian, a religion of the Western type, but its government was patrimonial and close to Oriental Despotism, whereas its cities, especially those in the Middle East prior to the Muslim conquest, retained much of the internal self-government inherited from the Roman period. This was partly a transitional situation which was moving in an Eastern direction, in a process that began in the late Roman Empire when the imperial form, practiced as a Principate, was giving way to the more Oriental form of the Dominate, as the Emperor was styled "dominus," and prostration in his presence became mandatory. The Byzantine emperors went further in this direction and subordinated the Orthodox Church in a Caesaro-papist system of ecclesiastical controls. Given such tendencies, Byzantium remains a mixed case, somewhere on the boundary between East and West.

Section V—The Boundary between East and West

The boundary between East and West was never clear-cut, either geographically or politically or culturally or religiously or in any other respect. Right at the start of Western civilization there seemed to be a sharp separation between the two civilizations of the Greeks and the Persians, and both sides were highly conscious of this. The Greeks were aware that theirs was a society of poleis, whereas that of Persia was focused on the court and the person of what they called the Great King. They distinguished themselves from those they considered to be barbarians in numerous ways, and there are many Greek anecdotes to this effect. In nuce, the conception of an Oriental Despotism already dates back as early as that, and with it came an awareness that their city civilization was quite different from a court civilization.

However, they were also aware from early on, perhaps as far back as Homer, that there was another society of cities in the Mediterranean that matched their own, that of the Phoenicians. In our terms, it too must be counted as a city civilization. Outside the Persian Empire, in the western Mediterranean, a whole network of cities under the leaderships of Carthage constituted a counterpart to the Greek cities in the same area. In fact, the two systems of cities were closely integrated, especially in Sicily. When Rome challenged Carthage for domination of the western Mediterranean, the leading Greek cities, such as Syracuse, were on the side of the Carthaginians.

Nineteenth-century historians presented the Punic wars as a battle for Western civilization. To do so, they based themselves exclusively on Roman sources, which are obviously biased in this respect, and also on the nascent racial theories of the time that pitted Aryans against Semites, such as expounded by Gobineau, Renan, and the others we discussed in chapter 2. However, a closer look at the situation of the Punic wars makes it clear that, whatever might have been the racial differences, they did not count for much since the Carthaginians were defending Greek civilization against the Romans. It was the Romans, after all, who killed Archimedes and destroyed Syracuse. From what we learn about Carthage from other sources, such as Aristotle's account of its political constitution, it is apparent that at the time it shared in a common classical civilization to a greater extent than did Rome.

Both this example of Carthage and the case of Byzantium previously discussed demonstrate that one must beware of simple dichotomies of East and West, and of drawing sharp boundaries on this basis. The old racist dictum that East is East and West is West and never the twain will meet is false, for the twain will meet and mingle and interpenetrate in numerous ways. Nevertheless, there is an East which can be distinguished from a West, and we have labored to make the distinction is a number of different ways. It is the difference that historically underlies the present-day separation between the West, now represented by America and Europe, and the East, represented primarily by China, India, and Islam, or what we have called the Third World. Despite globalization and the pervasive postcivilizational condition into which the world has entered, such past historical differences still matter, as we shall go on to show in the following chapters.

The distinction between East and West became much clearer at the start of the period of Modernity, around about 1500. By that date, the intermediate realm of Byzantium had been eliminated, though its successor, Muscovy, was starting to emerge; and a violent opposition between Muslim and Christian established the frontline as the boundary between them. The East was simultaneously consolidating itself into the five empires we previously referred to: Ottoman, Safavid, Mughal, Ming, and Tokugawa. But at the same time the West had burst out of its European fastness where the Muslims had hemmed it in and spread itself across the globe to confront all the five empires in the contest of colonialism that would go on for four centuries, leading to their collapse at the start of the twentieth century.

What made the victory almost foreordained was that the West was alone able to originate and develop the Forces of Modernity—capitalism, the rational legal state, science and technology. And a large part of the reason why the West was able to do this was the fact that it was a civilization of cities, one that never unified into a single empire, but remained a multiplicity of states. These sociopolitical factors gave it enormous advantages over the East. A city bourgeoisie played a crucial role in the rise of capitalism and science and technology, as numerous authors have described. It was not the aristocracy, as Elias and his followers imagine, but the bourgeoisie, as the Marxists have insisted all along, who were the main actors in founding Modernity, the latest stage of Western civilization. The feudal aristocracy ensured, however, that a multistate system of kingdoms would arise out of which the modern rational-legal Absolutist state developed.

In the Orient, within the imperial systems, both of these factors were lacking. The aristocracy had no independent existence; they were courtiers and servants of the king, if not actually slaves as in Muslim sultanates. They were fully absorbed in the rituals of the court and its culture of refinement that emphasized qualities called in Arabic *adab*—that is, precious arts, such as poetry and calligraphy; martial arts, such as horsemanship and archery—and placed great emphasis on grace of bearing, elegance, deference, dignity, decorum, protocol, and avoiding loss of face and loss of status. The court could grow to enormous dimensions; in China it housed the entire Ming government, including twenty thousand palace eunuchs and imperial workshops employing up to fifteen thousand skilled men. As David Robinson notes: "The varied cast of actors also produced a cultural milieu that provided ample opportunity for the transmission, adaptation, and interpenetration of sartorial, linguistic, gastronomic and artistic traditions."[101]

City-dwellers in the Orient, furthermore, were unable to match those in the West, because they could not constitute a bourgeoisie. As merchants, traders, manufacturers, and financiers they could grow rich and prosperous, but they had no share in government to any degree, nor did they contribute to or take part in the culture of the court. They could patronize the popular arts and even develop new forms of their own, such as the theatre and novel in China, but these were always considered inferior to the court arts. In China, too, they could seek to educate their sons to pass the imperial exams to qualify them as mandarins. But that is as far as such families could go. In Islamic cities they could also attend the mosques and study religious literature, and even take part in the controversies that this generated. But the possibilities of any major innovations, as in the West, were not open to them.

The dominant role of the court in determining civilization in non-Western societies, and the relatively subsidiary role of the cities, provides a large part of the explanation for the fall of these civilizations. It is a general feature of all court civilizations that they are vulnerable to decapitation. Once the head, the emperor, is removed, and the limbs, the court, is dispersed, then the whole body politic is helpless to resist the invader. This is what the Spanish *conquistadores* discovered in America when dealing with the native civilizations. Later colonialists did not behave as crudely and barbarically as the earlier, preferring to maintain the local rulers as puppets whom they controlled and in whose name they ruled or exercised influence; so the British kept Mughals on the throne long after they occupied India. They sustained the Ottoman caliph, the so-called sick man of Europe, as well as the Persian shah and the Chinese emperors. But nevertheless a kind of slow strangulation was taking place. The imperial systems on which these civilizations depended was shown up as helpless and unviable. Its court culture was gradually infiltrated and displaced by European culture. Its courtiers were Europeanized as were the ablest people in the empire, the ones with an eye to the future. Only those unable or unwilling to change were left to hang on to the civilization of the past.

Once the courts were gone, the civilizations withered. Not everything vanished at once, but a process of elimination began that gradually over the course of the twentieth century reduced them to vestiges of their former selves. In most cases what remained were the religions, particularly so in Islam and India, where religion was best able to resist the forces of secularization. In China, during the Maoist period, it looked as if not even the religious dimension of Chinese civilization would survive, but since then there has been a rapid reversal as the ancient Chinese religious practices have returned, especially in rural areas.

However, the persistence of religion must not be confused with the survival of civilization, and the reassertion of religious fundamentalism does not mean the revisal of civilization, as Huntington maintains. On the contrary, it is rather indicative of the death of civilization, not of its resurrection. In the history of civilizations in general, it is a well known fact that religions often outlive the civilizations that gave them birth. Thus Christianity has had a long history since the decease of the ancient classical civilization in which it first developed, and this is also the case with Buddhism. Indeed, Toynbee has made this fact a cardinal feature of his whole theory of civilization. Hence, it could well be the case that what we are now witnessing in the current religious revivals is some variant on this historical phenomenon.

It has long been a matter of intense debate why the non-Western civilizations fell so easily to the inroads of colonialism. Those who first maintained the theory of Oriental Despotism, such as Mill and Marx, assumed that these non-European civilizations were doomed to perish both because of the superiority of Western civilization and because of their own petrified and sclerotic state. They were, supposedly, incapable of change and therefore of progress; they were dead civilizations kept alive only because they had not yet been put out of their misery. But it was only a matter of time before they all disappeared before the march of Progress—and their religions along with them.

This is, of course, a travesty of history that nobody now shares. Unfortunately, however, there are signs that some of it remains in Wittfogel, and these elements of his analysis need to be exposed and expurgated. He writes as follows:

> Hydraulic society is the outstanding case of social stagnation. Probably originating in several ways and under favorable circumstances developing semi-complex and complex patterns of property and social stratification, hydraulic society did not abandon its basic structure except under the impact of external forces.[102]

He compounds this indictment by asserting that hydraulic society, that is Oriental Despotism, was incapable of initiating major changes of its own accord:

> The history of hydraulic society records innumerable insurrections and palace revolutions. But nowhere to our knowledge did internal forces succeed in transforming any single-centered agro-managerial society into a multi-centered society of the Western type. . . . More specifically: neither in the old nor in the new world did any great hydraulic civilization proper spontaneously evolve into an industrial society, as did, under non-hydraulic conditions, the countries of the post Medieval West.[103]

The latter point, that the West, not the East, developed industrial society is historically true, but is no more than a truism. The interesting question is why this happened in the West and not in the East. Wittfogel's argument that the East was constitutionally incapable of such a development and that it could never have happened there is fallacious. There were undoubtedly periods when the East came close to an industrial breakthrough; Sung dynasty China is usually now given as the main instance of this, and this was also the time when technology and science made their outstanding discoveries, according to the extensive study made by Needham and his team after Wittfogel wrote. Hence, there is nothing in principle that would have prevented an Industrial Revolution taking place sooner or later in China.

But in fact it did not turn out this way; China went backward in industrial development, as in science and technology, after the Sung. And it is generally true that all the major empires in the East were beset by social stagnation after about 1500, as Wittfogel claims. This happened in India and Islam as well. Why did this occur? It is not for the reason that Wittfogel adduces.

One crucial reason, perhaps the most important, is that the East was subject to repeated and constant invasion from Central Asia; of the major areas of civilization, only Europe and Japan were spared. First the Turks in numerous waves and then the Mongols in one huge surge swamped all the adjacent lands throughout the Eurasian continent. The cumulative effects of these invasions—especially that of the Mongols—would last for centuries and completely transform the political and social systems of all the countries subject to them, inflicting horrendous slaughter and depopulation in the process. The era of Genghis Khan in the East is the closest the world has come to the twentieth-century totalitarianism in the West.

Wherever the Mongols took control they established regimes of Oriental Despotism that were the harshest, cruelest, and most repressive ever devised until then. In the first instance, they were predatory rulers mainly intent on dominating and exploiting a subject population. Later, when they had settled down, they did acquire some of the trappings of the civilizations they occupied, but they still kept many of the tribal traditions and barbarous habits of their forebears. They acquired the native religions, mainly Islam, which they maintained with an inflexible orthodoxy. As foreign conquerors they were averse to change of any kind, fearing that this might delegitimize their authority. Hence they were particularly repressive and rigid in their opposition to any innovation. The long-term result was civilizational stagnation, as indeed Wittfogel asserts, but quite different explanations from the ones he gives must be provided.

The influence of the Mongol form of rule would continue ever after in the East, because of its effect on all rulers in the ensuing centuries. As David Robinson explains:

> The Mongols established standards by which future rulers in Eurasia would measure themselves.... Whatever other indigenous traditions rulers exploited for legitimacy and power, the Mongols and their legacy represented a critical source of political capital for ambitious dynasties across Eurasia. No one who aspired to power at home or in the greater state of Eurasia could ignore that repository of imperial glory.[104]

Robinson quotes Marx in support of his contention, arguing that "even regions which had not been within the Mongol empire were engaged with the Mongol legacy. The Delhi sultans, the Ottomans, the Mamelukes, and the Turkomen dynasties of western Iran were conscious of their origins in the steppes and formulated their genealogical and political claims with an eye to Mongol traditions."[105] It needs to be remembered that Timur or Tamerlane, who devastated so much of Asia, claimed descent from Genghis Khan. It is true that once the Timurids, his successors, settled down, some of them proved enlightened patrons of the arts and sciences, as, for example, Ulugh-beg (1404–49) in Transoxania, who furthered Muslim architecture, philosophy, and science. But these were like oases in a desert. The overall impact of the Mongols and their imitators such as the Mamelukes on Islamic civilization was in the long run stultifying.

Much the same was true for China. After the initial burst of activity, commercial and cultural, due to China's opening to the world under Kublai Khan, which so impressed Marco Polo, the Yuan dynasty followed the usual Mongol pattern of exploitative rule. Their successors the Ming, a native dynasty, followed Mongol precedents and if anything proved even more repressive and authoritarian; they were utterly averse to change in almost every respect. The founding Hongwu Emperor (1328–98) has been called "the harshest and most unreasonable tyrant in Chinese history."[106] He can only be compared to Stalin in our time, for like Stalin he instituted a massive purge of his officials, killing many thousands of them. According to Frederick Mote, "He terrorized the whole world of officialdom."[107] In this way, aristocratic families, who had exercised an important political and cultural role, were eliminated and had no further influence. The court became all-important. And there, also like Stalin, the

Hongwu Emperor was the sole authority and judge on all matters, as Robinson explains:

> A prolific writer, the founder penned scores of admonitions that his descendants and their courts follow his will in everything from hair ornaments, styles of gowns, and the frequency of audiences with officials to diplomatic relations with neighbouring countries, the role of eunuchs in the palace, and investiture titles for imperial clansmen.[108]

In this respect he did much better than Stalin, for his successors of the Ming dynasty followed his precedents; China was locked into a rigid, highly authoritarian Oriental Despotism that shunned any major change. The usurpation of the throne by the Manchus, if anything, made matters even worse, for they were determined to prove more Chinese than the Chinese and maintain all established traditional procedures. So it is true, as Wittfogel claims, that China could not change, except through the exertion of outside force. But since it had locked itself into that impasse, it could also have released itself from it.

Europe, as we noted, was spared a major Mongol invasion or occupation. What would have ensued if that had happened is amply demonstrated by the effect of the Mongols on Kievan Rus and the subsequent Mongol yoke on the whole of Russia. Their closest collaborators, who modeled themselves on their system, were the rulers of Muscovy, a distant city that grew from strength to strength and evolved into the czarist empire. As Wittfogel and many others have argued, czarism was a Mongol-inspired version of Oriental Despotism. This remained the legacy of Russia ever after, despite all its Europeanizing efforts from Peter the Great onward; and he himself was another variant of an oriental despot, though more enlightened than any before him. And even today President Putin is cast in the same mold. On the other periphery of Europe, in the Balkans, where once the Byzantine Empire flourished, a few centuries of Ottoman rule show the long-lasting effects of Oriental Despotism on a European people. Hence, one must ascribe Europe's salvation from the Mongol yoke to something approaching sheer luck. If Europe had not been so lucky, who knows where the Industrial Revolution would have first occurred. All that is certain is that the world would have had to wait a long time for it to happen.

Section VI—Colonialism and Modernization

We have concluded our presentation of the precolonial history of the Third World: China, Islam, and India. With the arrival of the Europeans and the onset of colonialism, a new epoch in their history began. They were dragged into Modernity, generally against their will, and started to participate in globalization in its first phase. Initially this was purely economic, as the Europeans used their sea power to establish a world trade system that gradually encompassed the productive capacities of people all over the globe. This began as a form of mercantile capitalism that eventually became industrial as well. In an inversion of the usual dictum, it was the flag that followed trade, since colonial possessions were established in those countries where trading monopolies already existed. Those countries that proved too difficult to conquer were divided up into spheres of influence. Thus India became an outright colonial possession, but China was partitioned into spheres of influence; in the Islamic world both types of arrangement were current, so that Algeria and Indonesia, at the two extremes, became colonies, whereas Persia was divided into zones dominated by Britain in the south and Russia in the north.

The remarkable ease with which the Europeans came to dominate the Third World was not merely due to their technological, military, economic, and presumed cultural superiority, but also to the debilitated state into which these Oriental Despotisms had fallen. The Mughal Empire was the first to disintegrate and proved easy prey for the British. The Qajar dynasty in Persia just barely hung on, saved by the rivalry of Britain and Russia. The Ottoman Empire, the sick man of Europe, was propped up by the active intervention of Britain and France to counter Russia inroads. In China the Qing dynasty was beset by constant rebellions and insurrections, the largest of which, the Taiping uprising, laid waste to large parts of the country and killed more people than anything in Europe until the Second World War.

When opposition was eventually roused against the Europeans, it did not come from the old established elites, who tended to collaborate with the colonialists, but rather from new elites who had risen as a direct result of colonialism itself. These were the Western-educated groups who had been schooled in the educational institutions established by the colonial powers or by Christian missionary churches, or at technical training schools that the local governments had founded in a belated bid to modernize their armed forces. All of these entailed a process of Europeanization. So by a supreme irony of history, it was the Europeanized elites who turned against the Europeans. This came first through the adoption of the most prevalent European ideology—nationalism. Later, the newer ideologies of Bolshevism and Fascism were added to this, both masquerading under the guise of Socialism.

Unfortunately, nationalism did not suit all non-Western societies equally well. It suited the Japanese best of all, for they were an insular, homogeneous people with long-established xenophobic tendencies, who had modernized themselves largely through their own efforts, once they had been forced to open themselves up to the world. Nationalism in Japan was so successful that they soon began to outdo the colonialist rapaciousness of the Europeans. After their victory over the Russians in 1905, they embarked on an aggressive colonialist policy that eventually led them to the folly of trying to conquer China, with all the well-known consequences.

China was less well suited to nationalism than Japan, for it had been a far-flung empire of many types of people who did not speak the same language, though they had the same script, and who adhered to numerous different religions. However, nationalism could also be sustained in China because the Han people predominated, and unity under the empire for so long had endowed them with a sense of their own exclusivity based on a common culture and the Confucian ethos. Chinese nationalism proclaimed itself with the establishment of a republic in 1911. It affirmed itself in 1919 with the May the Fourth Movement among students and intellectuals, protesting at the way China had been treated at Versailles. At that point in its history China might have been expected to follow Japan, modernize rapidly and soon emerge as a major world power with profound consequences for the whole world. But this was not to be, as China was dragged into a long and utterly debilitating civil war between the Nationalists and the Communists, the two major European ideologies, which battled it out in China as they did in many parts of Europe. The eventual victory of the Communists brought China a form of Bolshevik totalitarianism, which together with its own tradition of Oriental Despotism gave it perhaps the most tyrannical regime in human history and held it back for many decades.

India was less suited to nationalism than the others. It is a land of many peoples, many languages, many religions, and little to keep them together. In fact, the nationalist movement for independence in the Indian subcontinent very soon split it in two, and then in three, with further schisms just barely averted and a continuing state of simmering conflict; this still prevails, as irredentist tendencies have not been allayed. Whether all this could have been avoided with wiser statesmanship is a difficult hypothetical matter to settle. Nevertheless, India remains a democracy, though Pakistan has succumbed to dictatorships on numerous occasions. Socialism was preached and practiced in India, but fortunately only in its milder form, so that it did not lead to dictatorship, except for one bad moment under Indira Gandhi. Since India abandoned its planned economy with state controls—which it did belatedly, following China—and opened itself up to the forces of globalization, it has prospered. Unfortunately, this new-won prosperity is very unevenly distributed, and mass poverty still prevails.

Nationalism was least suited to the Islamic countries and brought them nothing but misfortune, except for a few rare cases, such as Turkey and Indonesia. Islam is a universal religion that cannot possibly be the basis for a single nation, as it embraces such a large geographic span inhabited by so many racially and ethnically diverse peoples, speaking utterly different languages, coming from diverse cultural backgrounds, and sharing nothing with each other except a common faith, but even that divided into different denominations. The dreams that some Muslims entertain of a universal caliphate are nothing but that—mere dreams. But at the same time, the Islamic world, especially its Arabic heartland, has been unable to separate into completely independent countries that have their own distinct national identities. They have too much in common to live apart and too little to live together. As a result there have been constant attempts at unity, sometimes embarked on by military means, and a constant breakdown of unity. Hence the Islamic world has been riven by conflict and beset by revolutions and upheavals. These are continuing at present with no end in sight.

Apart from nationalism, Socialism was the ideology that prevailed after independence in all the Third World countries. This came in many shades, ranging from the mild Fabianism of Nehru at one end to the Marxist-Leninism of Mao at the other extreme, with all kinds of variants more or less dictatorial or totalitarian in between. In most of the countries, especially in the Islamic world, Socialism was a prescription for military dictatorships where the military usually ended up running the economy as well, largely for their own benefit. The economic consequences of Socialism were invariably disastrous for state-run industries led to waste and inefficiency, not to speak of corruption on a vast scale and outright kleptocracy.

Corruption was, of course, one of the inherent features of all Oriental Despotisms, so it is little wonder that it has been inherited by the modern regimes that succeeded them. In fact, it served a useful social function, acting as grease in a political machine that would soon seize up without it, given the rigid controls exercised on all aspects of life. Historically, various forms of corruption were prevalent and well known. They are listed in the *Arthashastra*, the ancient Hindu handbook on statecraft that is highly realistic in assessing what that involves, and, according to Weber, outdoes even Machiavelli in this respect. Corruption was a fine art among the mandarins in China, as it always has been among traditional officials everywhere at all times. Tax farming, extensively employed by all older regimes, lends itself particularly well to graft and extortion. Mulcting private people and milking state coffers are age-old procedures. The fact that primary loyalties were to family, sib, clan, and tribe, especially in Muslim lands, meant that corruption was endemic, as unbiased, impersonal administration was very rare.

All such activities have been resurrected in Third World societies, especially after globalization and a free market ensued, bringing such a great deal of wealth, ready for the taking. Corrupt practices now bedevil all such countries and seem to be increasing the more successful they become. Corruption in China, India, and the entire Islamic sphere, even at the very highest levels, becomes newsworthy only when it involves high personages and vast sums; otherwise it is an ongoing daily occurrence the brunt of which is born by ordinary people, especially the poor. Eliminating it seems almost impossible; even lessening it considerably will be a very difficult task. But if nothing is done about it, then the whole project of founding a modern economy in a modern state will founder. Where there is too much grease, the machine ceases to function for nothing moves for lack of traction.

The heritage and historic memory of millennia of Oriental Despotism, in both its good and bad aspects, cannot be thrown off by a mere century or two of colonialism and postindependence modernization. No matter how hard a nation strives to abandon its past and remake itself as a modern nation-state, the past will invariably return in one guise or another to haunt the present. Thus we now witness the return of the hereditary principle in Third World countries, especially in politics. This has happened both in democratic and authoritarian regimes at once. In democracies, veritable dynasties have established themselves as certain select families have assumed the right to rule, so that sons follow fathers in office, or where sons are missing then daughters or widows or other close relatives; even children inherit seats in parliament in which they are guaranteed election. In authoritarian states it is much the same, assuming a grotesque form in North Korea, where the

Kim dynasty rules, and a more moderate form in China and Vietnam, where the children of the revolutionary heroes frequently rise to the top and acquire all sorts of other benefits and privileges. The oxymoron of a Communist aristocracy seems to be coming into being.

The irony of history is that the more a society attempts to rid itself of its past, the more that past is likely to return in monstrous form. China is a prime example of this: Mao sought to completely wipe out the old China, to eradicate the "four olds" and erase the memory of Confucius, but what he brought about was a modern version of Oriental Despotism reminiscent of that of the first emperor Qin Shih Huang-ti and the Legists. As Zhengyuan Fu puts it, "after various attempts to achieve a 'revolution' from above, Mao Zedong revitalized Chinese autocratic tradition in the name of 'socialist transformation.'"[109] Similar phenomena have arisen in the Islamic world, where something akin to sultanism was reestablished in the name of Socialism, with every such ruler attempting to establish a dynasty, such as the Assad family in Syria, which seems to have succeeded where many others failed, though not for want of trying.

What the future holds for the Third World in the long run is, of course, unpredictable. But to a large extent it will depend on how these countries deal with their past—whether and how they can integrate it into Modernity. At the same time, it will also depend on how they relate to and deal with the West—that is, both the New World of America and the Old World of Europe. The issue is not merely economic, one of who can outproduce whom, but also a civilizational matter of how different cultures can cooperate while preserving their own identity. Both East and West are confronted with the same challenge from the globalization that is pushing them all into a postcivilizational condition. Can they collectively overcome that threat, or will they succumb to the entropy of homogenization that is cultural death?

Notes

1. See Harry Redner, *Beyond Civilization: Society, Culture, and the Individual in the Age of Globalization*, op. cit.
2. François Furet, *The Passing of an Illusion: The Idea of Communism in the Twentieth Century*, op. cit., p. 370.
3. Gilbert Rozman (ed.), et al., *The Modernization of China* (Free Press, New York, 1981), p. 3.
4. See Karl August Wittfogel, *Oriental Despotism*, op. cit., pp. 161, 205–6.
5. Romila Thapar, *Early India: From the Origins to AD 1300* (California University Press, Berkeley, 2002), p. 8.

6. Quoted in G. L. Ulmen, *The Science of Society*, op. cit., p. 217.
7. Karl August Wittfogel, *Oriental Despotism*, op. cit., p. 418.
8. Marx Weber, *The Sociology of Religion: Economy and Society*, Vol. I, op. cit., p. 449.
9. Ibid., Vol. II, p. 1013.
10. Ibid., p. 1052.
11. Ira Lapidus, *A History of Islamic Civilization*, op. cit., p. 260.
12. K. A. Wittfogel, *Oriental Despotism*, op. cit., p. 101.
13. Ibid., p. 101.
14. Zhengyuan Fu, *Autocratic tradition and Chinese politics* (Cambridge University Press, New York), p. 119.
15. Max Weber, *Economy and Society*, Vol. I, op. cit., p. 819.
16. K. A. Wittfogel, *Oriental Despotism*, op. cit., p. 102.
17. Ibid., p. 101.
18. Ibid., p. 101.
19. Charles Lindholm, *The Islamic Middle East: Tradition and Change* (Blackwell, Malden, 2002), p. 123.
20. Ibid., p. 178.
21. Ibid., p. 178.
22. See Pierre Brant, *From Cyrus to Alexander: A History of the Persian Empire*, trans. Peter T. Daniels (Eisenbrauns, Winona Lake, IN, 2002).
23. Max Weber, *Economy and Society*, Vol. II, op. cit., p. 1044.
24. Ibid., p. 1044.
25. Ibid., p. 1047.
26. Charles Lindholm, *The Islamic Middle East*, op. cit., p. 38.
27. Ibid., p. 35.
28. Ibid., p. 35.
29. Ibid., p. 35.
30. Ibid., p. 101.
31. Ibid., p. 80.
32. Max Weber, *Economy and Society*, Vol. II, op. cit., p. 1162.
33. Ibid., p. 1162.
34. Ibid., p. 1161.
35. Ibid.. p. 1161.
36. Max Weber, "Sociology of Religion", *Economy and Society*, Vol. I, op. cit., p. 568.
37. Ibid., p. 449.
38. Ibid., p. 447.
39. Ibid., p. 448.
40. Ibid., p. 448.
41. See Harry Redner, *Beyond Civilization*, op. cit., Chap. 2.
42. Max Weber, "Sociology of Religion," op. cit., p. 441.
43. Ibid., p. 442.
44. Ibid., pp. 552–5.
45. Ibid., p. 551.
46. Ibid., p. 625.
47. Ibid., p. 556.
48. Ibid., p. 623.
49. Ibid., p. 624.

50. Rémi Brague, *Eccentric Culture: A Theory of Western Civilization*, trans. Samuel Lester (St. Augustine's Press, South Bend, IN, 2002).
51. Ibid., p. 61.
52. Ibid., p. 64.
53. Ibid., p. 119–20.
54. Ibid., p. 125.
55. Ibid., p. 122.
56. Ibid., p. 134.
57. Henri Pirenne, *Medieval Cities: Their Origins and the Revival of Trade* (Doubleday, New York, 1956), p. 925.
58. Clifford Geertz, *Negara: The Theatre State in Nineteenth Century Bali* (Princeton University Press, Princeton, 1980), p. 13.
59. Charles Lindholm, *The Islamic Middle East*, op. cit.
60. Max Weber, *Economy and Society*, Vol. II, op. cit., p. 1228.
61. Ibid., p. 1228.
62. Max Weber, *The Religion of China: Confucianism and Taoism*, trans. H. H. Gerth (Free Press, New York, 1951), p. 13.
63. Ibid., p. 15.
64. Cho-yun Hsu, *China: A New Cultural History*, trans. T. D. Baker and M. S. Duke (Columbia University Press, New York, 2012), p. 284.
65. Ibid., p. 537
66. Mark Elvin, *The Pattern of the Chinese Past* (Eyre and Methuen, London, 1973), p. 22.
67. Ibid., p. 177.
68. Ibid., p. 177.
69. Romila Thapar, *Early India: From the Aryans to AD 1300* (University of California Press, Berkeley, 2002), p. 370.
70. Ibid., p. 370.
71. Ibid., p. 259
72. John Tolan, "Saracens and Ifranj: Rivalries, Emulation and Convergences" in John Tolan, Gilles Veinstein and Henry Lawrence (eds.), *Europe and the Islamic World: A History*, trans. Jane Mary Todd (Princeton University Press, Princeton, 2013), p. 70.
73. Ira M. Lapidus, *A History of Islamic Societies* (Cambridge University Press, New York, 2002), p. 34.
74. Ira M. Lapidus, *Muslim Cities in the Later Middle Ages*, (Harvard University Press, Cambridge, MA, 1967), p. 185.
75. Ibid., p. 185.
76. Ibid., p. 185.
77. Ibid., p. xv.
78. Ibid., p. 7.
79. Ibid., p. 8.
80. John Toland, *Europe and the Islamic World: A History*, op. cit., p. 86.
81. Charles Lindholm, *The Islamic Middle East*, op. cit., p. 28.
82. J. F. Richardson, "The Formulation of Imperial Authority under Akbar and Jahangir," in Muzzafar Alam and Sanjay Su Grahmenyan (eds.) *The Mughal State* (Oxford University Press, Calcutta, 1998), pp. 130–1.
83. Ibid., p. 136.

84. Jack Goody, *The East in the West* (Cambridge University Press, Cambridge, 1996), p. 228.
85. Ibid., p. 228. See also K. I. Gillion, *Ahmadabad: A Study in Indian Urban History* (University of California, Berkeley, 1968).
86. Ibid., p. 228. See also William T. Rowe, *Hankow: Commerce and Society in a Chinese City, 1796–1889* (Stanford University Press, Palo Alto, CA, 1984).
87. Ibid., p. 228.
88. Sunil Khilnani, *The Idea of India* (Penguin, London, 2012), p. 112.
89. Ibid., p. 114.
90. Ibid., p. 116.
91. Ibid., p. 112.
92. Ibid., p. 112.
93. William T. Rowe, *Hankow*, op. cit., p. 13.
94. Ibid., p. 11.
95. Ibid., p. 30.
96. Ibid., p. 20.
97. Ibid., p. 20.
98. Ibid., p. 20.
99. Ibid., p. 10.
100. Ibid., p. 10.
101. David M. Robinson, *Culture, Courtiers, and Competition: The Ming Court (1368–1644)* (Harvard University Press, Cambridge, MA, 2008), p. 15.
102. Karl August Wittfogel, *Oriental Despotism*, op. cit., p. 420.
103. Ibid., p. 227.
104. David M. Robinson, (ed.), *Culture, Courtiers, and Competition*, op. cit., p. 366.
105. Ibid., p. 366.
106. Frederik Mote, "The Growth of Chinese Despotism," in F. M. Mote and D. Twitchett (eds.), *The Cambridge History of China*, vol. 7 (Cambridge University Press, Cambridge, 1988), p. 28.
107. Ibid., p. 28.
108. David M. Robinson, *Culture, Courtiers, and Competition*, op. cit., p. 2.
109. Zhengyuan Fu, *Autocratic tradition and Chinese Politics* (Cambridge University Press, New York, 1993), pp. 1–2.

8

China

Section I—China under Mao

Today China stands at the peak of its power, second only to America in the world. By sheer quantitative measure, its economy will soon surpass that of America. Its population is still young enough to assure it of labor capacity for a long time ahead, unlike the rapidly aging populations of Japan, Russia, and Europe. The material standard of living of its people is rapidly increasing, though very unevenly, with growing disparities between the middle classes in the cities and the still impoverished peasants in the countryside, especially in the interior of the country. But China has the means for bringing all its people up to an advanced level, just as Taiwan and South Korea have done. It has huge financial resources, so much so that it has become the largest creditor to America, and that the European countries, after the Global Financial Crisis, are lining up cap in hand in Beijing.

It is still not the case that scientifically and technologically China is up with the Western powers. However, some commentators, such as Niall Ferguson, point to the number of patents being issued in China as grounds for maintaining that it will soon catch up with America in this respect as well. Other commentators disagree, arguing that quantity does not equal quality. Hence the debate is still open whether and when China will also become a supreme scientific and technological power. But there is no disputing that it is rapidly moving ahead. Some of the best technical universities in the world are in China, and the schools in some of its cities are second to none. What might not such a highly educated people in huge numbers achieve in the future?

All this has been achieved in less than forty years, since the time that Chairman Mao died and left China virtually destitute. At the end of the totalitarian period the new rulers of the Chinese Communist Party presided over a country almost in ruins. Its economy was nearly at a standstill, with many factories lying idle; they had been

233

built under Russian supervision when the Soviets and Chinese were still allies, but after the split between them, the Russians refused to provide spare parts. Agriculture had barely recovered from the devastation of the Great Leap Forward and was providing just enough to avoid famine. The whole education system was in total disarray after the rampages of the Red Guards who had terrorized teachers and closed schools and universities. Scientific and technological research faltered, except in military-related institutions, for the best scientists and teachers had been sent to the countryside to learn from the peasants, but not to teach them. The environment was devastated by deforestation, and the desert was encroaching on arable land. All in all, if a mad dictator had wished to ruin a country he could not have done a better job of it than Mao. He held complete sway over everyone, like the most tyrannical emperors of old: while he was alive none dare to criticize him; only after he was dead could others begin to pick up the broken pieces of a devastated country and begin to put them together again.

The man who achieved this daunting task was Deng Xiaoping, under whose tutelage China began to move in a very different way and different direction. Under his urgings and guidance the Chinese Communist Party shifted from totalitarianism to subtotalitarianism. For let there be no mistake about this, China did not then and is not now tending toward liberal democracy; the events on Tiananmen square in 1989 demonstrate that Deng had no such intention in mind, and neither have the current rulers of China, as Hugh White comments:

> China remains a classic Leninist one-party state. The CCP is ruthless in preserving the monopoly of political power, and no system as repressive as China's has ever survived long in a country as rich as China has now become. Does this mean that the Chinese system is headed up the rocks? Not necessarily. Rather than presaging its downfall, the fact that no Leninist state has ever grown as rich as China might cut the other way and explain why its political system could survive. Nothing builds legitimacy like prosperity. No previous Leninist political system enjoyed the legitimacy that only economic growth can bestow. Perhaps China's leadership will be the first of its kind to remain in power over a successful modern economy, because it has been the first of its kind to build a successful modern economy and deliver so much prosperity to its people.[1]

Nevertheless, though its structure has not changed, the mode of operation and functional goals of the regime have altered drastically.

This began with the Third Plenum of the Eleventh Central Committee in December 1978, when Deng's way triumphed. Jonathan Fenby writes:

> 'Socialist modernization' became the watchword, with decentralization, rationalization, performance-linked reward and management responsibility at its core. Mass movements were to be abandoned, and collective leadership adopted, along with legality and Communist-style democracy.[2]

These are the features of subtotalitarianism with Chinese characteristics. One of these features introduced by Deng was not only to open up China to the world but also to open up the world to the Chinese. He sent ten thousand students abroad, but 80 percent of them were scientists, indicating clearly that it was pragmatic utility and not cultural enlightenment that was his main interest. Most of these went to America, the erstwhile ideological enemy that would become China's closest partner. However, none of this gave any indication that China would move to a posttotalitarian condition, as Russia did after Gorbachev. And as Hugh White argues, there is no necessity that it must do so.

For theoretical reasons we shall proceed to outline the metamorphic transformations of Chinese totalitarianism in terms of the stages we set out in chapter 3. Briefly and schematically put, the period from the May Fourth movement starting in 1919 down to the end of the Long March in 1936 can be treated as the pretotalitarian phase of ideological strife, tragically in China's case during a period of developing civil war. The next period of proto-totalitarianism started approximately from the point when Mao assumed leadership of the CCP after his arrival in Yan'an. At this time the Party ruled over a small area of northwest China, but gradually in the course of the war with Japan its territory extended over many more "liberated" areas in various provinces. Eventually, at the conclusion of the civil war, fought against Chiang Kai-chek's Kuomintang regime, the whole of China was under its sway. At that point in 1949 the regime mutated into totalitarianism proper. Its character changed dramatically; the regime dropped its libertarian pretense; it was no longer indulgent to religious minorities or any religious practices whatsoever. Mao then became the supreme Leader, and a cult of personality was instituted. But what marked the transition to totalitarianism most decisively was the perpetration of radical evil, the execution at public show-trials of landlords and other supporters of the old regime. This was the baptism by blood of a period of depredations rarely equaled in history, one that only came to an end with Mao's death. Predictably, this event brought about the subtotalitarianism that started with Deng and collective leadership we have just described. Of posttotalitarianism there is as yet no sighting, nor must we assume that it must necessarily ever come about.

Both the totalitarian and subtotalitarian forms of the Chinese Communist regime evince distinct likenesses to native traditions of Oriental Despotism. This has been argued at length by Zhengyuan Fu in a work entitled *Autocratic Tradition in Chinese Politics*.[3] As he states unequivocally:

> Politics in the People Republic of China cannot be and has not been detached from the autocratic imperial tradition. Although the Chinese Communist Party leadership brought new political styles and rhetoric in terms of organization and ideology, during the past four decades (1949-92) more and more evidence appeared showing the persistence of traditional values underlying institutional and behavioral patterns. Furthermore, the structure of the PRC state, which was erected by the CCP, has a centralized hierarchical authority pattern similar to the traditional Chinese imperial political system.[4]

According to Fu, in all crucial respects Communist systems of rule continue traditional oriental despotic patterns, and in this context he explicitly refers to Wittfogel's theory.[5] He provides the same account of the role of law in Communist China as Wittfogel does for Oriental Despotism:

> Throughout the two thousand years of Chinese imperial history, law was a tool wielded by the ruler to safeguard his rule. . . . [Under Communism] law continues to be seen as a penal tool of the ruler for the governance of the populace and the maintenance of his power. Due process, procedural rationality, sanctity of law, and judicial independence have remained alien to Chinese legal thinking and practice.[6]

Fu goes through numerous aspects in which the modern Communist regime mirrors traditional imperial rule. He mentions such things as "literary persecution, purges of the bureaucracy, court intrigue, elite faction conflict,"[7] as well as "control of most aspects of social life including the local community, the economy, and ideology."[8] His conclusion is that this regime "is both a reversion to and revitalization of traditional Chinese imperial autocracy."[9]

However, tradition was combined with modernity as imperial autocracy was overlaid with totalitarianism. Mao told Kissinger that "China's government requires a combination of Marx's methods and

Qin Shihuang's."[10] By Qin Shi Huang's methods he meant traditional Oriental Despotism. By "Marx's methods," which do not exist, he meant "Stalin's methods," of which he was an apt pupil. Everything Stalin did Mao imitated, usually on a larger scale. Thus Stalin's collectivization campaign was carried out by Mao as well, though with fewer and much larger collectives and the peasants reduced to a reserve army of laborers, working on whatever projects the administrators could think up to please Mao, usually inefficiently and wastefully to no lasting effect. The Great Leap Forward was a scheme that even exceeded Stalin's imagination, for Stalin was too rational to entertain such a futile effort. There was no limit to Mao's madness.

The losses China suffered as a consequence of Mao's delusions are truly immeasurable, they defy the calculations of statisticians. R. J. Rummel has sought to tabulate the losses of human life, and the figures he provides are only conservative approximations of what might have been the real tally.[11] It has proved impossible to state exactly how many died during the Great Leap Forward, with some statisticians quoting a figure of forty million and others "only" twenty-seven million.[12] The issue of whether the majority of these deaths constitute manslaughter—that is, they were not deliberate—rather than murder can also be debated. But there is no doubt that other campaigns unequivocally constitute murder, as, for example, when Rummel states that "7,474,000 were murdered by the Party during the collectivization period."[13] Even those who survived, the great majority of Chinese, were forever psychologically as well as physically scarred by the traumas of this whole period, for almost no one was untouched from the highest to the lowest. As Rummel describes it:

> All such human beings were sacrificed toward the most massive, total social engineering project ever forced on any society in modern history. Its means was the forceful imposition of command power over half-a-billion peasants; the destruction of the independent landlord, "rich" peasant, and gentry; the forced, temporary redistribution of land to the peasants to buy their acquiescence to the party; and the subsequent nationalization and seizures of the land for communes, a military-like factorization of the peasant and farming. Further, this social engineering required total power over the family and even its mating practices; the full control and nationalization of private contracts and businesses, "and the eradication of any possible opposition to party doctrine and policies of intellectuals and scholars."[14]

But by a horrible irony of history, it was precisely intellectuals and scholars, European ones, who first initiated such social engineering schemes. Translated to an Asian context and imposed on a massive scale, we find here Trotsky's original plans for the militarization of labor and Jünger's romantic ideas of total mobilization, which we discussed in chapter 3.

The damage this caused China was not just human and material but also moral and cultural, which in a way is far worse, for the former can be repaired over time; the latter is irreparable and so permanent. There is no doubt that it was deliberately done. As Rummel points out, "the party tried to achieve total control over all behavior and thought in order to completely demolish China's institutions, culture, and traditions, and completely rebuild these into a communist utopia."[15] The devastation of Chinese civilization that resulted was more thorough than the destruction of any other civilization. In this respect, Mao exceeded both Stalin and Hitler. Stalin maintained much of traditional Russian culture, except for that which had a direct religious message; he certainly kept nearly all the aristocratic bourgeois culture of nineteenth-century czarism, and even tried to continue it under Soviet auspices. Hitler, too, kept almost everything from the past, except the works of Jews or Communists, his presumed ideological enemies. But Mao destroyed much more. He declared that whereas Qin Shi Huang, whose avatar he felt himself to be in modern times, killed only six hundred scholars and burned only a thousand books, he boasted that he would kill and burn a thousand times that number. As he told André Malraux in 1965:

> The thought, culture and customs which brought China where we found her must disappear, and the thought, customs, and culture of proletarian China, which does not yet exist, must appear. Thought, culture and customs must be born of struggle, and the struggle must continue for as long as there is still the danger of a return to the past.[16]

The struggle he was referring to was the Cultural Revolution, which he launched when the total failure of his economic policies was evident even to his closest collaborators, and he feared for his position. So he enlisted students and schoolchildren to humiliate and degrade all those who might form an opposition. Once set loose, these so-called Red Guards, on Mao's command, attacked their teachers and vandalized their schools. All study and research stopped in China for nearly a decade. As if that was not enough of cultural destruction, Mao told them to "smash the four olds," meaning "old thinking, old customs, old habits, and old culture." He also instituted the anti-Confucius campaign to eradicate traditional religion with the result that "rural communal religion and its temples were almost completely obliterated for more than a decade," as Gosseart and Palmer report.[17]

Old objects, too, were only fit for destruction. As Rana Mitter notes, "Red Guards went to China's finest monuments and landmarks and systematically defaced them."[18] Kissinger states that "in Beijing Red Guard assaults destroyed 4922 of the capital's designated 'places of cultural or historical interest.'"[19] The Forbidden City itself was reportedly saved only on Chou Enlai's personal intervention. According to Mitter, in the Red Guard's view "for an item to give aesthetic pleasure without greater social utility was a crime in itself, and the guilty objects—statues, porcelain, books—were destroyed for their temerity."[20] Perhaps worse of all was the damage done to language itself, for many words lost their meanings, as Mitter reports:

> Terms such as "class," "bourgeois," "demon" or "capitalist-roader" could take on whatever meaning a group or person in control chose to assign them. "Humanist" and "compassion" could become hideous insults; "destruction" could become a term of immense praise. . . . A society in which language divorced itself so thoroughly from meaning, particularly in relation to terms that contained value judgments, was one that ended up by abandoning responsibility. . . . If you do not mean what you say, because what you say has no meaning beyond the immediate present, then it is impossible to imbue language with any system of values. . . . This led to the overall moral nullify of the Cultural Revolution during its most manic phase.[21]

We know from other sources that similar phenomena of language abuse occur in all totalitarianisms. Language becomes so debased that it is no longer possible to make any clear distinctions between truth and lies. Taken to its logical conclusion, which is a kind of reductio-ad-absurdum, we end up with the language "reforms" in Orwell's *1984*.

Of all the aspects of Chinese civilization, the one that was most thoroughly annihilated was traditional religion. According to Gosseart and Palmer, "the Cultural Revolution produced the most thorough destruction of all forms of religious life in China and, perhaps, in human history. . . ."[22] However, they continue their statement as follows:

> . . . it was far from being a secularization movement. Rather, it represented the apotheosis of a parallel trend of political sacralization, which had roots in imperial Chinese political and religious culture, as well as in utopian and apocalyptic dimensions of modernist

revolution. The modern Chinese state, in its various incarnations, had always incorporated, in its identity, in its ideology, and in its practices, many elements that bear functional and structural similarities to a religious institution—a pattern which climaxed with the CCP revolutionary eschatology and with the Mao cult.[23]

Once again we confront here the old question whether ideology can ever constitute a religion or even a political religion, an issue we have already debated in respect to the views of Emilio Gentile in chapter 2. Judging by the fact that soon after Mao's death mass disillusionment ensued very rapidly and the Mao cult collapsed, his ideology was thoroughly discredited and hardly anyone, except for some sentimentalists, continues believing in him, we are inclined to the conclusion that he was not a prophet but merely an ideologue whose message was abandoned as soon as it was seen to fail politically and economically in practical terms. It is true that in China religion and politics are closely intertwined, as the cult of the emperor demonstrates. However, not even that persuades us that Mao had become a sacred figure like an emperor. Hence, whatever might be the structural and functional analogues between Communist ideology and traditional Chinese religion, their meaning and how this was believed in by Chinese people is completely different. Structure and function do not trump meaning and significance.

The present Chinese regime has adopted almost the opposite policy to Chinese traditional religion to that prevalent in Mao's time, as we shall see in section IV. All the authorized traditional faiths can be freely practiced, and Confucianism, too, is making an officially approved comeback. Now it is Maoism that is condemned, though not Chairman Mao himself, whose portrait still hangs overlooking Tiananmen Square, where democracy was crushed in his name. The Party still needs his name and its own past history to legitimate itself. But any attempt to use that name to stir up resentment against the regime, as Bo Xilai tried to do, brings swift retribution. Nevertheless, the Party is itself reappropriating Mao who has become a symbol of egalitarianism for all those left behind in the race for prosperity.

This concludes our brief outline of the tumultuous period of Chinese history in the twentieth century, when it went from Oriental Despotism through the various stages of totalitarianism to the present subtotalitarian regime, which under the new leadership of Xi Jinping is at present becoming more repressive rather than more liberal. The historical question that shall concern us next is why China went through such an erratic and traumatic course in order to emerge as a modern society. The key to an answer lies in the belated nature of the modernization process in China.

Section II—Modernization Delayed Is Modernization Denied

China's modernization process was extraordinarily delayed. It came later than that of any major country—later than India, Japan, or even the Ottoman Empire. There was strong reluctance to modernize in China for reasons we shall presently explore. Only dire necessity and the threat of occupation by the foreign barbarians eventually forced the Chinese to accept the unpalatable fact that to survive they would have to imitate the aggressors. These were the old colonial powers—Britain, France, and Russia—and the new ones—Germany, America, and Japan. Why were the Chinese so averse to modernization?

The reasons mainly have to do with the fact that China was the oldest and most established civilization of all. It was a single unified empire that considered itself to be the Middle Kingdom, the center of civilization surrounded by various types of barbarians, among whom were the sea-barbarians—that is, Europeans. The traditional role barbarians were expected to play was to render homage to the emperor of the Celestial Kingdom. It took the Chinese authorities a long time to realize that the Europeans were different and could not be put in their place or kept out.

A country in China's position, dealing with stronger powers besieging it, has an invidious choice between self-denial and self-assertion. As Henry Kissinger argues, the leader or representative of such a country can follow a policy of accommodation to or rejection of the foreign:

> He can attempt to close the culture gap, adopt the manners of the military stronger and thereby reduce the pressures resulting from the temptation to discriminate against the culturally strange. Or he can insist on the validity of his own culture by flaunting its special characteristics and gain respect for the strength of his convictions.[24]

Japanese statesmen took the first course. Being a homogeneous and unified country not in any danger of division or occupation, they could afford to take this risk, which in fact paid off for them, as they rapidly Europeanized and industrialized. Chinese statesmen, such as Li Hongzhang, in effect the foreign minister, took the second course, but rather than gaining the respect of the Europeans, it brought them a whole string of defeats and failures. They were doing so because they feared that adopting barbarian ways to fight the barbarians was already to lose all that they were seeking to keep. As Kissinger explains:

> A segment of the Qing ruling class wrote eloquent memorials in the classical style about the challenges posed by the West, Russia, and rising Japan, and resulting in the need for China to practice "self-strengthening" and improve its own technological capacities. But China's Confucian elite and its generally conservative populace remained deeply ambivalent about such advice. Many perceived the importation of foreign-language texts and Western technology as endangering China's cultural essence and social order. After sometimes bruising battles, the prevailing faction decided that to modernize along Western lines was to cease to be Chinese, and nothing would justify abandoning its unique heritage. So China faced the era of imperial expansion without the benefit of a modern military apparatus on any national scale, and with only piecemeal adaptations to foreign financial and political innovations.[25]

Chinese leaders were also faced with the realization that to defend the empire and keep it unified they would need to preserve the imperial system and the position of the emperor, who ruled by the mandate of heaven. To weaken the cultural basis of the regime through innovative modernizing policies risked its legitimacy—that is, losing the mandate of heaven, and so might precipitate a struggle for power that would divide the empire and bring on another "time of troubles" such as China had experienced in the past. During the course of the nineteenth century, China had already been convulsed by a number of large-scale rebellions, the largest of which was the Taiping uprising, which provoked a civil war that killed as many people as the Second World War did in Europe and devastated the central provinces of the country. And in a way they were right: once imperial rule was overthrown, China did descend into the chaos of warlords battling for power; of civil war between the two major parties, the Kuomintang and the Communists; and ultimately of totalitarianism. It took the best part of three-quarters of a century for China to settle down again under a new imperial regime. What they did not realize was that modernization was unavoidable, and that by postponing it for so long they had only made the process of adopting it that much more traumatic and chaotic.

Abandoning the imperial system was in the long run inevitable. But this was fraught with enormous dangers to Chinese civilization, for, as in all Oriental Despotisms, the civilization was largely identical to the court culture. Once the court was, as it were, decapitated, it would be next to impossible to reestablish it on any other basis, especially if modernization ensued—that is, the importation of a foreign and utterly different culture, that of Europe. To modernize was impossible, but not to modernize was also impossible: this was the extraordinary dilemma the Chinese confronted.

Perhaps if Chinese civilization had been in a more vigorous and stronger state, as in many ways Japanese civilization was in the nineteenth century, it might have been possible for it to modernize on its own terms. To a considerable extent the Japanese succeeded in just such a compromise: they Europeanized, but only to an extent that they did not abandon their own unique cultural heritage, which at least in symbolic terms was enacted by the Meiji restoration in maintaining the position of the Emperor as a representative of the national spirit. The Japanese were also in a better position to Europeanize because almost imperceptibly they had begun to learn from Europe, mainly from the Dutch, during the long centuries of their self-imposed isolation. Thus, for example, they were much closer to industrialization than China. The Chinese might have been in a position to reach a better accommodation with Europe if their own civilization and its court culture had been in such a vigorous and strong state. But unfortunately it was not.

Chinese civilization was in an arrested state; it had already become largely decrepit and petrified even before it had to face the full brunt of the European challenge. As Cho-yun Hsu writes, starting as far back as the origin of the Ming dynasty under Zhu Yuangzhang, the Hongwu emperor, "Chinese culture and society moved step by step towards rigidity."[26] This was evident in just about every aspect of culture and society, and it was true in government, in education, and in technology; what little advance there was in science had been brought by the Jesuits. The main reason for this immobility was the explicit policy of the Ming emperors, which the Qing also maintained, that no innovation was to be allowed in any respect. This was initiated by Zhu Yuangzhang himself when he ordered in his will that his "Ancestral Injunctions" be maintained by all his successors, which put a brake on any major changes in government.

Zhu Yuangzhang established a particularly tyrannical form of Oriental Despotism. He concentrated all power into his own hands by abolishing the office of chief minister. He purged the mandarin bureaucracy by killing thousands of officials in a way reminiscent of Stalin. The result of this concentration of power in the palace was that either the emperor himself made all the decisions when he was a man capable of doing so, but when he was not, then the deciding authority fell to the palace eunuchs. As Cho-yun Hsu comments, "the greatest harm brought about by the Ming eunuchs' usurpation of authority was not their terrible corruption but that they destroyed the vitality of Chinese culture and thought."[27]

Stagnation in education was perhaps as much responsible for rigidity and insularity as anything else. The bureaucracy was monopolized by Confucian literati selected by an examination system based on the Confucian classics. But even these could not be freely interpreted, for "Zhu Xi's neo-Confucian interpretation of the classics was adopted as orthodox."[28] The examination itself was required to be answered with the so-called eight-legged essay (*bagu wen*), which made for total conformism both in form and content. Apart from such certified traditional knowledge, there was just a smattering of modern European knowledge, mainly in astronomy, brought in by the Jesuits during the Ming. But during the Qing even that was lost, as the Jesuits were stifled in the course of the so-called Rites controversy between the Vatican and the emperor, which led to a ban on missionary work during the Kansei reign in 1715. The Vatican itself forbad further Jesuit activity in 1755.

Missionary activity returned to China in full force during the nineteenth century as a direct imposition by the colonial powers, who set the terms for peace to the Chinese government following its defeat in numerous wars, starting with the Opium wars, initiated by the British in 1839. This is how modern knowledge entered China and how the modernization process began. As Gilbert Rozman writes:

> Missionary schools became gateways to the languages and knowledge of the modern world. Together with their employees and converts, missionaries translated a good deal of the literature of the West, and by the end of the nineteenth century individuals like Timothy Richards were important forces for reformation and change through their personal influence and their publications.[29]

Based on such missionary endeavors, secularly inclined schools and eventually universities were set up in China following the Japanese example of absorbing European knowledge. Thus the Shanghai Polytechnic Institute was established in 1874, to be followed by St. John's University and by the imperial Capital University (now Peking University) in 1898. These were mostly dedicated to the study of science and technology, though the Chinese students themselves evinced a preference for the humanities and social sciences, which were closer to the traditional studies. At the same time many of these students went abroad to study, mainly to Japan, as, for example, Sun Yat-Sen, the initiator of the revolution in 1911. These students became a disaffected group of intellectuals during the late Qing era because they were not allowed to return to their provincial homes, lest they infect the people there with foreign ideas, but had to be quarantined in the newly arisen westernized coastal or riverine cities, where they plotted revolution.

Such cities, among which are nearly all of China's major capitals—Shanghai, Shenyang, Guangzhou, Xiamen, Qingdao, and others, with the sole exception of Beijing and Nanjing—arose out of the trade locations or treaty ports forcibly extracted from China by the colonial powers, primarily Britain. Before this forcible entry by dictate backed up by force, trade with China had been severely restricted, just like trade with Japan. Like the Tokugawa shoguns, the Chinese emperors—starting in 1523 during the late Ming and continuing under the Qing—restricted foreign trade to just a few entry points. It took the Opium wars, starting in 1839, to compel China to open itself up for trade with the world.

But once established, trade became the second major route for the entry of Modernity into China. The treaty ports, with Shanghai in the lead, "served as the entry points for Western influence—commodities, industries, political systems and ideas—into the Chinese interior. In the process of modernization, these great treaty ports were the chief conduits of the new and the modern."[30] In such cities the Chinese experienced for the first time a modern way of life with all its attractions and sufferings. All the amenities and entertainments of European city life were available, but at the same time there was all the toil and squalor of capitalist exploitation of cheap coolie labor. The Europeans who inhabited these cities lived apart from the Chinese in their own enclaves, which had extraterritorial rights, making them exempt from Chinese law. For the Chinese revolutionaries this became a source of national humiliation and a strong motive to reassert Chinese sovereignty under a new, modern form of government once the antiquated imperial system had been overthrown.

The empire itself made one last, desperate attempt at modernization in the Japanese manner, but that failed after just a hundred days. On June 11, 1898, the Guangxu emperor (1875–1908) asserted himself over the Dowager Empress Cixi and the traditionalists behind her and attempted to institute a comprehensive reform movement. Advised by his ministers, Kang Youwei and Liang Qichao, he launched the "convert temples to schools" movement. According to Gosseart and Palmer, it "was an attack on the religious foundations of China's traditional social organization":

> This was the first wave of political and cultural reforms and revolutions that spanned most of the twentieth century, each of which involved the rejection of Chinese religion and the construction of a new spiritual civilization, through either secular substitutes to religion or modern reinvention of Chinese religious traditions. The goal of these projects of social, cultural, and political modernizations was to overcome China's weaknesses in the face of foreign powers and establish its position as a strong and independent member of the world community of nations.[31]

As it happened, the attempt failed and ended after only a hundred days. The traditional forces proved too strong even at this late date; they rallied behind Cixi and by means of a new army commanded by Yuan Shikai, they took power and placed the emperor under house arrest. Had he succeeded, China might have been spared much turmoil and suffering, and emerged as a major power at least half a century before it did so.

With the failure of modernization from above, the only other recourse was revolutionary activity from below. This eventuated in 1911 with the deposition of the child emperor Pu Yi and the inauguration of the Chinese republic under Sun Yat-Sen. However, the main impulse to modernization did not come until the New Culture Movement was inaugurated on May 4, 1919. It began as a protest by students in Beijing against what they perceived to be mistreatment of China at the Versailles conference. They launched the so-called May Fourth movement for the complete Europeanization of China and the extirpation of traditional Chinese religion and culture. Cho-yun Hsu sums up its main program as follows:

> First, the rejection of traditional Chinese culture, with some extremists calling for total Westernization and throwing Chinese string-bound books into manure pits. Second, advocacy for vernacular (*baihua*, plain talk) writing. Third, Hu Shi's (1891–1962) proposal to import "Mr De" (democracy) and "Mr Sai" (science) in order to save China.[32]

This was the program of the New Culture movement that aimed systematically to destroy Confucianism, identified with Chinese religion, and to replace it with all the then current European ideologies of scientism, Social Darwinism, Marxism, and so on. It was the beginning of the pretotalitarian ideological battles that convulsed China in the twentieth century just as they roiled Europe, and also led to civil war and totalitarianism of a Chinese variety.

The Communist Party of China was founded at this juncture by leading intellectuals Chen Duxiu, a professor at Peking University, and Li Dazhao, together with the young Mao Tse-tung. They argued for the abolition of religion and propounded an atheist (*fei zong jiao*) policy, as expressed in Chen Duxiu's essay "On Smashing Idols." According to this, Confucianism belonged to an outdated feudal order that had to be completely extirpated if a new society was to arise. So, step by step, the Communists set about destroying Chinese religion and the culture associated with it; at first for tactical purposes, they allowed some aspects of popular religiosity to continue in areas under their rule, but eventually when the whole country was in their control, the all-out attacks on religion and so-called superstitions began, culminating in the vandalizing rampages of the Red Guards during the Cultural Revolution. All that was allowed to remain of culture were the "secularizing and nationalizing elements of traditional culture such as folk arts, storytelling, opera, martial arts, Chinese medicine, and body cultivation traditions."[33]

In fact, that was all that remained of Chinese civilization as well, for this was a court civilization closely bound up with the imperial form of rule, the religious role of the emperor and the Confucian mandarinate based on the examination system. Indeed, if one wished to find a specific date for the end of Chinese civilization, it would be 1905, when the examination system was finally abolished. But in general, it was the decapitation of the court that brought the civilization to its conclusion, for the imperial state was central to the whole moral order of Chinese society. The emperor was "mandated by Heaven to enforce the moral order of the cosmos, the imperial regime was based on religious underpinnings."[34] Once these were removed the civilization was left without any further supports, as Gosseart and Palmer put it, "the liturgical continuity from the emperor to the village was a major cause for the religious cohesion of the empire, which was brutally severed in the early years of the twentieth century."[35] These were the wages of sin as far as the traditionalists were concerned, and they were right. But what other course was possible if China was to modernize? And there was no choice about that.

Section III—Religion in China

Can the civilization of China recover anything of its former self after the utter devastation it suffered at the hands of Mao and his totalitarian regime, and in general during the "time of troubles" in the twentieth

247

century? It was perhaps more ravaged than any other civilization in this period; hence the problem of restoring anything of it will be even more difficult to overcome than elsewhere. There is, of course, no question of a complete recovery, since China no longer has its traditional imperial court, merely that of conserving what is still left of the fragments of Chinese civilization, many of them better preserved outside mainland China, such as the tenets of Confucianism.

Religion will no doubt be the main means of restoring something of the old civilization to mainland China. Religion in Chinese terms means something very different than what it means in the West, with its monotheism and clear-cut separation of church and state. Religion in China includes all kinds of beliefs and practices that in the West would be classified as cults, superstitions, quackery, "sciences," bodily techniques, and even gymnastics. At present in China there are the five officially sanctioned creeds: Buddhism, Taoism, Catholicism, Protestantism, and Islam, which are recognized religions in the Western sense, a view of religion that the regime has tried to impose on Chinese society, but without much success. For apart from the authorized versions, there is also a myriad of other, more traditional forms of religiosity such as rituals, ceremonies, divinatory practices, spiritual mediums, feng shui geomancy, funeral rites, good-luck procedures, medical nostrums, and quackery of all kinds, as well as a huge variety of meditations and bodily exercises. Through all these channels civilization is starting to seep back into China. Sometimes one or another such pathway is blocked by government action, as when Falun Gong was banned and the whole *qigong* movement was temporarily discouraged. The Communist authorities had good reason for doing so, for as often in the history of China new creeds were the inciting causes of insurrection, and so were considered politically dangerous. The separation between politics and religion is also not as distinct as in the West. However, despite such setbacks, religion in China will grow and spread further, for it is a movement that can be contained but not extirpated, except by the most draconian measures that no Chinese government can afford to undertake any longer. Besides, in some respects the Party is backing religion now that Communism has become a dead letter.

Already under Deng Xiao Ping a temple restoration movement had official sanction, and this has since become widespread, especially in rural areas of the hinterland, and with it has come not only architecture and art, but also much traditional lore and folk customs that had been lost. Gosseart and Palmer write that "all the ritual specialists promptly reappeared since the late 1970s and played a crucial role in the revival of ritual life, both in its communal forms (temple festivals, New Year celebrations, prayers for rain) and in services to individuals and families (healing and death rituals.)"[36] At the same time, all kinds of artistic practices believed to be lost during the Marxist interregnum, were also resurrected, for "aged artisans still able to create statues, paintings and other religious artwork had to be found, sometimes from far away"; though, unfortunately, mass production methods arose in the heady commercial market climate, "since the 1980s large statue factories have emerged to cope will the demand, and had changed styles and tastes."[37]

There have been considerable social and moral benefits from the restoration and erection of temples, as this has been a cooperative communal endeavor financed by individual contributions, usually from local villages, though occasionally also from expatriate Chinese sources. Temples lead to be formation of temple associations that play a significant role in bringing together all the people of a local community, including government officials, as Gosseart and Palmer explain:

> Temples and village-wide lineages are solidarity groups that encompass all villages and embed local officials within them, providing the common moral obligations and incentives to perform, cooperate and comply.[38]

Thus some government officials have supported such endeavors, seeing them as expressions of local culture and the preservation of "intangible cultural heritage" according to UNESCO norms, which the Ministry of Culture has endorsed. At the same time temples and their rituals draw overseas tourists, especially wealthy Chinese from the diaspora and thereby provide added income as well as establishing linkages with expatriate overseas communities, such as those in Taiwan and Singapore.

Religion in China has suffered the consequences of rapid urbanization, as it has in every other society. Masses of people have moved from villages in diverse places to be housed together in row upon row of featureless apartment blocks in metropolises of varying sizes. In such an urban cultural wasteland, all local attachments are lost and local culture in general disappears; thereby "a growing proportion of Chinese lost any connection to the villages and, by extension, to the communal religious life which characterized local culture."[39] However, even under such unpropitious conditions, the growing shoots of religious life have broken through from beneath the concrete that blocked out the light of the spirit. In the cities there has been an extraordinary interest in all manner of religious literature, including that of foreign cults, such as Scientology. "Bootlegged *feng shui* manuals, divinatory almanacs, and *qigong* handbooks were among the main offerings of street-side vendors during the 1980s and 1990s."[40] At times it was "in practice easier to find religious materials than the works of Marx and Mao."[41] Later, when the megastores called "book cities" were established, these "provided a growing selection of academic works on the *Book of Changes* (*Yijing*), as well as all five of the officially recognized religious traditions."[42] As well as such hard copy, the Internet provided an almost unlimited amount of religious information online. Thus at least some knowledge of Chinese religion has been recovered.

There are also forms of Chinese religion that are inherent in the ordinary-life activities that many people pursue even in the cities. In themselves they would not qualify as religious in a Western context, but in terms of traditional Chinese beliefs, they undoubtedly must be so considered. They concern such things as martial arts, healing and health prescriptions of medicines and regimens, the practices of divination and horoscopy, and food fads, such as vegetarianism. Many of these were resurrected even during Maoist times as part of a general *qigong* movement that sought to assert a peculiarly Chinese way of doing things as opposed to those introduced from the West. Thus Chinese therapies were encouraged as a form of alternative medicine, and attempts were made to place them on a supposedly "scientific" basis. Thus the merits of acupuncture were extolled and near-miraculous achievements ascribed to it, which were subsequently circulated throughout the Western press. The martial arts and other forms of bodily exercises were similarly propagated and acquired a following in the West. In China, "the martial arts subculture became a major gateway into the religious universe of traditional China,"[43] and the same also holds for the healing traditions. This whole *qigong* movement was the most salient feature of religion to survive during the Maoist period, albeit in a disguised form and under strict government control. However, once the loosening of repression under Deng occurred, all these practices, freed from government controls, began to reassert their original religious character and to explore the beliefs, previously branded as superstitions, associated with them. Masters arose who promulgated their own doctrines, such as that of *qi*, and gained a huge following. Among these was Li Hongzhi, who emphasized *dong*, and who founded Falun Gong; and with his numerous followers began mass opposition protests. The government took fright and banned it, as well as other similar cults.

But other practices of a quasi-religious nature continued and are still widespread in China. The new capitalism made life and fortune extremely uncertain, so many people have recourse to traditional forms of divination and to the *Book of Changes* (*Yijing*) in order to read their fates. Geomancy in the form of *feng shui* became very prevalent, as many could now afford to build their own homes. Other aspects of traditional Chinese religion emerged from the shadows, either openly or in a disguised form. Vegetarianism became popular among those with a Buddhist inclination. Those intent on meditation followed Chan Buddhism, and those attracted to mystery took to Tibetan Buddhism, which was an officially recognized creed. As Gosseart and Palmer comment, "all these movements described here provide pathways for living and affirming Chinese identity and moral values in the chaotic amoral environment of capitalism."[44] Furthermore, they contribute significantly to the constitution of a "civil society" of free associations that had completely disappeared during Maoist times. Whether such religious tendencies will be allowed to develop much beyond this incipient point will depend on the policies of the new administration of Xi Jinping.

In respect of traditional Chinese civilization, it is most significant that Confucianism is making a comeback, especially after the Falun Gong fiasco that discredited the whole *qigong* movement, and that it is gradually becoming appropriated by the regime itself as part of an attempt to invoke traditional forms of legitimacy, given that both Marxism and Maoism no longer command much credence. Hu Jintao spoke of the new ideal of government as forming a "harmonious society," with clear connotations of Confucian precepts. Such a recourse to Confucianism will most likely continue under Xi Jinping, but it remains to be seen what forms it will take and how it will be melded with the Communist ideology on which the CCP still relies.

As is so often the case with religious developments within the Chinese sphere, the impetus to Confucianism at a state level has come from the outside, from the politics of Taiwan and Singapore. In Taiwan Confucianism continued unabated; it was spared the anti-Confucius campaigns that Mao launched in mainland China in the course of the Cultural Revolution. It also flourished as part of redemptive societies, the largest of which was Yiguando, which spread from Taiwan among Chinese throughout the world, and eventually also to the mainland. It promoted what has been called a "Confucian work ethic" and became an ingredient of popular religion. It helped spawn a Confucian revival in China after Deng, in the early 2000s, which took many varied forms. Mostly it involved study of the Confucian classics and other traditional texts. These were utilized at an elementary level for the moral education of children. This degree of Confucianism was acknowledged by the government itself, as in Hu Jintao's speech of December 18, 2007, when he allowed that religion could have a morally beneficial effect on society.[45]

Confucianism is, of course, the mainstay of Chinese civilization, yet the restoration of Confucianism does not mean that a resurrection or some kind of renaissance of civilization is taking place. As we have already stressed, religion can survive the demise of a civilization; and in China it was not just the case that civilization just about perished but that religion itself was gravely endangered and almost disappeared during the Mao years. The subsequent tentative revival of religion, salutary as that might be for cultural reasons, does not amount to any full restoration of civilization. At best, it recovers some limited aspects of civilization in so far as these are encapsulated within religion, especially so in Confucianism.

All these religious developments are beneficial for Chinese society, and they promise the restoration of cultural normality after the chaos of upheavals of the twentieth century. Materially China has advanced, but morally it has gone backward. Religion offers some prospects of moral improvement. This is perhaps the most intractable of all of China's problems that we shall consider next.

Section IV—China's Future

China bears the burden of an extremely troubled modern history of almost two centuries. During this period it suffered massive devastation in all respects, not only in loss of life but also in respect of culture and nature. It now faces the daunting task of having to repair a shattered civilization and a wasted environment. Its authorities must confront a multitude of problems, both material and moral, both cultural and spiritual where they concern religion. In keeping with its huge size, its difficulties are equally gargantuan. How its leadership deals with all these problems will affect not only China itself but also the whole world, to which China has become pivotal.

Some of the material problems have already been dealt with in spectacular fashion: hundreds of millions of impoverished peasants have been moved from the countryside into the cities and provided with work. But, as Jonathan Fenby remarks, "this may have been the easy part. Transforming this into a long-term, viable social and political system is likely to prove much tougher, particularly because of the highly complex heritage bequeathed to the Fourth Generation of leaders by events since the nineteenth century."[46] The heritage of events he refers to is precisely what we were concerned with in the previous two sections. He goes on to spell out what this means:

> China's future will be built on that deeply flawed past. Behind the booming statistics and the enormous challenges, this is the basic issue facing a country that has taken on a global role without having sorted out its own evolution from the history that still prevails.[47]

One of the key issues for the Chinese leadership to settle, once they have openly acknowledged it, which they refuse to do at present, is how far they wish to continue their rule as a modern version of Oriental Despotism. It is true, as we have previously pointed out, that this could continue almost indefinitely, but this is bound to lead to serious problems and shortcomings. Some of these are already surfacing. China's rulers are rapidly transforming themselves from Party apparatchiks to a self-perpetuating elite that is increasingly assuming a hereditary cast as the children and grandchildren of former revolutionaries accede to their positions and a "red aristocracy" of princelings is emerging who take it for granted that they are born to rule. They have also taken Deng's assertion that "to grow rich is glorious" as their birthright to be rich. And so they act accordingly, as Fenby points out:

> Today those impelled by the rush to the market and material self-improvement march increasingly to their own drum. Interest groups, individuals and competitive power centres proliferate within the overall supposedly unitary structure. State-owned enterprises join private firms in playing the stock exchange and using their position to maximize profits. The result is an authoritarian state which increasingly lacks authority, an empire without an emperor.[48]

As a result of these developments, China is now plagued by massive problems of corruption and an ever-growing inequality between rich and poor. Constantly, new scandals and unsavory revelations are coming to the attention of the Western media, for it is forbidden for the Chinese media to report them. As John Garnaut reports:

> The political explosion of Bo Xilai is blowing open the black box of Chinese politics and laying bare a world of staggering brutality,

corruption, hypocrisy, and fragility. For the first time, the walls of power and money that bind and also divide China's red aristocracy are being exposed for the world to see.[49]

And not just at the top levels of society but at the lowest levels as well, corruption, intimidation, and gangsterism abound. Peasants are everywhere being forced off their land with little or no compensation, for land-tenure and ownership is unclear in China; as Tom Millar points out, this is a huge nationwide problem:

> First, around 300 million farmers need to move from their villages and into cities. To ensure that farmers are not forced off their land with little compensation, China must abandon the principle of collectively owned land and give farmers secure private property rights.[50]

The battle over the land is causing mass incidents and protests all over China, some of which degenerate to armed clashes in which "crime syndicates and underworld networks acting in a sort of symbiosis with local states" are intimidating villagers, according to a study published in *Comparative Politics*.[51] But not all are intimidated; many react in self-defense. According to John Garnaut, "the number of loosely defined 'mass incidents' has doubled to more than 180,000 in the five years to 2010. Security sources have told me more than half of those incidents, including most of the increase, was generated by conflicts over farmers and households defending their land."[52]

But at the same time as corruption and civil unrest grows, so, too, does repression. Under the new leadership of Xi Jinping and Li Keqing, censorship has reached new levels not seen since Mao's time. A new secret document issued by the Party to hundreds of officials, entitled "2013 National Conference of Propaganda Chiefs: Briefing in the Ideological Situation of the Present Time," sets out new rules for China's universities that ban any discussion of so-called "evil subjects." These include "universal values, Western ideas of freedom of the press, civil society, civic rights, historical mistakes of the Communist Party, crony networks, and judicial independence."[53] These are precisely the issues that China needs to confront if it is not to move backward into its traditional past of Oriental Despotism. However, it is not yet clear to what extent China's rulers are committed to going into reverse.

They are certainly going forward in dealing with the material problems of rural poverty by moving three hundred million peasants into megacities of enormous size. This new wave of urbanization is set out in the twelfth Five-Year Plan that runs from 2011 to 2015. It is a gigantic undertaking such as only the Chinese state can undertake and carry through successfully. By comparison, India seems utterly incapable of any such project to resettle its impoverished peasant masses, who now drift into the cities in a completely unplanned, unorganized, and chaotic way. But if the planned exodus from the countryside succeeds in China, then this would have global implications for China's position in the world, as Tom Millar explains:

> If China's leaders get urbanization right, they may succeeded in tilting the world's second-largest economy away from its reliance on investment and manufacturing towards greater consumption of goods and services. But if China's leaders get it wrong, the country could spend the next 20 years languishing in middle-income torpor, its cities pockmarked by giant slums. If China gets urbanization right, it will surpass the US and cement its position as the world's largest economy. But if it turns sour, the world's most populous country could easily become home to the world's largest urban underclass.[54]

Whether or not China will become the largest economy in the world, which many maintain is inevitable but some dispute, is an issue that concerns its relation to America, on which hinges the future of world affairs. And if it does become the largest economy, then how it will use that wealth will be of crucial concern. If it converts it into military power so as to contest American supremacy, then great global instability will follow. China might succeed, where the Soviet Union failed, in challenging America, but at a huge expenditure that would be the burden its people would have to bear for the global ambitions of its leaders.

However, it is extremely debatable to what extent the Chinese will be able to surpass the Americans in any of the measures that matter in the modern world, such as military force, science, and technology, which are all closely connected, and the so-called "soft power" influence of global culture on which so much of America's prestige depends. Even the question of economic superiority has by no means been settled. There are those who believe China's GDP will surpass America's, but they differ widely as to when this will happen: "The *Economist* believes China will pass the US to become the world's biggest economy in 2018. Goldman Sacks thinks it will be more like 2027. . . . HSBC predicts that China's economy will be only 10 percent larger than the US in 2050, with the US streets ahead of India in third place."[55] The ex-prime minister of Australia, Kevin Rudd, a China expert, has stated unequivocally that "very soon we will find ourselves at a point in history when for the first time since George III a non-Western, non-democratic state will be the largest economy in the world."[56] But how soon is very soon?

A no less knowledgeable American expert, Thomas Barnett, argues that such a historical moment will never come:

> The World Bank recently recalculated the purchasing power of China's economy and found it to be about 40 percent smaller than we imagined. China won't be overtaking the US economy any time soon, if ever. Moreover, while we may fret over Beijing's dollar reserves, you have to remember that China's rapid industrialization has been built on very shaky environmental and demographic foundations, meaning most of the economy's vast liabilities have been pushed into the future on a scale that makes our Social Security overhang look modest by comparison. China will grow old before it gets rich, and it'll become increasingly unhealthy before it superfunds its environmental cleanup."[57]

In any case, it can be argued that even if China does surpass America in sheer GDP, how will this redound to its superiority in any other respect? If it stays at its present stage of economic development, relying on labor power alone to produce an even larger volume of goods to be exported abroad, mainly to be sold on markets in the West and Japan, then it will still remain a dependent economy, even as the indebtedness of its customers grows. It might be caught in the trap of high output without being able to move up to higher forms of production.

There are optimists and pessimists about what the rise of China signifies and what might be its continuing relation to the United States. The optimists view the China and America relation as a wonderful symbiosis of two complementary economies, each sustaining the other, and together constituting a new global Leviathan. Niall Ferguson and Moritz Schularik have dubbed this mythical beast Chimerica, and they describe it as composed of West Chimericans who spend and East Chimericans who save, both together being the two complementary halves of a conjoined body politic. But is Chimerica really a chimera, an unnatural amalgam of body parts? Another author who writes in the same optimistic vein is Zachary Karabell; he expresses much the same ideas of economic complementarily of the two partners as a kind of fusion that he calls "superfusion" and describes as follows:

> No one aspect of the relationship was sufficient to meld the two economies. It wasn't foreign direct investment alone, or low-cost production, or an emerging Chinese middle class, or the purchase

of US Treasuries, or the currency, or any other single factor. It was the unique combination of all of them. Any one facet would simply have meant a dynamic bilateral relationship between China and the United States. All of them together led to a superfusion that turned the two economies into one unit.[58]

Another author, Handel Jones, also foresees a bright future for the China-America partnership, but only in the short term while China must still rely on America for technology and to educate its scientists and engineers. But in the long run he foresees competition and conflict because China is itself moving into the field of technological development; its "latest initiatives are in high technology, including electronics, automobiles and aircraft."[59] And this is where he perceives the eventual threat to America and other countries will come:

> China will become a high-technology society that is a formidable competitor in the global market. By having the large local market and competitiveness in manufacturing, the Chinese corporations will be able to gain high market share worldwide. The large market inside China and the methods used to protect this market will result in more conflict with other countries.[60]

Whether such fears of high-tech competition will eventuate and, even more crucially, when this is likely to take place is hard to determine. Much will depend on whether innovative scientific inquiry and technological research can take place in an authoritarian society. The precedent of the Soviet Union is not very encouraging for the Chinese in this respect. At present the outcome of China's technological and scientific development is still largely unpredictable.

All the American authors we have so far considered predictably focus on the China-America relationship to the exclusion of all others. But in a globalized economic world, China need not be tied uniquely to America; it can gradually pivot in all kinds of other directions. Perhaps equally crucial is its relationship to the three East Asian neighbors, Japan, South Korea, and Taiwan, all of whom are democracies—which goes to prove that Oriental Despotism is not the fate of all Asians. Whether China, as a subtotalitarian regime, manages to cooperate with its near neighbors and allay their fears of its military might will be one of the decisive issues for the future. The other neighbors it needs to work with are Russia to its north and the ASEAN countries to its south, particularly Vietnam. And still further away there is India, with whom economic relations are rapidly developing, even though there are still unresolved border issues.

It is this whole America-China-Asia complex that needs to be managed if disastrous conflicts are not to eventuate. Any attempt by America to contain China by surrounding it with its allies will sooner or later lead to a disastrous showdown. Wise statesmanship on both side with a clear awareness of where the other side's vital interests lie and what, therefore, the one can and can't expect or demand of the other is the key to handling the relationship. That old and seasoned American statesman Henry Kissinger, who was himself instrumental in establishing the China-America nexus some four decades ago, provides some guidelines as to how this is to be done:

> The appropriate label for the Sino-American relationship is less partnership than "co-evolution." It means that both countries pursue their domestic imperatives, cooperating when possible, and adjusting their relation to minimize conflict. Neither side endorses all the aims of the other or presumes to total identity of interests, but both sides seek to identify and develop complementary interests.[61]

This view of the relationship is far from any ideas of "Chimerica" or "Superfusion" or any other such extravagant terms, but it seems far more realistic when it speaks of "less partnership than co-evolution." China and America can grow together cooperating in some areas, competing in others, both partners and rivals at once.

But, as Kissinger also makes clear, such a relationship can only work if it is embedded in a larger context of other neighboring nations, which he calls a "Pacific community," punning on the first word:

> An aspect of strategic tension in the current world situation resides in the Chinese fear that America is seeking to contain China—paralleled by the American concern that China is seeking to expel the United States from Asia. The concept of a Pacific Community—a region in which the United States, China, and other states all belong and in whose peaceful development all participate—could ease both fears. It should make the United States and China part of a common enterprise. Shared purposes—and the elaboration of them—would replace strategic uneasiness to some extent. It would enable other major countries, such as Japan, Indonesia, Vietnam, India and Australia to participate in the construction of a system perceived as joint rather than polarized between "Chinese" and "American" blocs.[62]

A leading Australian China expert, Hugh White, has come up with a similar proposal to Kissinger's. White, however, is much more forthright than Kissinger that America will need to accept China as it is—as it were, to paint it warts and all—and not seek to make it look better than it can be:

> The United States would need unambiguously to accept the legitimacy of the present system of government of China, including the monopoly of power of the CCP. This would be a big step.... American attitudes to China reveal doubts about whether the CCP is legitimate, and that it is proper to overthrow non-democratic regimes and replace them with democratic ones. This thought for example, flowed through many passages in President Obama's speech in Australia, in November 2011.[63]

Some might criticize this as a policy of appeasement, but short of a military showdown sooner or later, which must be avoided at all cost, there is no other way for dealing with China peacefully.

Notes

1. Hugh White, *The China Choice: Why America Should Share Power* (Black Ink, Melbourne, 2012), p. 39.
2. Jonathan Fenby, *The Penguin History of Modern China: The Fall and Rise of a Great Power, 1850–2008* (Allen Lane, London, 2008), p. 539.
3. Zhengyuan Fu, *Autocratic Tradition in Chinese Politics* (Cambridge University Press, New York, 1993).
4. Ibid., p. 1.
5. Ibid., p. 1.
6. Ibid., pp. 3, 115.
7. Ibid., p. 3.
8. Ibid., p. 87.
9. Ibid., p. 145
10. Henry Kissinger, *On China* (Penguin, New York), 2011, p. 93.
11. R. J. Rummel, *China's Bloody Century: Genocide and Mass Murder since 1900* (Transaction Publishers, New Brunswick, NJ, 1991).
12. Ibid., p. 248.
13. Ibid., p. 244.
14. Ibid., p. 206.
15. Ibid., p. 206.
16. Quoted in Henry Kissinger, *On China*, op. cit., p. 93.
17. Vincent Gosseart and David A. Palmer, *The Religious Question in Modern China* (University of Chicago Press, 2011), p. 165.
18. Rana Mitter, *A Bitter Revolution* (Oxford University Press, Oxford, 2004), p. 212.
19. Henry Kissinger, *On China*, op. cit., p. 194.
20. Rana Mitter, *A Bitter Revolution*, op. cit., p. 212.
21. Ibid., p. 209.
22. Vincent Gosseart and David A. Palmer, *The Religious Questions in Modern China*, op. cit., p. 167.
23. Ibid., p. 167.

24. Henry Kissinger, *On China*, op. cit., p. 72.
25. Henry Kissinger, *On China*, op. cit. p. 59.
26. Cho-yun Hsu, *China: A New Cultural History*, trans. Timothy D. Baker Jr. and Michael S. Duke (Columbia University Press, New York, 2006), p. 339.
27. Ibid., p. 337.
28. Ibid., p. 336.
29. Gilbert Rozman (ed.), *The Modernization of China*, op. cit., p. 44.
30. Cho-yun Hsu, *China: A New Cultural History*, op. cit., p. 539.
31. Vincent Gosseart and David A. Palmer, *The Religious Question in Modern China*, op. cit., p. 3.
32. Cho-yun Hsu, *China: A New Cultural History*, op. cit., p. 548.
33. Gosseart and Palmer, *The Religious Question in Modern China*, op. cit., p. 140.
34. Ibid., p. 27.
35. Ibid., p. 29.
36. Vincent Gosseart and David A. Palmer, *The Religious Question in Modern China*, op. cit., p. 248.
37. Ibid., p. 250.
38. Ibid., p. 258.
39. Ibid., p. 273.
40. Ibid., p. 276.
41. Ibid., p. 276.
42. Ibid., p. 276.
43. Ibid., p. 277.
44. Ibid., p. 305.
45. Ibid., p. 327.
46. Jonathan Fenby, *The Penguin History of Modern China* (Allen Lane, London, 2008), p. 681.
47. Ibid., p. 681.
48. Ibid., p. 679.
49. John Garnaut, *The Age* (Melbourne), 26 October, 2012.
50. Tom Millar, *China's Urban Billion* (Zed Books, New York, 2013), p. 10.
51. Quoted by John Garnaut, *The Age* (Melbourne), 10 May, 2013.
52. Ibid.
53. Michael Sheridan, *The Australian*, 20 May, 2013.
54. Tom Millar, *China's Urban Billion*, op. cit., p. 20.
55. Geoffrey Garret, *The Weekend Australian*, 26–7 May, 2012.
56. Kevin Rudd, *The Australian*, 14–15 July, 2012.
57. Thomas Barnett, *Great Power: American and the World after Bush*, op. cit., p. 183.
58. Zachary Karabell, *Superfusion: How China and America Became One Economy and Why the World's Prosperity Depends on It* (Simon and Schuster, New York, 2009), p. 326.
59. Handel Jones, *ChinAmerica: The Uneasy Partnership That Will Change the World* (McGraw Hill, New York, 2010), p. 199.
60. Ibid., p. 199.
61. Henry Kissinger, *On China* (Penguin, New York, 2011), p. 526.
62. Ibid., p. 528.
63. HughWhite, *The China Choice*, op. cit., p. 146.

9

Islam

Section I—Violence in the Islamic World

No contrast between major political entities in the world is as great as that between China and Islam. Though their populations are roughly similar—1.3 billion as opposed to 1.5—in every other way they are fundamentally different. China is a unified and coherent nation ruled by a godless secular regime of subtotalitarian Communism. Islam is a huge variety of societies scattered across the low latitudes of the world, under many kinds of regimes ruling separate states, comprising people who are different in almost all respects except one: they are all adherents of the one religion. Religion and denominational differences play the major role in the self-definition of all these people, distinguishing them not just from non-Muslims but also within themselves as between Sunni and Shia and many other minor offshoots and sects. Religion, as we shall see, is the most important factor in the Islamic world, much more so than in any other part of the world.

Historically considered, the current situation of the Muslim people is the outcome of the breakup of the Islamic world through the inroads of European colonialism and the power plays of the major European states. The three empires—Ottoman, Persian, and Mughal—that dominated the Muslim ecumene for centuries past were dispersed, starting with the Mughal in the eighteenth century and the Ottoman, bit by bit, in the nineteenth and early twentieth centuries. This gave rise to many states with purely arbitrarily designated borders that have proved highly unstable. Other Muslim lands were left as independent states with antiquated monarchies that have persevered; or they were colonized, as happened in Africa, Central Asia, and Southeast Asia, and these invariably became military dictatorships on gaining independence.

This historical outcome has resulted in a very unusual political situation. There are very many states in the Islamic world, but there is no single state or even several states that exercise a leading role.

All these states are formally independent but not truly separate from each other; their societies have too much in common in terms of religion, culture, and history to go their own ways. Hence what happens in any one of them very rapidly spreads to many others. Disturbances hardly ever remain purely local; they tend to spread across the region. This is particularly so in respect of the Arab states, whose people speak the same language and were for half a millennium under Ottoman rule. They have too much in common to separate but too little to be welded into a unity—they are neither one nor many, but remain suspended in some kind of limbo of indefinite relatedness.

Hence all these states in the Islamic world are highly volatile and unstable. Each one is pulled up from the top by overarching unities, belonging to the same community or *ummah* of Islam with all its religious, cultural, and historical commonalities; but at the same time, it is pulled down from the bottom by the local loyalties and adherences of its people to family, tribe, and sect, and in some places also to city or region. Under such conditions nationalism and devotion to the nation-state cannot acquire much of a grip on the primary loyalties of people, despite the best efforts of propaganda and education expended by many military regimes in the recent past. Only where there are distinct ethnic identities, such as among the Turks and Persians, can any national feeling obtain. The Western ideology of nationalism has served the Muslim people very poorly, whereas it has served the Chinese and even the Indians quite well, in some respects too well—dangerously so.

It is this uncertain and unstable political situation in Muslim states that explains why violence is endemic and prevalent in the Islamic world—drastically distinguishing it from both China and India. As Steven Pinker points out:

> Though a fifth of the world's population is Muslim, and about a quarter of the world's countries have a Muslim majority, more than half of the armed conflicts in 2008 embroiled Muslim countries and insurgencies. Muslim countries force a greater proportion of their citizens into their armies than non-Muslim countries do, holding other factors constant.[1]

If anything, the extent of the violence has worsened since 2008. There are both large-scale wars as well as small-scale unrests occurring at present. In the last half-century or so there have been numerous wars, both civil wars and wars between states. It can be said, almost without exception, that every Muslim state has been in some kind of war with every other neighboring state, whether Muslim or non-Muslim. Muslims in all kinds of non-Muslim countries have also been up in arms. Muslim jihadi terrorism has prevailed throughout the Western world and in many other places besides.

What is the reason for this prevalence of endemic violence in the realm of Islam? One reason, to which we have already alluded, is the artificial nature of many of the Muslim states, which tend to contain people of varied religious, ethnic, linguistic, and cultural backgrounds who cannot really abide each other or get along together. Since dictatorship is the predominant form of government, this often means that minorities of one type tend to rule majorities of another. Thus, for example, the rule of the Ba'ath Party, supposedly a secular party, in both Iraq and Syria really amounted to a Sunni minority ruling a Shia majority in Iraq, and an Alawite (a Shia offshoot) minority ruling a Sunni majority in Syria. Both countries have been beset by civil wars of great ferocity and intensity. The Sunni and Shia split, which goes back almost to the very foundation of Islam, is the main axis of conflict both between states, as in the long-lasting Iran-Iraq war, and within states where there are Sunni and Shia living side by side, as, for example, in Lebanon. The presence of Christians in large numbers in some Muslim countries, such as the Copts in Egypt and the Maronites in Lebanon, has also been a constant cause of friction and civil strife. And, of course, the existence of the Jewish state of Israel is totally unacceptable to Palestinians and all other Arabs; it has resulted in numerous wars and continuing violent hostility.

The upsurge of Muslim fundamentalist movements of various kinds, such as the Wahhabis, Salafis, the Muslim Brotherhood, and the terrorist organization Al Qaida, has certainly aggravated the violence and made fundamentalist Islamists more ready to take up arms or to fund those that are prepared to do so. All such groups can find ample sanction for violence in their traditional religious sources. They can readily quote from the Koran or the Hadith, the sayings and doings of the Prophet, to justify themselves. This does not mean that Islam as a religion has been any more violent than any other—than Christianity, for example, which proclaims itself to be a religion of peace and love yet has such a bloody past. But it does mean that those who wish to resort to violence, for whatever reason and in defense of whatever cause, find it much easier to justify themselves in religious terms if they are Muslims than if they are Christians. And besides their religion, Muslims usually subscribe to an honor and vengeance code, deriving from their tribal background, that makes it easy to slide into defensive or retaliatory violence and difficult to settle for accommodation and compromise through negotiation. When Muslims find themselves on the losing side, they tend to nurse a festering sense of humiliation that can persist for generations. Hence, they harbor all kinds of grudges against the West, whether this be against the old colonial powers, Britain and France, or against America, which, in fact, strove for their liberation. These are atavistic attitudes that make it very difficult for Muslim governments to work pragmatically in the best interests of their people, especially so in the modern world where other societies have long abandoned such views.

Besides these basic grounds for a resort to violence, there is one other singularly important political factor: most governments in Muslim countries are based on force and have little claim to legitimacy since they are military dictatorships, or at least were so until very recently. And since what is established by force can also be overthrown by force, there has been a constant round of coups, uprisings, rebellions, and revolutions, and now even mass street demonstrations to provoke a regime change. Except for a few rare recent instances, democratic transfers of government have rarely occurred. Where a government has been democratically voted into power, usually on behalf of an Islamist party, it tends to try to hang on to power by constitutional dodges, as the Muslim Brotherhood in Egypt sought to do, and as the Justice and Freedom Party in Turkey seems to be attempting. But mostly it is dictatorships or traditional absolutist monarchies that prevail, with just a few successful transitions to democracy, as in Indonesia. The promise held out by the Arab Spring to democratize the Arab world has not come to fruition. In Egypt the army is back in power.

Illegitimate military rule based on naked force, usually in the past with a fig leaf cover of Socialism to hide its shame, has been conducive not just to violence but to wholesale corruption. In the Islamic world autocracy rapidly gives rise to kleptocracy, since the ruler is backed by his extended family and all his relatives, by his tribal or regional associates, and by hordes of clients and supporters all looking to the government for opportunities for peculation, business monopolies, contracts without tenders, and all the other means of dishonest gain. Patronage becomes all-important for economic advancement, especially through family connections. The hereditary principle subtly reasserted itself as all dictators groomed their sons for succession. It is true that most have failed—that neither Saddam Hussein nor Hosni

Mubarak has been succeeded by a son, but Hafiz Assad's son is still hanging on. The effect of all these corrupt practices—which the people more or less condone, for that is what they normally expect of their rulers—is that it is difficult for leaders to arise who can unswervingly pursue policies in the best interest of the people and the country. And when such a leader does arise, such as Sadat in Egypt, he tends to be assassinated, again following long-established precedent. Under such conditions the safest prescription for ruling is to do as little as possible and make the fewest changes.

The economic situation in most of the Islamic world is very conducive to the condition of corrupt military dictatorship or even more corrupt monarchical rule, and the frustration of any initiative for change, especially modernization. From one end to the other, literally from Nigeria to Indonesia, the Islamic world floats on oil, and without oil to sustain it, would rapidly sink into destitution. For most of these oil-producing states, it is the main commodity to garner export earnings—in most cases the only one, apart from tourism, that is very uncertain, as tourists can quickly be frightened off by terrorism. Agricultural products are the other main resource, such as Egyptian cotton, and native handicrafts—for example, Persian carpets—but these do not earn very much. There are no manufacturing export industries, no service providers, none of the other productive sectors of an industrial society. Oil is all-important; it flows through pipelines laid by the state so foreign companies can export it and pay royalties into the coffers of the state. But all too often this ends up in the pockets of the rulers who control the state. Thus wealth is still only flowing into the state, and out again, as in the Oriental Despotisms of old. Consequently, the battle for control of the state becomes the key not only to all power but all wealth as well. There is thus a strong incentive to hold on to state power by force, or to capture it by force since there is no other way.

Since oil gushes from the ground and not much more is required to make it flow into the hold of oil tankers than some help from hired foreign experts, there is little need to establish industries, even ones based on oil itself. Such industries have in fact not arisen, and neither have any others. This is the curse of oil money, it stifles productive capacity, for there is so much of it that the rulers can afford to buy anything they fancy, either in their own countries or abroad. And in fact, most of the profits from oil have been invested abroad in Western countries. Some of it is used at home, of course, to ensure that the people can be kept satisfied and potential rivals or even enemies can be bought off, both locally and in other Muslim countries. This is how Saddam Hussein used his wealth—that is, Iraq's wealth—but that is a distinction without a difference, as Gilles Kepel reports:

> Fear was not the only instrument of power at Saddam Hussein's disposal, however. Like other rulers in the Middle East, he had so much oil money during the second half of the 1970s that he could buy allegiance far beyond the circle of his direct supporters. Journalists and Arab papers published in London or Paris, poorly-paid novelists and essayists from Morocco or Yemen, and over-the-hill filmmakers in Cairo all benefited from Saddam's generosity. He bought the services of secular nationalists in the same way that Saudi Arabia bought those of religious clerics. . . . Businessmen, oilmen, weapons manufacturers, and contractors from around the world flocked to Iraq's modernizing, solvent leader, who was busy erecting his country's civilian and military infrastructure.[2]

All that carefully erected civilian and military infrastructure was smashed in numerous wars, and all the money, in effect, squandered.

In most Muslim societies everyone becomes directly or indirectly dependent on the state, and therefore eventually on oil. Those who have no oil in their own countries go to work in the oil fields of other countries, where millions of foreigners are employed. Those who wish to get good jobs in their own countries must rely on contacts with the power-holders, which ultimately works to the advantage of the ruling families. Direct state employment becomes the preferred mode of work for those with educational qualifications and suitable family backgrounds. Such jobs are doled out as a form of patronage, and the more such semi-sinecures a state can afford, the larger the ranks of those who will support its ruling regime. As a result, the bureaucracy becomes bloated and swells to bursting point, and the state must use most of its resources to pay its own officials, leaving little for other programs. Any idea of state-promoted development goes by the board. This breeds a mentality of living off the state and not risking anything independently. In fact, under such conditions capitalist entrepreneurship is doomed to fail unless it has state backing, namely the support of those in power or their hangers-on. This was especially so where the state was declared to be Socialist, and private enterprise was either banned or discouraged. The result is invariably economic stagnation; and with a static economy no development in other spheres is likely.

The economy might be at a standstill, but the population keeps growing. It is true that fertility rates in the Islamic world have fallen drastically from their previous high levels, as is the case in the rest of the world, but that, too, brings problems. The fertility rate in Muslim countries used to be among the very highest in the world, about six or seven children per family. But now it has fallen to less than two children per woman in countries like Iran and Turkey, despite the exhortations of their leaders for women to breed more. If this continues it will in time lead to a huge drop in the numbers at work compared to those too old to work, which will make caring for the latter almost impossible, especially in such nonproductive economies. It is beyond our capacity to predict how this will be resolved.

In the meantime, however, these countries face the problems of overpopulation in the youth sector, the maturing children born to the old-style families with six to seven children each. A so-called "youth bulge" of unemployed young people has arisen as they emerge from schools and universities in their thousands, poorly educated and with no job prospects in their own societies. As Walter Laqueur comments:

> Some one hundred million jobs will be needed during the next ten years to solve this problem but they are unlikely to be created. This unemployment issue in North Africa and the Arab East (the "youth bulge") has been called a time bomb, and there is the question whether it will explode in the Middle East, Europe, or perhaps both regions.[3]

What Laqueur means is that such desperate young people will seek to migrate to zones of affluence, mainly to the welfare states of Europe that are closest to them, but also to other Western societies further afield, such as Australia, where they have already been arriving in boats. Can Europe or the West in general cope with such an influx?

These are the kinds of young people who have been at the forefront of the Arab Spring. When they find that revolution brings no jobs and no personal prospects for the future, how will they react? Will they turn violently against their own states and produce social and political turmoil? Or will they seek to turn their rage outward against the West, which is likely to restrict their entry? Will the ranks of Al Qaeda swell as a result of such deep frustration? Is the Muslim world about to face a catastrophe?

We cannot predict the answers to such questions, though we know that they point to problems that must somehow be resolved. There are numerous such problems, some immediate, requiring urgent treatment, and other distant, calling for long-term solutions. The problem of the youth bulge is immediate; that of the ratio of working to retired people is long term. The dependence on oil is also a long-term problem that might not eventuate this century, for oil will still be in demand until then, unless some unforeseen technological breakthrough occurs to generate cheap energy. However, sooner or later the oil resources will be depleted, and there are no prospects for any alternative sources of revenue in Islamic world. The reason for this is that Muslim societies have failed to modernize; indeed, they have been averse to modernizing, perhaps more so than any other major group of people. Why this is so we must consider next.

Section II—The Failure to Modernize

Modernization in the Islamic world has been going on in one way or another for two centuries, but it must now be admitted that it has largely failed. To say this is not to refuse to acknowledge that many Western-type institutions have been established in Muslim countries, such as military academies and universities, and that great technical progress has been made in running huge technological enterprises, such as electricity-generating plants and nuclear facilities. Nor is it to deny that as individuals many people of Muslim background, whether or not practicing Muslims themselves, are in the forefront in all modern developments, whether in science or literature or the intellect in general. However, Muslim societies have not been transformed sufficiently to make them qualify as modern societies, for the masses have hardly been touched by modern ways of thinking and acting. The proof of this is a report issued on behalf of the United Nations in 2002, written by a group of Arab intellectuals on the state of modernity in the Arab world. This has been summarized by Steven Pinker as follows:

> The authors documented that the Arab nations were plagued by political repression, economic backwardness, and oppression of women, widespread illiteracy, and self-imposed isolation from the world of ideas. At the time of the report the entire Arab world exported fewer manufactured goods than the Philippines, had poorer Internet connectivity than sub-Saharan Africa, registered 2 percent as many patents per year as South Korea and translated about a fifth as many books into Arabic as Greece translated into Greek.[4]

All these are symptoms of a widespread failure to modernize.

These statistics alter somewhat when we take the whole Islamic world into account, but not by all that much. There are at least three Muslim countries that have modernized much more extensively than the Arab ones: Turkey, Iran, and Indonesia. Turkey and Iran did so starting after the First World War under dictators who promoted wholesale secularization, to an extreme degree under Atatürk in Turkey and much less so and less successfully under Reza Khan in Iran. But in both these countries it was largely the elites that were transformed, not the masses. Now, Iran has been going backward under the rule of the ayatollahs and does not appear capable of breaking out of the isolation resulting from its determination to produce nuclear weapons. Turkey, under the Islamist Freedom and Justice Party, is still pursuing a modernizing course and is continuing efforts to enter the European Union, though it looks unlikely that this will succeed, as it is at the same time becoming more embroiled in the Middle East. The question therefore arises of whether it will revert to a more Islamic stance, especially if the ruling party were to institutionalize itself as the permanent government. In the case of Indonesia, where Islam takes a somewhat more eclectic and moderate form than elsewhere, there has also been an attempt to break away from the Islamic bloc and join up with non-Muslim countries making up the Association of Southeast Asian Nations. Its fate therefore depends on whether ASEAN proves viable and stable.

The failure to modernize by the large bulk of the Muslim countries means that the Forces of Modernity have not developed to any significant extent. When compared to China or India or any of the other fast-developing Asian countries, the so-called Asian "tigers," the Islamic world is still way behind in all the respects by which Modernity is measured in a globalized world. Industrial capitalism has not gone very far, as we have already shown, and has been inhibited by many factors. Reliance on oil as a purely extractive resource under the control of a militarized state or of traditional monarchies makes a manufacturing economy almost impossible. There are all kinds of religious barriers to this as well, such as low productivity during the whole month of Ramadan and restrictions on the employment of women, especially as they are often illiterate. The state has taken a highly bureaucratized but not a rational-legal form, which has bred corruption and inefficiency, as we have already explained. Whether the need to maintain some features of *sharia* law, and the resultant influence of the *kadis* on private affairs, has an impact on the functioning of society is a difficult matter to establish and would involve a longer discussion than we can embark on here. It certainly has a considerable restricting effect on science education, especially in the social sciences, and this contributes to the scientific and technological backwardness of Muslim societies.

Modernization has been going on for a long time but has not taken hold in these societies. All three of its forms have been successively tried: Europeanization, Sovietization and Americanization. Europeanization began in the nineteenth century with the inroads of the colonialist powers into the Islamic world at all points of its wide extent, in North Africa, the Balkans, the Middle East, Central Asia, and Southeast Asia. This was followed by Sovietization when independence was attained, as Socialism seemed the panacea to all problems of development. Since the collapse of the Soviet Union, and in some cases even before that, Americanization in the form of free-enterprise capitalist economics has been attempted. Modernization in all these three main forms has clearly not been successful, as our previous account substantiates, and why this has happened needs to be established, for that might provide clues as to how it might be better pursued in the future. We shall attempt to do so in reverse chronological sequence.

Modernization *à l'américaine* is at present not succeeding in the Islamic world in general, though in some cases it has made its mark. Business in Indonesia, which is managed to a considerable extent by indigenous Chinese, has done very well, though largely on the basis of an extractive economy of oil, timber, and agricultural products. But Americanization—or globalization, as it is now called—received a major setback in the Islamic world when the shah was dethroned in Iran. He was attempting to institute modernizing reforms in secularizing society and introducing land reforms. That brought him in direct conflict with the religious establishment who had the support of the pious of all classes, especially of the *bazaaris*, the middle-class shopkeepers, and he was overthrown through mass demonstrations. This was a great setback to American influence in the whole Islamic world and to the process of Americanization there. It put into effect a kind of Islamic counter-crusade initiated by Ayatollah Khomeini and then taken up by fundamentalist Jihadis throughout the Arab regions, which eventually led to the Al Qaida attacks on America and other Western countries. This is more or less where the situation remains at present, and how and when further Americanization or globalization will proceed is uncertain, especially given the prevailing violence now sweeping the region.

The previous modernization effort through Sovietization had completely failed. There were great hopes advanced after Muslim states had been liberated from colonialism that Socialism according to the Soviet model was the right course to follow, for it promised rapid industrialization. But it also justified the entrenchment of military juntas and dictatorships in one-party states; and it signified opposition to Western interests thinly disguised as Third Worldism. Nasser in Egypt was the main exponent of this approach, and the completion of the Aswan dam with Soviet finance and engineering was seen as the great accomplishment of his policies. It was supposed to lead to industrialization in general, but that never happened. Instead, widespread nationalization ensued, which placed the economy in military hands. Even now much of the economy of Egypt is still under military control. There was an analogous outcome where ever the Soviets gained a foothold. On the whole, the effect of Sovietization was counterproductive to any real economic development that could be pursued independently of Soviet aid and technical assistance, for once this was withdrawn development ceased.

Europeanization is the much older and longer process of the influence of European Modernity and European power on the Islamic world that began three centuries ago with the Turkish withdrawal from central Europe under military pressure, and only ceased with the end of colonialism after the Second World War. The Suez Canal war of 1956 was, at it were, its last gasp and occurred in Egypt, significantly so, since the first major incursion of Europe into Muslim lands occurred there as well. This was Napoleon's invasion of 1799. It was the Ottoman Empire that came under attack there, and it was there that the initial failure and eventual modest success in modernizing played itself out.

We can follow the story of what the Ottomans learned and failed to learn from the Europeans in Bernard Lewis's book *The Muslim Discovery of Europe*.[5] Here we shall concentrate merely in general terms on his one chapter dealing with science and technology where one would have expected there was most to be gained from the Europeans and least reason not to learn from them. But as it happened, the Ottoman sultans made only one serious attempt to keep up with the Europeans, and that was in the area of military technology. In almost all other respects, with the partial and very late exception of medicine, all new European scientific and technological developments were condemned as innovations to the authorized corpus of knowledge and practice and banned by the religious authorities. Thus it was religion, whether in itself or as interpreted at that time, that stood in the way of Europeanization, even in respect of the most urgent and useful matters.

Bernard Lewis explains how and why even very essential technologies, such as printing presses and clocks, with the almost sole exception of military weapons, were proscribed:

> In the Muslim tradition, innovation is generally assumed to be bad unless it can be shown to be good. The word *bid'u*, innovation or novelty, denotes a departure from the sacred precepts and practices communicated to mankind by the Prophet, his disciples, and early Muslims. Tradition is good and enshrines God's message to mankind. Departure from tradition is therefore bad, and in time the word *bid'a*, amongst Muslims, came to have approximately the same connotation as heresy in Christendom.[6]

It is even worse if innovation comes from the infidels, particularly the Christians, the major enemies of Islam throughout history. Imitating the Christians is a "particularly objectionable form of *bid'a*," as Lewis explains:

> According to a saying ascribed to the Prophet, "whoever imitates a people becomes one of them." This has been taken to mean that adopting or imitating the practices characteristics of the infidel amounts in itself to an act of infidelity and consequently a betrayal of Islam. This dictum and the doctrine that it expresses were frequently invoked by Muslim religious authorities to oppose and denounce anything which they saw as an imitation of Europe and, therefore, as a compromise with unbelief. It was a powerful argument in the hands of the religious conservatives, and was frequently used by them to block such westernizing innovations as technology, printing, and even European style medicine.[7]

The attitude to knowledge that arose on this religious basis was completely inimical to science and the whole scientific approach. The idea of entertaining hypotheses, of testing them by experiment, of amassing empirical data as evidence, of debating rationally according to methodological precepts the superiority of one theory as against another—all this was foreign to the Muslim mind; indeed, it was utterly obnoxious. Instead, "knowledge was conceived as a corpus of eternal verities which could be acquired, accumulated, transmitted, interpreted and applied but not modified or transformed."[8] Hence, scientific works of the Ottoman period consist solely of compilations drawn from earlier Muslim sources in Persian or Arabic. The idea of deriving anything from Europe was anathema.

One of the reasons why the Muslims were so averse to Modernity in general was that it came from Europe—that is, from the land of the

Christians, the *Dar al-Harb* (House of War) that was seen as the opposite of the *Dar al-Islam* (House of Islam) in every way that counted for anything. Had it come, for example, from China it would have been another matter. The pious Muslim mind found it difficult to separate Modernity from Christianity, since both came from the same source. In Egypt, Napoleon tried to win local support and overcome this misapprehension by deceitfully claiming that he and his troops were anti-Christian and ready to convert to Islam, but this equivocating trick did not fool the mullahs in Cairo for long. Inevitably, he and his men were seen as newfangled crusaders from the West, which they were not. Even now any incursion of Western forces into Muslim countries is seen by fundamentalists as another crusade designed to conquer land and convert its people. This was the problem the Americans faced in Iraq and Afghanistan. These days, of course, they are no longer feared as Christian missionaries but as leading to unbelief and licentiousness, to *jahiliyya* or the state of ignorance before the revelation given to the Prophet, as the main ideologue of the jihadis, Sayyid Qutb, spelled it out. The jihad being waged against the Americans and their European allies at present is seen by them as the latest manifestation of the age-old war in defense of Islam against the Christian crusaders.

With this background of intractable religious animosity, it is little wonder that European science appeared to Muslim minds as "dangerous knowledge" to be kept out as far as possible and only resorted to in dire necessity. Hence it was admitted in fighting the infidels with their own weapons, or of fighting disease where Muslim medicine had no cure, as in syphilis, the so-called Frankish illness. Eventually useful technologies such as clocks, printing presses and eye-glasses were also allowed, but that was about it, until defeat after defeat of the Ottoman armies in the eighteenth and nineteenth centuries forced the adoption at least of the military sciences necessary for handling modern weapons, above all artillery. But all else was excluded until almost the twentieth century, as Lewis notes:

> The system of filtration, designed to exclude those imports which might have threatened the traditional way of life, remained effective against the more dangerous penetration of ideas—of Western conceptions of inquiry and discovery, experimentation and change which underlay both the science of the West and the technology to which it gave rise. The products of Western technology might, after due consideration, be admitted; the knowledge achieved by Western science might in certain cases be applied; but that was the limit of their acceptance.[9]

When science and technology did reach the Ottoman Empire, it was in the first place taken up by the *dhimmis*, the protected people of the Book—that is, Christians and Jews. Apart from military matters, the Muslims were loath to learn anything from the Europeans until late in the nineteenth century. It was rarely the case that they travelled to Europe to study or even on business. Breaking through Muslim indifference to anything outside their own religion, language, and knowledge was no easy matter. Their own civilization, they felt, contained all that was needed for life in this world. They were convinced of the superiority of their way of life, founded on the only true faith, to all others. It took severe blows on the field of battle before they began to change their attitude, starting with the elites and only slowly proceeding downward, with the masses often changing little until now.

As with so many other things, the big transformation came with the First World War. It was only then that the ruling elites realized that they must Europeanize or perish. And so there took place the radical secularization revolution in Turkey and to a lesser extent in Iran. Many of the old and new Arab countries fell under the colonial yoke, and Europeanization was imposed on them whether they wanted it or not. As usual, it was the elites who took to it, and the others resisted with grim determination. But at this point, too, a religious countermovement began that sought for a revised version of Islam to make it capable of resisting European ideas and cultural influences. We shall come to it in the next section.

Having discussed the failure of modernization in the Islamic world even in respect of such mundane and practical matters as science and technology, we will next proceed to discuss it in more general terms. Once again we shall structure our exposition in reverse chronological order so as to establish first what ensued in recent times, and then seek to explain why it did so by locating its causes in the historical background.

Section III—Sources of Unrest

Despite the violence sweeping it at present, Islam as a religion is still largely intact and of late becoming much more assertive in the Islamic world. That in itself has contributed in a large measure to the prevailing instability. However, Islamic civilization is no longer extant. As we argued previously, religion alone does not constitute a civilization. In fact, the presence of a religion on its own usually indicates that a civilization has been destroyed. This is what we see in the Islamic world.

Formally speaking, the end of the Caliphate was the official con-clusion of Islamic civilization. That occurred in 1921 and was swiftly followed by the proclamation of the Republic of Turkey under the leadership of Kemal Pasha, later known as Atatürk. Kemal made it quite clear that civilization for him meant one thing only: European or Western civilization, and he recognized none other. He said, "the suc-cess that we have won until today has done no more than open a road for us toward progress and civilization."[10] He saw what we call Islamic civilization, that of the Caliphate, as past and superseded by the march of progress that led inexorably toward European civilization, the only possible one for the future. Like Peter the Great in Russia, he turned Turkey toward the West.

Also like Peter the Great, he was not against religion, as Bernard Lewis notes:

> The basis of Kemalist religious policy was laicism, not irreligion; its purpose was not to destroy Islam, but to disestablish it—to end the power of religion and its exponents in political, social and cultural affairs, and limit it to matters of belief and worship. In thus reduc-ing Islam to the role of religion in a modern, Western nation-state, the Kemalists also made some attempt to give their religion a more modern and more national form.[11]

This is precisely the view of religion that the governing Justice and Freedom party of Erdogan is seeking to undermine and to reinstate traditional Islam as the established religion of the state. In Iran the religious authorities, the ayatollahs, have gone much further than that; they staged a revolution against the quasi-Kemalist regime of the shah and have themselves captured power and exercised it in the name of a religious nationalism based on the Shiite version of Islam. However, any idea that this betokens a revival of Islamic civilization is deluded, and shares this delusion with the ayatollahs and their ideological apologists. *Pace* Huntington, there is not and there cannot be any such revival of a medieval civilization in the modern world.

When we say that Islamic civilization officially died with the Caliphate in 1921 this is, of course, a purely conventional dating. The reality behind it is that this was when the Ottoman dynasty court rul-ing an empire from Constantinople was officially wound up and for a civilization like that of Islam, which is largely based on the court and its aristocratic culture, the cessation of court life becomes the final event in the passing of the civilization. But in actual fact, this had already been taking place in gradual stages for many centuries past. Islamic civilization had been slowly and almost imperceptibly withering away in the three empires: the Ottomans, the Safavids and their Qajar successors, and the Mughals, who had lost their court with the defeat of the Indian Mutiny in 1857.

As we have already shown, the process of Europeanization, which was meant to take the place of Islamic civilization, has proved extremely difficult and tortuous in the Islamic world, perhaps far more so than in any other. Even under Atatürk in Turkey, where it was undertaken by force against much resistance, it has only had limited success. It certainly succeeded among the elite in Constantinople but not among the peasants in Anatolia, who are now making their voices heard as they move into the cities and have the numbers to elect the government of their choice. Whether Turkey joins Europe or drifts toward the Arab Middle East will depend very much on this confrontation of these two opposed parts of society. The fact that this is happening in Turkey, the most modernized of all Islamic societies, is indicative of how far modernization still has to go. The disparities are far greater in all the other Islamic countries, where fierce battles over Modernity are raging in all of them, with uncertain outcomes in each one. How the Islamic world as a whole will go remains to be seen, and no sure predictions are possible. How and why the Islamic world has come to this predicament, long after the issue has already been decided in the rest of the world, requires an explanation that only extensive sociological and historical research into its historic background can provide.

The problem begins with Islam as a religion itself. It is not a religion of faith alone, but one of daily ritual and practice, like Orthodox Judaism. It is not a religion where the Christian principle of "render unto Caesar what is Caesar's and to God what is God's" can be applied, because it rejects any separation of the realms of Caesar and God. Atatürk's attempt to separate state and church, so to speak to disestablish religion and to give it a modern, national form came up against tremendous opposition from the 'ulama and could only be implemented by force. It has only partially succeeded in Turkey, and elsewhere in many countries, above all Iran, it has completely failed. Everywhere in the Islamic world there is the demand that the Sharia be instituted as the official law and the basis of all legislation. Most governments have come some way toward meeting such demands. The result is that the clergy has gained considerable power in being able to veto most government decisions and by means of *fatwas* to impose their own requirements. This has given them a controlling influence on public and private life: the media, public education, the publication of books, all have to conform to religious rulings. As Muslims, whether they choose to or not, all individuals must subscribe in public to the beliefs and practices of the religion, which allows no criticism and can interpret any infringement in thought or deed as blaspheme. Women, in particular, must keep to their allotted inferior role, which, in fact, many of them are glad to do for so their upbringing has taught them. Such a religion is wholly incompatible with a modern society. But any thought of reforming the religion is out of the question, for even to utter such an idea is to risk punishment in most Muslim countries.

From the very start Islam as a religion stood firmly against any modernization even when Islam as a civilization was in favor of it: the 'ulama generally opposed what the court proposed in the way of introducing modern methods or institutions coming from the Christian West. And the clerics tended to prevail against the will of the ruler, the caliph himself, because they had the city mobs on their side. The deep division within Islam between the ruling court and the mosque, which carried with it the city faithful, who could be so easily stirred up by the Friday sermon, usually went against the court as the rulers feared to provoke riots and even insurrections. Thus the forces of civilization localized in the court tended to give way to those of the religion located in the city. Hence, the civilization could not modernize and keep up with what was taking place in Europe.

However, despite such opposition from traditional quarters Modernity did succeed in seeping through the cracks that had opened up in Ottoman society under the pressure of European imperialism. The elite, who were faced with the practical problems of administering the defending the Ottoman state from Western incursions as well as internal insurrections and de facto secessions, such as that of Egypt, had to find the means that would work. Invariably these were modern methods of European origin that only Europeans could impart to the locals. Such people, trained in the European technical professions who had perforce to mix with Europeans, inevitably also acquired a modicum of European culture. In the forefront were the military officers who had to be taught the sciences on which the modern arts of war and weapons depended, especially the artillery. But, as Ann Lambton notes, both in Turkey and in Persia "military reform, however, in the absence of administrative and financial reform proved abortive."[12] Hence, once the changes began to take place, largely during the second half of the nineteenth century, one kind of reform compelled other kinds to take place in parallel. This, of course, met with opposition and generated turmoil and upheaval within these societies.

There were many forces arrayed against each other. At the two extremes were the Westernizers and the Traditionalists, as Ira Lapidus explains:

> The elites generated two principal responses to European pressures. One was the response of the political classes and the newly formed intelligentsia trained in Western techniques and enamored of Western cultural values and nationalist concepts of the future of Muslim societies and tended to redefine Islam to make it consistent with European forms of state and economy. The second response came from the tribal leaders, merchants, and commercial farmers led by the 'ulama and the Sufis, who espoused a reorganization of Muslim communities, and the reform of individual behaviour in terms of fundamental religious principles.[13]

A third group, who tried to mediate between these contrary responses, were the Islamic modernists. They sought to keep the best features of both Modernity and Tradition and to combine them in a unique synthesis. Jamal al-Din al-Afghani and Muhammad Abduh, his Egyptian disciple, "called for an Islamic rejuvenation that was going to return to the pure seventh-century roots of Islam, and, at the same time was going to retain a spirit of innovation."[14] They were the founders of the Salafi reformist strain of Islam. They influenced Hassan al-Banna, who initiated the Muslim Brotherhood in Egypt in 1928 and was assassinated by the Egyptian secret police in 1949. At present it is the Muslim Brotherhood that briefly held power in Egypt after the ousting of Mubarak, one of the military strongmen who came to power after independence. Now it has been forcibly displaced by the military in a familiar pattern of Arab power politics. But what is unusual is that the Muslim Brotherhood encountered fierce opposition from the Traditionalists of Saudi Arabia, the guardians of orthodoxy.

The Westernizers, the Traditionalists, and the Salafis or Muslim Brothers are all fundamentally opposed to each other. The Salafis and assorted other religious modernizers against Sufism and cultic practices advocate a purified Islam based on the Koran and the Hadith made compatible with the modern forms of state and economy that had become mandatory. They are now coming into their own after a long period when the Traditionalist or the Westernizers were dominant. Starting with Atatürk in Turkey and to a lesser extent with Reza Shah, who seized power in Persia in a coup in 1921, Europeanization was embarked on by the Westernizers. Modernization and secularization followed apace; for example, the clergy was curbed perhaps for the first time ever.[15] However, as we now know it proved unavailing; in Persia the Traditionalists seized power from Mohammed Reza Shah and have held it ever since, and in Turkey moderate Islamists, the Justice and Freedom Party, have won a number of elections and are very gradually and cautiously trying to undo secularism from public life, though against considerable protests from the Westernizers.

In most of the other Muslim states that emerged out of colonialism in the period following the Second World War the Westernizers prevailed in the form of military dictatorships or in the form of ideological secularist parties such as the Ba'th in Syria and Iraq. Under the guise of Socialism, the dictators who seized power undertook a program of nationalization and Sovietization that everywhere spelled ruin for the economy. Nowhere was this more graphically illustrated than in Egypt under Nasser. In Indonesia, after Sukarno was ousted by Suharto, capitalism was promoted, and this had better economic results, though at the cost of enormous corruption. In Pakistan military dictatorship was interspersed with democratic elections, and a gradual Islamization ensued after the rule of general Zia al-Haq. As we shall see in the next chapter, Pakistan's development contrasts markedly to that of India, for whereas India has maintained its democracy uninterruptedly since independence and embarked on ambitious projects of modernization and economic development, Pakistan has failed in all these respects.

Pakistan was not unique in its turning to Islam, for starting from the 1970s all kinds of religious revival movements swept the Muslim world, such as those of the Wahhabis, Salafis, Muslim Brothers among the Sunnis, and others among the Shia. Some of these had led an underground existence, repressed by the military dictators or other secularizing rulers, such as the shah of Persia, for some decades past. In the 1970s they began to come into their own and exert a strong influence on the masses, especially after the shah was ousted and the Soviets were defeated in Afghanistan. There were also many social reasons for this development. By this stage it had become obvious that Sovietization in the guise of Arab Socialism had failed to improve the lives of the masses. But at the same time more and more of them were moving from the rural villages where tradition held sway to the burgeoning and overcrowded cities where they were open to the call of radical types of religious preachers with a more modern message. Greater numbers of the middle classes undertook technical and professional forms of education in universities and higher schools, a form of education that in no way disturbed their religious orientation. Such people could often not find suitable employment. All these developments brought about a huge mass return to Islam in response to the siren calls of the imams that Islam is the answer to all problems. Ira Lepidus explains how this took place in Egypt:

> In the 1970s Islamic revivalism appealed especially to students and professional people—engineers, school teachers, and white-collar workers—often from rural backgrounds and from upwardly and geographically mobile, but socially conservative, families. [In Egypt] student enrolment in the universities had grown from less than 200,000 in 1970 to more than half a million in 1977. . . . Many young professional people also came from rural backgrounds and acquired a technical or professional skill without going through a deep process of social or cultural adjustment. In Cairo they found themselves, despite their high professional qualifications, without a place in society, living in marginal districts, alienated by inadequate salaries and stressed by the moral corruption of the big city.[16]

Here we encounter a peculiar paradox, that in the Islamic world modernization can lead not away from religion but back toward it, as it is merely superficial. A little modernization is a dangerous thing. Particularly paradoxical is the fact that not only Muslim men but also educated Muslim women turn back to Islam, even though they would seem to have all of their freedoms to lose by this move. But they are the ones who don the veil and shapeless clothes to emphasize their sexual unavailability, and so, too, presumably to protect their marriage prospects. Thus in Egypt the Muslim Brothers built up a huge and devoted following among such people. Under Mubarak they controlled most of the professional associations, student associations, and university faculties. They carried out extensive social services among the poor. After Mubarak they won the first open democratic election in Egypt. The Salafis in Algeria would also have won the election there twenty years ago if the army had allowed it to take place. Instead, the military cancelled it and provoked a civil war that is still ongoing.

Violence on a large scale has been the main consequence of the coming to power or of the removal from power of previously banned and repressed religious movements. One of the main effects of this struggle was to open up the age-old fault line of conflict, the Sunni and Shia split. No sooner did Ayatollah Khomeini take control of Iran than he aroused the fears of Sunnis, especially Saddam Hussein in Iraq, where a Sunni minority ruled a Shia majority. To counter the apparent danger he invaded Iran, and a bloody war ensued of eight years duration and hundreds of thousands of casualties on either side. This has enlarged into a general Sunni-Shia struggle taking place throughout the Middle East, and now centering on Syria, where a proxy war between Iran on one side and Saudi Arabia and the Gulf Sheikdoms on the other is being fought by the Allawites, together with the Hezbollah from Lebanon, against the Sunni majority rebels. In Iraq it is the Shia majority government confronting the Sunni minority unwillingness to accept their dominance. In Lebanon a repeat of the old civil war between these factions seems to be fast approaching.

This is but one of the many sources of violence that rack the Islamic world. In almost every country there are internal as well as external conflicts apt to generate more violence on a small or big scale. Extremist movements of the Jihadi type circulate through all of them and are always ready to perpetrate more outrages against their follow Muslims or to engage in international terrorism generally against America and Britain. These movements gain much of their leverage from the civil wars in failed states, such as Afghanistan, Somalia, and Yemen. They have now extended their reach deep into Africa in Mali and Nigeria, where they are intent on reigniting the old civil war between Muslims and Christians. As well as all these battles between Muslims themselves, there are still unresolved territorial struggles against outsiders, such as the long war over Palestine against the Jews and that over Kashmir against the Indians, either of which could break out into all-out battles with all the dangers of resorting to nuclear weapons.

Given all this prevailing violence, predicting what the future may have hold for the Islamic world is a foolhardy venture. Regimes rise and fall continually. So-called failed states abound. Except for Turkey, Indonesia, and Malaysia, where there is at present stable government, not even economic development can be undertaken, not to speak of extensive modernization. In all these respects the Islamic world stands in contrast to India, which we shall examine next.

Notes

1. Steven Pinker, *The Better Angels of our Nature*, op. cit., p. 362.
2. Gilles Kepel, *The War for Muslim Minds: Islam and the West*, trans. Pascalle Ghazaleh (Harvard University Press, Cambridge, MA, 2004), p. 216.
3. Walter Lacquer, *After the Fall*, op. cit., p. 233.
4. Steven Pinker, *The Better Angels of our Nature*, op. cit., p. 364.

5.   Bernard Lewis, *The Muslim Discovery of Europe* (Norton, New York, 1982).
6.   Ibid., p. 224.
7.   Ibid., p. 224.
8.   Ibid., p. 229.
9.   Ibid., p. 234.
10.   Quoted in Bernard Lewis, *The Emergence of Modern Turkey* (Oxford University Press, Oxford, 1968), p. 480.
11.   Ibid., p. 212.
12.   Ann K. S. Lambton, "The Breakdown of Persian Society," in P. M. Hold, Ann K. S. Lambton, and Bernard Lewis, *Cambridge History of Persia, Vol. I* (Cambridge University Press, Cambridge, 1970), p. 439.
13.   Ira Lapidus, *A History of Muslim Civilization,* op. cit., p. 457.
14.   Paul Berman, *The Flight of the Intellectuals* (Scribe, Melbourne, 2010), p. 28.
15.   See Cyrus Ghani, *Iran and the Rise of Reza Shah* (I. B. Tauris, London, 2000).
16.   Ira Lapidus, *A History of Islamic Societies* (Cambridge University Press, New York, 2002), p. 530.

10

India

Section I—India under the Nehru Dynasty

At first glance it would seem that India sits somewhere in the middle between China and Islam, though it is far from being the happy mean. Where China has succeeded so well in economic and technological development and Islam has failed over all, India has done moderately well. And where Islam has retained its religion together with some of its traditional culture, and China has largely lost both, India has also kept some of its traditions intact. In politics, however, India has succeeded where China and Islam have both failed; it has become a stable democracy, though, as we shall see, a democracy of a peculiar kind, one that has proved ineffective in dealing with some of its main problems.

India has still not overcome its crucial shortcomings, which, according to Sunil Khilnani, are "gender inequality, illiteracy and hunger."[1] Gender inequalities are far worse than in China, though perhaps not as bad as in most Muslim countries. Illiteracy, too, is far worse than in China and among women at least not as bad as in Islam. Hunger, however, is worse in India than in either of the others, for it still holds a considerable proportion of its poor, especially the poor peasants in the countryside numbering hundreds of millions, in its relentless grip. India's economic and technological advance has benefitted its society in an extremely uneven way.

These are some of the many paradoxes that characterize India, where nothing is quite what it appears, where every dark cloud has a silver lining and every ray of sunshine casts a dark shadow. Perhaps the most peculiar of these paradoxes is that the poor, who are there in such large numbers, have the vote but can do so little with it to ameliorate their condition. The still-prevailing norms of caste discrepancy and the ingrained habits of oriental despotism are clearly a large part of the explanation. Most people look to dynastic succession for legitimacy in government, as is so commonly the case throughout democratic

Asia, and cannot rid themselves of this assumption despite being often disappointed by the outcome. They look to the state as the all-powerful authority regulating and controlling their destiny.

Nevertheless, despite its multitude of problems, India has held up well. It has neither broken up along the many fault lines and fissures dividing its people along linguistic, ethnic, religious, and cultural differences, nor has it fallen into the endemic violence perturbing the Islamic world. It has not suffered the totalitarianism of China or succumbed to dictatorship, except very briefly as an emergency measure. There was, of course, the violence of Partition, the wars with Pakistan, and now there is the still-festering insurrection in Kashmir. But Indian politics offers a pleasing contrast to that of Pakistan, which has remade itself into a Muslim country with all the troubles that this move has brought along. India remains largely secularist. Despite frequent communal riots and the occasional pogrom, religious minorities have been tolerated. This augurs well for its future as it guarantees social peace.

Perhaps the main bar to India's development has been political incompetence, stemming from a lack of effective political leadership after Nehru. The principle of dynastic succession in the Congress Party and the completely splintered opposition have ensured that few, if any, able leaders could emerge in the following period. Indira Gandhi, Nehru's daughter, did not prove herself up to the role in which she was cast. She kept herself in power by illusory populist promises and by emergency measures. She dismantled her father's party and created her own, so that, as Khilnani comments, "by kicking down the inherited Congress apparatus Mrs. Gandhi appeared to enjoy freedom and immediate control: she exuded absolute power."[2] Just as it was once said of czarism that it was absolutism tempered by assassination, one might say of Indian politics that it has become incompetence tempered by assassination. Not that either Indira or her son Rajiv deserved to die, but their deaths undoubtedly brought benefits to India. By getting rid of Indira, the assassins relieved India of a particularly bad economic manager, who also corrupted the apolitical civil service inherited from the British; and by removing Rajiv, they opened the way for P. V. Narasimha Rao, whose most important act was to appoint Manmohan Singh to the Finance Ministry. Singh subsequently became prime minister through the patronage of Sonia Gandhi, and has proved a very able economic manager. This was the point at which the Indian economy was reformed and began to globalize after the quasi-socialist, Nehru-inspired policy of state controls was abandoned. At present

Singh has bowed out from the leadership to make way for the next Nehru dynasty scion.

The main failure of leadership in India is reflected in the mismanagement of the economy. This had already begun with Nehru, though only free-marketeers would have blamed him for the course he pursued in the 1950s. Socialism seemed the panacea for underdeveloped nations at the time, and this meant that the state played the leading role in the economy; though in India, unlike many other ex-colonial countries, this did not amount to outright nationalization of banking and heavy industry, often called the commanding heights of the economy. However, Stalin's Five-Year Plans were undoubtedly Nehru's inspiration, for as a young man in the 1930s he was much impressed by the industrial development of the Soviet Union. Electrification and the steel industry were also his main goals. Unfortunately, Soviet-style economic development did not work in India. "The economy created in the name of the intellectual blueprint of the 1950s, state-directed and regulated, founded on heavy industry, has not delivered its promises. . . . Poverty in the countryside and the city continues to destroy the lives of hundreds of millions."[3] The close military and economic alliance with the Soviet Union in the whole subsequent period meant that India was locked into that type of slow and cumbersome development and found itself on the wrong side of the Cold War, at least economically, as China recognized much sooner.

Nehru entrusted the task of economic development into the hands of a Planning Commission that exercised an extraordinary powerful influence within the whole political system. At its head was a small group of technocrats who operated behind the scenes in setting targets and goals. Their chief planner was Prasanta Chandra Mahalanobis, a statistician by profession, who "was to become the single most important individual in directing Indian development planning and transforming a vision of India's progress into a technical model that directed state policy."[4] As Khilnani goes on to note, "the Planning Commission became the exclusive theatre where economic policy was formulated. The subject was removed from parliament and cabinet."[5] Furthermore, Mahalanobis enjoyed Nehru's complete trust, so he could proceed as he pleased.

A key example of the disaster of such economic planning and state industrial development is the Heavy Engineering Corporation set up with Soviet support in 1958. According to Patrick French, "the Heavy Engineering Corporation is one of the most extreme examples of how big dreams in India went wrong. A lot of what it could make was not wanted or needed."[6] French states that the heavy machine–building plant operated on average at a capacity of 21 percent during the period 1965–1980, "so year after year, the gargantuan enterprise lay idly and bleeding public money."[7] Only in 2006–7 did it finally come into profit.

After this bad start under Nehru, the real damage to the economy was inflicted by Indira Gandhi. As John Keay reports, in 1969 "she then revived the radical agenda of the 1950s and announced the national-ization of the banks, the cancellation of the privileges and stipends of the princes when they opted to form the Indian union, new legislation on land holdings, corporate profits and personal incomes."[8] She also introduced protectionist policies when international trade was boom-ing in the 1970s. The state bureaucracy grew by leaps and bounds and controls and regulations increased, the so-called license raj came into being. At the same time restrictions were introduced on foreign invest-ment. Only the Green Revolution saved India from dependence on food imports and possible mass starvation. India's rate of growth between the 1950s and 1980s was around 3 percent per annum, far lower than that of the Asian "tigers" or eventually China.

On the political front, under Indira populism triumphed over policy, as everything became geared to winning elections. As Keay puts it, "Mrs. Gandhi's Congress itself swiftly degenerated into an unaudited company for winning elections."[9] Politicians tried to appeal to the electorate by outbidding each other in public generosity and further-ing sectional interests. Indira herself began to resort to the patronage and power of office to reward loyalty to herself and to her party. State governments were routinely dismissed by decree of Presidential Rule whenever they were seen as hostile. At the same time corruption increased and has kept on growing ever since.

Economically, at least, India gradually and belatedly lifted itself out of the doldrums of the so-called Indian rate of growth and attained a healthy rate of around 7 to 8 percent, below China's but adequate for its society. Rajiv's accession had already made a difference as he made the key policy change by abandoning Socialism and beginning liberalization. He introduced such reforms as lifting licensing requirements and restric-tions on investments; quotas, taxes and other business disincentives were also removed. Furthermore, Rajiv laid the basis of India's high-tech IT industry. Later, when Singh was appointed finance minister, liberaliza-tion began in earnest, and with it growth picked up astonishingly fast.

Politically, however, the disarray continued. Corruption grew as everything was staked on winning elections and the party in power thought of nothing but the next election. Parties became election-contesting machines; little else seemed to matter. Increasingly they had to form coalitions by appealing to a wide diversity of groups: caste, class, language, ethnic, tribal, rural, urban, and so on. Identity politics became uppermost. Such groupings tended to break up as easily as they could be formed. A bewildering array of parties and coalitions came to contest elections and hold power at the federal and state levels. As Maria Misra comments:

> It is possible, though unlikely, that India will develop a west-European style of politics, in which voters and parties form broad coherent left and right blocs. More likely, however, is the continuation of government by an ever shifting kaleidoscope of unlikely coalitions which seek to harness a vast array of diverse castes, regional and community groupings heedless of the ideological incompatibilities. The rather hesitant pace of economic liberalization that follows from this causes frustration to some who demand that India free up its labor markets, slash social expenditure and open itself fully to the global economy. But there are some advantages to India's haphazard and wayward trajectory. Unlike China, India is an open, pluralistic and highly diverse society, and from these virtues flows great creativity—a commodity that even the mighty Chinese may be lacking in their own more streamlined development drama.[10]

For most of the period since independence, the Congress Party in its various incarnations and reincarnations has been in office. This has meant rule by the Nehru dynasty with the well-known advantages and disadvantages that court politics brings with it. The succession is assured for as long as heirs or heiresses are born, which means that there is no struggle for power at the highest level. However, at the levels just below the top there is a constant jockeying for position to become a favorite and win the good graces of the ruler or the heir apparent. Flattery, currying of favor, and all the other well-known ploys of courtiers are utilized to gain an advantage. As a result, leaders cannot emerge from below and their competence cannot be tested in the usual democratic way through the formulation and implementation of policy. This is a large part of the explanation for the incompetence of India's political leadership.

The opposition, particularly the Bharataya Janata Party (BJP), which briefly held office in the intervals between Congress periods in power also has problems of leadership. It has to appeal to an almost exclusively Hindu constituency by stressing *Hindutva* or Hinduness, which more or less equates religious and national identity, so that Muslims or Christians or Sikhs or Buddhists or any others are excluded. It depends on launching strategically targeted agitations for mobilizing support, usually directed against Muslims, such as the vandalism perpetrated on the mosque at Ayodhya in December 1992. This was followed by communal riots and pogroms against Muslims in Bombay, Surat, Ahmedabad and Calcutta. The BJP Party leadership is made up of demagogues and agitators who stir up crowds by means of religious symbols and symbolic acts. Thus Lal Krishna Advani, the leader of the BJP who was instrumental in the desecration at Ayodhya, displayed himself as the god Rama with the symbolic bow and arrow in hand. The present contender for this position, Narendra Modi, now chief minister of Gujarat, is blamed for stirring up anti-Muslim animosity and not giving them police protection during the post-Ayodhya riots and murders. With such leaders one can only take a dim view of the BJP coming to power in the near future.

If India does not succumb to religious nationalism, sectarianism, and the divisiveness arising from the multitude of separate interests, if it maintains national unity and stable government, and if, by some lucky chance, effective leadership can emerge, then it will be in a good position of becoming the world's fourth and eventually third most powerful country after China and America. It is already entering into close bilateral relations with China and America. According to Edward Luce, "the growth in volume of trade between India and China will make it one of the most important trading relationships in the world. Eventually, demography suggests it will be the world's largest trading relationship."[11] The economies of India and China are highly complementary, for "India's facility with both the English language and information technology is not matched by China."[12] At the same time, India is developing close relations with America, both economic and political. Following the collapse of the Soviet Union, until then India's main economic partner and political ally, India has been drawing closer to America. The Americans are keen for the Indians to play a balancing role in Asia to counter China's growing power. How this will work itself out only time will tell, and time seems to be on India's side, provided it continues to grow and does not disintegrate or provoke nuclear war with its archrival Pakistan.

Section II—Religious Nationalism

A rising shadow looms over the politics of India: Hindutva, which is a form of religious nationalism parallel to those that have arisen throughout Islam, including Pakistan, as well as in other places throughout the world, including a Judaic version in Israel. Religious nationalism is no stranger to Europe, in the form of so-called "clerical fascism" based on Catholicism; it was very prominent between the two great wars, and parties acting on such ideologies assumed dictatorial power in a number of countries, such as Austria, Hungary, Slovakia, Spain, and Croatia during the war. It had precursors before the First World War, such as Action Français in France. It died out in Europe after the Second World War. But then with de-colonialization, something analogous arose in Third World countries based on other religions.

Hindutva is the religious nationalist ideology behind the BJP that was in power under the prime ministership of Atal Bihari Vajpayee, starting in 1998, and once before under another name in the coalition of the Janata government from 1977 to 1980. Now it seems poised to take power again under Narendra Modi. He has presided over an extremely successful program of economic development that has made the state of Gujarat, with its capital Ahmedabad (which we have already discussed from an historical point of view in chapter 7) the most economically successful in all of India. The other successful and modernizing state, Karnataka—which contains the cities of Bangalore and Mysore, where the IT industries are located—has also fallen under the rule of the BJP. It is also strong in Maharashtra with its metropolis Mumbai (once Bombay) and threatens to sweep the Gangetic plain, areas where the Congress Party used to dominate. Hence, the curious political anomaly arises that it is precisely in the most economically developed and modernizing states, where normally one would expect secularism to predominate, that Hindutva holds sway instead, and the BJP has won elections. How is this paradox to be explained?

A large part of the explanation is that Hindutva is a modern development, precisely because it is a form of religious nationalism that arises only under modern conditions. To fully understand this we must show how Hindutva arose historically and trace its origins right back to the colonialist era. This account will also explain why the so-called Saffron Revolution has been taking place of late.

Hindutva means equating Indian identity with Hindu religiosity—which logically implies that all non-Hindu religious minorities—Muslims, Sikhs, Christians, and tribals—are excluded from the *Volksgemeinschaft* and only tolerated as protected minorities, or Hindu variants of dhimmis, and in any case relegated to second-class citizenship status. What takes place when such an idea arises is the following set of ideological moves, as Peter van der Veer explains:

> What seems to happen in religious nationalism is that ideological movements give a new interpretation to the cosmological understandings communicated in religious ritual. The nation is presented as the extension of the self and nationalism as part of religion, dealing with the shame and honor, the illness and death, of the person.[13]

Hindutva or Indian religious nationalism shares these characteristics with other such forms, including the Islamic ones we studied in the last chapter. Like these, it too arises out of modernizing reform movements in religion. It is the religious modernizers who give rise, intentionally or not, to religious nationalism as a political ideology. This will become apparent when we examine the religious reform movements that preceded and fed into the BJP.

One of these key reformist precursors was the Vishwa Hindu Parishad (VHP), a Hindu evangelical movement founded at a conference in Bombay in August 1964. Peter van der Veer describes it as follows:

> My argument here is that the VHP (Vishwa Hindu Parishad founded in Bombay 29 August 1964) tries to create a modern Hinduism as the national religion of India. In this way nationalism embraces religion as the defining characteristic of the nation. The VHP is certainly not an "antimodern" movement. In fact, if nationalism is the discourse of modernity, the VHP project is fundamentally modernist. As I have argued earlier, Hindu nationalism articulates certain long-term transformations in Hindu discourse and practice that feed upon orientalist underpinnings of India and are as such deeply enmeshed in Western conceptions of modernity.[14]

We shall presently explore these suggestive comments, but before we do so, it is imperative to mention that the VHP is often viewed as a religious front organization for the Rashtriya Swayamsevak Sangh (RSS), a straight-out militant political movement directed mainly at Hindu youth. It was founded in1925 at a time when such fascist, Communist, and nationalist youth movements were quite common throughout Europe, and it manifests similar militant features, such as physical training in camps, saluting-the-flag ceremonies, and celebrating Shivaji, the Hindu warrior who fought the Muslims. Most of the senior leaders of the BJP derive from the RSS.

These were the political forces behind the events in Gujarat in which Modi is implicated, and they are also the ones behind his rise to power.

The massacre in Gujarat stemmed directly from a previous incident at Ayodhya. Some Hindus who had vandalized the mosque at Ayodhya, on the assumption that it stood on the site of a temple of the god Ram, were killed in an accidental fire on the train in which they were returning to Gujarat, which was falsely blamed on the Muslims as deliberate arson. This demonstrated to the Muslims that the state government could not or would not protect their persons and the federal government their sacred sites.

Why is it then that the middle classes and upwardly mobile groups in general have voted a party of this kind into power in Ahmedabad as well as in Delhi, and might well do so again? The answer lies precisely in their upwardly mobile aspirations. As van der Veer remarks, "if there is a 'mainstream' constituency for the VHP's discourse or spiritual Hinduism as India's 'national identity', then it is the middle class, together with those who aspire to this status."[15] Those who want to make a success of their lives and to show that they have been successful turn to religion to demonstrate this fact. But they do not return to the ancestral practices of their forebears, rather to a much more modern version of that faith, one that has been spiritualized and moralized, brought much closer to Western-style religion. In this form religion begins to approximate to nationalist religion and, therefore, becomes implicated in politics.

This is a phenomenon that, as we have seen, is also common in the Muslim world, where particularly the lower middle class is behind the fundamentalist governments in Iran, Egypt, Turkey, and elsewhere. It is also the case in Pakistan that professional groups of lawyers, doctors, and teachers support Islamist parties. A certain minimal degree of education, of a modern technical kind, makes people who are sufficiently literate, and intent on a search for meaning, turn to the sacred texts of their religion. It also motivates them to express their newfound interest in their social deportment and political allegiance. Similar manifestations of religiosity are to be found in India among the professional and technical elites. With people on both sides of the India-Pakistan border intent on affirming their religious identity, no peace can ever be secured, and the probability of future wars increases—wars that will be so much more dangerous now that both sides have nuclear weapons. And in this context it is important to note that it was Vajpayee, as the new BJP prime minister, who launched a round of nuclear testing almost as soon as he came to power in 1998, and that this was then followed by Pakistan in reply. What is likely to happen in the next round of the nuclear arms race, especially if the BJP under Modi comes to power?

All these present troubles of the subcontinent arose from the calamity of the Partition, when the old India was ripped in two; the wound never healed. Religion brought it about, just as it now prevents any lasting reconciliation taking place. Indians and Muslims had lived together for at least a millennium and continued to coexist more or less amicably under the British Raj. Yet it was during this colonial period that a process of modernization occurred that transformed the two religions, Hinduism and Islam, in a way that made them antagonistic to each other and eventually, by gradual stages, led to the separation of the two communities, which eventuated in the political and human tragedy of Partition.

Indian nationalists and anticolonialists in general tend to blame the British for this development. But they forget that their own nationalist aspirations were as much responsible for the rift with the Muslims as any of the often well-intentioned, but wrong-headed policies of the British administrators. It is true that they introduced census classifications based on caste and religion; it is true that they introduced separate electoral rolls for Hindus and Muslims, thus dividing the communities. It is even true that Lord Curzon, the viceroy, split Bengal in half along religious lines at one point, thereby paving the way for the later division.

But the British did not create the *gau mata* (mother cow) movement, "one of the most important issues in an incipient nationalism between 1880 and 1920,"[16] that demanded, unsuccessfully, the legal prohibition of the slaughter of cows. As van der Veer goes on to comment: "The movement created a rift not only between Hindus and the British but also between Hindus and Muslims, since the latter acted as butchers and also used the cow as sacrificial victim in their celebration of Bakr-Id, a festival commemorating Abraham's offering of Ishmael."[17] The Arya Samaj, the foremost Hindu religious reform movement, made protecting the cow its most important practical imperative. It became the constant source of conflict with the British administration and the Muslim community, both castigated as cow butchers.

The British did not initiate the movement for independence, which inevitably split into a Hindu and a Muslim party: the Indian Congress Party and the Awami Muslim League. The former was clearly dominated by Hindus, mainly upper-caste Brahmins like Nehru. Even Gandhi, though devoted to the cause of Indian unity, and ultimately sacrificing his life to prevent the mutual slaughter at independence, nevertheless contributed to the separation of the two communities. He was a Hindu saint, who had "his predecessors in Hindu saints like Vivekananda and

Aurobindo."[18] And although "he proclaimed an all-embracing Indian spirituality . . . [h]is discourse practices were recognizably Hindu, that did not fail to alienate Muslims, who had their own discourse of universal religion."[19] His assassin, Nathuram Godse, was a member of the RSS, which showed clearly that a Hindu militancy had already developed by this stage that would not countenance any form of accommodation with the Muslims. Hindutva was already well and truly instituted and able to inspire action, no matter what the consequences. But it was not yet strong enough to seize power.

Hindutva arose out of the very attempts at the reform of Hinduism to turn it into a modern religion undertaken by Gandhi's precursors such as Vivekananda (1863–1902), Aurobindo, and many others. It was Vivekananda, the founder of the Ramakrishna Mission, who was the main exponent of the idea of a unique Hindu spirituality, which he contrasted and considered superior to "Western materialism." Many Westerners came to accept this view and were drawn to Hinduism, including Madam Blavatsky, the founder of theosophy, and a number of British novelists, such as E. M. Forster. In our own time many gurus have been able to sell "transcendental meditation" to a youthful Western public eager to imitate the example set by the Beatles. But before any of this commercialized debasement of Hindu spirituality, Vivekananda had worked with a much higher purpose in mind. He emerged out of the Bengali renaissance when Indians were first exposed to and took advantage of Western education provided by the British. He used this learning to make Hinduism respectable as a religion by Western standards; his "typical strategy was to systematize a disparate set of traditions, and make the result intellectually available for a Western audience and defensible against Western critiques."[20] But the ultimate outcome of this attempt was to "create a discourse that became fundamental to Hindu nationalism. It was specifically developed by Mahatma Gandhi, but it was also a major source of inspiration for the RSS/BJP/VHP brand of Hindu nationalism," as van der Veer comments.[21]

This was even more so the case with the Arya Samaj movement of Dayananda Saraswati, founded in 1875: "It urged Hindus to abolish image worship, a crucial feature of devotional literature, to abolish caste divisions, and to change their rites of passage,"[22] namely, to become more like a Western religion. Behind this call to reform stands the influence of Western orientalist scholarship: "the emphasis on Vedic *texts*, reconstructed by historical research, the message of socio-religious reform, and the rejection of contemporary Hindu discourse and practice are all supported by orientalist knowledge."[23] In a partially oral culture like India, there were no set authoritative texts; any given work existed in many different local versions, often at odds with each other, both oral and written. It was the orientalists who systematized these different sets of materials into unified "critical editions," such as those of the Mahabharata and Ramayana. This produced the illusion that such unified texts had existed from the start, as it were, way back in a pre-Muslim past during the golden age of Hindu history. This is the illusion cherished by Indian nationalists, who, ironically, are thereby made dependent on orientalist scholarship, archaeology, and other Western sciences. But an unfortunate result, as van der Veer notes, is that "the Muslim presence in India is ignored or marginalized."[24]

Section III—Hindus and Muslims

Indians look back to a time before the Muslims to a golden age of Hindu civilization, to the Guptas, the Mauryas and even further back to Harapa and Mahenjo Daro of the earliest Indus Valley civilization. Few of them realize how much of this past civilizational history is, in fact, the reconstruction of Western orientalists, archaeologists, philologists, numismaticians, art historians, and other such scholars. For this glorious Indian past was overlaid and forgotten; some of it, such as the Indus Valley civilization, was lost completely without trace, though monumental remains and texts from the later civilizations did survive. All in all, during the nearly thousand-year rule of the Muslim conquerors of India, there was even less left of its past civilization than in other such situations of Islamic occupation, such as, for example, in the Balkans, where apart from the Orthodox Church not much remained of Byzantine civilization.

This, once again, prompts us to consider the well-established historical phenomenon that religion invariably outlasts civilization. There is no doubt that Hinduism as a religion is alive and flourishing, but equally little doubt that Hinduism as a civilization is dead and gone. The disparity between Indian religion and civilization is perhaps sharper than elsewhere, for such a long interval has elapsed since the civilization perished in the Indian heartland of the Ganges valley, though it did survive for much longer in the Dravidian South. Indian civilization is not completely dead, like that of ancient Egypt, but it only lives on in so far as it is inherent in the religions to which it gave rise: Hinduism, Buddhism, and Jainism, particularly in the sacred texts of these religions.

The reason so little is left of Indian civilization is not only that it was destroyed by the Muslim invaders who supplanted it with their own Perso-Islamic civilization, which they brought with them from Afghanistan and Central Asia. Perhaps even more decisive was the fact that the Indians made so little effort to preserve their own past. In fact, they had little interest in the past as history. They preserved all kinds of religious and literary texts, but those of an historical nature were not amongst them, for they wrote no history. Hence, it is very difficult and frequently impossible to date the origins of these texts, to know who their authors were or say anything about them, and, what is most important, to place them in their socio-cultural context. These surviving texts are messages from a distant past that has almost vanished, like the light from a long-dead star that reaches us only now.

The Indians wrote no history in the way that the Greeks, Romans, Jews, Chinese, and Arabs did. Even chronological records of the simplest kind, such as the names and dates of kings, are missing, not to speak of detailed historical accounts. Most of what we know of Indian history comes from travelers' reports written by Greeks, Chinese, Arabs, and Persians. There are certainly no speculations about history such as we find among these other peoples. This lack of an interest in history has been the subject of much disputation, and two main reasons are generally adduced: the first is technical and concerns writing, and the second is religious and concerns the Hindu worldview.

On the technical side is the fact that India remained an oral culture throughout most of its history, even though writing was known and widely used. However, oral culture persisted in that the sacred texts, primarily the Vedas, were taught and learned by word of mouth, as is the case even at present. Even such huge epics as the Ramayana and Mahabharata were learned by heart and mainly transmitted orally.[25] Ancient secular texts, such as Panini's grammar, that exist in written form are still taught orally. The causes of this adhesion to orality have much to do with the monopoly that the Brahmins have exercised on all textual matters, insisting that they must be taught by a guru in person, and thereby securing their own indispensable position and employment opportunities.

Religion is the other source of a lack of interest in mundane affairs, including history. If life is seen as a veil of illusion (*maya*), a passing show and mere link in a chain of being (*samsara*) on the way to rebirth in a higher state or to extinction in nirvana, then what does it matter under which king, or in what city or country this takes place? So why should anyone bother recording such irrelevancies? Where Indian historical texts exist, they are invariably of a very late date, and most probably owe their existence to outside influences. A case in point is the *Rajatarangini* of Kalhana, a history of Kashmir written in the twelfth century. Kashmir borders on the Muslim sphere of Afghanistan, from whence no doubt the inspiration for such a work derived.

The instigation to write history would have lapsed once there were few Hindu rulers or dynasties, when the Muslims established the Sultanate of Delhi early in the thirteenth century. Clearly, the Indians took little interest in the conquests and affairs of these foreign rulers who did not partake of their religion or culture. The idea of recording such things for posterity would have been incomprehensible to them. Of course, the Muslims themselves wrote extensive and detailed histories of India, but only of their own sultans and Sufi saints; they had no interest in their Hindu subjects.

It was not until the British, who ousted the Mughals and removed or reduced in status the other Muslim rulers, that the history of India as a whole, and particularly the Hindu past, began to be written. This was also when all the other types of historical research began to be undertaken. The British colonialists were not just high-minded scholars of history; they had their own motives in resurrecting the past. As we have already seen in chapter 2, they were intent on cultivating the Aryan myth because that seemed to give them a direct racial kinship with the Indians, especially with the lighter-skinned Brahmins of good *varna* who were their natural assistants in administrative matters. It meant that their usurpation of the Muslim conquerors and rulers from Central Asia, with their Mongol background, could be interpreted as racially justified, for Aryans were once again ruling India. And what is more, they were restoring to India the long lost glories of its past civilizations prior to the Muslims by the modern means of orientalist scholarship, archaeology, et cetera.

The British had little interest in the Perso-Islamic civilization that the Muslims had brought to India and cultivated there to such a pitch of perfection. As long as the East India Company was in charge of India, something of this Perso-Islamic culture was maintained. The Mughals were not officially dethroned, and their titles and honorifics were recognized, a small role was allotted to the throne holder, and Persian remained the language of administration. But all this ceased after the Indian Mutiny of 1857, whose main aim, in fact, had been to restore the Mughals, and this had the support of Muslims, Hindus, and Sikhs. Once India became an imperial possession, the process of Europeanization became official policy, and everything was done to repress and obliterate the former Perso-Islamic practices and prerogatives. This was the historical background for the eventual partition of India, which does not mean that the British are solely to blame.

The British tended to favor the Hindus rather than the Muslims in a process that began as soon as the East India Company took over. The Brahmins proved very useful in helping the British rule India. They were useful above all because they were literate; they provided the ancient Sanskrit texts on law and caste that the British colonial officials consulted in drawing up their new administrative measures. Also, being literate they were willing to learn English and take up the lower-level administrative post, thereby becoming so-called *babus* in the British system. They tended to be supportive of British rule and sent their sons to English schools and universities, even those in England itself. This is how Nehru was educated as a dusky-skinned English gentleman who hardly spoke any Hindi. Ironically, the British were educating the anticolonialist India nationalists who would eventually clamor for independence.

The Muslims on the whole were far less compliant. English education was not attractive to them, for they saw it as a danger to religion. As the viceroy, the Earl of Mayo, in office from 1869–72, remarked: "There is no doubt that, as regards the Mohammedan population, our present system of education is to a great extent a failure."[26] However, in time the elite among the Muslims also sent their sons to English schools and universities and established their own as well. This is how Jinnah was also educated as an English gentleman, and not much of a Muslim in practice. How it came about that two such gentlemen, Nehru and Jinnah, could not overcome their backgrounds and reach an understanding on keeping India united is a difficult historical question to answer, and much partisan controversy is still excited by the question of who was to blame. It is known that as late as 1946, Jinnah was still proposing a federal system for all of India. However, it is almost impossible to ascertain how and why this final opportunity to avoid Partition was not seized. Perhaps all those involved believed that Partition would not matter all that much—but how wrong they were. The British, in the person of Lord Mountbatten, were to blame at least to the extent that he too readily acceded to such proposals.

However, the British made a lasting contribution to India through the historical recovery of its lost civilizations, whatever their mistakes and misdeeds. India's awareness of itself as a nation would not be as filled with pride as it is now, if not for this history. And the pride is fully justified. The two peaks of Indian civilization during the Mauryas and the Guptas are as shining and brilliant as those of any other civilization. Unfortunately, between these peaks lies a murky trough that the light of historical research can barely penetrate. It is a feature of Indian history that it very rapidly goes from light to darkness and back again. Thus, between the death of Ashoka in 231 BC and the beginning of Gupta rule in AD 320 there was a five-hundred-year gulf that John Keay has called "India's Dark Age." But on either side of that divide, both before and after there were outstanding civilizational achievements.

All in all then, Indian civilization was prolific in many endeavors and reached an extremely high standing in most of them. Yet it was so quickly and apparently easily destroyed by the Muslim invaders. How was this possible? Why was it that only its religious forms were left, whereas all the other manifestations disappeared almost without trace?

To answer these questions we must once again return to Wittfogel's theory of Oriental Despotism and our own elaboration on that in the theory of court civilizations discussed in chapter 7. Indian nationalists and historians have baulked at this whole approach, and even the levelheaded Romila Thapar has objected to it and sought to refute it by reference to Marx's original version, rather than the much more sophisticated one presented by Wittfogel, which we previously considered. In this form, the approach fits Indian civilization particularly well. There seems little doubt that India was a court civilization. The graces of civilized living were carried on at court in the society of courtiers attending on a king or emperor. The cities played only a minor subsidiary role in providing the necessities of court life. In imperial times, according to Keay, "what distinguished an imperial court politically, and especially one whose king claimed to be a universal king of India, was that it was primarily a society of kings."[27]

The court was so important that cities seem to have declined during the Gupta period. Romila Thapar states that "archaeological evidence has been used to suggest a decline in urban centres during the Gupta period, thus questioning the claim to being an age of considerable urban prosperity."[28] In any case, a highly precious and refined culture couched in Sanskrit, no longer the demotic tongue, could hardly have circulated beyond court circles, "for Sanskrit was understood only by that minute percentage of the population whose sophisticated tastes and opulent life-style are so vividly portrayed in the Ajanta frescoes," as

Keay notes.[29] Hence the broad-based public of the cities was excluded, and could take little part in this type of civilizational endeavor. The contrast with civilization in the West is particularly startling.

A court civilization, as we argued in chapter 7, is particularly vulnerable to decapitation. Once the head is gone, the rest of the body politic quickly withers. The civilization cannot survive the loss of its courtly centers. And this is precisely what happened in India. Once the Muslim invaders began raiding and then occupying the Indian heartland of the north Gangetic plain, the courts of the Indian rajas went into decline or disappeared. Starting with Mahmud of Ghazni they plundered and burned, and eventually with Mohammed of Ghor they occupied and settled. They established their own courts based on the Perso-Islamic civilization they brought with them, and, of course, following their Muslim faith they despised the idol-worshipping Hindus. There was little from Indian civilization that they wished to take on and adopt as their own. Thus, with the foundation of the Delhi Sultanate the gradual elimination of Indian civilization took place in stages as the Muslims penetrated deeper south into India. It is true that here and there Hindu rajas survived and maintained their courts, but these were invariably based on the dominant Muslim models. "The Rajputs, Jats, Marathas and Sikhs who carved out independent principalities followed the broad pattern of Mughal administration and welcomed the presence of talented Muslims at their courts," as Rizvi writes.[30]

There were, of course, Hindu military reactions to Muslim rule, and in any case the Muslim conquest of India was never complete; places like Nepal and many others never fell under Muslim rule. Perhaps the most serious attempt at a return to pre-Muslim rule was that made by Jai Singh of Jaipur (1688–1743), who tried to "create a society based on Hindu ideology (*varnashramadharma*)," according to Peter van der Veer:

> There can be no doubt that Jai Singh tried to implement Brahmanical political theory (varnashramadharma) by demanding that the communities follow caste regulations and that ascetic celibacy be postponed until the last stage of life. His own role was clearly that of *dharmaraja*, the "righteous king" and "protector of the socio-religious order." But this attempt at religious state formation proved abortive.[31]

But even if it had succeeded, by that late stage it could hardly have brought back Indian civilization, which was mostly forfeited.

Given Muslim monotheistic exclusivity and intolerance, there was little chance that a syncretic Muslim-Hindu civilization could arise.

There were some syncretic attempts at a fusion of faiths at the lower levels of folk religiosity, as when the shrines and tombs of Sufi saints were used for worship by all, but this did not go very high or very far. Akbar might have had schemes of uniting all his subjects in the one faith just as Mehmet II did after he conquered Constantinople, but such ideas proved utterly abortive. The 'ulama would never countenance such things. As Qureshi explains, "by the time of Jahangir's accession the orthodox party had gained sufficient influence to defeat the machinations of their rivals. . . . [I]t culminated in the orthodox measures of Aurangzeb."[32] The Muslims, of course, were not interested in converting the Hindus; they were quite content to let them practice their heathenish religion unmolested, provided they paid the head tax (*jihza*) incumbent on all nonbelievers. This was the traditional way of dealing with the *dhimmis*, the people of the Book; its extension to the *kaffirs*, the idolaters of India, was at first resisted by the 'ulama, but they eventually acquiesced because of the overwhelming power of the sultan.

There are interesting comparisons to be drawn with other civilizations that have been destroyed, but were survived by their cognate religions; this occurred under Muslim rule in the Balkans as well as in India. The Ottoman rulers destroyed the Byzantine civilization they encountered in the Balkans but allowed their Greek subjects to freely practice their Orthodox Christian religion. To some extent the Orthodox Church preserved elements of Byzantine civilization, as it were, encapsulated in its scriptures, liturgy, and artistic styles, but that is about all. The Church acted as the mausoleum of the civilization in which its dead remains were preserved. There was of course no question of resurrecting the civilization at any future time. For even on gaining independence from Ottoman rule, the Greeks made no attempt to become Byzantines once again. If anything, they pretended to be reenacting the glories of ancient Greece, such as building in the Classical style and holding the first Olympic Games.

There is a similar story to be told of India as well. Any idea of a revival of the long-lost Indian civilization is pure nationalistic delusion. Certainly, that need not stand in the way of religious reassertion. And, indeed, as we have seen there has been a strong resurgence of *Hindutva*. But this, as van der Veer explains, is nationalist religion, a modern form of political religion; such political religions made their appearance in Europe, especially between the two great wars, and are also doing so now in all the Islamic lands, including Pakistan. But Pakistan can no more continue Perso-Islamic civilization than India can continue Sanskrit civilization.

This reassertion of nationalist religion in countries such as India and Pakistan has been completely misinterpreted by Huntington as signifying a revival of civilization. Because of it, he believes, a clash of civilizations results, such as that between India and Pakistan or the Islamic sphere in general and the West. By way of concluding this whole study of the Third World we shall take up Huntington's thesis next.

Section IV—Critique of Huntington

Huntington's thesis of a clash of civilizations depends on identifying religion with civilization. This enables him to argue that the religious militancy evident throughout most of the Third World signifies a civilizational renewal. India is the prime example of the falsehood of this argument, for it is clear that in India religion cannot be identified with civilization: Hinduism is alive and well, whilst the civilization of India is long dead. Indian civilization, that of its rulers, died at the hands of the Muslim invaders; the religion survived among the people.

This argument can be extended to all the cases in which Huntington assumes that a civilizational resurrection is taking place in our time. Buddhism as a religion still flourishes in many parts of East Asia, but to assume on this basis that there is a Buddhist civilization current in the world is clearly nonsense. In fact, the one and only Buddhist civilization occurred in India at the time of Ashoka. It is true that many other civilizations were still present as late as a century ago, but that does not mean they are still here now. The traumatic twentieth century has just about destroyed them all, as this book has shown. Not much is left of the civilization of China after all the depredations of civil war and Maoist totalitarianism, as we argued in chapter 9. Even religion in China was left in a sorry state after the Red Guard rampages. By contrast, the religion of Islam is still fully intact, but not so the civilization that it sheltered in the past; that is gone. With the passing of the Caliphate and the Ottoman Empire, as well as the other Muslim imperial courts, there was no longer any basis for the civilization, as we argued in chapter 10.

Arnold Toynbee's thesis is that a religion can survive the demise of the civilization that gave it birth. It is based on the history of Christianity that arose in the Roman Empire in the Classical civilization but continued on, in the form of what Toynbee calls a universal Church, after the empire and its civilization were long gone. What was left of the civilization was only as much as was encapsulated in Christianity and in this form retained and maintained by the Church during the long interval of the Dark Ages. In this way it was passed on to the succeeding Western civilization of Europe that rose much later on the basis of Christianity. Whether this model holds for all major religions, as Toynbee believes, or only for Christianity as a unique case, as we tend to hold, is irrelevant to our argument. What this historical example shows conclusively is that religion can survive the demise of civilization, and that, therefore, religion and civilization cannot be identified, as Huntington assumes.

It thus remains an open question whether anything will remain of the civilizations that brought the still-extant religions into being. It is possible that only those features of a civilization that are encapsulated in its religion will be all that remains in the near future, provided that the religions themselves do not disappear. However, it is also possible that a sustained effort at cultural conservation will succeed in retaining much more of the recently disrupted civilizations than that small remainder. Many aspects of Chinese civilization can be recovered, especially those that are still current in the Chinese territories and communities outside Mainland China. Japan has demonstrated that it is possible to retain much of an ancient civilization even within a highly modern society where the Forces of Modernity are as well developed as anywhere else. Perhaps the Muslim countries, too, will embark on a similar effort once the prevailing violence in the Islamic sphere has been contained and a proper course of development undertaken.

The conservation of what is still left of civilization is a very different project from civilizational reassertion through aggression, as Huntington conceives of it. On the contrary, the reaffirmation of civilization can only be carried out as a pacific undertaking, premised on global cooperation. For no such attempt at conservation can be achieved in isolation; in a globalized world it must depend on support from comparable undertakings carried out in relation to other civilizations. It must become a joint global effort for it to succeed. It is in this kind of endeavor that the West, meaning both America and Europe, has an important role to play. It can set an example of cultural conservation that will be taken up by others once their modernization problems are over. The New World and the Old World might come to the rescue of the Third World.

At present, religious nationalism is the great danger the world faces, and it comes from all quarters—most visibly from Islamic Jihadists, because their activities feature almost daily in the media, but also from the other fundamentalists such as the political exponents of *Hindutva* that we examined in this chapter. Huntington's thesis that they represent a clash of civilizations plays into the hands of such extremists by providing them with an intellectual rationale for their terroristic activities. In fact, some of them have read or heard of Huntington's thesis and used it to justify themselves. To assert that they are engaged in a battle of civilizations ennobles their cause, for it is nothing more than an ideologically inspired grab for power.

Not only do such movements not signify a revival of civilization, they do not even amount to a religious renewal. As the work of Peter van der Veer and many others shows, the fundamentalist insurrections are largely political in character, and they have been inspired by Western ideological movements. They do not have much to do with traditional faith and piety. Their more intellectual exponents have almost invariably arrived at their fundamentalist ideology after passing through a Western-style political party, most frequently Communism or some variant of nationalism. By disguising their cause in religious terminology and by utilizing traditional religious symbols, they seek to gain support or at least sympathy from the credulous masses that are still bound to religious traditions. Such tactics have worked in the Islamic world, and they seem to be working in India as well, though the damage there is still much more limited.

Huntington misconstrues this whole political phenomenon when he states that "the Islamic Resurgence and the economic dynamism of Asia demonstrate that other civilizations are alive and well and at least potentially threatening to the West."[33] Everything we have so far established about the Third World shows the falsehood of that assertion. Neither the so-called Islamic Resurgence nor the economic dynamism of China demonstrates that Islamic civilization or Chinese civilization is alive and well. And whatever it is that is threatening the West, it is not these other civilizations. Of course, the threat to the West from the Islamic Resurgence is utterly different from and bears no relation to that emanating from China's economic development. The latter is by far more serious than the former: China is threatening America's economic position and political hegemony in the world, but not by military means; the military threat coming from Jihadi terrorism is a nuisance, but almost trivial by comparison.

How Huntington arrives at his extraordinary view becomes evident from the argument leading up to the statement we have quoted:

> The West obviously differs from other civilizations that have ever existed in that it has had an overwhelming impact on all other civilizations that have existed since 1500. It also inaugurates the process of modernization and industrialization that have become worldwide, and as a result societies in all other civilizations have been attempting to catch up with the West in wealth and modernity. Do these characteristics of the West, however, mean that its evolution and dynamics as a civilization are fundamentally different from the patterns that have prevailed in all other civilizations? The evidence of history and the judgment of the scholars of comparative history of civilizations suggest otherwise. The development of the West to date has not deviated significantly from the evolutionary path common to civilizations throughout history. The Islamic Resurgence and the economic dynamism of Asia demonstrate that other civilizations are alive and well and at least potentially threatening to the West.[34]

Apart from the opening two sentences, which are evidently correct, all the other statements in the quotation are patently false. It is true that the West has affected all other civilizations since 1500, almost fatally so; it is also true that the West initiated modernization and industrialization. But that very fact contradicts everything that Huntington goes on to say about it. The West does deviate from the patterns that have prevailed in all other civilizations precisely by its inauguration of Modernity, especially the Forces of Modernity, to which Huntington seems to be referring with the words "modernization" and "industrialization." This was a unique occurrence in history, one that marks a new stage in the historical development of humanity, as we argued extensively in *Beyond Civilization*. It is responsible for the disastrous impact it had on all the other civilizations, whose survivors must now follow the Western lead in modernizing and industrializing.

In making his deflating statement about the West, Huntington is relying mainly on American scholars of the comparative history of civilizations, such as Matthew Melko and Carroll Quigley. Such authors have expounded a conventional cyclic view of the rise and fall of civilizations reminiscent of Spengler: as one civilization falls after going through its developmental cycle, so another civilization rises and begins the cycle anew. Such an approach to civilization is completely contrary to that taken by major European thinkers such as Marx and Weber. Neither of these historical sociologists took the view that civilization follows a cyclic course; on the contrary, for them the West represented a new and different course of history that made it impossible for new civilizations to emerge or the old civilizations to reappear. The very processes of modernization and industrialization, not to speak of the other Forces of Modernity, made that unthinkable.

Huntington believes that such a possibility is always open because he draws a purely arbitrary and artificial separation between "modernization" and "westernization." He states that "modernization involves industrialization, urbanization, increased levels of literacy,"[35] and so on for all the factors we have placed under the Forces of Modernity. By contrast to this, he equates "westernization" or Western civilization in general with the cultural and religious aspects of the West, such as "Greek philosophy and rationalism, Roman law and Christianity."[36] He thus comes to hold that "modernization" is a detachable component of development that can be attached to any civilization without necessarily involving any "westernization" whatever and without apparently affecting the civilization to which it is applied. It is made to seem like a neutral pragmatic technical process that takes no account of the nature of the civilization involved. Hence, any non-Western civilization can be modernized without forfeiting any of its essential characteristics or having to accept anything else from the West. If this were true, it would be very comforting for all those opposed to Western influence.

Unfortunately for such opponents of the West, this is far from being the case. Modernization, or the Forces of Modernity in general, is a Western product that arose in the context of Western civilization and can only be transferred to the people deriving from other civilizational backgrounds by a process of Europeanization, such as the colonialist powers imposed on their subjects or as the self-modernizers such as the Russians, Japanese, or Turks undertook on their own behalf. Invariably this meant having to adopt European ways in most respects, including the cultural aspects of Western civilization. This, of course, had a profound impact on their own native civilizations, which did not need to be completely abandoned, but had to be partially transformed and severely curtailed. This is what the Japanese succeeded in doing very successfully: they both Europeanized and retained their own native culture in many respects, but obviously not all. The Russians were less successful in that they became almost completely Europeanized. The Turks attempted to pursue a similar course and ended up by splitting their society into a Europeanized elite in Constantinople on the one hand and a still-Islamic mass in the Anatolian hinterland on the other hand. However, it is clearly a misconception that any of these nations could have modernized without Europeanizing, or as Huntington calls it "westernizing," at least to a considerable degree.

However, once modernization is defined not as full Europeanization but as Americanization, or even Sovietization, it becomes a somewhat different process, as we have already argued, but one that still requires some westernization. Americanization restricts itself very much to the Forces of Modernity, which is obviously what Huntington has in mind when he equates it with "industrialization, urbanization, literacy," and so on. Sovietization is also a highly limited and partial form of modernization, also focusing on the pragmatic technical aspects, though with an infusion of Marxist ideology, which is a European cultural product. And something similar applies to Americanization, which is also accompanied by cultural features, such as democracy, liberalism, individualism, global culture, and so on. It seems, therefore, that every form of modernization involves some degree of westernization. This becomes even more evident when science, a crucial part of modernization, is considered, for science cannot be taught, acquired, and practiced without some degree of cultural immersion, and that necessarily involves westernization.

All Third World countries have experienced Europeanization, Sovietization, and Americanization, to varying degrees, usually in that order. Hence they have all been westernized to that extent. Any further processes of modernization will involve further westernization, which now mostly calls for Americanization. Cooperation with America is the main way in which Third World countries are pursuing their present goal of developing the Forces of Modernity. Such cooperation takes place on numerous levels, ranging from the education of students in American schools and universities to technology transfers and scientific publication. In time, of course, they will themselves take over these processes, but that will only attest to their own westernization, because modernization and westernization cannot be severed, as Huntington imagines.

Notes

1. Sunil Khilnani, *The Idea of India*, op. cit., p. 101.
2. Ibid., p. 47.
3. Ibid., p. 62.
4. Ibid., p. 81.
5. Ibid., p. 85.
6. Patrick French, *India: A Portrait* (Knopf, New York, 2011), p. 139.

7.   Ibid., p. 137.
8.   John Keay, *India: A History* (HarperCollins, New York, 2000) p. 523.
9.   Ibid., p. 523.
10.   Maria Misra, *Vishnu's Crowded Temple: India Since the Great Rebellion* (Allen Lane, London, 2007), p. 446.
11.   Edward Luce, *In Spite of the Gods: The Strange Rise of Modern India* (Little, Brown, London, 2006), p. 280.
12.   Ibid., p. 279.
13.   Peter van der Veer, *Religious Nationalism: Hindus and Muslims in India* (University of California Press, Berkeley, 1994), p. 84.
14.   Ibid., p. 132
15.   Ibid., p. 137.
16.   Ibid., p. 86.
17.   Ibid., p. 86.
18.   Ibid., p. 94.
19.   Ibid., p. 95.
20.   Ibid., p. 69.
21.   Ibid., p. 69.
22.   Ibid., p. 65.
23.   Ibid., p. 65.
24.   Ibid., p. 196.
25.   On issues of orality and writing see Peter van der Veer, *Imperial Encounters: Religion and Modernity in India and Britain* (Princeton University Press, Princeton, 2001), Chap. 5.
26.   Quoted by A. A. Rizvi, "The Breakdown of Traditional Society," in D. M. Holt, Ann K. S. Lambton, and Bernard Lewis (eds.), *Cambridge History of India* (Cambridge University Press, Cambridge, 1970), p. 82.
27.   John Keay, *India: A History,* op. cit., p. 140.
28.   Romila Thapar, *Early India,* op. cit., p. xxi.
29.   John Keay, *India: A History,* op. cit. p. 152.
30.   S. A. A. Rizvi, "Breakdown of Traditional Society," in *Cambridge History of India,* Vol. II, op. cit., p. 75.
31.   Peter van der Veer, *Religious Nationalism,* op. cit., p. 48.
32.   I. M. Qureshi, "India under the Mughals," *Cambridge History of India,* Vol. II, op. cit., p. 61.
33.   Samuel Huntington, *The Clash of Civilizations and the Remaking of the World Order* (Simon and Schuster, New York, 1996), p. 302.
34.   Ibid., p. 302.
35.   Ibid., p. 68.
36.   Ibid., p. 69.

Conclusion

Inconclusive

We have completed our studies of the civilization-destroying consequences of totalitarianism, colonialism, and globalization in the Old World, New World, and Third World. All three of these destructive agents derived from the West: colonialism, totalitarianism, and globalization in its earlier phase came from Europe, whereas the latest phase of globalization emerged from America. This does not mean that Third World countries have been completely virtuous and uninvolved, mere innocent victims of the depredations of Western imperialism, as their defenders try to present them. For, once they were freed from Western tutelage, they were all too ready to replicate all the Western failings in their own way. Japan showed them the way by demonstrating that a non-Western country can be just as ruthless and rapacious as any colonialist power. European totalitarianism was in vogue all over Asia and Africa. And now globalization is being largely pursued in the very same areas, most often on the heels of totalitarianism.

It is understandable that this should be so, for globalization offers all the fruits of the Forces of Modernity: productivity, power, and all the other benefits deriving from industrial capitalism, a bureaucratic state, science, and technology. The origin and development of the Forces of Modernity was the main manifestation of Modernity in the West, and their extension to the Third World is what is meant by modernization. These constitute the underlying historical condition for the rise of colonialism, totalitarianism, and globalization, the agents of civilizational destruction. This does not mean that the Forces of Modernity were the direct causes of the agents of destruction or that civilizational destruction necessarily followed from the Forces of Modernity; the relationship was far more mediated and complex than any such simple connection suggests. However, the agents of destruction arose in the context of the expansion of the Forces of Modernity and can only be understood against that background.

Thus colonialism has to be seen in relation to the global expansion of capitalism; the growth of state power and its imperialist ventures in a sequence where first the flag followed trade and then trade followed the flag, and science and technology, especially in their military applications, gave the European traders and armies superiority over the native ones in the colonies. Totalitarianism was made possible by the very same Forces of Modernity that came into play during the First World War: a vastly expanded state machinery engaged in the total mobilization of all people and resources, complete dedication of the productive capacity of a capitalist economy to the one supreme goal of winning the war, and the utilization of all available scientific and technological talent to devise the weapons necessary to achieve this end. Globalization results when the Forces of Modernity, once fully established, are directed to the very different end of capitalist expansion, thereby raising the living standards of a mass population by means of a worldwide capitalist market in the hands of multinational corporations; the state takes its main aim to be the provision of welfare to its people; and a science and technology apparatus develops that is intent on technifying all the processes of daily living. Such, in barest essentials, are the interrelations between the Forces of Modernity and the agents of civilizational destruction. For a fuller treatment we direct the reader to *Beyond Civilization.*

As we argued in our previous work, with globalization the world has entered into a new phase of human history, that of postcivilization. Civilization, as we have demonstrated, is largely a matter of culture, of ethics, rationality, and high literacy, as we spelled this out in the Introduction. This is the reason that a "technological civilization" is impossible by definition and the expression itself is an oxymoron. What people mistakenly call a technological civilization, alluding thus to the approaching technification of the world, is really a post-civilizational condition.

A postcivilizational condition is approaching because culture is rapidly declining and assuming a secondary position in relation to the Forces of Modernity. As culture ceases to matter, civilization recedes. This does not mean that civilization is at an end, for there is still much of it left, but it no longer plays a primary role in human affairs, as it did in the past. All the major aspects of civilized life—its standards, values, and aspirations—have become optional for most people; they are no longer necessities of life, but things one might choose to indulge in for a time, or one might not do so. They have become more like hobbies or fads rather than vital concerns. This holds not only for the graces of living, such as the arts or manners, but even for morals themselves. Beyond what the law prescribes, some people choose to uphold moral standards, and some choose not to do so. This is a sure symptom of the waning of civilization into irrelevance.

There is no way now of reversing this process and bringing about a civilizational renaissance. What has been lost is beyond recovery, but what is still here can be retained and maintained. A civilization-conserving effort can be launched as a worldwide endeavor to save what can still be saved before it is lost forever. It can be directed at all the forms of the major civilizations examined in this work: the West, China, India, and Islam. Obviously, it will need to take a different course in each of them, for what still survives in each is very different. We shall forbear to debate the issue of which of them has retained most of its civilizational resources. But since we write from a Western perspective, we will argue that the West is best placed to maintain itself because it can cope better with the Forces of Modernity, to which it alone gave rise, than any of the others. But this is clearly a moot point, and we expect rejoinders from authors who derive from a different civilizational background.

The main joint task facing all of humanity is how to deal with the Forces of Modernity. Any attempt to defeat or override the Forces of Modernity is a completely quixotic undertaking. We cannot go back to simpler modes of life. The attempt to do so could provoke human catastrophes. Instead, our aim should be to prevent the Forces of Modernity from bringing down all human life to the same homogenous level everywhere on the globe, for this is the ultimate effect of globalization. The Forces of Modernity tend to promote sameness and equalization, for they are themselves universally the same. They extirpate anything that makes for difference. Since they are themselves ubiquitous and uniform, they create near identical conditions in respect of economy, bureaucracy, law, technological infrastructure, social services, educational systems, and much else right across the globe. Cultural or civilizational differences are irrelevant to such developments, for there can be no such thing as Chinese or Indian or Islamic Forces of Modernity. Where attempts have been made to erect culturally specific variants of such universal factors, these have been ideological delusions or pure pretense. Aryan science is an example of the former and Islamic banking of the latter, and there are many more such that nobody can take seriously.

311

The real differences that still remain between societies derive from the cultures that survive from the old civilizations and other such traditional roots. These cultural differences stand in opposition to the global culture that is an adjunct of global capitalism, particularly of the media linked to the advertising industry. The battle between these two forms of culture is now an ongoing struggle, as people everywhere seek to protect their heritage from global commercial interests that threaten to overwhelm all local traditions—that is, to consign them to museums as relics of the past. The loss of the past is manifest in all sorts of ways, ranging from the wrecking of old buildings to the desuetude of old customs. And with the oblivion of the past, civilization also vanishes.

Obviously, not everything of the past can be retained; wholesale conservation is impossible; much has to be relinquished. But the essentials that define civilization must be maintained even at the cost of efficiency. Language is one such. It might be much more efficient and facilitate communication if everyone spoke a global version of English, a kind of Esperanto devised for this purpose, but this would amount to the final blow to civilization. So much of the culture of a civilization is inherent in its language when this is practiced at a level of high literacy. It is the repository of meanings derived from the past, mainly from literary traditions, congealed in metaphors and expressions. Once language is, so to speak, sanitized, cleared up for purposes of universal communication, its very soul is destroyed. Hence, maintaining languages in their traditional usages is one of the main tasks in preserving civilization. All languages must be safeguarded, for the loss of any one renders the total stock of human culture all that much poorer. No language is an island, but part of the main.

The main threat to language also comes from the Forces of Modernity. In this respect it is science that assumes the leading destructive role. This occurs when the technical vocabularies derived from the sciences, particularly from the social sciences, invade ordinary modes of speech, supposedly in order to clarify meaning, but the effect is just the opposite; meaning is obfuscated. The result of the scientification of language is to replace specific, homely, and realistic words with generalizations and vague abstractions. Thus, for example, our rich moral vocabulary of good and evil, virtues and vices, and so on is gradually being replaced by the jargon of values, preferences, and options derived from a bastardized sociology. Or consider the flagrant misuse of the ordinary word "information." Bureaucratic discourse adds its own technical flourish to this linguistic debasement. The sloganeering of politics and advertising is a further source of harm. From every such quarter language is besieged and reduced to ruin under the battering.

The maintenance of a language is primarily the task of those that speak it. It is difficult for others to join this endeavor, unless they happen to be bilingual. The same is true of many other features of civilization, which belong exclusively to the people who have been brought up in it. Thus it is up to the Chinese to exert an effort to sustain Chinese civilization, Indians Indian civilization, and so on. However, this is not the case for all aspects of a civilization, for in many respects it is possible for people to take an interest and be involved with maintaining the practices of a civilization that is not their own native one. Thus, for example, Western classical music has become the preoccupation of people all over the globe; it flourishes particularly among those in the Far East, among Japanese, Koreans, and Chinese. On the other hand, a great many examples of the fine arts of these societies have been collected and preserved in the West.

In a contemporary situation, civilizations are no longer the self-isolating spheres they used to be in the past. They have become permeable and interpenetrate each other. They absorb influences from outside and carry on exchanges with one another. Many of these communications between civilizations are mediated by translators and other intermediaries such as cultural scholars, art critics, and intellectual interpreters. Such people now assume an increasingly important role since each civilization must also look to outside supports to sustain itself; it can no longer rely completely on indigenous resources. Outside help functions in a multitude of ways: it brings world attention to despoliation of monuments, it makes important works known and appreciated throughout the world through the work of translation, it lends prestige and appreciation to local efforts to maintain traditions, and it can lessen the ravages of unrestricted tourism. Civilizations now belong to the entire world, not just to the people who originated them, and their preservation is the duty of the whole of mankind.

As far as we can look into the future, it seems that the Forces of Modernity will remain dominant. Feeding, housing, educating, finding jobs, policing, regulating, and all the other necessary functions of ordinary life under modern conditions require the optimum cooperation and close coordination of the Forces of Modernity. This has already taken place in the so-called developed countries; it is proceeding in the developing ones and failing to do so in the underdeveloped ones, leading to excruciating human misery. In such places as the latter the issue of civilizations might come to seem a luxury that few can afford. This is what the Chinese authorities argued when China was still very poor, when they focused solely on economic development to the exclusion of all other considerations. To some extent this view was justified, though it was also a rationalization in defense of a subtotalitarian regime still intent on keeping itself in power and on maintaining its ideology. However, their concentration on economy to the detriment of ecology and culture has now come back to haunt them. They face overwhelming ecological as well as social problems. Had they undertaken a more balanced development, paying due regard to the environment as well as the essentials of Chinese civilization, China would now be a much better place. On the other hand, to neglect material development, as many Muslim societies are doing when they give primacy to fundamentalist religion, risks incurring the opposite dangers of permanent poverty and unrest.

The fate of mankind will be determined by the interplay between globalization and civilization. This is the titanic struggle between the universalizing tendencies of the Forces of Modernity and the particularizing ones of local culture that reach back into the past. It is in deciding what is universal and what is particular that most of these disputes turn. There are those who maintain that everything should be universalized and that the world will attain complete unity as the one global civilization. Thus Francis Fukuyama argued for the end of history in which American-style liberal democracy and everything else pertaining to it would be universally prevalent right across the world. In direct contradiction to this view, Huntington asserted that the world was bound to break up into separate and mutually warring civilizations because all their basic values were particular and in opposition to each other, so that there was little that was universally shared. Clearly both of these theories are mistaken; the world is neither one, nor is it many things, with little in common. Globalization ensures that a considerable degree of cooperation, integration, and unity is bound to be maintained, but cultural differences will work against complete fusion and will separate distinct regions and countries from each other. These are the centripetal and centrifugal forces that are pulling in opposite directions. What the resultant outcome will be will depend on their relative strength, which is bound to vary from region to region, and cannot be predicted in advance. The one thing we can predict is that, as always in history, the future will prove different from what we expect it to be. This is the nub of the inconclusive conclusion on which we end.

Index

scientific establishments of, 124
and totalitarianism, xv, xvii, 18, 97
Franklin, Benjamin, 127, 128–129, 132
Free-market capitalism, xvi, 94
French, Patrick
on Heavy Engineering Corporation of
India, 285–286
French Revolution, 31, 65, 79, 90
Friday sermon, Islamic civilization, 277
Friedman, George, 160–161
Friedrich, Carl, 23, 25
Führer, xix
Furet, François, 16–17, 28, 33, 98–99

G

Galton, Francis, 46
Gandhi, Indira, 226, 284
Gandhi, Mahatma, 292–293
Gandhi, Rajiv, 284
Gandhi, Sonia, 284
Garnaut, John, 253–254
Gau mata (mother cow) movement, 292
Geertz, Clifford, 205
Gehorsamkeit, 86
Gender inequalities, India, 283
General Agreement on Tariffs and Trade,
102
Gentile, Emilio, 24–25, 26, 63–65
Gentile, Giovanni, 22, 33, 65
Geomancy, 251. *See also Feng shui*
German Geist, 41
Germany
anti-Semitism in, 40–47
approach to science and law, 14
Christians in, 57
colonialist race of, 111
movies made in, 106
moving towards revisionism, 100
postwar totalitarian regimes in, 74
scientific establishments of, 124
and Social Darwinism, 34, 46
Spartacists in, 47
totalitarianism and civilization in, vii,
viii, xviii, 5, 6, 8–11, 14, 19, 21, 23,
26, 28
universities, American students
attending, 130
and West, liberal democracy teach-
ings, 105
Gestalt psychology, 159
Glaubenskrieg, 4

Gleichschaltung decrees, 10
Global culture
described, 104
emergence in Europe, 104
generation by the U.S., 104–105, 125
and media companies, 104–105
Global Financial Crisis, 103
Globalization, xx–xvi, 71, 94–95, 122. *See
also* Americanization
America after Second World War, xvi
and cultural problems for Europe,
104–108
defined, 101
and European colonialism, 102
Europe's contribution to, 103–104
and New World, 102
and Old World, 102
totalitarianism effect on, 112
U.S. role in, 102–103, 116
Godse, Nathuram, 293
Goitein, S. D., 197
"Golden Age of the Press," 149
Gorbachev, 28
Gospels, 39, 64
Graubart, Stephen, 143, 144
Great Awakening, 138
Great Britain
admitted to Common Market, 103
and bankruptcy, the U.S., 99
colonialization of India, 123
and colonial possession, industrializa-
tion, 111
eugenics in, 46
scientific establishments of, 124
scientific racism in, 46
The Great Depression, xvi, 6, 18, 25
Great European Renaissance, 203
Great King, 168
Great Leap Forward, 81, 234, 237
Great War. *See* First World War
Greece, 107, 129, 169, 216–217
city civilizations, 203–204
Greeks, 43, 129, 168, 216–217
Greenberg, Clement, 163
Green Revolution, India, 286
Grossman, Vasily, 58
Guangxu emperor, 245–246
Guggenheim, Peggy, 163
Gujarat, communal riot/massacre in, 288,
290–291
Gulag, 19

Index

Achaemenid emperors, 191
Bab, 60
  colonialism, 224
  kingship, 192
  monarchy, 192
  Qajar dynasty, 224
Perso-Islamic civilization, 295
Peter the Great, 55
Philosophical refugees, 159
Physics, high-energy, 152
Pinker, Steven, 3–4, 262
  on modernity of Arab states, 268
Plekhanov, Georgi, 34, 50, 52, 56
Polanyi, Karl, 12, 13
Political failures, of American civilization, 141–147
Political hegemony. See Hegemony
Political liturgy, 65
Political religions, 300–301
Pollock, Jackson, 163
Postcivilization, ix, xiii, xvi, xxi, 22, 177, 183, 217, 228, 310
Pound, Ezra, 162
Pre-Homeric Dark Age, 196
Pretotalitarian ideologies, 31–38
Pretotalitarianism, 26, 27, 36, 235, 246
Preuves, 165
Primus inter pares or figurehead, 27
Proletarian violence, 15–16
Propaganda warfare, 33
Protocols of the Elders of Zion, 40
Proto-totalitarianism, 26–27, 55, 69, 74–79
  full totalitarianism, transition to, 81
  leader's power in, 80
  and Mao, 81
  totalitarianism proper vs., 79–84
Psychology, Gestalt, 159
Punic wars, 217
Purges, 9, 13, 88, 236
Putnam, Hilary, 154
Pu Yi, 246

Q
Qajar dynasty, 224
Qigong movement, 250
Qing dynasty, 244–245
Qin Shih Huang-ti, 228, 237
Quatre, Henri, 205
Quigley, Carroll, 304
Qutaybah, Ibn, 201
Qutb, Sayyid, 273

R
Racism, xix, 16, 27, 41, 46, 83
  Nazi version of, xix, xvii, 10, 11, 12
Radical evil (das radikal Böse), xix, xv, 15–22, 18
  alternative versions of socialism, 15–16
  Americanization, 21–22
  features, 19–20
  First World War and civilization, 17–18
  Second World War and civilization, 18
Rajatarangini (Kalhana), 296
Ramakrishna Mission, 293
Ramayana, 295
Rao, P. V. Narasimha, 284
Rashtriya Swayamsevak Sangh (RSS), 290
Rational-legal bureaucratic state, 142
Rayfield, Donald, 77, 90
Red Army, 35
Red Guards, 234, 238–239
Refugees. See also European refugees in America
  and American science, 152, 155–158
  critics and litterateurs, 159–160
  philosophical, 159
Reich, 34, 86
Reine Intelligenz, 165
Religion(s), 11, 24, xii. See also Chinese religion; Hindutva; Indian civilization
  consumption prohibitions of, 199
  Eastern, xix
  East-West dichotomy, 194–203
  Erzatz, 58
  and Hitler, 13
  and ideology, 56–65
  marriage and sex practices, 199–200
  political, 13, 24, 64
  secular, 65
Religious literature, 219, 250. See also Literature
Religious nationalism, India, 288–294. See also Hindutva
Renaissance, 127
Renan, Ernest, 45
Representatives, House of, 143
Revisionists, 37
Revolutionary Socialism, 12
Richardson, J. F., 212
The Ring (Wagner), 46
Risorgimento, 86
Rites controversy, 244
Robinson, David, 218, 224

327

civilization in Eastern Europe during, 8–9

civilization in Germany during, 9–10

civilization in Russia during, 9

cultural devastation in China during, 10

cultural devastation in Germany during, 9–11

in Eastern Europe, 6–7

freedom of expression during, 7–8

religion under, 13–14

Towns and cities. *See* Cities and towns

Toynbee, Arnold, 301–302

Trade, China, 245

"*Trahison des clercs*", 101

Treaty ports, China's modernization and, 245

Trente année glorieuses, 100

Trotsky, Leon, 33, 35, 47, 56, 77–78, 90–91

Truman Doctrine, 97

Tsarist Despotism, 52

Tucker, Robert, 55

Turkey, 264

   Europeanization, 276

   modernization, 269

   Ottoman Empire. *See* Ottoman Empire

Twain, Mark, 108

"Two nations," 145

"2013 National Conference of Propaganda Chiefs: Briefing in the Ideological Situation of the Present Time," 254

The Tyranny of Greece over Germany (Butler), 43

U

Ulugh-beg, 222

Ulyanov, Alexander, 49

United Nations, 102

United States. *See also specific* American entries

   acquisition of its colonies, 100

   development of, 126–131

   economic rescue of Europe, 99–100, 123

   and failure of totalitarianism, 123, 130

   and global culture, 104–105

   and globalization, 102–103, 106, 116

   and Great Britain bankruptcy, 99

   OECD, establishment of, 102–103

   origin of, 131–139

   rise of, 121–126

scientific and industrial advantages over Europe, 124

version of Forces of Modernity, 98

University system, American education, 160

Unsere Kampfstellung, 78

Untermenschen, 83, 88

Untermenschen or human animals, 19

Urbanization, China, 249–250, 254–255

Utopias, 37

V

Vajpayee, Atal Bihari, 289, 291

van der Veer, Peter, 290, 291, 292, 294, 299, 300–301, 303

Vedas, 42, 295

Vereinigung, 86

Vernichtungsbefehl, xvii

VHP. *See* Vishwa Hindu Parishad (VHP)

Vienna circle, 159

Vishwa Hindu Parishad (VHP), 290, 291

Vivekananda, 293

Volksgemeinschaft, 58, xix

Voltaire, 39, 88

von Neumann, John, 153

voting cynicism, 143

W

Wagner, Richard, 44, 45, 79

Water-management, 186

Weber, Max, 60–63, 76, 79, 110, 131–133, 136–137, 156–158, 186–189

Wehrmacht, 35

Weininger, Otto, 39

Weltanschauungen, 32

Werth, Nicolas, 90

Western civilization, 11, 12, 14, 16, 17, 20–22, 21, 22, 28, x, xix, xviii, xx

Westernization *vs.* modernization, 305–306

Western morality, 12, 201

West Germany

   as American ally, 21

White, Hugh, 235, 258–259

Whitefield, George, 138

Wilde, Oscar, 106

Wirtschaftswunder, 100

Wittfogel, Karl August, 48, 52, 86, 157, 186–193

Wittfogel's theory, 236

World Bank, 102

World Trade Organization, 102

World Wide Web, 122